TEXAS SHOUT:
HOW DIXIELAND JAZZ WORKS

by

Tex Wyndham

Illustrated & Published by Dan and Sis Polin
LIGHT, WORDS & MUSIC
16710 16th Ave. NW
Seattle, Wa. 98177
Phone: 206-546-1498   Fax: 206-546-2585
E-Mail: SisP@aol.com

Copyright © 1997 by Tex Wyndham & Light, Words & Music Publishing. All rights reserved, including the right to reproduce this book or any part thereof in any form, except brief quotations for reviews, without the written permission of the author and publisher.

Every effort has been made to locate the copyright holders of the photographs used in this book that are not in public domain. Omissions brought to our attention will be credited in subsequent printings. Grateful acknowledgement is made to those photographers, relatives and collectors who asked that their ownership and courtesy be noted.

Printed in Canada
ISBN Number: 0-9645795-1-0
Library of Congress Catalog Card Number 96-079296

Published by Light, Words & Music Publishing
16710 16th Ave. N. W.
Seattle, Washington 98177
Phone 206-546-1498   Fax 206-546-2585
E-Mail: SisP@aol.com

Cover Photo: Louis Armstrong and The Dukes of Dixieland
courtesy of Hank O'Neal, Chiaroscuro Records
Photographer Unknown

TABLE OF CONTENTS

ABOUT THE AUTHOR vii
INTRODUCTION ix
CHAPTER 1 .... "DIXIELAND" 1
CHAPTER 2 .... UNAVAILABLE RECORDS 5
CHAPTER 3 .... HOT DANCE 9
CHAPTER 4 .... READING, SOLO & ENSEMBLE SKILLS 13
CHAPTER 5 .... NON-GENRE MUSIC 17
CHAPTER 6 .... HAND-HELD LIVE TAPES 21
CHAPTER 7 .... SUBUNITS 25
CHAPTER 8 .... CONTEMPORARY CLASSIC COMBOS 29
CHAPTER 9 .... ENTERTAINING THE AUDIENCE 33
CHAPTER 10 .... REVIEWING RECORDS 39
CHAPTER 11 .... WOMEN IN DIXIELAND 45
CHAPTER 12 .... PLAYING THE STANDARDS 51
CHAPTER 13 .... BOOKS ABOUT THE MUSIC 57
CHAPTER 14 .... HOW TO IMPROVISE SOLOS 61
CHAPTER 15 .... WHY YOUTH DOESN'T LIKE DIXIELAND 67
CHAPTER 16 .... FAVORITE MUSICIANS 71
CHAPTER 17 .... CHICAGO STYLE 81
CHAPTER 18 .... CHRISTMAS RECORDS 91
CHAPTER 19 .... DIXIELAND vs. RAGTIME 95
CHAPTER 20 .... POPULAR HISTORIES 105
CHAPTER 21 .... ECONOMICS OF DIXIELAND 109
CHAPTER 22 .... NJJS HALL OF FAME 117
CHAPTER 23   PICKING TUNES YOU CAN SWING 121
CHAPTER 24 .... CREATIVITY/REPERTORY BANDS/
                                IMAGINATION 125
CHAPTER 25 .... "STORYVILLE BLUES" 131
CHAPTER 26 .... WHITE NEW ORLEANS 137
CHAPTER 27 .... WEST COAST REVIVAL 145
CHAPTER 28 .... PERIODICALS 155
CHAPTER 29 .... ENSEMBLE SKILLS 161

TABLE OF CONTENTS (Continued)

CHAPTER 30..... JAZZ SINGERS 167
CHAPTER 31..... WESTERN SWING/SPANISH TINGE 175
CHAPTER 32..... BLUES 181
CHAPTER 33..... REFERENCE BOOKS 187
CHAPTER 34..... DOWNTOWN NEW ORLEANS................................. 191
CHAPTER 35..... UPTOWN NEW ORLEANS....................................... 197
CHAPTER 36..... BRITISH TRAD..207
CHAPTER 37..... WILL DIXIELAND COME BACK? 215
CHAPTER 38..... MOVIES 225
CHAPTER 39..... RECORD REVIEWING REDUX 229
CHAPTER 40..... COMMON THEMES 239
CHAPTER 41..... ROUTINES 245
CHAPTER 42..... "TRADITIONAL"..251
CHAPTER 43..... FATS WALLER, ETC. 255
CHAPTER 44..... LEARNING TO PLAY 263
CHAPTER 45..... JOHNNY ONE NOTE 275
CHAPTER 46..... CONTEMPORARY RAGTIMERS 279
CHAPTER 47..... AGING MUSICIANS..285
CHAPTER 48..... GOVERNMENT SUBSIDIES 293
CHAPTER 49..... "DIXIELAND" REVISITED 299
CHAPTER 50..... SUBSTITUTES 307
CHAPTER 51..... MELODIC IMPROVISATION 311
CHAPTER 52..... MAJOR LABELS 317
CHAPTER 53 .... CDS: IMPORTANT VS. "GOOD" 323
CHAPTER 54..... ART FORM VS. FUNCTIONAL.................................327
CHAPTER 55..... LAST MONTHLY COLUMN 333

Tex Wyndham *Photo by Andrew Wittenborn*

ABOUT THE AUTHOR

Tex Wyndham is a recognized authority on ragtime and early jazz. He has played them on over 30 recordings and at national festivals, jazz clubs and cruises as cornetist/leader of The Rent Party Revellers and The Red Lion Jazz Band, as a band pianist and as a ragtime soloist.

Since 1966, Tex has written columns and reviewed ragtime and classic jazz recordings for several publications including *The American Rag, The Mississippi Rag, Coda, The Second Line* and *Rag Times.* He wrote the introduction, and acted as consultant, for Hal Leonard Publishing's music folio "The Definitive Dixieland Collection". Reproductions from his extensive sheet music collection have appeared in a number of folios and scholarly musical books.

In 1974, Toronto's Ragtime Society presented Tex with an award "in grateful recognition of his contribution to ragtime". In 1992, he was the first recipient of the Pennsylvania Jazz Society's musician's Jazzer Award "for his contribution to the preservation, promotion, and presentation of traditional or mainstream jazz music". Also in 1992, Tex acted as the Sacramento Jazz Jubilee's Festival Jazz Education Coordinator and, in addition, was the luncheon speaker and a panel discussion leader at the annual convention of the American Federation of Jazz Societies. Tex is the only jazz writer to place among the top three in the "Favorite Jazz Critic" category of the 1985 and 1996 Jazzology Record Polls (none occurred 1986-95).

Tex's recordings on the Dan Jazz label of the three Dixieland/ragtime appreciation shows he wrote for presentation at festivals and cruises have been broadcast on jazz radio programs throughout the English-speaking world. Titled "The Sources of Dixieland Jazz", "A Guide to Dixieland Jazz" and "A History of Ragtime", they have been used in musical courses from elementary school to college.

Contact Tex Wyndham at:
P. O Box 831, 632 Hillendale Road
Mendenhall, Pa. 19357
Phone: (610) 388 6330

INTRODUCTION

The text of this volume speaks for itself. However, to orient you properly, I should tell you a little about the source of that text.

This book presents, in the order of their publication, all of the "Texas Shout" columns I wrote for *West Coast Rag/The American Rag* from the column's inception in the November/December 1989 issue through the August 1996 column that marked its conclusion as a newly written every-issue feature. (To be precise, one column was not newly written. January 1990 was reprinted from the August 1989 *Jersey Jazz*.)

No attempt has been made to update these columns to the present. First, doing so would involve too much rewriting. Second, if we did try, something would go out of date before the final printing anyway. Thus, you will see references to recordings and other products that may no longer be on the market; prices, addresses and phone numbers that may not be current; musicians who are no longer among the living; bands that have disbanded; etc.

The columns were meant to be self-contained and to be digested, not in one gulp as you are about to devour them, but over a period of nearly seven years. Thus, you will find points repeated in summary form that were made in earlier columns but resurrected to support the argument of a later one. Again, an attempt to minimize such repetition would have essentially involved starting from scratch to reorganize and rewrite the entire text.

West Coast Rag began as an eleven-times-a-year tabloid published by Woody and Pat Laughnan. It acted as a social calendar for the Dixieland and ragtime festival scene on the West Coast.

While retaining its basic focus on festivals, it quickly became national in scope and increased its circulation until it was one of the country's two leading independent periodicals focusing on Dixieland and ragtime. In mid-1995, Don Jones took it over from the Laughnans, renaming it *The American Rag*.

"Texas Shout" is based on two of my most deeply held beliefs: (1) The more you know about something, the more likely you are to enjoy it and stick with it. (2) Dixieland jazz and ragtime, like all other valid art forms, are not in any way dated.

Specifically, Dixieland and ragtime are worth pursuing for their own sakes and have much to say to a contemporary listener who understands them. If artists from the turn of the century could use the conventions of these two musics to create something timeless in its appeal, then today's artists can do the same thing provided they approach the task with searching creative spirits.

| TEXAS SHOUT: HOW DIXIELAND JAZZ WORKS |

"Texas Shout" drew on my experiences over the decades as a writer, bandleader and performer of Dixieland and ragtime. This background was utilized to organize and discuss these musics along the above lines.

In doing so, I reached certain conclusions that are at odds with the conventional wisdom in the field. Therefore, I suspect that a number of readers will disagree with some or all of what I have to say.

Whether you agree or not, I'll have accomplished my purpose if this volume causes you to think through your position in a new way. I hope that the exercise will broaden your ability to appreciate music that has brought me and many others a great deal of pleasure.

This book would not exist without Dan and Sis Polin, of Dan Jazz Enterprises, my friends and producers. Dan, who believes that there are enough of you who care about what I have to say regarding Dixieland and ragtime (music that has all but disappeared from the general musical marketplace) to justify this tome, has acted as jack-of-all-trades in the production, illustration, layout and other hard work involved in preparing a book for publication. Sis has done the painstaking data input and other detailed labor required to get the text onto computer discs in a format ready for reproduction in a published form.

Nor would this book have come to pass without three people whose unquestioning support of my interests in obscure old music, movies and fiction enabled me to get deeply enough involved in them to form opinions about them: my parents, Charles (deceased) and Louise Wyndham, and my wife Nancy. Mom and Dad, bless their hearts, never really understood much about jazz. However, if I wanted to play it, that was fine with them. They were proud of whatever I did, no matter how arcane.

Nancy is perceptive and knowledgeable about Dixieland and ragtime. In addition to her dedicated toil as my wardrobe mistress, sales manager, etc., she has been a very valuable sounding board as well as de facto editor for my writings.

In the 1960's, except for an occasional local gig, my musical activity consisted of amusing myself in the music room and basement of my Wilmington, Delaware home. I would still be in that position except for many generous people, some of whom have since departed this world, who opened their homes, sheet music collections, etc., to me, and who undertook to get me out into the larger musical community.

Space prohibits naming all of them, so the following short list will have to act as a surrogate for the complete registry: Fred and Anna Wahler, Johnson and Liz McRee, Shannon Clark, Keith Miller, Jack and Jean Cuff, Roger Hankins, Mike Montgomery, Charlie Rasch, John Arpin, Bill and Mary Cay Donahoe, Bill and Mimi Barnes, Alan Granruth.

On the technical side, typographical and proofreading errors appearing in the original published columns have been tacitly corrected. We hope no new ones

Introduction

have been introduced, although our four-person proofreading team is inevitably not as eagle-eyed as that of, say, a major pubishing house.

Quite a few columns ran over more than one issue of *West Coast Rag/TheAmerican Rag*. In those cases, we have indicated where the original breaks occurred by use of the following: ◊ ◊ ◊.

I did not title the original columns. However, so that I could find relevant columns easily for reference purposes, I kept offhandedly-fashioned working titles on a sheet of paper. These titles have been included here for whatever use they may be to you.

We have not indexed this book for two reasons. First and foremost, I don't consider it to be the type of reference book for which an index is necessary; the chapter titles should get you where you want to go. Second, none of us is willing to do the work required to compile an index.

In closing, as this is probably the only time when I'm going to have a chance to mention special people in a book of mine, I would like to say that my two children, Buck and Susan, have been steady sources of pride and joy in these quarters. I won't keep you from the rest of this volume any longer. Keep swinging.

Tex Wyndham

September 1996

| TEXAS SHOUT: HOW DIXIELAND JAZZ WORKS |

Sacramento Dixieland Jubilee   *Photo by Dan Polin*

CHAPTER 1   "DIXIELAND"

Not so long ago I undertook an assignment to write some liner notes. Everyone seemed happy with the result, except that both the producer and the artist took issue with my use of the term "Dixieland" to describe the music with which they were involved.

I asked each to define for me what he thought "Dixieland" was. I got two very different answers, one of which went into such things as the clothes worn by the musicians on stage.

This incident caused me to reflect on the way, over the years, the term "Dixieland", when used by people who have a deep commitment to the music normally covered by the *West Coast Rag*, has become a pejorative word. Interestingly enough, these people rarely go much beyond that point in refining their thinking about "Dixieland". It's as if they are saying: "I recognize that music which is heavily informed by devices used by jazzmen during the twenties may be categorized into several styles. I know which of those styles I enjoy. The other styles are 'Dixieland'."

Thus, I have Person No. 1 telling me that "Dixieland" is "solo-oriented" twenties-style jazz, meaning (in this person's case) what we generally refer to as Chicago style, a type which this person doesn't like much (he prefers an emphasis on ensemble playing with carefully-worked-out routines on little-known titles). However, some well-known Chicagoans are reputed to have expressed a dislike of "Dixieland" and a preference to avoid playing with "Dixieland" musicians (meaning exactly those (usually) part-time organized bands preferred by Person No. 1). Obviously, both can't be right.

The short answer is that none of these attitudes, though quite prevalent among the cognoscenti, makes musical sense. If "Dixieland" refers to a style of music, then there must be a musical definition of it - that is, we should be able to tell if a band is a "Dixieland" band just from hearing it, without needing also to see what it's wearing, how it moves on stage, etc. Also, if "Dixieland" refers to a style of music, then there must be varying levels of performance of it, from excellent to inferior - that is, there must be good Dixieland as well as bad Dixieland.

Yet, those who resist use of the term "Dixieland" usually do so because, whatever it is, they want to dismiss all of it. At any rate, I have never heard such a person admit that there is a Dixieland performance that he really enjoys.

I submit that denigration of the term "Dixieland" reflects sloppy thinking on the part of the folks who desire to do so. Worse, it is counterproductive to the effort in which we are all engaged to attract more people to an enjoyment of our music.

We should recognize that there is no need for us to preach to the converted. Instead, we should want to present ourselves, via our music, our terminology, etc., so that we can most easily reach the ones who have not yet come to appreciate the merits of twenties-style jazz.

If so, let's face up to the fact that the most commonly understood term for our music, to those outside the field, is "Dixieland". How many times have you had to

TEXAS SHOUT: HOW DIXIELAND JAZZ WORKS

explain to someone what "classic jazz" is? ("No sir, it has nothing to do with classical music".) Or "traditional jazz"? (After all, bop has been around for nearly 50 years, and I have met bop musicians who consider themselves to be playing "traditional jazz".) If someone not close to twenties-style jazz is going to associate any term with it at all, I think you'll find overwhelmingly that the term which makes that association for them is "Dixieland".

Moreover, to the civilians outside our hallowed halls, "Dixieland" does not have the negative connotations described above. They may not know exactly what Dixieland is, or be able to define it with precision, but they usually have an upbeat image of it, an image that suggests a good time.

Producers of the large festivals have frequently been quick to perceive the positive effects of "Dixieland" on general audiences. The largest, best-attended jazz festival in the world calls itself the "Sacramento Dixieland Jubilee".

I'm sure all of us can name many other festivals which go out of their way to make sure that the public knows that they are a "Dixieland" or "Dixie" festival (San Diego, Central Ohio, Shasta, Santa Rosa, etc.). The producers of these festivals know that they need the attendance, not only of the small number of traveling jazz fans and jazz club members who read the genre publications, but also of the public as a whole.

I think it is time for our community to stop trashing a term that works on our behalf. This word helps us get gigs and helps us get audiences into those gigs where we then have the opportunity to expose them to quality older-style music.

In short, "Dixieland" is not a synonym for bad jazz. It is a very useful umbrella term for describing the type of music played at our favorite festivals, music which is comprised of several styles, all of which can be played badly or well.

(As an aside, I can't help but be amused at the inconsistency displayed by certain fans and musicians who claim to hate "Dixieland" but who nevertheless take great pains to plan trips to attend - or get invitations to perform - at - festivals that proclaim themselves to be "Dixieland" festivals that hire "Dixieland" musicians. How does such a person justify his own presence? Do such musicians make a point of telling the festival chairman, when the invitation comes in, that they really shouldn't be invited because they don't play "Dixieland", or do they take the gig under false pretenses?)

For my own part, my Red Lion Jazz Band's business card states that we play, "Authentic Dixieland". When people ask me what kind of jazz I play, I respond "Dixieland"; that answer usually strikes sparks of recognition, and of a positive type.

In the quarter-century the Red Lions have been together, we've never once, to my knowledge, lost a booking because the person who got my name decided he wanted a "classic jazz" or "traditional jazz" band and not a "Dixieland" band. Quite the contrary: I always point out to any potential client who's never heard the RLJB that we are a Dixieland band, and he often responds with a sigh of relief and says that's just what he wants.

We then go and play our regular show in which we perform as honestly, sincerely and uncompromisingly as we know how to do. Most of the time, both the crowd and the musicians leave with smiles of satisfaction on their faces.

"Dixieland"

Do yourself and the whole genre a favor. The next time you're discussing jazz, don't twist yourself into a pretzel trying to deny that you're involved with "Dixieland" and trying to persuade others that they should investigate what they may perceive as an esoteric music described by a term they don't know. Tell them up front that you like "Dixieland" (adding any other descriptive words, such as Chicago or uptown New Orleans, as you wish) and see if you don't find yourself reaching a common understanding with them a lot faster than before.

Red Lion Jazz Band   *Photo by Nancy Wyndham*

TEXAS SHOUT: HOW DIXIELAND JAZZ WORKS

Unavailable Records   Photos by Dan Polin
From the collection of John Ochs

Jan. 1990 West Coast Rag
*Reprinted from Aug. 1989
Jersey Jazz*

CHAPTER 2   UNAVAILABLE RECORDS

It hardly needs to be said that you learn how to play jazz by listening to jazzmen perform. It also goes without saying that, if you want to play jazz well, you need to listen to the greatest artists in the field. If you have not heard the best, and if you do not fully understand what makes them the best, the odds are that you will not move your own talents in the proper direction, nor stretch your skills to their maximum potential.

Where classic jazz is concerned, most of the truly lustrous names can be heard only on recordings. Bud Freeman and Wild Bill Davison are about the last active practitioners from the twenties. If you want to study with Oliver, Bix, Louis, Bessie, Fatha, etc., you need to look toward your record player as a classroom.

Unfortunately, there no longer is any reasonable accessibility to the acknowledged masterpieces in the vintage discography. Go into your nearest record store and try to find any pre-swing jazz at all, much less music recorded in the twenties (regarded today, I suppose, as being in unacceptable fidelity). Although some of this material is beginning to appear on CDs, there is not as yet a whole lot of it, and as far as I know, mall stores, which usually go for high-volume, fast-turnover items, aren't rushing to stock up on what has been issued.

Similarly, the large domestic corporations with rights to, say, the OKehs, Victors, Vocalions, etc., have minimal interest in producing recordings that will have low-volume sales to a decreasing number of fans of older-style jazz. Further, small collectors' labels, for understandable reasons, tend to focus on really rare 78s that have never been reissued.

Thus, the budding vintage jazzman who needs sources is cut off at the knees. Seasoned collectors know that classic stuff can be obtained, often on foreign labels, through specialty mail-order houses, but how many of today's players even know about the limited-circulation publications in which such recordings are advertised?

The net effect of this dearth of masterworks is a change in the nature of the jazz being played. It is only too obvious that many of today's organized bands are learning licks and tunes not from the originals but from each other, especially at festivals (about the only place where much interchange of ideas can occur these days, or where recordings can be bought in any quantity or variety). If you hear Band X play Tune Y, and you like the tune or it gets a good crowd response, you take the chart, using your hand-held cassette machine, and eventually show up with that tune played much that way in your own book. A natural enough thing to do, and where else can you find new titles and figures?

So far, so good. But the problem is that the guys on the next bandstand, though certainly capable enough, are probably themselves part-timers just like you. Without demeaning their talents, we still know that few of them deserve to be mentioned in the same breath with the Hall Of Famers. They may have graduated from more modern forms of music in which amplification and heavy rhythm are

~ 5 ~

TEXAS SHOUT: HOW DIXIELAND JAZZ WORKS

taken for granted.* How likely is it that your own performances are going to be much improved if you follow their lead?

Thus we have, as once was noted in the letters column of *The Mississippi Rag,* some bands getting standing ovations today that would have been laughed off the stage twenty years ago. This situation is not their fault. Most of them in that category, I'm sure, are playing as well and honestly as they can. However, their growth has been stunted through lack of opportunity to understand what they're supposed to be doing via intimate familiarity with the great recordings in the idiom. Audiences conditioned to a steady diet of amorphous music on the radio and in commercials, movie and TV sound tracks, etc., are in the same position and respond enthusiastically to a type of pre-swing jazz that is becoming increasingly hybridized.

Perhaps there is nothing wrong with this development. Perhaps all music should change over time. Perhaps it is just fine for musicians to play what they want to, and audiences to enjoy it, regardless of what it's called.

Personally, though, I have some trouble with the way things are going. If our music is going to change, I don't think it's right that older-style jazz should become something else either without realizing that it is doing so, or without changing what it calls itself.

As one who was lucky enough to amass a collection of music during a time when great material from the golden age was reissued in abundance, I get discouraged at the current flow of recordings from artists who too often have nothing to say, nothing to add to what's gone before. And yet I think they would have much to contribute, if they only knew how to go about it - as can be demonstrated by a relatively limited number of contemporary musicians/bands (Vince Giordano's Nighthawks, The Jim Cullum Jazz Band, Warren Vaché, Jr., Howard Alden, and Kenny Davern, among others, are names that come quickly to mind that will be familiar to readers of *Jersey Jazz*) who have developed personal and valid styles within the bounds of traditional jazz. Which brings me back to the points in my first paragraph. With no solution to my concerns, that's as good a place to stop as any.

---

*As an aside, a good classic-style combo shouldn't need amplification, except for vocals and announcements, on a typical indoor gig - i.e., one that isn't in a large auditorium. Its instrumentation took shape at a time when sound equipment wasn't available, and that's why banjos, tubas, trombones and other instruments that can easily be heard without amplification wound up in Dixieland bands in the first place. Nevertheless, how many of you have seen bands that always operate with each man's axe stuck into a turned-up mike? Can that kind of music be likely to "swing" in a jazz sense? Or will its rhythmic intensity and excitement be more likely to resemble that of rock rhythm?

Unavailable Records

Unavailable Records   *Photos by Dan Polin*
From the collection of Bert Barr

TEXAS SHOUT: HOW DIXIELAND JAZZ WORKS

Duke Ellington and his Washingtonians 1926
Photo courtesy of Riverside Records

The Coon-Sanders Original Nighthawk Orchestra 1930
Photo courtesy of The Record Changer

CHAPTER 3   HOT DANCE

Festivals wishing to present the full spectrum of pre-swing (i.e., Dixieland) jazz styles, customarily include combos playing "hot dance" music. Like many terms emerging from popular culture, "hot dance" is not the best name that could have been selected for the particular type of jazz it describes.

As a result, I have encountered some misconceptions about hot dance music which I'll mention and try to clear up below. In addition, I've never seen anyone attempt a useful working definition of "hot dance" in musical terms. So, for the benefit of festivalgoers and other interested listeners, I'll provide you with one:

> *"Hot dance" is a pre-swing, or Dixieland, jazz style in which the ensemble passages are generally arranged (either via written scores or memorized voicing), leaving only the solo passages available for improvisation.*

To properly understand that definition, you should be sure not to confuse an "arrangement" with a "routine". A routine is a common understanding among the musicians as to when certain strains of the selection will be performed, where the key changes and breaks are, and which instruments are to be playing at which times. It need not involve an arrangement.

All jazz performances have to have routines, even if they are the common ensemble-solos-ensemble jam formats handled spontaneously on the bandstand by having the leader point his finger at the next soloist. Many Dixieland standards have very complex routines. "Tiger Rag" is an example of a tune that has an extremely tricky routine - one which all seasoned Dixielanders know, but which is rarely rendered via an arrangement.

Musicians will sometimes casually refer to the routine as the "chart" or, less accurately, as the "arrangement". However, an arrangement, in the sense we are using it here, applies to musical passages which are voiced in advance so that the instrumentalist is given little or no choice as to the notes he is to play during those passages.

With those ideas in mind, let's address two misconceptions regarding hot dance. The first is the notion that hot dance is an exclusively big-band idiom. The second is the notion that hot dance is not jazz, or that it has some lower amount of jazz content than other Dixieland styles.

It is true that a large group playing twenties-style jazz will be a hot dance band. Once you have more than eight instruments, you pretty much have to voice the ensembles to keep everyone from getting in each other's way. In that sense, hot dance may be thought of loosely as the big-band jazz style of the twenties just as swing was the big-band jazz style of the thirties.

However, a smaller combo may elect to arrange its ensembles on some or all of its tunes, and will thereby become a hot dance band, just as there are swing combos

TEXAS SHOUT: HOW DIXIELAND JAZZ WORKS

that have fewer sidemen than a typical thirties swing band. The Stomp Off label has, in recent years, released a number of fine hot dance albums by groups using the conventional seven-or-fewer Dixieland lineup. One of the most popular thereof is the Hot Antic Jazz Band which uses the doubling talents of its five (sometimes six) musicians and very intricate arrangements to evoke the feeling of a larger unit.

To address the second misconception, hot dance is most emphatically a jazz style. In fact that's what the word "hot" tells you. If the performance is not a jazz performance, then it is ordinary dance music. Thus, it is not proper to use "hot dance" as a catchall term for any twenties-style pop music.

How do you tell if you're hearing a hot dance performance? First, you satisfy yourself that it is, on the whole, a jazz performance - i.e., its main focus is on using jazz licks and jazz phrasing, played with a jazz feeling. Second, you satisfy yourself that it is a Dixieland performance - i.e., it deliberately avoids the jazz licks and conventions of swing or of other advanced jazz styles. Third, you listen to try to determine whether the ensembles you're hearing, for the most part, must have been voiced in advance. If all three tests are passed, you have hot dance.

That third test will be the toughest. It might not always be possible to determine the presence of an arrangement just from hearing the performance.

In most cases, you will be able to detect an arrangement fairly easily - usually there's not much point in arranging something unless you're trying for an effect that wouldn't happen spontaneously. However, if the band is doing a note-for-note re-creation of a performance that was originally fully improvised - let's say the 12/8/27 OKeh 78 of "China Boy" by McKenzie and Condon's Chicagoans - the results ideally would sound just the same as the original.

Why, you may ask, should a style of jazz be defined in a way that might not make it identifiable from listening to it? One answer to that question is that, whether one realizes it or not, all jazz styles can only be validly defined in terms of what the musicians are trying to do.

Musicians who operate under exactly the same rules and objectives are inevitably playing the same style of jazz - some better, some worse, some bringing their own distinctive sounds and ideas to it, but they could all sit in with each other's bands and get along. It's only when you change one or more of those rules, say to put more emphasis on soloing, or on fancy repertoire, etc., that you move to a new style. Usually, those changes will be fairly obvious to a seasoned listener, but that need not necessarily be the case.

Another answer to that question is that the skills required to play hot dance are substantially different from those required to play other styles of Dixieland jazz. To function effectively in hot dance, a musician must be able to execute written or memorized arrangements with a proper jazz phrasing and a feeling of spontaneity. For other styles of Dixieland, a musician need not be able to read music or to fit in with scored voices. In Chicago style, for example, where the solo is the focus of the performance, it will be sufficient if he is a talented and creative soloist. (By the way, the subject of Dixieland skills is really a larger one that needs a column of its own.)

Note that it is the performance, not the band, that determines the style of jazz. Most bands can only play convincingly in one style and are not interested in playing other styles, so that it would be proper to refer to them as "uptown New Orleans" or

Hot Dance

"West Coast revival" style bands. Other groups, however, may take a more eclectic outlook.

One such group, fondly remembered as one of the best of the twenties white hot dance bands, was the Coon-Sanders Original Nighthawk Orchestra. However, listening to its overall output reveals that many of its recordings are straight non-jazz dance music. It wasn't until the Nighthawks began waxing jazz-permeated material like "High Fever" and "Roodles" that they became a jazz - i.e., a hot dance - orchestra.

This characteristic is more typical of groups that like to play hot dance. Some of their selections will be hot dance numbers, some (if the band is small enough) might be fully improvised, and some might be conventional dance tunes. Failure to notice this difference causes bands like, e.g., Paul Whiteman's twenties band, to be too casually referred to as hot dance bands. Actually, most Whiteman performances are not primarily focused on jazz, despite the presence of Bix and other famous jazzmen. They are essentially ordinary dance music, spiced up in isolated portions by an overlay of jazz.

One point may bother some of those who have wanted to dismiss hot dance as being some kind of weak sister in the Dixieland field. The pre-swing recordings of the great Negro orchestras such as Moten, Ellington and Henderson are properly characterized as hot dance sides. That is, from a technical point of view, the members of those orchestras were given exactly the same assignment as the Coon-Sanders musicians - read the arrangement and play hot solos.

Calling early Ellington and Henderson "hot dance" may disturb fans who feel that such outstanding groups should not be lumped into the same category as the lesser-quality white hot dance bands. In this instance, one needs to realize two things: (1) In all styles of jazz, there will be musicians who are much, much better at what they're doing than other musicians. (2) In the twenties, the Black jazz orchestras were so far ahead of their white counterparts that comparisons are hardly possible.

Black bands displayed a much more pervasive jazz feeling, and far superior soloists, than the whites. Had Ellington's crew waxed the Coon-Sanders arrangement of "Brainstorm" while the Nighthawks were waxing the Ellington score of "The Mooche", each would have known exactly what it was supposed to do. However, in that case, I feel sure that the Ellington rendition would have been so superior that today's Dixielanders would have made "Brainstorm" into the quasi-standard that "The Mooche" has become, and the latter tune would have fallen more by the wayside.

By the way, I would like to emphasize that my use of Coon-Sanders for illustrative purposes here is not meant in any way to denigrate the output of a band whose best records are every bit as memorable as its many present-day fans testify. One hardly needs to apologize for not consistently operating at the level of an Ellington.

Finally, and most importantly, what is the best way to enjoy hot dance? You do so, by focusing mostly on the arrangement. Has the arranger made imaginative use of his resources, giving you a pleasing yet distinctive mix of sounds? Has he found combinations that bring out the special features of the composition, or shown you a vision of it that you hadn't anticipated? Does the band handle the arrangement

TEXAS SHOUT: HOW DIXIELAND JAZZ WORKS

crisply, with the sections functioning as a unit with no rough edges? And, with regard to solos, do the soloists have the skill to carry their passages and provide the build that the arrangement contemplates?

Developing an appreciation of such matters will more than compensate you at your next festival when you decide to take off a set from a diet of free-wheeling, let-it-all-hang-out jamming to catch the hot dance combo. Anyway, for fans or would-be fans of hot dance, I hope that the above provides you with a basis for more easy access to a fine and valid Dixieland style.

Devil Mountain Jazz Band   *Photo by Dan Polin*
Known for some of their "Hot Dance" numbers

CHAPTER 4   READING, SOLO & ENSEMBLE SKILLS

In my last "Texas Shout", I mentioned that the skills required to play hot dance jazz are substantially different from the skills required to play other types of Dixieland. Actually, there are three main skills utilized in playing the various styles of Dixieland jazz. For purposes of today's column, I'll call them "reading skill", "solo skill" and "ensemble skill".

Reading skill is the ability to execute a written or memorized arrangement with the proper degree of jazz phrasing and feeling. As explained in my previous column, it is the most important skill in the hot dance style of Dixieland.

Solo skill is the ability to conceive novel and interesting improvisations, together with the instrumental ability to execute those improvisations as they are conceived. Although soloing is important in all jazz styles, solo skill is most highly valued in Chicago-style Dixieland, where the solos are the focus of the performance.

Ensemble skill is the ability to listen at once to as many as seven other musicians improvising simultaneously while, at the same time, conceiving and executing an improvisation that will enhance and complement their efforts, making the whole greater than the sum of its parts. This is the most highly-valued skill in the other styles of Dixieland, such as uptown New Orleans, West Coast revival, etc.

Many Dixielanders possess all three of these skills to some degree. However, it should be noted that being particularly proficient at one of these skills does not necessarily guarantee adequate performance at either of the other two.

That is the reason why so many hand-picked all-star bands fail to jell as units. All-stars are usually selected for their superior solo skills. However, a group of outstanding soloists may include several artists with below-average ensemble skills. In a Dixieland band, even one performer who functions poorly in an ensemble can bend the overall results out of shape.

Sidney Bechet, for example, though arguably the finest soloist Dixieland jazz ever produced, was a relatively weak ensemble player, being a flamboyant artist who tended to dominate ensembles. Bechet's best ensemble recordings were made on those occasions when he was matched with other top players who were equally strong-willed, and who could stand their ground with Bechet in an ensemble context.

A player in a hot dance band should practice by spending time sight-reading, or by going over any memorized arrangements to be sure his notes are fixed in his mind and can be instantly executed. Depending on the difficulty of the scores, and on the other instruments with which he has to blend, he may also need to work on range and tone.

A player desiring to practice ensemble skills should seize every opportunity to play with other improvising Dixielanders, in as many different combinations and styles, with as varied a repertoire, as possible. Failing that, ensemble practice could be gained by playing along with a good variety of recordings.

TEXAS SHOUT: HOW DIXIELAND JAZZ WORKS

A player practicing solos is going to work on developing licks and creating logical melodic lines. Playing with records is suitable for this purpose, but a sufficiently broad-based musician might be able to get by practicing with a metronome (or without one, if he has a sure enough sense of rhythm).

A professional musician will often need to attain a professional standard in all three areas. He will have the time to do the required practicing and will usually have to be proficient at reading, soloing and ensemble playing if he is to compete successfully for whatever gigs may come his way.

The problem is that these days, except for a few areas like Orlando or New Orleans where nostalgic music is either an important part of the entertainment scene or part of the area's tourist-attraction heritage, it is next to impossible for a musician to make a secure full-time living playing Dixieland. The overwhelming majority of Dixieland musicians seen at local jazz clubs and festivals today are semi-pros who depend importantly on full- or part-time non-musical jobs for their livelihood.

Most part-time musicians simply do not have the practice time available to become accomplished in all three areas described above. This fact has some impact on the quality of the music provided by the average Dixieland band we hear today.

Let's start with soloing, which is the most discouraging area. Becoming a consistently creative soloist requires constantly working to expand one's ideas and to extend one's self. A musician who practices an hour or two a week and then plays a gig or two on the weekend is very unlikely, unless unusually gifted, to do more than get himself back to where he was last weekend by the time he finishes his weekly cycle. He will spend most of his solo time reworking favorite figures and standard licks that lie comfortably under his fingers.

Unfortunately, and it pains me to say so, the level of soloing we hear these days from the part-time bands is pitifully weak, even from many of the best-known players and combos. As a record reviewer over the past twenty-plus years, I've heard a pretty representative sampling of what's out there. I'd be hard put to name more than a small handful of part-time Dixielanders who manage to get through a record (or a festival set) without substantially repeating themselves as soloists and leaving me with an uncomfortable sense of deja vu.

Whether you like the all-star jam sets or not, the fact is that if you like consistently inventive soloing, you're much better off to spend time with the name pros on the all-star festival sets, even if their ensembles seem chaotic. Similarly, if you are a budding Dixielander who wants to learn to solo, the records of your favorite organized bands are not going to teach it to you as well as the records of the famous professional soloists.

The news is much better in the other two areas. In particular, I've observed that the typical format for West Coast Dixieland jazz club meetings almost always includes several informal jam sets for the members. In those cases, a person desiring to jam will be matched, from month to month, with a wide variety of players, of all levels of ability and in a mix of styles.

This admirable practice not only helps involve people in the music, to insure some sort of steady supply of players, but it is ideal for developing ensemble skill. I feel sure that this factor is an important one in the relative health of Dixieland jazz on the West Coast as compared with the rest of the country (where the informal jam session is generally not an integral part of local jazz club meetings).

Finally, most players learned their instruments in school, where they were also taught to read music. If the school had a stage band program, they were also taught to read with a jazz feeling and to read more complex licks than are usually found in a Dixieland arrangement.

After leaving school, such players can gravitate rather easily to Dixieland, which is all to the good for our music. There are quite a few bands out there which are either reading their charts or obviously performing memorized arrangements, and doing a most effective job thereof.

So-called purists may scoff at Dixieland that isn't fully improvised, but as I pointed out in my previous column, hot dance is a perfectly valid Dixieland style. In today's climate of part-time musicians, the presence of arrangements provides a way for a band to play a much broader and more varied program than it could if the sidemen were required to memorize the entire band's book in the limited practice time available to them. Also, the presence of the arrangements makes it possible to bring younger musicians, fresh from their stage-band training, into a Dixieland situation that allows them to feel comfortable and be productive while learning the rules of the music.

None of the foregoing remarks is intended to be critical of the scene or of the players that comprise it. They're designed more to help the non-musician fans in the crowd better understand what's going on onstage. Once you've grasped the dynamics of the situation, I think you're likely to be more forgiving of any weaknesses caused by the circumstances under which we all have to function today, and thereby enjoy yourself more. And what should Dixieland be all about, if it isn't enjoying yourself?

TEXAS SHOUT: HOW DIXIELAND JAZZ WORKS

Sidney Bechet 1952 "Solo Skills"   *Photo by Robert Parent*

Uptown Lowdown Jazz Band "Ensemble Skills"   *Photo by Dan Polin*

CHAPTER 5   NON-GENRE MUSIC

In recent years, I have noticed that non-genre music is becoming a larger part of the Dixieland festival and club circuit. Producers are booking non-genre bands, some of which are proving to be their most popular draws. Some of today's Dixieland bands include in their sets a few non-genre performances, which are also meeting with favorable crowd response.

There is a significant element of the Dixieland community which is unhappy about this development. I am no longer one of them, and I do not propose to use this space for complaints. However, because the controversy still rages, I am going to make my points without naming names, lest someone conclude that I am criticizing where no criticism is intended.

What I would like to do today is share with you my views on how this situation came about. Those of you who know me very well won't be surprised to read that I believe there is a musical reason for this changing emphasis.

First, let's be sure what's meant when I say "non-genre" music. I am talking about performances at Dixieland festivals that are not, and make no real claim to be, Dixieland performances. ("STAD", as my dear friend Anna Wahler would put it, but propriety precludes setting out the full translation in this column.) Examples that come to mind include the booking at major "Dixieland" weekends of groups that play mostly or exclusively swing, country/western, blues and/or salsa.

I am not talking about what are commonly referred to as "show" bands. These are Dixieland bands that package their product with a keen eye for high production values, for ear-catching numbers with a substantial orientation toward excitement and accessibility.

Some purists turn away from the show bands, asserting that they are shallow and commercial. As a general proposition, I disagree. If any of you have seen The Rent Party Revellers' "Guide to Dixieland Jazz" show, or heard it on audiocassette, you know that (as explained in an early part of the show) I consider entertainment for its own sake an authentic and valid function of Dixieland jazz.

The "show" bands, in my view, if they are playing Dixieland jazz and not some other music, belong at a Dixieland festival. To be sure, some of them have not yet developed the skill needed to entertain without being shallow and commercial. However, the better ones (which, I am pleased to say, include most of the really popular show bands) deliver the goods when they start to play, offering creative charts, a high level of musicianship, and well-knit ensembles.

In short, the show Dixieland bands are operating within a branch of Dixieland jazz that, like any other style (uptown New Orleans, Chicago, West Coast revival, hot dance, etc.) can be played badly or well. As long as they play Dixieland, they should be represented at Dixieland festivals.

Now back to non-genre music. When I came to Dixieland jazz, in the pre-rock-and-roll days, the other people at a Dixieland concert would be fairly knowledgeable

TEXAS SHOUT: HOW DIXIELAND JAZZ WORKS

about Dixieland. They were there because they knew what Dixieland was, and they wanted to hear it on that occasion vs. other available kinds of pre-rock music, such as swing or country/western or urban blues.

At that time, as I covered at some length in a column in the January 1987 issue of *The Mississippi Rag,* all types of popular music used the same fundamental building blocks - such as four-or-eight-bar phrases and circle-of-fifths chord progressions. With all of us, consciously or not, having become acclimated to these common elements, the differences between, say, Dixieland and swing were easier to perceive. We could tell them apart more easily and deliberately chose the music that most appealed to us.

Rock, which has dominated the pop charts for the past 35 years or so, has reversed this situation. Its current musical vocabulary is completely different in every respect - melody, rhythm, dynamics, chord progressions, whatever - from any type of popular music and jazz that preceded it in this country.

Rock is so radically different in these respects, and is so overwhelmingly popular, that it has crowded virtually all non-rock popular music and jazz into the same corner. As a result, to many people (particularly if they are not deeply into music) the pre-rock forms of music are less distinguishable than they used to be. Dixieland, ragtime, swing and vintage popular songs, because of their common elements mentioned above, now seem a lot like each other when compared to rock music. The differences between them are harder to discern when rock is the commonly-accepted standard of measurement.

Further, rock today is ubiquitous. It's all over the airwaves, on film and TV soundtracks, in commercials, everywhere. More than half the people in the U. S. have lived their entire lives during the rock era, absorbing rock that comes at them from every direction. Naturally, most people whose musical tastes are conditioned in this fashion have great difficulty relating to music that doesn't have electrified sound, high volume, heavy back-beat and the other accoutrements of rock.

What about the rest of us, usually folks past middle age who had our musical tastes formed before rock took over? Today, if someone wants to get away from rock music, he may well investigate a Dixieland club or festival. Whatever else he knows about Dixieland, he'll know that it came before rock.

Anyone from pre-rock times who investigated the Dixieland scene would discover, and would have discovered at any time in the last twenty-five years that it consisted largely of persons of his age or older, generally well-behaved, fun-loving people. He would have discovered music to which he could relate, and ballroom dancing of a type that he grew up with. He would not feel assaulted by the youth/drug culture, by humorless lyrics that centered totally on adolescent concerns, etc.

It doesn't surprise me at all that so many mature people who, if rock had never appeared, would be listening instead to today's equivalent of Dinah Shore, Eddy Arnold or Harry James, have now gravitated to the Dixieland scene. However, we should keep in mind that these people are not there because they had any advance commitment to Dixieland as an art form. Many of them will be perfectly happy with any kind of music that they can dance to that isn't too loud. And if the truth be told, many of them would probably rather hear something that's more reminiscent of Xavier Cugat or Sammy Kaye than of Turk Murphy.

Non-Genre Music

I believe that this element of the Dixieland community is a large and growing segment of our audience. It may even now be the largest segment - after all, dedicated Dixieland devotees never were more than a small proportion of the overall population.

At any rate, and probably without realizing why this audience is out there, Dixieland club officers and festival producers have obviously become increasingly aware that a major part of their crowds wants very much to hear, at least once in a while and maybe more than that, non-genre music. One can hardly blame them for booking acts that satisfy the demands of their patrons.

So far, so good. Anything that attracts people to a Dixieland environment is going to benefit our music, bringing financial and other resources to it, even if some of those people don't spend much or any time listening to Dixieland when they get there. If the addition of an element of non-genre music makes those folks happier and helps keep them around, it's O.K. with me.

I am concerned, though, about what these people think when they open their "Dixieland" festival program and find that the headline artist is a pop singer from the thirties, or learn that the most crowded venues are the ones with the country/western band. Are they going to conclude that these attractions, being heralded as the top or most popular names, are what Dixieland is all about? Not being told otherwise, will these people perceive that the real Dixieland bands, perhaps not being headliners or not drawing as well, are somehow not doing their jobs correctly?

You may scoff at such concerns, but I could cite some examples where just such misconceptions have occurred. Those of us with a deep commitment to Dixieland ought to want the public to have a better understanding of what Dixieland is and to have a better ability to appreciate good Dixieland. To that end, I have a mild suggestion that might reduce confusion without interfering with anyone's good time.

I would like to see the festivals and clubs that sponsor events where Dixieland is a principal attraction make a point of identifying non-genre music in their advertisements and program notes. There is no reason why such identification has to be done in any sort of negative way. For example, the ads could list Dixieland by Bands A, B, C, and D; Swing by Bands E and F; Ragtime by Band G; etc. The program notes should make a point of stating what type of music each band plays without somehow trying to sneak in some marginal relationship to Dixieland where none actually exists, and should clearly point out that the event offers a variety of musical styles for those who don't want to spend every minute listening to Dixieland.

Such a policy would help educate the audience about what it's hearing, would help attendees plan their listening schedules and would help those who might be considering a long trip decide more easily which events on a potential itinerary are most likely to offer the mix of music that they prefer. It would also help bandleaders evaluate which festivals and clubs to contact regarding possible gigs by putting into clearer perspective the different types of music on which a given organization focuses.

Further, a practice of identifying non-genre music might help the clubs and festivals define their own roles more clearly. There are "Dixieland" festivals out there now hiring so much non-genre music that, perhaps, they should be calling themselves by names that more accurately describe to prospective attendees what to expect on the bill. Such festivals might be better off to openly acknowledge that they are now festivals of "American music", or "Dixieland and vintage pop", or "1920s-30s jazz", or whatever.

At any rate, such a change would go far to reduce any valid reason for the hard-core Dixielanders at such events to gripe about the performers. Since festivals and club concerts are, above everything, supposed to be fun for all, anything that raises the level of good cheer has to be a plus.

CHAPTER 6   HAND-HELD LIVE TAPES

Hand-held tape recorders are ubiquitous. Everything played these days by any jazzman from the stage of any festival or sizeable jazz club is recorded by someone and exists somewhere in one or more living rooms.

Of course, this situation has created a nightmare for discographers, but that's not what I want to discuss today. After all, discographers, invaluable though they are, seem to enjoy impossible assignments that no one in his right mind would undertake. Instead, I want to talk about the effects of this boom in private recordings on the music that's heard on the Dixieland circuit.

Many musicians object in principle to having their music recorded by individuals in the audience. I am not one of them. If you've paid your money to see my show, and you want to take my music home with you to re-hear in your home for your own enjoyment, it's OK with me. I feel rather complimented, in fact. Now that you know where I stand on this commonly discussed aspect of portable recorders, let's move on.

Many musicians and record producers point out that, to the extent that people elect to do their listening to their in-person tapes, the market for sales of commercial recordings will be damaged. There can be no question that this point has merit.

If you would otherwise have purchased a recording by the artist, and you decide not to do so because you're just as happy with the tape you made from your seat, overall demand will be reduced with the inevitable result that fewer commercial recordings will appear. Those that are issued will need to be more cheaply produced in order to be economical in a shrinking market. Further, this reduction in demand will tend to diminish whatever minimal incentives still exist to encourage musicians to play Dixieland vs. whatever other music they might choose.

However, while I do regret such developments, I can't weep too much about them. Except for the veteran jazzmen who have always made their living playing Dixieland and can't really do anything else (and few of them survive at this writing), Dixieland jazz today is almost 100% a hobby music. It has not been commercially viable for decades. Most younger musicians who enter the field full-time do so with their eyes open to the hazards thereof. The overwhelming majority of Dixieland musicians and record producers are persons who do not depend on jazz for their livelihoods.

In that situation, the diminution of the market for recordings means that, for many Dixielanders, their hobby will cost them a little more than it would have otherwise. Because they never went into Dixieland for the money anyway, and because Dixieland records haven't sold in enough quantity recently to provide much of anyone with significant financial rewards, the economics of the record marketplace shouldn't detain us for long.

What bothers me is the effect on the aesthetic sensitivity of the audience as it becomes increasingly conditioned to appreciating music via amateur in-person

TEXAS SHOUT: HOW DIXIELAND JAZZ WORKS

tapes. I will categorically say that any tape made from a seat in the audience, or from a table at a jazz club, will not contain the musical subtleties that were played by the musicians on stage. Those nuances, those fine points that separate the ordinary jazz from the truly outstanding, are lost in the echo, crowd noise, chatter, poor balance, tinkling of glasses, etc., that invariably appear on material recorded from a spot in the crowd.

If essentially all of your listening library consists of such recordings, I can confidently state that you have not fully learned how to appreciate Dixieland jazz and that you do not understand it as well as you think you do. You are not in position to request producers to book the best bands, because you are not entirely able to distinguish which ones they are.

To the extent that this situation is becoming more prevalent on the circuit, a standard is being established that settles closer to mediocrity. If a band has simply mastered the surface characteristics of the music - the only elements of it that will carry through into microphones sitting offstage -, many listeners will have no basis for distinguishing it from a combo that has depth. Producers, in many cases, will naturally come to disregard depth in hiring musicians if the audience doesn't particularly want depth and if depth costs more money.

There is, however a simple solution to this problem. Listen to your amateur tapes and enjoy them, by all means. However, do yourself a favor and be sure to buy, on some kind of regular basis, commercially-produced recordings and give them a fair listen as well. If you particularly like live sessions, that's fine - the commercially-produced ones will typically be made from onstage microphones which, though some problems of balance may still obtain, will screen out extraneous sound and give you a chance to understand all of what's happening. It won't be long before you'll be able to tell the difference in musical quality, and the extra fun you'll get from the music will more than repay you for the cost of the recordings.

Once you've done that, I have one small favor to ask. After you've taped my show, and taken it home and enjoyed it, please, please don't make dubbings of the tape for other people. Just listen for your own amusement.

Here's why I ask this favor. When you listen to your tape of a show you've seen, the tape brings back your memories of the in-person event. You don't really hear the crowd chatter, the echoes, the fluctuations in level, because you've mentally been taken back to the scene where the recording was made.

I can understand why you might want to share that good time with your friends. However, it's not possible to do so because they weren't there. They have only what's on your tape to hear, maybe by themselves in the cold surroundings of an expensive hi-fi set up without the benefit of the drinks, friends, and congenial atmosphere that you remember when you hear your tape.

Believe me, in those circumstances your friends will notice any acoustical deficiency in the recording as if it were fingernails across a blackboard. Their adverse judgment thereof is very likely to fall on the artist, not on your recorder.

Thus, you do not do a jazzman a favor by mailing around home-made recordings of his shows. In fact, you are very likely to have exactly the opposite result. I can cite examples of excellent bands that were passed over for festivals because well-meaning fans had sent the producers, without the band's knowledge, amateur tapes of the groups accompanied by requests that they be invited. The tapes sounded so bad that the producers resolved to waste no more effort on those bands; years elapsed before the producers could be persuaded to take up the subject anew in a proper way.

If you really want to help, believe me, you're better off if you stick to praising your favorite artists verbally to your friends and to jazz show producers. An additional step you could take would be to find a way to get such people to hear commercially-produced recordings by those artists.

Finally, remember that paying to see a show does not create an automatic right to record it. If the club or festival has rules on the subject, cooperate with them. If you do record, don't do anything that interferes with the ability of the other paying customers to enjoy the show (such as by putting mikes on booms or high stands that block a clear view of the stage, by running wires across the floor, by using an adjacent chair for sound equipment unless you buy an extra ticket for it, etc.). Don't put recording gear on stage where the musicians will have to step around it, particularly in situations where there is not enough room for everyone with a recorder to exercise the same prerogative. And take the long view - after all, if you don't get this particular session, there are plenty of others coming up on the calendar.

In short, let's handle our hand-held recorders in a way that helps us improve the quality of the music and enjoy ourselves at the same time. If we do so, we'll get more happy and knowledgeable jazz fans in our neighborhoods and we'll all be better off.

TEXAS SHOUT: HOW DIXIELAND JAZZ WORKS

Art Hodes, Rod Cless and George Brunies 1940 "Subunit"
Photo courtesy of Metronome Magazine

Jim Cullum Jazz Band "Subunit"
Photo by Dan Polin

LIGHT, WORDS and MUSIC PUBLISHING
BOOKS • JAZZ RECORDINGS • NATURE & TRAVEL PHOTOGRAPHY
16710 16th Avenue N.W.　　　　(206) 546-1498
Seattle, Washington 98177　　　Fax (206) 546-2585

11-23-97

Jim Cullum Jazz Band

Hi Jim,

Enclosed is your free copy of Tex's new book. Note your photos on pages 24 & 116.

Let me know if you can promote this book or write a review for publication.

Thanks again,

Dan Polin

CHAPTER 7   SUBUNITS

The High Sierra Jazz Band, a sextet without a clarinet, is one of the most popular bands on the festival circuit. Turk Murphy for years led a band regarded as one of the best extant, often without a drummer. Some of the finest uptown-style New Orleans and British trad records are by piano-less sextets. Jimmie Noone's immortal classic period six-man lineup omitted both trumpet and trombone. A typical Chicago sextet, such as the one led by Jack Teagarden near the end of his career, will not have a guitar.

Among the great quintets, Louis Armstrong and his Hot Five functioned without either bass or drums. Soprano Summit usually had neither brass nor piano on stage. The Original Dixieland Jazz Band worked without banjo or bass.

We could go on down through the various small bands that have recorded through the years. We'd wind up with piles of marvelous duet recordings, such as those by clarinetist Kenny Davern and pianist Dick Wellstood, organist Dick Hyman and cornetist Ruby Braff, and violinist Joe Venuti and guitarist Eddie Lang. The possibilities seem endless.

Well, not quite. If I've counted correctly, there are 131 different instrumental combinations that the seven instruments (not allowing for any doubling) in a typical Dixieland band could present to its audience. I get 1 septet, 7 sextets, 21 quintets, 37 quartets, 37 trios, 21 duets, and 7 unaccompanied solos. We could also count utter silence as a 132nd possibility, something which may result from the judicious use of space during a performance.

By now, you should have taken my point. Any mixture of the instruments in a Dixieland band is capable of playing valid, full-bodied jazz if given a chance.

A few bands (it seems to me that they tend to be among the top-ranked outfits) do pay some attention to this fact. One which comes readily to mind is Jim Cullum's Jazz Band, a full-time professional crew of first-rate jazzmen, all of whom are highly accomplished technically. Listen to them in action, say on their excellent "Super Satch" album for Stomp Off, and you'll hear all kinds of bands-within-a-band showing you new and different facets of the selections as you go along.

Unfortunately, most of the combos you'll hear today barely make use of one-tenth of the 131 available combinations. Listen to a typical Dixieland septet throughout an evening and, for about 99% of the time, you'll hear either the full ensemble or the seven soloists with whatever instrumental backup the group is used to providing for them (generally the full rhythm section for the horns, sometimes special settings for certain rhythm section soloists). That's a total of eight configurations. Add a passage or two where the trumpet drops out while the clarinet or trombone takes the lead, and a couple of groupings where one or more horns may play with just the banjo behind them and that's about it.

Why do we get so much unimaginative programming? I suspect that many leaders are not fully aware of the musical resources within their ranks waiting to be

TEXAS SHOUT: HOW DIXIELAND JAZZ WORKS

tapped. And yet, as I have previously discussed at length in the June 1988 issue of *The Mississippi Rag,* Dixieland players have, in general, the most widely-developed ensemble skills of any style of jazz. A Dixieland band should be an ideal laboratory for varying the tonal mixtures.

(Other ways to use the instrumental resources at hand include dynamics - how many bands anymore play those really quiet but highly-charged ensembles, such as those you frequently heard on Kid Ory's revival-period recordings? - and chase choruses. However, for today's column, let's stick to the variety that can be obtained through subunits.)

Such variations do much to keep the audience interested over the long haul. If your first few tunes suggest that, for the rest of the night, it's going to be either full ensemble or solos with rhythm, the fans will soon realize that all you're going to do from here on out, on each tune, is the same thing you just did but on a different chord pattern and at a different tempo. Will they then start to table-talk a little more?

I firmly believe that, once the listeners think they know what you're going to do, they will listen to you less intently. If you keep surprising them, they won't chatter as much because they won't want to miss something special.

Further, deploying your musicians in novel ways keeps the sidemen alert and stretches their abilities, two things that will guarantee the steady improvement of your lineup. It's easy for a horn player to get lazy on his solos if he knows he'll have four sidemen filling out the sound - he can't hide as well if the only instrument behind him is a tuba or a string bass or just the drummer's brushes.

But do all of these different combinations sound good? Sure they do, with a little practice and if you don't overdo them. There's no reason why your trombone and clarinet can't learn to play a short passage of unaccompanied duet as a way of easing the steady pressure from the full rhythm section, or your tuba player can't step out for a brief interlude all by himself. A chorus by a trio of clarinet, banjo and piano - or a quartet of cornet, trombone, tuba and banjo - or, for that matter, whatever your sense of showmanship tells you might work at a given moment, is worth a try, and it'll be fun for musicians and audience alike.

Lest you think I am idly theorizing, I can tell you that the two bands I regularly lead, The Red Lion Jazz Band in my home town and The Rent Party Revellers at festivals and cruises, follow the principles set forth above and those principles work just fine. Each member of these combos may find himself playing all alone or together with any combination of the others at any time, and the response from the crowd and the musicians has been most satisfying.

To illustrate, one of the high points for me of the Revellers' appearance at the 1989 South Coast Metro festival came near the end of our last set, while we were playing "Faraway Blues", a tune that's been in our book since we first got together. Just to try something a little different, we decided, while the performance was going on, to do a three-chorus routine consisting of an unaccompanied clarinet chorus, an unaccompanied clarinet-soprano saxophone duet, and a trio of clarinet, soprano saxophone and tuba. What came out was absolutely gorgeous, the audience listened so closely you could hear a pin drop, and the applause went off the meter when that spot ended. A fan later sent me a tape of it, and it stands up as well on repeated listening as I remembered it in the event.

Subunits

You can do the same thing with your band. All you have to do is remember that you're not leading one band, you're leading 131 different bands, and you should give many, if not all, of them a chance to play during the evening. If you do - trust me on this - you'll play a jazzier show, your sidemen will improve (at least the ones who want to improve will do so, the others may complain), and the audience will get more out of the experience. Shouldn't the prospect of such results be worth a try for a few times, just to see how it goes?

Uptown Lowdown "Group Sax subunit" (John Goodrich & Paul Woltz)
Photo by Dan Polin

TEXAS SHOUT: HOW DIXIELAND JAZZ WORKS

Kid Thomas Valentine Jazz Band   Preservation Hall 1967   *Photo by Ed Lawless*

New Black Eagles Jazz Band   *Photo courtesy of NBEJB*

CHAPTER 8   CONTEMPORARY CLASSIC COMBOS

There is a small body of recordings from the vintage years of Dixieland jazz that are regarded by everyone as being "classics". Included therein, for example, would be the 78s of King Oliver's Creole Jazz Band, Louis Armstrong and his Hot Five, Jelly Roll Morton's Red Hot Peppers, and Bessie Smith.

Various commentators, including myself, would add other names to the above list, but for today's purposes, I want to concentrate only on those about which there could be no reasonable disagreement. Indeed, I would go so far as to say that anyone unfamiliar with the works mentioned above, or who does not understand why they are universally considered to be "classics", does not have a sure grasp of what Dixieland jazz is all about.

When Lu Watters and his colleagues started the Dixieland revival in the early 1940s, they used recordings by Oliver, Armstrong, and other classic jazzrnen as a point of departure. At that time, Dixieland jazz was thought to have been out of vogue for a long time. These "classic" platters were disappearing relics of an ancient era.

Of course, these seemingly hoary discs that Watters was reviving were, when he began recording, only about a dozen years old. The revival he initiated has continued for 50 years now. If music that was only a dozen years old in the early forties could by then have attained classic status, isn't it time for us to begin looking back over revival-period recordings, some of which are now decades behind us, to see which ones should be added to the list of acknowledged classics?

That's what I'd like to do for the balance of this column, i.e., make a first step at designating a set of classic revival-period Dixieland recordings. Each of you will have his or her own favorites that I won't mention - as do I. However, for the benefit of those who would like to delve a bit deeper into the music, I think it useful to suggest some places to begin, with the hope that my selections will also be hard-core "classics" about which there should be little or no room for controversy.

Let's understand the ground rules. To me, classic status implies both skill and influence. Said another way, to be "classic", you must have (1) demonstrated the ability to play high-quality Dixieland consistently and (2) inspired a significant group of jazzmen to follow your lead. I think you'll find little disagreement with the position that these criteria are met by all of the artists/sessions suggested below as being revival-period classics.

The 1940s are relatively easy. Lu Watters' Yerba Buena Jazz Band defined the West Coast revival approach to Dixieland. The recordings by Bunk Johnson with George Lewis did the same thing for the uptown New Orleans style. Finally, the sides by Eddie Condon and his cohorts for Commodore (which began in the late 1930s and continued into the 1940s) crystallized, once and for all, the direction that Chicago style would follow. I can't imagine anyone disputing the classic stature of these sessions. Indeed, their frequent reissue supports the view that these are essential sides.

With the knowledgeable George Avakian producing its Dixieland material, Columbia dominates the 1950s. Turk Murphy's Columbias rank among the high points in his illustrious career; the 1950s Murphy sound has been echoed by San Francisco-styled combos all over the world ever since. One of the finest editions of Louis Armstrong and his All-Stars made a series of LPs for Columbia that were state-of-the-art downtown New Orleans. And the Condon jams for Columbia, in their way, are virtually the equal of his Commodores.

The 1950s were the heyday of the Good Time Jazz label, formed to preserve the exhilarating Firehouse Five Plus Two, whose loose-limbed straight-ahead two-beat and breezy presentation can perhaps now be recognized as the classics they are, in contradiction of the 1950s critics who seemed unable to forgive the septet for wearing firemen's uniforms on gigs. Certainly the FH5's vitality and humor survive today in abundance from the stage of virtually every festival that hires organized bands.

Good Time Jazz also housed, for a while, another giant of the downtown New Orleans style, trombonist Kid Ory. Of the long string of recordings he made from the mid-1940s to the mid-1960s, the Good Time Jazz sessions are probably the best and certainly the most influential.

When Bunk Johnson died, the baton of uptown New Orleans passed to his clarinetist George Lewis, whose septet towers over this branch of Dixieland in the 1950s. Of the many first-rate recordings they made, the three LPs on Delmark would rank near the top, catching the band in top form and, taken together, displaying its full range.

The 1950s saw the initial flowering of the variation of uptown New Orleans now known as "British trad". Trumpeter Ken Colyer's unimpeachable integrity makes anything by him worthwhile, but his early Deccas with Chris Barber and Monty Sunshine are especially choice. Barber's excellent initial series of albums on his own can still be heard in the playing of many bands today, though Barber's style later changed rather markedly.

Finally for the '50s, one of the finest combos of all time, the incomparable septet led by trombonist Wilbur De Paris started a long run at Jimmy Ryan's in New York and a series of albums for Atlantic that obviously were adored by many of today's Dixielanders. Speaking for myself, I do not have unqualified praise for De Paris, believing that his stop-and-go arrangements, and particularly his oddly-constructed compositions, reflect a flawed view of what Dixieland is supposed to be. However, when his band headed, without any constraints, straight into one of those good old good ones, it couldn't be beat. In light of its effect on musicians who came later, it is beyond doubt a "classic" team.

By the time the 1960s rolled around, Dixieland was in a bit of a decline. Rock had a firm grip on the pop charts, the veteran Dixielanders were starting to die off, the busy festival scene (which now provides a market for organized bands) was years in the future, and many outfits were jam bands of part-timers playing Chicago style on weekends at neighborhood taverns.

Contemporary Classic Combos

Out of this milieu, however, emerged Kid Thomas and his Algiers Stompers, a combo that had been operating for decades across the river from New Orleans. Thomas's direct, from-the-shoulder, back-alley sound got a degree of national distribution on Bill Bissonnette's Jazz Crusade label, moving on to world-wide fame and influence. As with Colyer, Thomas's tough-minded trumpet always satisfies, but the "classic" nod probably goes to a couple of platters for Riverside plus quite a bit of Thomas material now available on G.H.B.

Similarly, there is only one band from the 1970s which, from this perspective, can justifiably claim to be "classic". The New Black Eagle Jazz Band's best days occurred in that decade, during which its then-unique characteristics of delivering a four-beat feeling with a banjo-tuba rhythm section, its wide-ranging repertoire, and its occasional use of sub-units during a performance, single-handedly changed the way many Dixielanders think about their music. During those years, the Eagles maintained an amazingly high standard; you could buy virtually anything they waxed in the 1970s and mount a respectable argument for its "classic" status.

What about the 1980s? Too soon to tell, I think. There are a number of combos out there that are doing exceptional work, but none as yet has generated the type of following that I've indicated above as a prerequisite for "classics".

I'm sure you've noticed that I've chosen to concentrate primarily on full bands in developing this preliminary list, setting aside individual soloists, small combos, and chamber-jazz groups. However, not being quite sure whether the remarkable Soprano Summit would fall on the full-band side or the chamber-jazz side (where I'd put it), I can't close this column without a mention of one of the most distinctive and musical jazz organizations that ever took the field, one that left in its wake a few clearly Summit-derived reeds-with- rhythm units.

As I said, each of you will have your own favorites to add to the above selections. Personally, it grieves me to omit Bob Scobey's Frisco Jazz Band, Red Nichols' Five Pennies (its LPs for Capitol), the efforts of the Ohio revivalists (Gene Mayl, Carl Halen), the Bay City Jazz Band, the Teagarden-Hackett "Coast Concert" date, and many others. They produced great stuff that stands up marvelously decades later, as any "classic" should. However, good as they are, these sides have not yet exerted the strong effect on later jazzmen that I think the "classic" designation implies.

Making lists of this type is always fun. You probably started your own halfway through this column. However, I have a larger purpose in focusing today on this subject.

I have previously remarked in these pages that many people have become involved in today's Dixieland scene for a variety of different reasons. Some of these reasons are more social than musical - the chance to organize something, the chance to escape the electrified rhythms on the current pop charts, the chance to spend time within a gathering made up mostly of folks in one's own age group, the chance to dance in the pre-disco ballroom style, etc. I think that's great; anything that attracts people to Dixieland is fine with me.

However, I also think it's too bad that a number of fans become deeply immersed in aspects of Dixieland while not fully giving themselves a chance to appreciate the music at its best. Virtually all of your favorite bands on today's scene, whether you (or they) know it or not, derive from the artists mentioned in this column or others of comparable stature. Some of your favorites are clearly direct disciples of a specific classic player or band, some appear as bits of one great vintage musician modified by pieces of another, and some derive from these older artists but filtered through contemporary jazzmen on the next stage.

If you'll take the time to seek out and listen to a few of these "classic" combos and players, you'll discover the musical roots of your interest in Dixieland. I can't help but think that you'll thereby soon find a deeper satisfaction in hearing your own favorites, you'll be a more perceptive observer of the current environment, and you'll enjoy your hobby even more. As a further challenge, let me repeat my opinion that anyone unfamiliar with the works mentioned above (including the new entries I've made), or who does not understand why they are leading candidates for "classic" status, does not have a sure grasp of what the contemporary Dixieland scene is all about.

In any event, the names I've suggested will get you started, in case you need some direction, and you won't go wrong with any of them. Next time we're at the same festival site, tell me how it came out.

Soprano Summit   *Photo by Rollo Phlecks*
Courtesy of Chiaroscuro Records

CHAPTER 9   ENTERTAINING THE AUDIENCE

I have a Dixieland musician friend who, for purposes of today's column, I'll call "X". (The name is actually Y, but I don't like to get personal in print). X is a talented and experienced player who takes a strongly purist, jazzman-as-artist, the-music-is-everything stance toward Dixieland.

Because I believe that nothing should ever dilute the integrity of the music being performed, X and I are on common ground most of the time. However, I am more of a ham at heart than X; that fact causes me, I think, to spend more time than X does in looking at Dixieland from the audience's point of view.

X and I were working together on a gig not long ago. The leader on the gig likes to honor requests. As a result, we had just finished performing a tune that, it seems to me, gets requested every time this particular band plays. X and I were discussing whether the number in question had reached the status of being overplayed by the band.

During this discussion, I offered the view that the first and foremost thing a Dixieland band has to do, when it appears before paying customers, is entertain them. X's face fell. X, like many other jazzmen, tends to equate the word "entertain" with being "commercial" - doing a whole lot of things on stage that you don't much want to do, all of them at the expense of the quality of the music.

I don't see it that way. To me, any band that doesn't entertain its audience isn't going to get much work. The trick is to find a way to be entertaining while still playing the way you want to play.

Let's acknowledge our common purpose of increasing the paying audience for Dixieland jazz. Let's also recognize that, in order to do so, we are going to have to reach out beyond the tiny minority of persons who deeply understand and appreciate the music for itself alone. There aren't enough of them, and never has been, to keep a Dixieland scene alive.

If we are going to extend our message beyond the already converted, we have to do something to make that message easily accessible to more people. If we want to attract non-jazz fans, to get them to dress up, give up whatever other activity they might have available that evening, come to our show and spend thirty dollars a couple or more on drinks and food, and return for more at our next gig, we must focus on making those folks glad they came. That is, they have to leave with the feeling that they've been well entertained.

Thus, if we don't entertain them in the sense that I've described above, we aren't doing our job. Does that mean we have to compromise on the quality of our music? I don't think so at all. It does mean that we have to keep in mind that the average person does not instantly appreciate the merits of Dixieland the first time he hears it, and that we have to package it in a way that guides him along the true path.

TEXAS SHOUT: HOW DIXIELAND JAZZ WORKS

There are a zillion ways to package your musical product. None is more "right" than another, but they all require some effort and planning. If you want most people to go away feeling they got their money's worth, you need to think about such matters and pick a method of presentation with which you feel most comfortable.

You might begin by asking yourself if you would go out once or twice a month and spend thirty dollars to see your own band perform. If not, why not? Given the other combos that are on the bill at the festival you're playing, would you forsake the chance to see one that's scheduled against you for the chance to see your own? Again, if not, why not?

To name one of the non-musical settings in which Dixieland is frequently found, lots of bandleaders use the space in between tunes to tell jokes. Indeed, I've seen at least one band that regularly involves several sidemen in elaborate comedy routines. We can all think of very popular groups on the circuit that obviously attract many fans who prefer to get their primary entertainment value from comedy and high spirits and only secondarily from the music.

Such an approach may offend purists, but I think it's fine. Of the two bands I had in mind when I wrote the preceding paragraph, both - once the comedy is over - play good solid jazz that's well worth hearing. Exposing the public to Dixieland of that quality is what we all should encourage, and if laughs help do so, I'm all for them.

Other bands package their Dixieland in a "personality" atmosphere, wherein the announcer establishes a special rapport with the audience on a personal level. This approach might be coupled with encouraging requests, or remembering the special favorite songs of certain fans.

Yet another common tack consists of supplying the audience with a little background, e.g., telling them who wrote the tune that's coming up, who recorded it, or something historically interesting about it. Being a person who spends a lot of time thinking about how the music works and how it got that way, I find this an avenue that comes naturally to me, as anyone who's ever seen one of my shows will tell you.

Dixielanders recognize that the principal audience for Dixieland today consists of older folks who go back to the swing years but not back to the twenties. Accordingly, some bands include a few non-Dixieland tunes in their program - swing, ballroom dance, Latin, etc.

Who can deny that presenting a good-looking female vocalist will bring in some segments of the audience, or having a Red Hot Mama who flounces across the stage in a boa and sings naughty ditties? As long as you make sure she has musical talent, and the tunes she executes are worthy, so that you're not watering down your jazz, we can all - Dixieland buffs and civilians alike - enjoy her time at the microphone.

If you have no vocalist, do any of your sidemen have singing talent? If so, including a fair number of vocals in each set gives the neophytes in the audience something to which they can relate, a way of distinguishing one tune from the other. Besides, many of these old pops have great lyrics that will enhance your overall performance if properly utilized.

The point here is that, if you expect people to take the time and trouble and pay the money, to attend your programs, you should, whether you like it or not, pay

Entertaining The Audience

attention to all aspects of your programs, the musical and non-musical ones, and to the way they fit together. Your show is going to have some kind of presentation, and you can either do something to control and improve that presentation or not. If you don't, I'll bet that your show won't be as entertaining as the show of someone who does, even if both shows are indistinguishable musically.

You're probably thinking that what I've outlined sounds like extra work for you to do. Well, it is. But much of it involves activities that will get done by default if you don't grab the ball.

For example, how about the tune list? All of us have been bored to death at one time or another by bands that get on stage without any idea of what they're going to play, and then stand around trying to decide. You're going to pick the tunes sometime, so why not in advance?

Clothing? You're going to wear something on stage so you might as well give some advance thought to wearing apparel that will enhance your show in the eyes of the audience you're trying to reach. Many bands use distinctive uniforms in order to look neat and well-organized. Conversely, lots of "British trad"-style jazzmen, possibly in an attempt to focus attention on the music itself or maybe as a subtle way of reminding the audience of the folk origins of the uptown New Orleans Dixieland from which British trad derives, deliberately appear in casual clothes.

Timing? If you're playing a non-festival gig, you'll probably need to take some breaks. Do you have a clear idea of how long your sets and intermissions will last? Or is yours one of those bands that ends a set, gets involved in discussions with the customers and returns to the bandstand about ten minutes after half the audience has checked their watches for the third time?

Along the same lines, does your show start when it's supposed to? We've all been annoyed by situations where we've rushed to get to a tavern early to get a good seat, and then the band members drift in five minutes before the gun and yak away among themselves for twenty minutes or so before playing a note.

For the benefit of any Dixieland combos out there that are just getting off the ground, I'll use the balance of this column to share with you some of the principles I follow with the band I've led in Wilmington, Delaware, for over a quarter-century, The Red Lion Jazz Band. They'll provide a preliminary checklist of things you might want to think about. Though I find them useful, I hold no special brief for them. Keep in mind that there are lots of other ways to operate, and all of them can be successful ones.

The Red Lions appear in coordinated uniforms whenever we play. If we're appearing before a general audience, I think it helps get them in a mood to enjoy the music if we wear what they expect us to, which is colorful vests and string ties. For jazz clubs and festivals, our Red Lion polo shirts, or white shirts and ties, take over.

On typical-length four-hour gigs, we play five sets of thirty-five minutes each (the first one runs forty minutes), with four fifteen-minute breaks. Personally, I think the standard twenty-minute break is just a little long for the audience, and by structuring the gig this way, we try to keep it moving while taking about the same amount of total break time as other bands.

Our sets on such gigs run six numbers each, usually half vocals and half instrumentals. Tune lists are made up well in advance, with copies available to the sidemen (so the rhythm section can turn to the next tune in our chord books without delay while I'm making the announcement). I like to start a set with a fast tune (to get everyone's attention) and end the same way (to leave them on a high), but in between we play dance-tempo tunes at slow and medium tempos. If we're doing any special feature numbers, I keep them spaced throughout the evening.

In fact, I think some tunes work better early in a show and some later. I try to build the flow of excitement so that it peaks at the end of the fourth set, with the fifth (often a late set with only die-hards left at the tables) being a relaxed collection of danceable vintage pops.

I try to schedule at least two or three "familiar" tunes in each set, i.e., ones that most people with a working knowledge of Dixieland or older popular music will recognize and treat as old friends. I personally enjoy playing standards anyway, but beyond that, I think doing so helps keep the crowd listening through the several total obscurities we'll do that night. If we're playing a jazz club or festival, where the audience is more sophisticated jazz-wise and is often anxious to hear new material, I'll reduce the percentage of standards, but never take it down to zero.

I think that a show should be as unpredictable as possible. My view is that, once the audience thinks it knows what's going to happen next, its attention is likely to start wandering. If you keep things changing on stage, they're less likely to look away, fearing they'll miss something.

For that reason, I never program two consecutive songs in the same tempo or same key. Not only does this policy maintain variety, but it also helps challenge the part-time musicians who staff most Dixieland bands and who need every push they can get to avoid chord-running and over-reliance on favorite licks. Also, I think even a listener with a tin ear will eventually develop a sense of deja vu if you play too many tunes in the same key without a break. (I carry this fetish to what is probably a fanatical extreme by trying to avoid scheduling a tune that will begin with the same chord with which the prior song ended, or by avoiding two straight numbers that use either opening vamps or twelve-bar blues patterns.)

The Red Lions start and stop on time, and take our breaks on time, even if a sideman is late, or if there's practically no one in the room. That's what we're being hired to do, and if there's only one customer on hand, he's paid his money and he's entitled to the show he came to see. Personally, I have no patience with leaders who say "Let's not start until the room fills up a little more"; besides, who wants to walk in and sit down in a nearly-empty room in which nothing is happening?

If you've hired the Red Lions to play your private party, we'll play whatever tunes you want us to. However, during the years when we were playing Wilmington restaurants, I wouldn't take requests on our recurring monthly gig. We had too many regular fans who each had a special favorite tune, and we'd have played about half our program from their list every time. I felt that such repetition would not get the rest of the audience coming regularly, so I made sure that the tunes we played at our recurring gig didn't come up too often.

Those principles worked for us through eighteen virtually-uninterrupted years of first-Friday performances at four local watering holes - until downtown Wilmington at night went the ghost-town route of most older cities its size and the hotels where we played remodeled their dining rooms so that they no longer had space for a Dixieland band and dance floor. Following these practices, we found out something else, too - if the non-musical part of a show is crisp and tight, if the band looks and acts like it knows what it's doing, an audience is much more likely to forgive (or not even notice) some of those musical on-stage glitches that happen occasionally to all Dixieland bands.

To sum up, if I'm going to rent a movie, read a book, attend a concert, or spend money on any leisure-time activity, I expect to be "entertained" by it in the sense that I want to come away from it thinking that I got value for my investment. Dixieland bands are no exception to this rule. If we play well, we can expect to sell our recordings to Dixieland buffs. If those buffs don't get something extra, something entertaining beyond our music, when they come to see us live, we can expect that they will decide next time to stay home and listen to those records.

At the risk of beating this point to death, let me reemphasize that, to be entertaining, you don't have to tie a confederate flag on the end of your clarinet, or march around the room, or work the trombone slide with your foot (but if you really like to do those things, that's O. K. too). You can and should always play the tunes you prefer, as well as you're able. But if you want most of us to share your enjoyment in doing so, you really ought to use your presentation to give us some help in that direction.

You'll be pleasantly surprised at how quickly and eagerly we respond to such consideration. After all, we came to see you to have a good time, didn't we? We've arrived at your gig already disposed to enjoy ourselves. Meet us halfway; you'll find more of us returning next time.

Firehouse Five Plus Two at Disneyland   *Photo by Roger Marshutz*
Courtesy of Contemporary Records

TEXAS SHOUT: HOW DIXIELAND JAZZ WORKS

Spike Jones and his City Slickers   1950s
Courtesy of Past Times Publishing Company

CHAPTER 10   REVIEWING RECORDS

Today I want to talk a bit about reviewing records. Inasmuch as I do not review records for *West Coast Rag*, perhaps it is appropriate for me to explain to our readers why I feel qualified to talk about record reviewing.

My first published record review appeared in the November 1966 edition of the newsletter of the Toronto-based Ragtime Society. The story of how it came to be written appears in the October 1986 issue of *The Mississippi Rag*.

In the nearly quarter-century since, I believe that I have had published more reviews of recordings of ragtime, Dixieland jazz and related music than any other U. S.-based writer. All of these reviews have appeared in specialized, small-circulation musical periodicals, including *The Second Line, Coda*, the now-defunct *Jazz Digest* and *The Ragtimer, Rag Times* and, most particularly, the leading U. S. publication in the field, *The Mississippi Rag*.

My first published review for *The Mississippi Rag* appeared in the February 1978 issue. During the following dozen years, my reviews therein have covered over 600 recordings, between one-third and one-half of all recordings reviewed in *The Mississippi Rag* over that period. On the average, I review over one recording a week, week in, week out, holidays and vacations included.

I know of only one stateside readers' poll in recent years that has focused on Dixieland and has included a category of "Favorite Jazz Critic" - a poll taken a few years ago by Jazzology Records. Participation was limited, but I finished third in the category, behind *The New York Times*' John S. Wilson and *The New Yorker*'s Whitney Balliett, both of whom write for periodicals whose circulations dwarf any with which I'm involved.

Maybe the foregoing summary appears immodest to you, but I'm proud of that resume and it gives me reason to believe that I'm doing something right where reviewing is concerned. Against that background, let's talk about the role of the record reviewer in today's Dixieland/ragtime scene.

There are a number of purposes served by record reviews. For example, a review announces the release of a record, much like an ad, so that the artist's completist-fans can take steps to acquire it.

Because Dixieland is essentially a hobby these days for nearly everyone concerned with it, reviews serve an entertainment function, i.e., they should be written so as to engage the reader's attention. Some reviewers use their space to present chatty personal anecdotes, or to relate colorful incidents about the artists, composers, etc., as a way of increasing the review's entertainment value.

A review is a useful tool for educating the readership about what constitutes good Dixieland or where the music came from. Some reviewers take this latter goal to the extreme of spending more time on background than on the music being reviewed. Not long ago I read a review in which the reviewer, believe it or not, used

TEXAS SHOUT: HOW DIXIELAND JAZZ WORKS

virtually all of his space to cite discographical data about other artists' vintage recordings of the songs on the record, but failed to supply similar information on the record he was reviewing!

A review serves the purpose of gratifying the ego of the artist, producer or fan in that such persons get the reinforcement, in many cases, of knowing that a supposedly informed writer agrees with their musical tastes. Conversely, if the reviewer fails to provide such reinforcement, some readers consider his comments as nothing less than a personal attack on their values. My files contain, for example, an irate letter from an individual involved with an album to which I had given a favorable review, taking me most severely to task for expressing certain reservations regarding selected portions of the music thereon.

To me, however, the principal purpose of a record review is to give someone who has not heard the record a basis for deciding whether to seek out and purchase the recording. That factor is the one that determines whether what's being written is a "record review" as opposed to an announcement of newly-issued recordings, a discographical essay, or an historical article.

Dixieland record reviews are less important in that respect than they were in the pre-rock-and-roll era. Back then, most local record stores maintained a broad stock of all types of music. Dixieland musicians did not generally produce their own recordings, so any Dixieland records that were made usually wound up on nationally-distributed labels appearing in the racks of moderately-large record stores in good-sized cities.

When I was growing up in Wilmington, Delaware, I had little opportunity to hear Dixieland or ragtime live. (In fact, I was nearly 30 years old before I ever encountered, face-to-face, another pianist who sat down in front of me and played a rag.) Nevertheless, I was able to get a firm grounding in the music because both of my downtown record stores, between them, not only had the major labels, but also such smaller ones as Good Time Jazz (on which my beloved Firehouse Five Plus Two were heard). When the first big shopping mall in town opened, not far from my home, it had a sizeable record store that stocked, among other things, the marvelous series of LP reissues of vintage jazz on the Riverside label.

Handicapped by the then-typical youth's shortage of funds for as large an investment as an LP ($4.00-$5.00 then), I tried to get as much information as I could about what to buy. *Down Beat* covered Dixieland for a while, and had some good reviewers. *Coda* had not yet gone so heavily into modern jazz and could also be relied on. I paid attention to what they said, and eventually my own tastes started to take shape.

The scene is different now. Except for a very few specialty dealers in isolated spots around the country, most stores rarely stock any Dixieland records. The majority of such recordings today are produced by the artists themselves, and by far the largest portion of all Dixieland record sales are made at the sites of the artists' personal appearances.

In these circumstances, record reviews play less of a role than they used to. If the crowd is enjoying a performer at a gig, it will step up and buy a record without knowing or caring about what some reviewer may have said about it. Even a highly positive review in a respected Dixieland publication today produces mail-order sales of about twenty copies, hardly a dent in the customary initial pressing of 1,000.

Reviewing Records

(There are exceptions for recordings with unique characteristics - I was told by a producer that a favorable review I wrote of his LP by an extremely popular musician which was published shortly after that musician's death resulted in nearly 60 orders.)

So, why bother with record reviews anymore if Dixieland record reviews in genre publications aren't read by very many people and if reviews have little influence on record sales? Is the relevance of reviews further diminished because the recordings themselves are relatively minor purchases, only costing a few dollars, or because in most cases, even their most dedicated devotees don't take them off the shelf that often even after having owned them for a few months?

Answering for myself, I bother principally because I know there are avid Dixielanders out there who, like me years ago, can't get to the festivals and gigs where the records are sold, don't have access to well-stocked stores, and need some help in spending their limited record budgets. I'm still in that position myself regarding European releases; I rely heavily on reviews and ads in certain foreign periodicals in making up my want lists.

Those are the folks I write for. My reviews are aimed at bringing together people who've never heard the record, and may never have heard the artist, with recordings that they will feel are worth their money. Conversely, I try to assist people in identifying recordings that they won't like. Finally, I attempt to do both of those things without regard to my own feelings about the record.

For that reason, I try to include in each full-length review a fairly explicit description of the following items: the style of music that is played (the best Chicago-style recording in the world won't be welcome in the household of someone who is inalterably wedded to, say, Lu Watters or George Lewis as the barometer of good jazz); the positive aspects of the recording (no matter how bad I may think a record is, the artist has developed an audience or he wouldn't have made the record - my job is to help that audience realize that this is a record they'll like); and the negative aspects of the record (I may think the music on a given disc is so good that it overcomes inadequate fidelity, but a hi-fi addict probably won't).

Being specific in my descriptions is very important to me. I do not like to read reviews that talk in generalized terms about how great, or how bad, the recording is. Such an approach gives me no help, as a reader, in making my own decision about whether to put the album on my want list.

Thus, I think it is necessary to say in my review, if I like something about a record, exactly what it is I like and why. Similarly, if I dislike something, I feel obligated to indicate fairly clearly what I dislike and why.

Therefore, if I've done my job right, I've put the reader in position to make an informed purchasing decision, whether or not he agrees with me. For example, I recently reviewed a recording unfavorably because, in my opinion, much of the music on it was played too fast. The producer later wrote me, in a most friendly way to tell me that he's received about a half-dozen orders as a result of my <u>unfavorable</u> review. Obviously, those purchasers considered fast playing to be a plus. If my review helped them find a record they'll enjoy, I think that's great, even though the album didn't do all that much for me.

| TEXAS SHOUT: HOW DIXIELAND JAZZ WORKS |

Here's how the process goes from my end: Each review copy I receive gets two spins before I start to write. First, I play my cornet along with it - you can learn some amazing things about a recording by "sitting in". Next, usually after several days have passed (or weeks, if there are a lot of records ahead of it on my review shelf), I sit down with earphones and take detailed notes on everything I hear - and I break the listening session into at least two parts to try to give the album time to work on me. Then, a day or two later, I take my notes to a word processor and write, rewrite, edit and re-edit, striving to find terms that capture exactly what I'm thinking.

Space constrictions are severe in this business. Most Dixieland publications are too small, and have too many available records to cover, to allow a reviewer the luxury of discussing each track or each player individually. My longest reviews rarely exceed four paragraphs. Currently, *The Mississippi Rag* prefers audiocassette reviews to be capsules - one paragraph per tape.

Finally, before submission, my wife Nancy reads over what I've written. Although she usually has not yet heard the album, she understands jazz well and is good at catching possible ambiguities in phrasing or awkward sentence structure that might cloud the meaning of what I've tried to say. The words and ideas are always mine, but like any piece of published writing, they benefit from discussion with a good editor.

Anyone planning to try his hand needs to keep in mind that you can't review many Dixieland or ragtime records for very long without spending a lot of time reviewing the work of people you know, often close friends who are performers, producers, or otherwise deeply attached to the recording. This situation is no fun, believe me, because it often produces a no-win choice for the reviewer. Is it seemly to say anything at all negative about the product of your friends? Yet, can you live with telling that reader out there, who's counting on you to give him advice that's useful in dealing with his constricted record-buying budget, anything other than your honest opinion of the recording?

Some reviewers will not review recordings by their friends. Over the years, I have, on rare occasions, received a review copy directly from another reviewer with a note asking me to cover the album. In those cases, it's usually clear from the situation that the other reviewer was avoiding the prospect of giving less than a rave review to his friends' release. Trying to treat my reviewing professionally, I think it is unprofessional to refuse to do your job, particularly when someone close to the record has specifically asked you to write it up.

Some reviewers will not write unfavorable reviews. They concentrate on the positive aspects of the record, and leave it at that. Personally, I think that this "all records are good ones" approach does not supply the record-buying public with the sort of honest, balanced information it needs.

Most artists and producers take criticism in stride. They know that the readers will understand that a reviewer's opinion is still, no matter how well-informed, only one person's view. They also know that there is no record or artist destined to receive unqualified praise from every commentator. Finally, they realize that the reviewer's remarks are usually applicable only to one specific recording and should not necessarily be interpreted to mean that the reviewer would say the same thing about the artist on a more general basis.

Reviewing Records

Along those lines, I can't help digressing at this point to cite George Buck, who owns what is probably the largest active catalog of older-style jazz recordings ever assembled, as an example of someone who takes a thoroughly professional attitude regarding reviewers. I recall a conversation with George in which I expressed an interest in reviewing one of his new releases. George responded that the record wasn't one of his best ones, but he'd be happy to send it to me for review. When I hesitated to face the up-front probability of doing a review that seemed likely to be negative, George pressed his offer more strongly, saying that, if he released an album with weaknesses, he deserved to have reviewers say so. For my money, there's someone who takes the long view, and the right view too, in terms of educating the public to recognize and look for the best.

Now a word about the Record Review Police, the most relentless and merciless organization ever known. The RRP has operatives throughout the world, and it always gets its man, no matter how long it takes.

The RRP scans every word written in a published record review for factual errors. Let's say, for example, that I have said the reed player on an obscure vintage recording sounds like Adolphe Sax. If there is any shred of evidence anywhere in the universe to indicate that it is not Sax, the RRP will root it out and trumpet it before the world, usually in a "Letter To The Editor" that starts about like this: "Doesn't that Tex Wyndham know <u>anything</u>? A collector in Paris showed me, during my trip there thirty years ago, an interview with Sax which appeared in the February 1935 issue of the *Bombay Jazz Club Newsletter* in which Sax clearly states that he was vacationing in Antartica at the time that recording was made..."

The RRP do, however, keep all of us on our toes, and that's to the good. I maintain a sizeable shelf of jazz reference works simply to avoid the vengeance of the RRP (including each successive edition of the standard discographies). Though I have not always been able to run the RRP's gauntlet successfully, I think my batting average is as high as the next reviewer's.

Even beyond the RRP, I have received mail "correcting" information that was right in the first place. In that case, I had mentioned, based on recently-unearthed evidence regarding Jelly Roll Morton's date of birth (which still represents the latest accepted thinking on the subject, but which was not specifically cited by me in my review), Jelly's age at the time of his first recording. Shortly thereafter, I received a letter from a fan who assured me in friendly terms that Jelly was actually somewhat younger than I had stated.

Aside from corrections of facts, reviewers don't get much follow up mail, and almost all of that is argumentative. The person who sent you this album will sometimes drop you an amiable note to acknowledge the publication of a favorable review, but fans virtually never write you to tell you that they agree with what you said in a record review. The relatively few letters usually come when you have touched a nerve by stating an opinion at variance with someone's.

I'm an active correspondent, but there is a type of letter to which I do not normally respond - one that is written solely to register disagreement with what I've said in a review. I figure that I've had my say in the review, my reader is entitled to his say in his letter, so we're as even as we're going to get and let's stop there.

In closing, having taken the time at the top of this column to tell you why I feel qualified to write record reviews and to express opinions about them, I think it's only fair to balance the scales by presenting the position of someone who feels somewhat differently about my efforts. Thus, I will leave you with an except from a February 27, 1984 letter sent to me by a reader who, apparently having borrowed a copy of *The Mississippi Rag* (I verified that he was not a subscriber) in which he read my review of a recording that he liked better than I, addressed himself to my qualifications in terms that included the following constructive pleasantries:

"I... can not understand what could have led you to write such a wrong-headed, vicious and unprofessional piece of nonsense. ...(P)utting such a record out is largely a labor of love - love of jazz music, something you seem neither to love nor to understand.

"...I have listened to jazz since I was sixteen years old and certainly know more about it than you do. ...(Y)ou are apparently deaf and have some sort of axe to grind in this case. ...This is not professional reviewing: this is assassination. ... I suppose you may take pleasure in the fact that you have prevented a certain number of people from enjoying this superb jazz music.

"...(O)n the off chance that you are man enough to resent any little thing I have said please do not hesitate to look me up at the above address. I have had the pleasure of thrashing many a nasty little cur like you and would be overjoyed to oblige you at any time. ...

"In hopes that your teeth rot out and your fingers drop off, I remain..."

Nov. 1990 West Coast Rag

CHAPTER 11   WOMEN IN DIXIELAND

All of us would like to see more people involved with Dixieland jazz. To that end, I can think of just one simple little thing that would need to happen for the number of Dixieland musicians to double, approximately speaking.

I have been unable to figure out why it doesn't happen, so I thought I'd try discussing the subject with you. Maybe you can tell me what I'm missing.

What the Dixieland community needs is for women to become as interested in playing the music as men are. Almost all Dixieland instrumentalists are, and always have been, male. Why is that?

Are women less interested in Dixieland than men? I can't buy that. Women are just about equally represented in all aspects of the scene these days except playing. They run jazz clubs, edit and publish jazz newsletters and magazines, deal in vintage sheet music, produce jazz festivals, volunteer in all aspects of festival and club activities, and make up half the audience at performances.

Do women get less instrumental training than men? I don't think so, but let's examine that thought for a moment.

No one, neither male nor female, gets much training on two instruments commonly found in Dixieland bands, tuba and banjo. With few exceptions, these axes are "manned" by individuals who decided on their own to play those particular instruments. Such folks are typically self-taught or seek out lessons for the specific purpose of learning to play in a Dixieland context.

Why is such a self-starting thrust to play those two instruments so predominately male? Perhaps the size and weight of the tuba explains the dearth of distaff tubaists, but not of banjo.

To be sure, those women who play Dixieland are most likely to be playing banjo or piano (the instrument that, at least when I was a kid, was most commonly taught to youngsters of both sexes). However, the proportion of female pluckers and ticklers is nowhere near the 50% that you might expect. Why not?

The question is particularly puzzling when you consider the clarinet. Judging from the virtually all-female clarinet sections fielded by high school orchestras for several decades now, you might think the licorice stick has become an exclusively female preserve. And yet, looking at the festival stages, you'll see that essentially none of these distaff stickmen has felt a calling to continue on into Dixieland. How come?

I asked this question in the April 1987 issue of *The Mississippi Rag*. In that column, I discussed a point raised by my lovely bride Nancy, who observed that women of our age and older (50 and up, that is) were raised under circumstances where it was not considered proper for a female to do anything so unladylike as

~ 45 ~

playing Dixieland Jazz. On the other hand, it was considered proper for a woman to be involved in activities that might cover more social aspects of the music, such as running a jazz club.

The following month, *The Mississippi Rag* ran a response by "Sister Jean" Huling, a noted ragtime pianist who's been a friend of ours for years. I hope I am paraphrasing Jean accurately when I tell you that Jean said she agreed with Nancy, citing several instances in which she (Jean) felt subtle and sometimes not - so - subtle anti-female pressure from parents, other musicians, etc., when attempting to follow her heart and play Dixieland and ragtime.

Jean is obviously in a better position to address such matters than I, and I'm sure she is right in what she says. However, I am still not convinced that such pressure explains today's lack of female Dixieland musicians.

In most locales, Dixieland jazz is not as easily found today as it was when Jean, Nancy and I were in our youth. When Dixieland is performed, the setting is much more likely to be one where a woman can go while feeling both safe and respectable, i.e., a jazz club or a festival as opposed to a late-hours tavern in a potentially threatening downtown area.

Moreover, times have changed a great deal. I believe that people in general are much more accepting than they used to be of a woman who decides to do her own thing.

My Red Lion Jazz Band has had, for quite a few years now, a female banjo player. Pat Meitzler decided some time ago that she wanted to play Dixieland; began attending our rehearsals; developed into a light, steady and reliable rhythm banjoist; and took over the chair when Bud Ahern died. We consider ourselves lucky that she was available.

As the bandleader, I think I'd know if there is any sort of resentment of Pat's presence, but I've never felt a hint of any. However, just to be sure, while preparing this column, I discussed the subject with Pat.

She confirmed my view. Pat told me she's never sensed even a trace of sexist pressure.

In fact, her experience is quite the contrary. On the relatively few occasions when anyone has brought up the subject with her of a woman's playing in a Dixieland band, Pat reports that she's received universal approval and encouragement.

When a last-minute conflict required The Rent Party Revellers to recruit a new member to play piano on our first cruise, our choice was Rose Marie Barr, the excellent tickler with Seattle's Uptown Lowdown Jazz Band. Not only did the question of gender never enter our minds, but we were overjoyed that such an accomplished musician was able to adjust her schedule to join the band. Thus, from my experience at least, I have a hard time believing that the disproportionately low number of female players on today's scene is attributable in any significant way to anti-female attitudes.

Moreover, whether or not non-Dixielanders in general feel unduly bound by convention, Dixielanders almost by definition are unconventional - that is, choosing to become involved with Dixieland jazz these days is in itself an unconventional

Women in Dixieland

thing to do. The music is not commercially viable any more. Although some festivals attract thousands of attendees, it is still true that the Dixieland jazz community is a minuscule part of the total population. The people who don't care a fig about Dixieland are the "normal" ones - we are the oddballs in the crowd.

In these circumstances, a female who is deeply committed to the Dixieland club/festival scene, one who is interested enough to be reading these words, is already, in a sense, defying convention and swimming against the tide. Can there be any additional lingering conventions holding her back, if she's ever had any instrumental training (or even if she hasn't), from deciding to take just one more step and play the music itself?

On rare occasions, while getting ready to go out, and after I've gotten an update on the weather, I'll switch the bedroom TV over to MTV as a way of making sure I'm prepared for the enemy's next attack. I can't stay with 1990's rock for more than a few minutes, but I have noticed something about it that's relevant to today's discussion.

Rock is, as far as the division of the sexes is concerned, just like Dixieland. If you see a female on MTV, whether or not she has an instrument in her hand, she is almost always appearing primarily as a vocalist. The rockers who stay in purely instrumental roles are overwhelmingly male.

Now the rock scene, it seems to me, is about as unconventional and rebellious as you can get. If there's a way to thumb one's nose at the establishment in a musical context, I think you'll find plenty of rockers who will jump at the chance to do so with a vengeance. Moreover, the rockers are almost all of an age to have been born and raised in a context of open public discussion of women's lib.

Thus, I can't imagine that there is any sort of anti-female bias in the rock world against women instrumentalists. Still, there aren't any more of them than there are female Dixieland instrumentalists. Why not?

Just about everyone who plays Dixieland these days does so because he (or she) can't really do otherwise. Although there is no longer any appreciable fame or fortune in the music, something within us compels us to spend time learning to play it and, when our abilities have reached a certain point, to appear before an audience. Is there something about that activity that appeals more to males than to females? If so, what?

I've wrestled with this question for years, and have no answer that satisfies me. In bringing it up in these pages, I do not intend to imply any sort of sexist sentiments in favor of either gender. If I've inadvertently done so anyway, I sincerely apologize.

However, loving the music as I do, I am disturbed that there continue to be, even in this liberated age, virtually no females deciding to play Dixieland. Said another way, fully half of the potential performers of Dixieland are choosing not to do so, a situation that should concern all of us who care about the music.

How's about it ladies? Do you still have your high school clarinet in the closet? Why not dust it off, take it to the local music store if necessary to get the pads or keys spruced up, and start to play along with some of the easier tunes on your favorite Dixieland records?

| TEXAS SHOUT: HOW DIXIELAND JAZZ WORKS |

Several jazz clubs have regular jam sets as part of their monthly meetings, in which players of all levels of ability are cheerfully welcomed. Some also maintain chord books, and publish advance lists of suggested tunes for the monthly jams, to make it easier for neophytes to make their first steps onstage without embarassment. Surely you ladies can function in that kind of situation as well as men, right?

Why not give it a try? And men - husbands, boyfriends, whatever - get yourselves on board via encouragement for such activities as your lady's home practice, attending functions where your wife or companion wants to play, applauding good performances on stage or at jam sets without reference to the gender of the performer, etc.

Who knows? In a few years, we may have lots more Dixielanders out there. Isn't that a goal toward which we're all working?

Norma Teagarden   1976   *Photo by Ed Lawless*

Women In Dixieland

Pat Meitzler
Photo by Andrew Wittenborn

Rose Barr
Photo by Dan Polin

Cynthia Sayer
Photographer Unknown

Virginia Bonnel   Hot Antic Jazz Band
Photo by Dan Polin

TEXAS SHOUT: HOW DIXIELAND JAZZ WORKS

Lu Watters   Yerba Buena Jazz Band   1949
Photo from Ed Lawless collection

Bix Beiderbecke   1923
Photo from collection of Duncan Schiedt

CHAPTER 12   PLAYING THE STANDARDS

Chicago-style Dixielanders have never been reluctant to play "standards". Indeed, as will be explained below, it is the Chicagoans who created the body of evergreens that players of vintage jazz have come to regard as standards.

New Orleans-style jazzmen (including uptown, downtown, and the variation known as "British trad") have always understood that a leader's choice of tunes to play is less important than what his band does with those tunes. Moreover, Crescent City musicians, from Louis Armstrong, Bunk Johnson and George Lewis down to the present day, have always had a strong streak of showmanship in their presentations, of insuring that their audiences go away entertained.

Thus, while the New Orleans-originated groups have their favorite selections, most have never shown any particular aversion to the standard repertoire. Indeed, The Preservation Hall Jazz Band at one time made a point, and may still do so, of ending each concert with "Just A Closer Walk With Thee" followed by "When The Saints Go Marching In".

There is, however, one branch of Dixieland jazz that makes a conscious effort to cut itself off from a body of music that includes many of the best vehicles ever written in the idiom. It is the West Coast revival style. Combos of that stripe, including (for purposes of today's column) those hot dance bands that follow a West Coast lead, probably make up the majority of the Dixieland bands currently heard on the festival and jazz club circuit.

In my view, failure by these bands to play selections from the standard repertoire does a disservice both to our music and to the audiences for such combos. Moreover, I believe that it results from a basic misreading of the musical objectives of the original West Coast revivalists. Perhaps a little discussion of the background of the revival can put the picture in perspective.

When trumpeter Lu Watters and his Yerba Buena Jazz Band inaugurated the West Coast revival in 1941, swing was the prevailing jazz style. To the extent that Dixieland was heard at all, it was invariably Chicago style.

As I have mentioned in previous writings, Chicago is a solo-oriented style. The individual solos are the focus of a Chicago performance.

Repertoire is not particularly important in Chicago style. Chicagoans and their fans do not consider it repetitive if, for example, "Squeeze Me" is played at every performance because their main interest is in the solos, which will be different each time.

For that reason, Chicago jazzmen can and do function quite well with a book limited to fifty or so tunes that have proven themselves to be comfortable vehicles for improvisation. In 1940, when Watters was developing his musical ideas, such a

TEXAS SHOUT: HOW DIXIELAND JAZZ WORKS

group of tunes, which I will refer to in this column as the "1940 Standards", was the basis for just about all the Dixieland jazz being performed.

Watters was interested in restoring to the scene some of the breadth that Dixieland jazz had achieved during the twenties. He was attempting to balance the scales by giving exposure to Dixieland that was ensemble-oriented instead of solo-oriented, that used two-beat rhythm instead of the typical Chicago four-beat, that used a banjo and tuba in place of the usual Chicago guitar and string bass, and that gave some stage time to worthwhile tunes which were not commonly being rendered.

Watters, as we know, achieved his purposes with an impact that forever changed the course of Dixieland jazz and inspired disciples throughout the world. In doing so, he always remembered to maintain, in his own performances, the type of balance that was lacking in the Dixieland scene when he came to it.

Specifically, Watters did not turn his back on the 1940 Standards. Indeed, in the YBJB's first recording session, two of the eight tunes the octet waxed were 1940 Standards, "Muskrat Ramble" and "Memphis Blues". Throughout his career, he continued to record the 1940 Standards, his discography including, for example "Fidgety Feet", "St. Louis Blues", "Royal Garden Blues", "When The Saints Go Marching In" and "Tin Roof Blues".

Watters, of course, understood what Dixieland jazz is all about. He knew that a band should play the best tunes it can find, but should be sure to do so with originality, with a fresh vision of the material. No matter how many times you have heard a given Dixieland tune, when you finally hear the Yerba Buena version, you'll encounter a rendition with its own distinctive stamp; with a unique, instantly recognizable sound; and with a chart that shows you facets of the selection you've never previously seen.

Watters most famous alumnus, Turk Murphy, splendidly carried forward the Watters banner. Turk's recordings not only cover many of the numbers revived by Watters on disc, but also such 1940 Standards as "Bill Bailey, Won't You Please Come Home?", "Ballin' The Jack", "Wolverine Blues", "After You've Gone", "The Darktown Strutters' Ball" and "Baby, Won't You Please Come Home?".

Both of these great jazzmen are recognized as archetypes of musical integrity whose product made no concessions whatever to commerciality. Nevertheless, they continued to include 1940 Standards in their repertoires. Clearly, they wanted to play the best titles, and did so without regard to others who may have played, or were playing, the same tunes.

It is now a half-century later, and the scales badly need balancing in the other direction. First of all, many organized bands whose roots go back to Watters have distorted the revival's interest in expanding the repertoire into an emphasis on avoiding the 1940 Standards at all costs. Second, though to a lesser degree, these same bands have lost the idea of finding an original and fresh way to present their music. Instead, we have many bands re-creating figures from recordings by Morton, Armstrong, Beiderbecke, Watters and other favorite artists in the belief that doing so constitutes the "correct" or "legitimate" method of Dixieland performance.

To illustrate, two of the most frequently-played tunes on the circuit today are "Rhythm King" and "Since My Best Gal Turned Me Down", both excellent compositions. However, most bands have selected, from among a number of vintage-period recordings of those pieces, Bix Beiderbecke's as the ones to be frozen in interpretation.

Today's combos almost always open and close "Rhythm King" with the note-for-note front-line-only intro and tag from Bix's 78. Similarly, "Since My Best Gal Turned Me Down", a hard-charging set-closer if there ever was one, is constantly having its momentum cut off at the knees by regurgitation of the awkward and ill-considered stop-and-go ensemble from Bix's penultimate chorus.

In this process, West Coast revival bands have created a new body of standards that are not only being played unimaginatively, but also excessively in proportion to other quality tunes that have now fallen into relative neglect. Is "New Orleans Stomp" so superior to "Original Dixieland One-Step" that "New Orleans Stomp" needs to be performed by just about every organized band at every festival while "Original Dixieland One-Step" has virtually disappeared? Why is it justifiable to play "Canal Street Blues" over and over while 1940 Standards based on similar twelve-bar blues chord patterns, such as "Tin Roof Blues" and "Royal Garden Blues", are deliberately ignored?

Revivalist bands that boast of ignoring standards will often tell you that the standards (always meaning the 1940 Standards) are overplayed, or that they are "easy" and unchallenging. In case you ever hear such claims, take it from me, both are nonsense in today's scene.

The "overplayed" accusation, one that was certainly accurate fifty years ago, simply isn't true now. If you don't believe me, check it out for yourself the next time you attend a festival that concentrates on organized bands or when you're digging a West Coast-style outfit at your local jazz club.

During the event, count the renditions of "At The Jazz Band Ball", "Jazz Me Blues", "Beale Street Blues", "I've Found a New Baby" and "Sugar" vs. those of "Buddy's Habit", "Flat Foot", "Black Bottom Stomp", "Once In A While" and "Big Bear Stomp". After you've done so, ask yourself which group of tunes is overplayed.

As to the "easy" argument, let's begin by recognizing that some 1940 Standards are based on straightforward chord patterns and simple melodic phrases, just as are "Trouble In Mind", "See, See, Rider" and lots of other tunes played by the combos that claim to specialize in esoterica. However, many of the 1940 Standards, such as "Clarinet Marmalade", "Tiger Rag", "That's A'Plenty", "Royal Garden Blues" and "Eccentric", are as intricate, or more so, than the bulk of the selections typically played by revivalists.

The simple truth is that the 1940 Standards got to be standards because, whether complex or simple in construction, they proved themselves to be compositions that facilitate the performance of swinging Dixieland jazz. After all, nobody put a gun to the heads of the 1940 Chicagoans and forced them to play the 1940 Standards. Despite what the revivalists say, these tunes were played so frequently in 1940 because they are, on the whole, above-average compositions.

In fact, many of them are the cream of the crop from their source artists or composers. "Singin' The Blues" provided the platform for what is generally agreed to be the best solo that Bix ever recorded. "St. Louis Blues", "Memphis Blues" and

TEXAS SHOUT: HOW DIXIELAND JAZZ WORKS

"Beale Street Blues" are the core selections supporting W. C. Handy's well-deserved reputation as the Father Of The Blues. Fats Waller's formidable position as a jazz composer is firmly grounded on, to list a few of his best pieces, "Ain't Misbehavin'", "Honeysuckle Rose", "Squeeze Me", and "Blue, Turning Grey Over You".

Are we doing our audiences and our sidemen a service by teaching them that such immortal works ought to be banished from our stages? What conclusions will they then draw about the elements that constitute good Dixieland jazz? Are these conclusions likely to enhance their abilities to appreciate the best our idiom has to offer?

Along similar lines, combos also need to recognize that obscurity is not necessarily an indicator of quality - in fact, it may just as often suggest lack of quality. If you look through a pile of old sheet music, you will find that - along with about 99% of everything else that is a part of popular culture - just about all of it consists of ditties that never had any particular merit in the first place and have been forgotten for a good reason.

No one knows better than I that there are overlooked gems out there waiting to be discovered. However, no band has the rehearsal time to learn every tune ever written. Before deciding to add a selection to its repertoire, a band owes it to itself and to its audience to be sure that its time is going to be spent on the best possible material.

Thus, before scoring some ditty you've resurrected from a 78 or an old music stack, look at it critically and do the same with the 1940 Standards. Has your band yet learned "I've Found A New Baby"? Is your discovery really a better, hotter selection than "I've Found A New Baby"? Think over your answer carefully before you decide which one to start rehearsing.

Note that I am not saying that we should discard the wonderful discoveries of the revival, nor that we should abandon the search for more. I'm merely saying that we need to balance the scales in the 1990s, as Watters did in the 1940s, by giving tried-and-true material a fair share of playing time.

Frankly the 1940 Standards have so much to offer a creative jazzman that it's a shame to deny yourself the delights of playing them. I know I don't.

My Red Lion Jazz Band in Wilmington, basically a West Coast-style septet, has a book that I will match against anyone's for little-known titles. However, we also regularly perform and thoroughly enjoy such works as "Sweet Lorraine". "(Back Home In) Indiana", "(Up A) Lazy River", and "Bugle Call Rag". As far as we can see, our audiences respond positively to renditions of those numbers.

Similarly, if you have seen The Rent Party Revellers, you'll know that we're just as likely to play "That's A'Plenty" as "Meat Cuttin' Blues", or "Clarinet Marmalade" as "Shake Your Shimmy". If you have all of the Revellers' recordings, you not only have performances of "Here Comes My Blackbird", "Home Again Blues", "Brancusi Bird", "Forty and Tight" and "Kiss Me Sweet", but you also have Rent Party versions of "I Got Rhythm", "When The Saints Go Marching In", "Royal Garden Blues", "Sweet Georgia Brown", and "Jazz Me Blues". Again, this blend in our repertoire seems to meet with the approval of crowds and record reviewers.

Revivalist bandleaders, why not do your part to rebalance the scales? Play "Barrel House Stomp" and "South African Blues" by all means and I'll be there to

Playing the Standards

cheer you on. However, in between those two, why not count off "Jazz Me Blues" and let us hear your own distinctive version of it?

I'll pay attention to that one as well, and cheer it on if you try, as Watters did, to present it in a fresh costume. So, I hope, will the readers of today's column. And I'll bet you and your sidemen will have a lot of fun in the process.

TEXAS SHOUT: HOW DIXIELAND JAZZ WORKS

Books About The Music   *Photos by Dan Polin*

Feb. 1991 West Coast Rag

CHAPTER 13   BOOKS ABOUT THE MUSIC

There are piles and piles of books about jazz. A few are brilliant, many are execrable, but about 99.9% of all jazz tomes have one thing in common. They are popular histories of the music.

A popular history of music concentrates primarily on background. That is, we can find many books that will tell us such things as when King Oliver came to Chicago, how Fats Waller died, Louis Armstrong's favorite dish and the sad circumstances of Billie Holiday's girlhood.

Few of these volumes, even ones solely devoted to a specific artist, spend very much time trying to tell us exactly what musical things the great musicians did that distinguished them from ordinary mortals. You will come away from popular histories knowing which players are the ones you should follow up, but too often you'll only have a vague idea of why you should do so or of what you should listen for once you've located their recordings.

I have not re-read any of the books I'm going to discuss today for purposes of this article, but I don't think I need to do so. Over the four decades that I've been immersed in older-style jazz, ragtime and blues, I've only read a small handful of volumes that concentrated on the music. They made such an impression on me that I'd like to say a few things about them here for the benefit of those readers who are interested in delving into this part of the literature.

Some years back, Mike Mills, the trombonist in my Red Lion Jazz Band, brought a volume to a rehearsal that he'd received from a former colleague. It was about jazz, and Mike wanted my opinion of it. Not having heard of the book or its author , and having wasted many hours reading jazz books that are worse than useless, I had some misgivings, but I kept them to myself. After all, bandleaders do have some responsibilities toward keeping sidemen well-fed and content.

Thus it was that I became acquainted with *Jazz: A History*, by Frank Tirro. Not to put too fine a point on it, this is far and away the best book I have ever read from the viewpoint of explaining how the music should be approached by a critical listener.

Tirro, an educator, designed his volume to be used in connection with a course in jazz appreciation. He recognized that, in order to understand comments about jazz performance, one must be able to hear the performance being discussed. His problem was that jazz recordings go in and out of print with frustrating frequency.

In a stroke of inspiration, Tirro decided to key his book to a several-LP set of widely-recognized classic jazz performances produced by The Smithsonian Institution. He reasoned, and he's been right to date, that the Smithsonian, not being a record producer per se but a museum primarily focused on American culture, would keep the set available longer than the typical private record firm would maintain any group of jazz records on the market.

His book starts with ragtime and early Dixieland and progresses through the most advanced types of jazz. Tirro goes from performance to performance, telling you what parts of the rides are crucial, often setting forth the musical notation thereof.

I already owned, of course, all of the cited recordings in the styles that interested me, knowing them well enough that I could follow Tirro's text without specific need to refer to the records. I found his analysis so insightful, and so well written, that I couldn't put the book down, even when the chapters moved into forms of jazz that I don't care for at all. In fact, as Tirro discussed some of the most modern recordings, I found myself wishing that I could hear the passages, even while recognizing that I would probably hate them if I did hear them!

Despite the numerous musical notations, I think that Tirro's masterpiece could be grasped by someone who can't read music, provided he has access to the records. However, some of you may not wish to peruse a volume that spends over half its space on music that is well beyond the scope of *West Coast Rag*. In that case, you might look for what I believe is the only other volume that can rank with Tirro's, *Early Jazz*, by Gunther Schuller.

Schuller, also a music educator, focuses only on jazz prior to swing. His opening portion, covering pre-jazz musics and their contribution to jazz, is quite academic and very rough going even for a musician, but plow through it, skim it, or maybe skip it if you have no other alternative. The bulk of the volume discusses the kind of music covered every month in *West Coast Rag,* leading you through its development as found on records waxed during the pre-swing period.

As might be expected, Schuller (as does Tirro) sees our music evolving via the efforts of certain great innovators. He organizes most of his chapters to center on those great names - Original Dixieland Jazz Band, Louis Armstrong, Bessie Smith, Duke Ellington, etc. -, discusssing, frequently with musical notation, the specific innovations that these figures brought to jazz. Because Schuller underwent the daunting task of hearing every pre-swing jazz recording, he is well positioned to, and does, make sure you understand the musical context in which those innovations occurred.

As far as I know, these two volumes make up the top rank of books that cover our music other than as popular histories. However, if you want a few other suggestions of similar books in related areas, I'll mention three.

The Swing Era, by Gunther Schuller, does for jazz during the thirties and early forties what *Early Jazz* does for the preceding period. Because Schuller again tried to hear every recording, he had an almost impossible task. *The Swing Era* is rather lengthy, took him much longer to write than he expected, and probably because of the size of the undertaking and the text, is not quite as well-written or thought out as *Early Jazz*.

However, if *Early Jazz* rates an A-plus, *The Swing Era* rates no worse than an A. I hadn't planned to read it, both because it was so thick and because swing is not my primary area of jazz interest. However, once the rave reviews began to pile up, I capitulated and found, once again, that I was reading it compulsively.

Schuller's judgements are sound, informed and penetrating, usually in accordance with conventional wisdom but sometimes surprising (e.g., his well-supported conclusion that Cab Calloway was the most broadly gifted male vocalist of his day). There is a great deal in *The Swing Era* of direct relevance to fans of the music covered in *West Coast Rag*, such as the chapters on Louis Armstrong, Earl Hines and Red Nichols.

For those interested in ragtime, *Ragtime: A Musical And Cultural History* by Edward A. Berlin, stands astride the limited shelf in this field as the best non-popular history you'll find on the subject. With indefatigable thoroughness and keen musical understanding, Berlin has researched ragtime and the literature of the ragtime years. His slim but fact-filled volume describes how the music was perceived by the public and how it developed musical sophistication (his observations on mid-bar and cross-bar syncopations are a revelation).

(The best book ever written on ragtime, however, and one of the best books ever written about any kind of music, is still the pioneering *They All Played Ragtime*, by Rudi Blesh and Harriet Janis. However, it is a popular history - a wonderful, romantic, accurate, exceptionally readable popular history - and so beyond the scope of today's column.)

Finally, *American Popular Song,* by Alex Wilder, explains in musical terms what happened to take America's popular songs out of the European parlor ballad stage and make them uniquely American. Wilder, himself a composer of quality pops, exhaustively researched the song libraries of top Tin Pan Alley publishing houses and discovered that, in general, American popular song developed through the efforts of a limited number of inspired composers who appeared on the scene after the initial rhythmic breakthroughs inaugurated by ragtime.

Wilder's book is organized by chapters dealing with these composers, illustrating their innovations with portions of the music from the songs discussed. (An exception is Irving Berlin's chapter - Berlin would not permit short quotes from his works without payment of full royalties.)

American Popular Song kept me mesmerized throughout. I gained new perspectives on tunes I'd played for years, and also some leads to others I hadn't previously considered. I know of no other volume comparable to it. If you read it, you won't learn what George Gershwin had for breakfast, but you will learn exactly why, for example, "Some of These Days" was years ahead of its time and paved the way for similarly propulsive numbers that characterised the jazz age.

I have not listed publishers above because books, like records. go in and out of print in various formats from various publishing houses. However, I believe that all the books mentioned in this column are available, some of them in relatively inexpensive trade paperback editions.

Why do you need to read a book to learn about such matters? Since jazz is a matter of listening, why can't you find these subjects discussed on record or hear them at a concert?

Partly it's because so many of the historically-oriented musical shows you'll hear are themselves popular histories. The band will tell you who the ODJB was, and when it recorded, and then play an ODJB tune - in the style of the band putting on the show. Then it will tell you something about King Oliver, or Jelly, or Satchmo, and punctuate that discussion by playing tunes associated with those names, again in its own style.

Thus you'll certainly learn what the group you're listening to sounds like, but you're unlikely to learn much about the musical differences among the artists being discussed. Even when the band is playing transcriptions of the old recordings, which will give you a leg up in hearing the differences between the renditions, its spoken introductions too often concentrate on personalities rather than music.

I want to emphasize that today's column is not designed as a thinly-disguised elaborate lead-in to a plug for my own recordings. Nevertheless, to my knowledge, the only available records that attempt to teach the audience, via both spoken commentary and side-by-side musical demonstrations, how to listen to Dixieland jazz are the two jazz appreciation cassettes by The Rent Party Revellers produced by Dan Polin. I'd like to see more of that type of recording on the market, but I'm not aware of anything else that's around.

The books I've mentioned, though, should be easy to locate through any sizeable book store in your area, or maybe even your local public library. By taking them one at a time, reading them at your own pace, and digesting and thinking about what they have to say, I believe you will get even more enjoyment out of your recordings and out of the live concerts you attend. You might even find yourself liking a broader range of our music too. Why not give it a try?

CHAPTER 14   HOW TO IMPROVISE SOLOS

At Dixieland events I often find myself in discussions with fans who tell me that, years ago, usually at school, they played trumpet, clarinet, piano, or some other instrument. I always ask if they still play. Upon hearing a negative answer, I urge them to get out the instrument and join the action. Typically, they respond in a friendly way, but with a noncommittal remark conveying the notion that they probably won't do so.

Why don't more Dixieland fans who've learned the basic rudiments of playing music try their hands at the idiom? There are lots of answers, of course. We all have our priorities, matters that make demands on our time and leave us less opportunity than we'd like to indulge our hobbies.

However, I can't help but think that many would-be jazzmen are discouraged from trying to play by the gnawing fear that they will embarrass themselves in the process. They can get their old axes out of the closets - no trouble. They can find time to get their chops back into decent condition. They know a nearby jazz club that sponsors open jam sessions at regular meetings. But - they can't face what might happen on that first tune when they have to play a solo in front of other musicians and an audience of jazz fans.

I guarantee that the room will be filled with people who are on your side in such a situation. All the other performers went through the same process, and all the fans want to encourage new talent to play their favorite music.

You will be applauded. No one will laugh at you. However, that information may not be quite enough for you, because you still want to have some basis for believing, before you take the step, that you can meet some minimal standards, that you won't be off in left field somewhere.

If you are in this category, I am going to try to use today's column to help you. Without taking you through detailed, theoretical analyses of the music, I will give you a procedure to follow that will enable you to improvise a solo that will sound O.K. There are other ways of teaching this same skill, and mine is just one of them, but it will work.

I am assuming that you know how to play your instrument in the sense you are able to sound the notes and know which notes you're sounding. That is, if I tell you to play a B-flat (written "Bb"), you can do so.

On that basis, for each of the twelve notes of the tempered scale, you should learn one scale and five chords. They are set forth below in the key of Bb:

> Bb scale = Bb, C, D, Eb, F, G, A and Bb played in that order or in reverse order.

> Bb major chord (referred to as merely a "Bb" chord in fake books or chord charts) = Bb, D and F, sounded simultaneously.

Bb minor chord (Bbm) = Bb, Db and F, sounded simultaneously.

Bb seventh chord (Bb7) = Bb, D, F and Ab, sounded simultaneously.

Bb diminished chord (Bbdim or Bb°) = Bb, Db, E and G, sounded simultaneously.

Bb augmented chord (Bbaug or Bb+) = Bb, D and F-sharp (written "F#"), sounded simultaneously.

To discover the notes in the scale and the chords in the other eleven keys, transpose the foregoing data up and down the keyboard. It might help to write this information down on a piece of paper for each key.

You will eventually need to memorize this scale and these chords for each key, knowing them so well that they'll pop into your mind automatically when you think of the basic note (referred to as the "tonic" note - Bb in the above example). However, so that you can get started, Dixielanders should learn the scale and the chords for the twelve keys in the following order: Bb, F, Eb, C, Ab, G, Db, D, Gb, A, E, B.

That suggested order is given because it goes from the most common keys used by Dixieland bands to the least common. The vast majority of Dixieland tunes are played in Bb, F and Eb, while almost none are played in D, Gb, A, E and B. However, you will need to learn the scale and chords for all twelve keys because there will be occasions, even when playing in Bb, F and Eb, that you will encounter parts of tunes constructed on the tonic notes of A, E, B and the others.

Similarly, concentrate at first on learning the notes in the major, minor and seventh chords. Many Dixieland songs do not use either diminished chords or augmented chords. Of the two, the diminished chord is much more common than the augmented chord.

Advanced forms of jazz, and occasionally some Dixieland tunes, use more sophisticated chords. You may sometimes see notations for sixth, ninth, eleventh and other chords.

However, for purposes of Dixieland jazz, stick to the five chords I've mentioned. Any others, should you encounter them in a Dixieland context, will still sound O. K. harmonized with these five.

In order to begin improvising a solo, you'll need to know the chord pattern of the tune you're playing. As an example, let's use the basic twelve-measure, or twelve-bar, blues in Bb. The most common form of that tune has the following chord pattern:

Bar 1	2	3	4	5	6
Bb///	Bb///	Bb///	Bb7///	Eb///	Eb///
7	8	9	10	11	12
Bb///	Bb///	F7///	F7///	Bb///	Bb///

How To Improvise Solos

The "/" tells you to play another beat of the chord you've been playing, i.e., "Bb///" means the underlying chord for all four beats in that bar is Bb.

Note that each of the twelve bars has four beats. All Dixieland tunes have four beats in each bar.

Of the four beats in each measure, the first and third beats are, in Dixieland jazz, strong beats in feeling. The second and fourth beats are weaker in feeling.

That situation means that a discordant note (one not in the underlying chord) will make more of a clash - will be more likely to sound "wrong" - if it is heard on the first or third beat. An out-of-chord note heard on the weaker beats will not clash, but will create tension in the listener's mind which the listener will expect to hear resolved on the next strong beat.

Now you're ready to construct your solo. For each bar, regardless of the key signature of the tune, pay attention only to the underlying chord or chords. Construct a melody that will have, on the first and third beats, a note in the underlying chord being sounded. To close the gap between such notes, use notes in the scale of the tonic note of the underlying chord.

To illustrate: In our twelve-bar blues, you might start the first beat of the first bar with a Bb note, one of the notes in a Bb major chord. Let's say you've decided to work toward D, another note in a Bb major chord, as the note you'll hit on the third beat. How should you fill the time between the Bb you'll hit on the first beat and the D you'll hit on the third beat? You may do so any way you want to, provided you use only the notes Bb, C, D Eb, F, G, A and Bb. Got it?

Your transition notes can be quick ones, long ones, repeated ones, linear (along the scale), in leaps (jumping up and down between notes on the scale), anything you wish. Whatever you choose will sound O. K. against a Dixieland rhythm section, as long as it uses only notes in the Bb scale.

I recommend that you try this system out while practicing along with records. I have practiced along with records all my life. It's a great way to train your ear to hear chord changes, to learn tunes, to get a clearer understanding of what's going on in the band, and to try out some licks that the other musicians are using - all in a context where you're by yourself and can't be embarrassed. When you think you've got the basics, you're ready to try a live jam session.

When you get into a jam session, don't make the mistake many newcomers make regarding repertoire. They're afraid to admit they don't know the tune or the key that someone has suggested. They think they can "ear it in" after the first chorus. Instead, they wind up in over their heads.

Not even professionals will go on stage in front of an audience and try to play tunes with which they are unfamiliar. If you don't know a tune, or you don't feel comfortable trying the one mentioned, or you are uncertain about the key, say so and the band will pick something else (or you can suggest an alternative). Nobody will hold it against you for wanting to play material that puts you at ease.

I can't emphasize this point too strongly. There are thousands of tunes to play, and you're only going to be playing five or six of them during the set, so don't try to be a hero. If it makes it easier for you, say that Tex Wyndham told you not to try that tune until you've learned it better.

TEXAS SHOUT: HOW DIXIELAND JAZZ WORKS

Now assuming that you've memorized your scale and chords, and have some records with which to practice, how do you learn what the chord patterns of the tunes are? This can be a tough question in today's scene, where it is relatively difficult to locate music stores that stock any tunes from the early years of the century, let alone some of the Dixieland tunes that did not become hits with the general public.

However, many of the local jazz clubs have "fake books" that contain "lead sheets" (the melodies and related chord patterns) for standard Dixieland tunes. Perhaps you can obtain access to a copy.

Similarly, many Dixieland jazzmen possess such books. Perhaps a musician friend may be in a position to help.

Although Chuck might wind up bombarded with calls as a result of this reference, if all else fails, try contacting Charles B. Anderson, 3959 Kendall Street, San Diego, California, phone (619) 272-7690. Chuck is a retired musician and music collector who has been most helpful to many Dixielanders in the past by steering them toward sources of lead sheets.

The system I have just outlined calls for steady and dedicated work on your part. It will not turn you into the next Louis Armstrong via two weeks of five-minutes-a-day practicing. (For perspective, although I work a full-time non-musical job, I play my cornet nearly every day along with a recording, a procedure which consumes about 60-75 minutes total, including warm-up.)

However, if you want to participate in the considerable joys of playing Dixieland jazz, and you're willing to put in some time, this system will do the job. It will bring you to the point where you'll be able to get into a jam session with some confidence that you'll leave the stage with a sense of having made a positive contribution.

The system has a name. Musicians call it "chord-running," or "running the changes."

As you may have gathered, chord-running is a by-the-numbers, take-no-chances, play-it-safe, non-creative way to improvise. If you never learn to do anything other than run chords, you will never be regarded as anything other than a plain-vanilla-style Dixielander.

However, on today's scene, there are many instrumentalists out there, some of them with very popular bands, who have scarcely gone beyond running chords and reworking favorite licks. You can have a lot of fun without being the next Sidney Bechet.

Moreover, and this is the important thing, if you pay attention to what you're doing, and listen closely to those records as you play along, you will gradually learn when you can step away from the mechanical rules of chord-running, when you can set up those clashes on the strong beats, when to play notes that aren't in the scale or the underlying chord, when to keep the listener in suspense via a silent passage and then sweep him up with a fleet run, etc. You will do what all good jazzmen should do: find your own individual voice and your own vision of the material.

In the process, you'll be playing Dixieland jazz - some of the most satisying kind of music that there is-, playing an important role in keeping it alive as an art form, and earning audience applause. Have I got any takers?

How To Improvise Solos

    Next time we meet at a Dixieland show, instead of mentioning that you used to be a musician, tell me that you read this column, dusted off your instrument, learned some tunes, played along with some records, jammed with other musicians, and are having a ball keeping the flame burning. You'll make my day.

TEXAS SHOUT: HOW DIXIELAND JAZZ WORKS

Sacramento Traditional Jazz Society Youth Camp
Photos by James E. Jones

April 1991 West Coast Rag

CHAPTER 15   WHY YOUTH DOESN'T LIKE DIXIELAND

In recent years, the Dixieland community has come to realize that, if our music is to survive in its present form, a larger proportion of young people must become involved with Dixieland. I'd like to share with you today some thoughts on the magnitude of the task before us, including some musical reasons why younger folks are not attracted to Dixieland, plus my views on the area where we should be concentrating our efforts.

First, some background. The mid-1950s may be thought of as the real beginning of the rock era - that is, the first time in which more rock songs than non-rock songs appeared on the hit parade lists. Rock has dominated the pop charts ever since, meaning that well over half of the people in the U. S. have grown up in circumstances where their musical tastes were inevitably conditioned by the conventions of rock music.

What are those conventions and how do they differ from pre-rock music? Perhaps the most obvious difference to a non-musician is in the approach to rhythm.

Pre-rock popular music, not only jazz but folk, country/western, ordinary dance music, etc., normally presents melody mounted on rhythm that generates a feeling of buoyancy and springiness, that seems to get off the ground, that has the characteristic referred to by jazzmen as "swing" (when they are talking about rhythmic momentum, not "swing" when it means the prevailing jazz style of the thirties). Usually, the lighter and less cluttered the rhythm, the more likely it is to have this flavor. By contrast, rock rhythm is deliberately heavy and loud, going for power instead of swing.

Other basic differences occur in phrase lengths and chord patterns. Pre-rock music almost always consists of four-bar phrases, and is constructed of chords utilizing the "circle of fifths" pattern (that is, the ears of a fan of pre-rock are conditioned so that if, say, a G7 chord is played, he expects the next chord to be a chord with a root of C, five notes below G if you count G as the first). By contrast, since the Beatles revolutionized popular music in the sixties, a phrase may be any length (the first line of "Yesterday" is seven bars long), and chord patterns tend to be based on guitar shapes (that is, a chord made by placing one's fingers a certain way on a guitar fretboard may well lead to a chord which has the fingers placed about the same way one or two frets up or down the fretboard).

These are very fundamental differences. If your musical tastes were formed at a time when you were principally exposed to pre-rock music, you will have to make a conscious effort to adjust to and get comfortable with rock, and vice versa.

To illustrate this point, let's use the native music of India as an example. During the sixties, Indian raga music achieved a certain degree of exposure in the U. S., typically rendered by a trio of sitar, tabla and tamboura. Raga is very intricate and disciplined music, requiring hard work and practice to play properly, calling for a high degree of empathy among the performers.

TEXAS SHOUT: HOW DIXIELAND JAZZ WORKS

If any of us heard such a trio today, we might be entertained for a short time, and we probably would appreciate the high degree of musicianship required to play raga music. However, few of us would make much of an effort to seek it out, either in person or on record.

Why not? Easy question. Raga music doesn't speak to anything in our experience. We didn't grow up with it. We would have to make the same effort to get into raga that we'd have to make to get into rock.

Raga isn't around any more in the U. S. The general public in the sixties was not prepared to make that kind of adjustment, and the popularity of Indian ragas turned out to be a passing fad.

The same principle is true for people who grew up during the rock era. If Dixieland is going to become accessible to them, they'll have to make a considerable modification to their musical values, i.e., they'll have to do a bit of work to appreciate it.

For a couple of years, my Red Lion Jazz Band played once a month at a hotel in a room where, when we weren't appearing, rock was featured. From time to time, young folks would come in, not having checked the schedule and expecting to find rock. Often they would stay, dance, have a good time, and make a point of telling us at the end of the evening how much they enjoyed themselves.

However, they usually didn't come back. The next time they went out, they did the natural thing and sought out music with which they were more at home, that they could enjoy without making any adjustments.

As we know, rock is ubiquitous. Radio stations that used to be "easy listening" stations (in the sense that you and I understand the term - Mantovani, 101 Strings, etc.) have switched to "adult contemporary" or "oldies", both of which are essentially soft rock. Movie sound tracks contain rock, even when it's inappropriate (as for a story that takes place in pre-rock times). Commercials use rock music to get their messages across. The only forms of pre-rock music that are still popular are those that have co-opted rock devices, e.g., many country bands today have electrified instruments and drummers playing with a disco back-beat.

Why is rock so pervasive? As described above, the majority of today's potential audience for music - people aged about 45 or younger - have trouble relating to anything else. They aren't willing to do the work required to get into something like, say, Dixieland jazz, which is as alien to them as Indian ragas are to most of us.

I graduated from high school in 1954. I was already deeply into Dixieland and ragtime and was one of the youngest people I knew who was. Now I'm in my early 50s and I'm still one of the youngest. Nearly everyone in the audience or on stage at the Dixieland festivals, concerts and clubs I attend is older than I am.

That's a pretty scary situation, when you think of it in connection with the future for Dixieland. Indeed, as I have previously pointed out in this column, people are already starting to present as Dixieland, and accept as Dixieland, a significant amount of non-genre music within the Dixieland scene. As I look ahead to retirement, with the hope that I might be able to locate in a spot that will provide me with more opportunity to play Dixieland and ragtime, I find myself becoming

Why Youth Doesn't Like Dixieland

concerned that (1) what will be passing as Dixieland when I retire will no longer be anything I have any interest in playing and (2) there no longer will be a significant audience left that has much interest in hearing authentic Dixieland.

Quite a number of Dixieland jazz clubs have begun to address these concerns. They recognize that, if any substantial headway is going to be made, people must become involved in Dixieland when they are young, when their musical tastes are still being developed, and when they will not have to make a significant effort to adjust their ears to gain an appreciation of our music.

Involving youngsters in Dixieland is not going to be an easy job. In fact, two developments during the rock era show pretty clearly how difficult the task will be.

First, in the 1960s in England, there was a "trad boom" that lasted for a number of years. Dixieland was "in", Dixieland concerts featuring several bands were well attended, younger players entered the field, and Dixieland recordings appeared on the popular charts. In fact, British trumpeter Kenny Ball's rendition of "Midnight in Moscow" even crossed the Atlantic to become the last full-fledged Dixieland ride to head the U. S. hit parade.

Second, a similar thing happened with respect to U. S. ragtime in the mid-1970s. As a result of the success of the orchestral ragtime score to the hit film "The Sting", everyone - classical musicians, major record labels, music publishers, you name it - was climbing on the ragtime bandwagon. Scott Joplin's turn-of-the-century rag, "The Entertainer," was, for a while, the number one pop tune.

Both of these surges of popularity were beyond the wildest expectations of Dixielanders and ragtimers. However, even with the benefit of major media exposure, neither of these fads took root. The conventions of rock music had become too firmly entrenched, the adjustments required of the general public were too great, and both Dixieland and ragtime receded to the hobby-music status that they occupy today.

If national popularity couldn't resurrect our music, what tack can we take that shows promise? I think we could learn something from what's happened to big-band music.

Big-band is about the only kind of pre-rock music that has survived without substantial modification and continues to attract more than a smattering of the under-50 set.

Why? Because, for about thirty years now, nearly every sizeable high school has had a "stage band" program, one with the faculty, students and parents behind it, with its own regional competitions and prizes. These high school stage bands play, along with fusion (jazz licks plus rock rhythm) and progressive, plain old 1930s-type big-band swing and dance music. Thus, our young folks are discovering that they need make no listening adjustments to continue to enjoy big bands in their later years.

I would like to think that similar programs could be instituted in the public schools for Dixieland. As the oldest form of jazz, it has a legitimate claim on the attentions of students, particularly students in the U. S., where jazz originated.

There are, however, two problems that arise in teaching Dixieland that do not arise in teaching big-band. First, a Dixieland band will have substantially fewer

TEXAS SHOUT: HOW DIXIELAND JAZZ WORKS

members than a big band, thereby implying a smaller support base of student participants, parents, etc. Second, big-band can be taught in large part, or exclusively, from written charts, whereas Dixieland requires the teaching of improvisation.

Improvisation presents a special difficulty. The student can't simply come to his sixth-period Dixieland class and expect to get comfortable improvising the way he can get comfortable playing arrangements in the stage band. He'll need to work on his own to learn chord patterns and scales, and he'll need to do some listening to Dixielanders, in person or on record, to find out what improvising is all about.

Still, Dixieland is a subject that is being taught successfully. There is a summer Dixieland camp for young instrumentalists run by the Sacramento Traditional Jazz Society that develops several combos at once during a few days' intensive work. Southern Comfort has sponsored a contest for collegiate Dixieland bands that has produced both bands and individual players who have remained in the field. If I have my facts right, Bill Clark, tubaist for the Queen City Jazz Band, teaches Dixieland at the college level, while Dick Cruz, trumpeter/leader of the Fullertowne Strutters, took his Dixieland clinic on tour recently for young players up and down the West Coast.

This is the direction we need to take, I think, if we're going to keep the music alive in a meaningful way. We need to find secondary-school music teachers willing to recognize that jazz didn't start with Charlie Parker, and get them teaching their students not only to play Dixieland, but to play it for the remaining members of the student body and in regional competitions similar to those held for stage bands.

In short, as indicated above, occasional exposure of youngsters to Dixieland is not going to be enough, nor is the once-in-a-lifetime fad like the British "trad boom" or the Sting/Joplin craze. However, if Dixieland is something that our children accept as part of their daily lives, that is taught as part of their regular school routines, eventually it'll start getting back onto the airwaves, into record bins, and on the concert stages.

How can jazz clubs further the effort to get Dixieland into secondary school music curricula? Someone more familiar than I with the machinations of school boards and school administration will have to answer that one, I'm afraid. When the answer is provided, though, I'll do my part to help.

If you really want to keep listening to our music, you'll pitch in as well to help get it taught to youngsters when the opportunity comes. Otherwise, I fear that "Dixieland" events of the future are going to be featuring not the Dixieland you and I love so much, but bluegrass, Latin, urban blues and the latest thing in heavy metal.

May-June 1991 West Coast Rag

CHAPTER 16   FAVORITE MUSICIANS

Who is your favorite Dixieland musician? Who is your favorite living Dixieland musician?

The great thing about "Favorites" is that it's a game anyone can play. You don't need to be an expert to have a favorite. All you need is a musician who, for whatever reason you want to pick, rings your chimes more than any other. No one can tell you you're wrong, either.

Moreover, the musician needn't be an all-time great, or for that matter even a very good player. If a favorite had to be the greatest, the discussion would end right here, in fact - we'd all pick Louis Armstrong.

On that point, don't let anyone tell you different - Louis Armstrong was, beyond any reasonable controversy, the greatest jazzman who ever lived. As a technician he was not only far ahead of his contemporaries, but also of the majority of today's Dixieland cornet/trumpeters. He had a majestic, compelling tone as well. Satchmo was also a magnificent soloist, an unerring ensemble player and an instinctively infallible jazz vocalist.

There are a few other great jazzmen about whom most of those statements could be made, but the additional factor that sets Armstrong so far above the herd was his all - pervasive influence. More than any other jazzman, maybe more than any other American musician in or out of jazz, Louis Armstrong single-handedly changed the course of modern music.

First, his instrumental talent was such that he was a key figure in changing the direction of the ensemble-oriented jazz of the twenties to the more solo-oriented jazz of swing and later styles. More importantly, his way of phrasing against the rhythm was so far ahead of everyone else in the field that, due almost solely to Louis, jazz was able to free itself of the vertical up-and-down influences left over from ragtime and develop its unique momentum, the "swing," that distinguishes jazz performances from those of other musics.

It is no exaggeration to say that all jazzmen play some Louis Armstrong. In fact, one can find, in virtually any piece of contemporary music, from rock to country to current "classical" works, something that can be traced to Louis either because he did it first or because so much attention was paid to him that devices he adopted from his musical background were thereby given wider recognition in the scene.

There simply is no one else about whom such statements can be made. If greatness implies not only personal skill but also influence, Louis clearly leads the pack and by such a margin that we can't clearly discern who's running second.

Having said that, I'll tell you that I love listening to Louis, that I think there is no such thing as an Armstrong record which doesn't contain something worth hearing, that he is one of the few musicians whose autograph I sought (it's framed on top of my piano), that I didn't wash my hand for a day after first shaking hands with him, but that he is not at the top of my all-time favorite list. That honor belongs to Turk Murphy.

From the first day that I ran across (in the files of *WDEL* in Wilmington, where as a teenager I helped pull records on a Saturday afternoon call-in disc jockey radio show) a promotional 78 of "Creole Belles"/"The Pearls" by Turk Murphy's Jazz Band, I was mesmerized by the sextet's brassy well-knit ensemble, easy-rolling two-beat, and rusty-hinge tailgate trombone. When, a few years later, my parents gave me a table model Pilot LP player, three of the first platters I bought, starting a collection that now numbers about 4000 LPs, were Columbias by Turk.

I spent long hours playing my trombone along with those records, doing my best to get under the skin of the Murphy sliphorn. When my Red Lion Jazz Band first took the field in 1964, it was as close to the Murphy mold as I could make it. I even played trombone on its first two gigs, until I realized that, given the limited number of Dixielanders around Wilmington, Delaware, I would have to play the lead instrument over the long haul if I wanted a band that could perform the sort of repertoire I had in mind.

(Since our marriage in 1971, I had told Nancy from time to time that I was a good Dixieland trombonist, and finally had to take a trombone gig several years ago - my only one in about two decades - to prove it. I needed two weeks' advance work to get my trombone lip back in shape, but Nancy volunteered after the show that, to her surprise, I turned out to be a much more expressive trombonist than she expected.)

As the years went by, I discovered that, as far as my own playing was concerned, pure Murphyish West Coast revival wasn't exactly where I wanted to go. I like all the Dixieland styles and want the freedom to use figures from all of them, a method to which the relatively highly-structured routines of unadulterated Watters-Murphy do not easily adjust.

Thus, I doubt that anyone today would place The Rent Party Revellers, and probably not the Red Lions either, squarely in a Murphy groove. Still, he's my favorite. I respond more quickly and more emotionally to Turk Murphy than any other jazzman. I have all of his recordings that I can locate, and I'll buy without hesitation any further material on which he appears. (I even have an album by comic singer-songwriter Shel Silverstein that I bought solely because Turk's name is included in the credits - even though, if it is indeed he, his trombone is just barely audible for a few notes among party-type sound effects on one track.)

As favorites go, the choice of Turk is a pretty easy one to defend. His band is one of the most widely imitated in all of Dixieland jazz. He is one of the greatest ensemble Dixieland trombonists who ever lived, having a flawless ear for exactly the note needed to complement and enhance the work of the other sidemen. While Turk was perhaps a better ensemble player than soloist, his husky, shouting solo style is still one of the three most copied pre-swing trombone sounds (the others belonging to Jim Robinson and Jack Teagarden).

Still none of those elements necessarily require you to make someone your "favorite." Favorites are strictly personal. You can have a favorite in defiance of all logic.

Favorite Musicians

In fact, despite what I've said above, if I could only take one recording to a desert island, I wouldn't take one of my Murphys or Armstrongs. I'd take my Neovox audiocassette that contains all but two of the sides waxed in 1925-28 by cornetist Albert Brunies' Halfway House Orchestra.

There are those who criticize the HHO. I suspect that these people have some difficulty making their peace with the fact that Brunies and his cohorts didn't record much blues, that they did record pop tunes (many with sentimental titles), and that they were all white musicians.

However, to me the Halfway Housers did exactly what a good jazz band is supposed to do: generate a sweeping momentum without appearing to be working hard in the process; have a seemingly spontaneous loose-limbed ensemble that can sail through brief pre-planned effects without shifting gears or losing drive; and build its rides with a steadily escalating emotional pitch. In Albert Brunies, the band could boast a leader whose burnished tone sounds like a slightly warmer, southern edition of Red Nichols and whose solos are a model of how to play basic melody as red-hot jazz via inspired phrasing and accents. Its rhythm section sported tuba/string bassist Chink Martin, one of the most swinging bass men of his day.

In Bill Whitmore and "Red" Long, Halfway House had a couple of pianists who composed top-notch tunes for the band. Indeed, Whitmore's "New Orleans Shuffle" has become a standard on today's festival circuit.

Anyway, this business of favorites was going along swimmingly for me for decades. Then, after a long and productive career, Turk Murphy died. He didn't stop being my favorite jazz musician, of course. Now, though, all of a sudden, I was confronted with the question of whether I had a favorite _living_ jazz musician.

That term, I thought, needed a little definition. Nancy and I have been fortunate enough to become friends with lots of Dixielanders, all of whom might qualify as "favorites" in one respect or another. We enjoy seeing them play, hearing their recordings, and generally getting together with them. How does one begin to narrow down such a group?

I decided that my favorite living musician would be one, judged on the basis of music alone, whose records I would buy if I knew nothing more about them than that he was on them. Looked at from that viewpoint, the picture became clearer.

Wild Bill Davison and Dick Wellstood, along with a few other names, seemed to be the clear choices for me. On the basis of the difference in their ages, I went for Bill, thinking, incorrectly as it turned out, that there'd still be plenty of time for Dick to get to the top of my pile.

As you can surmise, it wasn't long before I went through this process again. This time Art Hodes wears the crown, and I hope he lives forever.

However, experience has taught me to be ready, so I've started kicking around some names. Toronto pianist John Arpin, is such a master of the keyboard, and such

TEXAS SHOUT: HOW DIXIELAND JAZZ WORKS

a consummate interpreter of ragtime, that I have to own anything he records falling within my ragtime/Dixieland orbit. However, though John can play superb vintage jazz, I believe that he has not yet recorded any, sticking essentially to ragtime when he ventures beyond his normal studio-type or hotel lounge environs. So I need to cast about among jazzmen.

Ralph Sutton and Sammy Price, though not as active these days as they used to be, are nevertheless going to be obvious candidates for someone who loves to play the piano as much as I do. Similarly, having so much respect for the integrity of the music as an art form, I find it easy to empathize with Kenny Davern's open-minded, searching approach while also appreciating his masterful reed-work. My record reviewing activities have taught me that the great bassist Bob Haggart and British trad drummer Barry Martyn are artists virtually incapable of making a recording that isn't a keeper. And there's Ernie Carson, Howard Alden, and many others whose names are no less deserving because space considerations prevent me from listing them here.

While I've been mulling this question over in my mind, I've become aware of something that prompted me to discuss the matter in today's column. My candidate list is overwhelmingly balanced in favor of veteran musicians, mostly ones who probably can no longer even be called middle-aged, much less young.

That fact disturbs me greatly. It puts me in mind of a remark recently made to me by a musician friend who said "There are no stylists left in Dixieland." What he meant, and there is a lot of truth in this thought, was that too many of today's Dixielanders are choosing to be derivative of their favorite players rather than finding their own distinctive voices.

Where are today's counterparts to such instantly recognizable jazzmen as Bix Beiderbecke, Louis Armstrong, Turk Murphy, Pee Wee Russell, Willie "The Lion" Smith, George Lewis, Ken Colyer, Kid Thomas, Sidney Bechet, Bessie Smith, and Jelly Roll Morton? That's a mighty tough question.

I have previously remarked in these pages that, of the three principal skills utilized in playing Dixieland (ensemble skill, solo skill, and - for hot dance bands - reading skill), by far the weakest in today's scene is solo skill. It's one thing to let yourself be influenced by your favorite artists from the past - we all do that, and in fact there's no other effective way to learn how to play Dixieland than by listening to others play it. However, it's quite another thing, once you've learned the rules, not to go on and accept the challenge of doing what the great jazzmen did, i.e., find your own personal mode of expression within the idiom.

It can be done. Trombonist Jim Snyder of the South Frisco Jazz Band has taken a basic Murphy approach and pounded it into a grindy, gut-bucket stew of rhythmic splatterings that not only works beautifully but, as far as I can hear, belongs to him alone. The marvelous reedman Sammy Rimington has forged his own personality on clarinet using George Lewis as a base and on alto saxophone using Cap'n John Handy. Bob Jackson's spare, tart trumpet goes its own way and does as much as anything to define the special sound of the Grand Dominion Jazz Band. Eli Newberger's deft tuba work with The New Black Eagles Jazz Band owes almost nothing to any particular Dixieland tubaist from the past.

I could think of some others from today's players, but not a lot of them, and almost none from the ranks of artists in their twenties or thirties (the age at which

Favorite Musicians

the Beiderbeckes, Armstrongs, etc., made their maximum impact). This situation bodes ill for our music as a viable art form, raising a prospect that Dixieland soloing may, through inattention to what's really important, turn into a stylistic and creative dead end.

With all the performers in all the Dixieland bands now out on the circuit, can't more of you become interested in taking some chances? In too few years, we're going to run out of originators from the early revival or the swing periods. When someone asks us, in 1995 or 2000, who our favorite living musician is, we'd like to be able to mention your name, instead of shamefacedly saying "Gee, I can hardly tell them apart these days. I guess I don't have one any more."

Louie & Duke   1953
Photographer Unknown

TEXAS SHOUT: HOW DIXIELAND JAZZ WORKS

Turk Murphy   1979   *Photo by Ed Lawless*

Abbie Brunies Halfway House Orch.   About 1923   *Photographer Unknown*

Favorite Musicians

Wild Bill Davison 1940s
Photo by J. Robert Mantler

Kenny Davern 1960s
Photographer Unknown

Bob Haggart & Ray Baudoc   About 1939
Courtesy Metronome Magazine

TEXAS SHOUT: HOW DIXIELAND JAZZ WORKS

Ernie Carson 1960s
Photo by Ross Kelly

Ralph Sutton 1980s
Photographer Unknown

Jim Snyder 1991
Photo by Andrew Wittenborn

Favorite Musicians

Sammy Rimington   1961
Photo by Ed Lawless

Howard Alden   1987
Photo by Andrew Wittenborn

Dick Wellstood   1950s
Photo courtesy of The Record Changer

TEXAS SHOUT: HOW DIXIELAND JAZZ WORKS

Eli Newberger   1980s *Photo by Dan Polin*

Bob Jackson   1990s *Photo by Dan Polin*

CHAPTER 17   CHICAGO STYLE

When I was five years old, Spike Jones and his City Slickers came up with their first big hit record, "Der Fuehrer's Face." I loved it, not only the comedy, but the musical parts as well.

At that time, as I have written before in these pages, the Dixieland scene was dominated by Chicago-styled-bands, which usually use a guitar and string bass in their rhythm sections. While commercial radio was then more broad-based than it is now, and played some Dixieland on occasion, bands with banjo-tuba rhythm sections virtually never appeared thereon.

Spike Jones, of course, made the funniest musical parodies of all time, gems of comedy that stand up beautifully today. His gags, however, were supported by a brand of pseudo-Dixieland that included banjo and tuba. Indeed, when the band wanted to (as airchecks of it prove), the City Slickers could play some formidable two-beat Dixieland.

For that reason, many revivalist Dixieland fans my age will tell you that Spike Jones's 78s were key elements in shaping their musical preferences. I collected those platters avidly, listening to them over and over until I knew every note by heart, and then still replaying them.

One day, browsing through one of my local record shops, I stumbled across "Tiger Rag/The World Is Waiting For the Sunrise" by The Firehouse Five Plus Two. Hearing it in the audition booth in the store, I felt that a bright light had been turned on. Here was a whole side of just the type of music I'd been responding to all those years, without the distractions of Jones's jokes (great though his jokes were)! I immediately started acquiring FH5 disks and playing my trombone along with every one as soon as I got home from school each day.

At about this time, I had learned that the music I liked was called "jazz" I went to the public library and tried to read something about it, to discover how it worked and where to find more of it.

My tastes at that time had been heavily conditioned in favor of the revivalist two-beat sound. I had discovered Turk Murphy (who instantly became my favorite musician) and Lu Watters, but my local stores carried very little of their styles in the racks. There was plenty of Dixieland, but its rhythm sounded too smooth to me and its ensembles too disorganized. I had trouble relating to it. What I was hearing was, of course, Chicago style.

Well, I tried to maintain an open mind and continued reading my way down the jazz shelf in the library, whereupon I ran across some books by a guitarist named Eddie Condon. Condon was a witty and erudite spokesman for older-style jazz, particularly the branch he played which, I later realized, was called Chicago style. I enjoyed his writing so much that I decided to seek out his recordings, hoping that they would be good, not knowing that any intelligently-compiled list of the all-time

TEXAS SHOUT: HOW DIXIELAND JAZZ WORKS

greatest Chicago sessions will be dominated with dates on which Condon was either the nominal or de facto leader .

As it happened, I started out with an LP called "Jammin' At Condon's" - which, in retrospect, turned out to be one of the best Chicago-style albums of its day. Again, that bright light flashed on. Hearing Condon's incomparable crew of rugged individualists performing at their peaks cut through the problem I'd been having with the sound and approach. I understood what this music was all about, that it was indeed the same Dixieland jazz I'd been enjoying so much. As before, I set out to understand it and to find more of that quality.

At the time of the West Coast and New Orleans revival in the early 1940s, the revivalists were trying to right the imbalance that then existed on the scene in favor of Chicago-style Dixieland. Today, it seems to me, the scales are heavily weighted in the other direction. There are pitifully few high-quality organized Chicago-style bands on the scene, and several misconceptions abound in the Dixieland community about Chicago style.

First of all, I have seen festivals declaring themselves to be "traditional" festivals, when they intend to say to the potential audience not only that they do not hire musicians who play swing and other advanced forms of jazz, but also that they do not hire Chicago-styled combos. This terminology fosters the wholly inaccurate idea that Chicago style is not "traditional."

To the extent that this point makes any difference to anybody, Chicago style is much more traditional than most of the so-called "traditional" styles prominently featured at "traditional" festivals. The "traditional" festivals regularly hire bands that play (1) uptown new Orleans style, a type of jazz that did not really come to public attention until Bunk Johnson began recording it in the early 1940s, (2) West Coast revival, a branch that originated with Lu Watters in the same early-1940s time frame and (3) British trad, a style that was developed in the 1950s by Ken Colyer, Chris Barber and other English revivalists.

By contrast, Chicago style was on the scene in the twenties, and was thriving before swing (and the changes in jazz that accompanied swing) had ever been thought of. If, by the word "traditional," you mean authentic Dixieland jazz of the twenties, Chicago has a better claim to be represented than most of the bands usually on the bill at "traditional" weekends.

Second, many fans today don't truly realize what Chicago style is. They're so used to hearing banjo-tuba bands that they lump together all guitar-string bass units. I could cite instances where I've seen references to "swing" when the context indicated fairly clearly that what was in fact being discussed was Chicago-style Dixieland. It seemed obvious to me that the commentator did not have a clear idea in mind of what constitutes Chicago-style Dixieland and how it differs from swing. Perhaps, therefore, it would be useful to mention some characteristics of Chicago style, together with some thoughts on why such characteristics developed.

Chicago style is, like the other six Dixieland styles I've been able to identify, a pre-swing form of jazz. That is, it uses the same musical vocabularly as uptown and downtown New Orleans, West Coast revival, hot dance, etc.

It does not use the thicker chords often heard in swing or other advanced jazz forms, nor does it use many chords that incorporate notes more than an octave above the tonic (i.e., not many 9th chords, no 11th or 13th chords, etc.). Similarly, Chicago jazzmen spend little time exploring the extreme ranges of their horns, in contrast to swing and more advanced jazz musicians, and play less cluttered, less extended lines than jazz players with a post-1930 orientation.

Thus, Chicagoans can, and do, perform from time to time, often as guest artists or sometimes in festival jam bands, with revivalist musicians and everyone gets along just fine. The main difference between Chicago and other styles is in the objectives of the musicians.

All improvised styles of Dixieland require musicians to reach competent levels of ensemble skills and solo skills. However, Chicago style is the only one of the seven styles where solo skills are more highly valued than ensemble skills. Hot dance, as I explained in my "Texas Shout" column in the February 1990 *WCR*, places its highest values on reading skills. The other five Dixieland styles place their highest values on ensemble skills.

Accordingly, to a Chicago musican, the solo is going to be the focus of the performance. In a typical Chicago format, the combo will play one or two ensemble choruses, and then each musician will take a turn soloing, attempting to find something distinctive, creative and personal to say about the musical material. Then the band will reassemble for a chorus or two to wrap it up.

The Chicagoans' solo orientation explains why Chicago bands, by the early 1940s, typically played a fairly circumscribed repertoire of tunes (which, as I have argued in the December 1990 "Texas Shout," are now unfairly ignored by the revivalist community). Because the rendition is going to center on the solos, during which the melody won't be heard much anyway, the Chicagoan is just as happy to work with a tried-and-true tune, one with which he feels comfortable. He plans to give you a brand new performance, a different improvisation, a fresh vision of it, from the one he gave you yesterday. He doesn't see it as repetitive to use that number again today.

Chicagoans prefer to work with the softer-edged guitar and string bass vs. banjo and tuba. Similarly, Chicago pianists often play light single-note-treble lines with occasional chordal jabs in the bass.

If you asked a Chicagoan why those things are true, he would probably tell you that he believes the soloist has more freedom in that context. The Chicagoan would go on to say that, if a soloist wishes to construct a line using a few out-of-chord notes, he wants a backup that will still swing hard, but which won't clash and drag him back into the basic chord the way the more insistent banjo, tuba and two-fisted stride piano will.

Along the same lines, Chicago-style bands, once past the opening ensemble, tend to play with a four-beat rhythm under the soloists. Again, my hypothetical Chicagoan probably believes that the soloist has more freedom that way - that is, he has more room to place his rhythmic accents where he chooses when his support is placing equal rhythmic accents on all four beats of the measure than if he is supported by two-beat jazz (which gives different rhythmic accents to beats one and three than to beats two and four).

I do not want to be in a position of setting up straw men here. Thus, I tested the preceding points with a friend of mine who is a fine Chicago musician. He confirmed that a typical Chicagoan would probably endorse them.

| TEXAS SHOUT: HOW DIXIELAND JAZZ WORKS |

Personally, I would not agree with our hypothetical Chicago jazzman on either one. I do not think that any particular combination of supporting instruments is more conducive to creative soloing than any other, nor do I believe that either two-beat or four-beat rhythm is inherently superior for that purpose.

The most important thing that a soloist's support can do to inspire good soloing is to be attentive and sensitive to the soloist. In my view, that factor dwarfs everything else you can name. I think most above-average Dixieland soloists would concur. As I see it, this point is, to a large extent, the key to Chicagoans' aversion to two-beat rhythm and banjo-tuba bands.

Over the past 20-30 years, an increasing proportion of the organized Dixieland bands consists of banjo-tuba groups which strongly emphasize ensembles vs. solos. Further, Dixieland jazz has become a music played principally by hobbyists. Even if they are full-time musicians, most Dixielanders make their living primarily from something other than playing Dixieland jazz.

Many of the best bands on the circuit, including a lot of my own favorites, are comprised of part-timers. Nevertheless, it is inevitable that the demands of a full-time non-musical (or non-Dixieland) job severely limit the time a hobbyist Dixielander can devote to mastering all the nuances of his music. If he chooses to concentrate the bulk of this limited time on developing ensemble skills, he is likely to be less attuned to the finer points of soloing.

An extensive essay could be written on the current state of soloing among such combos. Suffice it to say for now that these trends, in my opinion, have denigrated creative soloing on so much of the Dixieland scene that we now have quite a few bands out there - including some very popular ones - in which the musicians seem to have only a dim understanding of what a soloist is supposed to be doing with his time.

I suspect that it is the fallout from this unfortunate situation that has caused such deep-seated prejudice among certain Chicagoans against two-beat and banjo-tuba combos. A truly creative soloist is bound to feel hamstrung if he finds himself on stage with bands that are not properly sensitive to a soloist's needs, particularly if the bandsmen are wielding relatively hard-edged instruments (such as banjo and tuba) or playing forcefully (i.e., two-fisted stride piano vs. right-handed spare jabs).

If you're a festivalgoer, and/or a fan who listens to recordings in your living room, why should you take the trouble to condition your ears to enjoy Chicago style? I can think of several reasons.

You like Dixieland jazz and are spending a lot of your life involved in it. Why not like all of it? After all, Chicago style is Dixieland jazz, and it uses devices that you applaud when your favorite revivalist bands employ them. You should be able to enjoy those licks just as much in the context of a Chicago instrumentation.

Like all styles of Dixieland, Chicago can be, and is, played every way from superbly to atrociously. Why cut yourself off from the chance to hear a top-quality

Chicago band at a festival if the only other choices at that particular time slot might be revivalist bands with less promise?

In addition, Chicago musicians almost always are single-mindedly aimed at keeping the performances hot and hard-swinging. They are not derailed, as revivalists sometimes are, by a desire to play obscure material without sufficient regard to its potential as a vehicle for cooking jazz, or by a desire to replicate certain figures from vintage recordings without sufficient regard to whether those figures add much to the development of the rides.

Whether they're played slow or fast, soft or loud, hot performances that swing hard are, essentially, what Dixieland jazz ought to be all about. Chicago goes straight to the heart of the matter much of the time.

In fact, the Chicagoans regularly utilize effects that are aimed at keeping soloists on their toes and goosing the rides along. These devices include chase choruses and backup riffs behind soloists, two very effective heaters-up that are rarely utilized by revivalist bands. If you want to hear how these figures work, you'll probably need to catch the Chicago band at the festival.

Finally, as mentioned above, the revivalist movement in some quarters has emphasized ensemble playing to such a degree that soloing has been virtually ignored. I hear many revivalist musicians playing solos, and often getting warm applause, who hardly seem to know what the purpose of a solo should be. The current lack of standards for soloists offers little incentive on the revivalist side for a truly creative solo performer, someone who stands out from the crowd in what he is able to do on his instrument and what he wants to say with it, to remain with the revivalist camp.

As a result, the overwhelming majority of the truly outstanding Dixieland soloists today have been driven to Chicago, where their accomplishments are recognized and highly valued. If you want to hear performers who have learned to use their instruments to give you consistently inventive versions of the tunes, you are going to have to spend some time with the all-star Chicago jams.

Many of you know that I've been championing the full Dixieland spectrum for years and urging individuals to enjoy more of their favorite music by becoming familiar with all seven branches thereof. In particular, because Chicago style seems on the verge of invisibility at many festivals these days, I've tried to point some of you toward it.

From time to time, one of you will report back and say something like "I went to the all-star jam at the festival this weekend, but I simply couldn't stand all that endless soloing. Moreover, the ensembles were just a mess, with everybody blasting away. I guess this music isn't really for me."

I can understand your problem and your frustration. I had that same trouble until, as I mentioned above, I had a chance to hear some 100% undiluted Chicago-style jazz of the highest quality on the "Jammin' At Condon's" LP.

Unfortunately, many of the musicians appearing in the contemporary all-star jams are not true Dixielanders at heart. The top-name Dixieland soloists from the twenties who used to man the all-star sessions at Chicago-oriented festivals like the Manassas Jazz Festival are now all dead or inactive. Today's performers may indeed be all-star jazzmen, extremely capable instrumentalists with enviable reputations on the jazz scene. However, some of them made those reputations playing in big bands, or performing swing or progressive jazz.

These musicians, when soloing, have learned how to relate to their accompanying rhythm, and in ensemble have learned, to some extent, how to interact with the pared-down lineups favored by small swing or bop combos. In many cases, however, these artists have not learned the more complex ensemble skills that Dixielanders have - how to listen to as many as seven other improvising musicians playing at once, how to find the right few notes that will enhance and complement their activities, how to avoid moving up or down into the range occupied by another instrument, how to avoid using advanced chords that clash with the group's harmonic orientation, etc.

These non-Dixieland musicians can't be blamed, when they're sent on stage at a Dixieland festival, for playing the kinds of lines that brought them fame in the jazz field. However, it doesn't take many such players in a jazz band to reduce the proceedings to chaos during ensembles.

Thus, an all-star jam these days can be an iffy proposition for initiating your contact with Chicago jazz. If you've got a Yank Lawson, a Bob Haggart, a Kenny Davern, a Ralph Sutton, you can't go wrong. These great soloists, and others of their stripe, are also steeped in the Dixieland tradition. Other great soloists, not as well grounded in pre-swing jazz, cannot function as effectively in these types of Dixieland jam sets and can push the whole proceeding out of kilter.

At this point, some of you may be thinking: O. K., Tex, I hear what you're saying. I've never paid much attention to the Chicago bands, and I've been burned a few times wasting an hour in front of a group of disorganized all-stars. However, I'm still willing to give Chicago a try and to see if it really has as much to offer as you say. But I don't want to keep wasting my time and money groping in the dark. What do I do next?

Well, I can't tell you whether an all-star festival jam is going to be good or less so. However, there are a few organized bands out there that, from my experience, are ones where you can, as they say, shop with confidence.

Two are from the West Coast and are fairly active on the festival circuit. From Northern California, the Fulton Street Jazz Band plays Chicago style with cohesion and drive. From the other end of the state comes the aptly-named Chicago Six. This group's rather laid-back presentation may fool you but, based on the few times I've seen it, when the Six start to play, the band delivers pure, worthwhile Chicago style.

Though Swing 'N Dixie is made up of musicians from the East Coast, it has had substantial exposure on the West Coast and on cruises over the several years when it was named The Parke Frankenfield Dixieland All-Stars. I suspect that its name change reflects the fact that the combo is modifying its focus somewhat because the elderly folks comprising the bulk of the audience for older-style jazz these days grew up not during the twenties, but in the swing years. These people can relate more easily to the somewhat more polished and structured sound of swing and mainstream (improvised small-band jazz played by swing musicians) than to the raucous polyphony of Dixieland. As of this writing, however, my experience with Swing ' N Dixie is that it likes to nail those good old good ones to the mark in approved Chicago fashion.

Chicago Style

While we're on the East Coast, cornetist Eddie Polcer led the band for years at the revived Eddie Condon's in New York City. I'm not sure if Polcer has a regular working group with set personnel any more, but if he puts a band together it's going to speak fluent Condonese.

The foregoing list is not meant to be exhaustive. For example, I've not yet heard cornetist Tom Saunders' Wild Bill Davison Memorial Jazz Band. However, from my knowledge of Saunders and the sidemen he's using I expect that, when I do hear it, I'll hear some quality Chicago style.

Also, bright stylistic lines can't be drawn around every combo. The popular Hot Cotton Jazz Band plays jazz in which Chicago predominates, but with some revivalist leanings. The Garden Avenue Seven sports quite a few tightly-conceived production numbers, but will also slip its traces and lay down some blistering Chicago as a change of pace.

For those of you who don't get to festivals, or those who want to adjust your ears a bit in advance, how's about some records? The idea for this column, in fact, stems from the simultaneous arrival at my home of review copies of three recordings which, it seems to me, would be ideal starting points for a neophyte Chicagoist.

Normally I would cover them in my "This Month's Records" column for *WCR*. However, the underappreciation of Chicago style in today's market is a topic I've been meaning to talk over with you for some time. Reviewing these records in "Texas Shout" provides as good a springboard for that discussion as any.

Stash ST-CD-530, "The Definitive Eddie Condon And His Jazz Concert All-Stars, Vol. 1", is a compact disc containing material from two 1944 recording sessions for Associated Transcriptions. It would be an excellent introduction to Condonese for a number of reasons.

First, the personnel make up a pretty generous sampling of the Condon "barefoot mob". Although Wild Bill Davison and Bud Freeman are missing, you nevertheless will hear, among others, Bobby Hackett, Billy Butterfield, Pee Wee Russell, Ed Hall, Ernie Caceres, Gene Schroeder, Jess Stacy, Bob Haggart, George Wettling and Lee Wiley - that is, quite a few of the names that most quickly come to mind when the discussion centers on Condonland. Moreover, in 1944, these artists were in their primes.

Second, because these performances were designed for radio broadcast, they were not only recorded with then state-of-the-art fidelity, but also are relatively brief (usually two-to-three minutes). You will not hear endless strings of solos. On the hot selections, the band brings it in, gives some brief solo space to a few horns, and then roars on out.

Third, the 74-minute running time allows for a good variety in presentation while still leaving plenty of room for stomping versions of the tunes the Condonites most liked to play, like "That's A'Plenty", "At the Jazz Band Ball", and "Royal Garden Blues". In between, you'll hear features for individual sidemen, such as

| TEXAS SHOUT: HOW DIXIELAND JAZZ WORKS |

Butterfield on "What's New?" or Caceres on "Time On My Hands" (though these rides are basically pop-oriented dance material).

If I were reviewing this one in my "This Month's Records" column, I'd give it a top rating of five stars. It may not include Condon's all-time-greatest sides - more on those later - but there is so much good Chicago jazz here that, if you couldn't come away from this album believing that you got your money's worth, I'd guess that you never will come to enjoy Chicago-style Dixieland.

Stash ST-CD-530 is available @ $15.00, plus the shipping charges mentioned below, from Stash Records, 611 Broadway - Suite #411, New York, New York 10012. Shipping charges: Domestic - $3.00; Canada & Mexico - $4.50. Overseas - $5.50. New York residents add 8% sales tax. Charge customers may phone Tues-Thurs, 10-5, to (800) 666-5277.

FLLM Recordings, CM 2996, "Play Me A Trad Band Tune," by Swing 'N Dixie, would also, for a somewhat different reason, provide an excellent introduction to Chicago style. This 44-minute audiocassette captures a crackerjack Chicago octet (which, because three of the horn players double various saxophones, offers a broader-than-usual range of sound textures) playing a program of selections that, until now, have been the exclusive province of revivalists.

S'ND here does exactly what a Dixieland band should always be doing - giving us a brand new, and yet valid within the idiom, vision of its material. Its charts are imaginative, active, economical, and executed with panache, punch and well-knit integration.

How's about Turk's characteristic climbing break on "Ministrels Of Annie Street" done by unison tenor saxophones? Or Bechet's romantic "Love Me With Feeling" by a melting soprano saxophone trio? Or the two-cornet breaks on the intro of Watters' "Annie Street Rock" by a soprano-clarinet duet?

This marvelous five-star 2/22/90 session is filled with felicitous surprises, one right decision after another, with so much imagination on display that it puts most of today's organized bands to shame. It's $10.00 postpaid from Parke Frankenfield, 786 Camelia Lane, Vero Beach, Florida 32963. While you're at it, pick up a copy at the same price of the four-star companion audiocassette, FLLM Recordings CM 2997 "Play It The Chicago Way", on which S'ND delivers "Rosetta", "Riverboat Shuffle" and others in time-honored no-nonsense Windy City fashion, along with some smoother numbers for fans of 1930s music.

There are, of course, lots of other top-rank Chicago-style records available. If you're a retired millionaire and are wondering what alternative you have to buying a third Cadillac, or you're looking for a once-in-a-life-time Christmas or anniversary present for a Dixieland fan, or you're just a committed collector who would like to get a good library at once instead of one record at a time, I'll toss out a couple of expensive ideas.

Mosaic Records has been putting out magnificent boxed sets for a number of years now, each one a definitive job on its subject, including alternative takes and a comprehensive descriptive booklet. A few years ago, Mosaic undertook to issue the complete jazz records of Milt Gabler's historic Commodore label in three sets of 20-23 LPs each.

Chicago Style

Gabler had impeccable taste, everything on his label being quality jazz. Specifically, Commodore recorded loads of titles by the Condonites at a time when those musicians were in their most productive years.

Not to put too fine a point on it, if a representative group of Chicago experts were polled as to the all-time best recordings in the idiom, the results would unquestionably be heavily skewed with Commodore dates, the choicest probably being those by the lineup that was variously known as Wild Bill Davison and his Commodores and George Brunies and his Jazz Band. Personally, I collected Commodore reissues in their various incarnations for years, just to get more alternative takes by the Condon aggregations.

When these massive Mosaic sets appeared, costing about $200 each, I choked at first. However, when I learned that only 400 copies of Volume One were left (these are limited editions), I ponied up. After seeing the final product, containing piles of previously unreleased material, I'm delighted I did. Pick up a current Mosaic catalog and see how much of this is still around. It's Mosaic Records, 35 Melrose Place, Stamford, Connecticut 06902, phone (203) 327-7111, fax (203) 323-3526.

During the forties, the Condon crew put on a wonderful series of half-hour jam session broadcasts from New York's Town Hall. Jazzology Records is in the process of releasing these commercially, complete in chronological order, in double albums containing four broadcasts each. This set can be acquired piecemeal and thereby will be less pricey than the Mosaics, but you'll still be out more than a few bucks by the time the series is complete. You're hearing airchecks, not studio recordings, but for the most part the acoustics sound fine.

Jazzology was founded to preserve Chicago style, and there is a lot of good Chicago on it. The catalog is available from Jazzology Records, 1206 Decatur Street, New Orleans, Louisiana 70116, phone (504) 525-1776.

Basically, though, you needn't get in over your head all at once. I"ll settle for having you check out the Stash CD and the Swing 'N Dixie tapes described above. If you aren't glad you got them, and if you don't want to hear more of that kind of hot music after you've absorbed them, I hereby excuse you from paying any more attention to my proselyting for Chicago. However, I'll bet that, for a lot of you, the bright light that came on when I heard "Jammin' At Condon's" is about to flash one more time.

TEXAS SHOUT: HOW DIXIELAND JAZZ WORKS

Pee Wee Russell 1920s
Photographer Unknown

Eddie Condon 1940s
Photo - The Record Changer

Chicago Six Jazz Band 1990s

CHAPTER 18   CHRISTMAS RECORDS

I recently received a review copy of a compact disc of Christmas-related blues and jazz. Its arrival brought to ten the number of holiday-season jazz albums on the Wyndhams' shelves.

Things weren't always so good for Dixielanders at Yuletide. For many years, the only vintage jazz Christmas recording I knew about was <u>Jazzology J-9</u>, "Let's Have An Old-Fashioned Christmas", by George Jackson's Jazz Band.

<u>J-9</u> is a respectable journeyman session of brash Dixieland by a British band that maintains a nice balance between the Chicago and British trad styles. First thing each Christmas morning, I'd throw it on the turntable and we'd open our presents. It did a fine job of maintaining a festive spirit around the hearth in keeping with the general Dixieland orientation of our household.

The problem was that we only had the one record, but the holiday season lasts longer than just Christmas morning. Lots of activities, for which we wanted accompanying music, had been going on during the preceding weeks - addressing cards, trimming the tree, etc. - and would continue through New Year's.

Nancy and I like Dixieland, ragtime and related music so much that we've never discovered what, if anything, is second on our list. So, to keep some congenial sounds in the air, we'd wrap presents, make (Nancy) or eat (Tex) Christmas cookies, and follow other seasonal pursuits while listening to general material from our collection, nevertheless recognizing the incongruity of stringing Christmas lights to the tune of, say, "Send Me To The 'Lectric Chair" or "Satanic Blues."

I am pleased to report that, in recent years, the situation has improved. A satisfactory number of Christmas recordings have appeared that are aimed at the vintage jazz buff.

Nowadays we usually get out the stack in early December and go through it, often more than once, during the ensuing weeks. There is enough variety in these recordings, and we have a sufficient supply, to eliminate monotony. They speed our holidays along most agreeably. Further, they are of a high enough average quality that, when guests arrive, we feel comfortable playing them in the background, thereby exposing our friends to our favorite music in a suitably seasonal way.

If you subscribe to this publication, you have a higher-than-average committment to pre-swing jazz and ragtime. Thus, you may also find it pleasant to have some Christmas Dixieland on hand for the holidays. For whatever use it may be to you, I'll take the balance of this column to pass along some thoughts on the recordings with which I'm familiar.

One word of caution, though, before we begin. You might think that a Christmas Dixieland album would be an ideal gift for your fellow Dixieland fan, or even for a non-Dixielander you'd like to rope into our circle. Most of the records discussed in today's column are items you can safely give, but if I were doing the giving, they wouldn't be my first choices.

| TEXAS SHOUT: HOW DIXIELAND JAZZ WORKS |

Why not? Because the typical Christmas song is not constructed in a way that makes it a preferred vehicle for jazz performance. The bulk of the Christmas repertoire consists either of fluffy ditties designed to bring a quick smile or tear to the Christmas audience or of carols or religiously-tinged music, some of it composed centuries prior to the development of jazz. Such material calls for a higher level of thought and creativity from the musicians if rides thereon are to emerge on a par with jazz performances of more compatible compositions.

By contrast, quite a few of the Christmas Dixieland albums capture the artists relaxing and playing for their own special pre-sold fans without particularly trying to wring every ounce of jazz out of their programs. For that reason, the Christmas Dixieland albums, while usually worthy enough, do not typically rank with the best in the artists' discographies and, judged strictly on their jazz content, are less desirable as gifts than other, better recordings by the players involved.

With that caveat, let's move to the discs. So as not to neglect my job, I'll begin with a review of the CD that prompted me to pick up my pen this morning.

JASS, J-CD-3 "Santa Claus Blues" is a 69-minute compilation of 23 cuts taken from Stash/JASS's two previous Christmas LPs, ST 125 and J3. Unlike this firm's previous theme compilations, which have as much or more appeal to blues fans than jazz buffs, this one is almost all jazz. Further, there is a surprising amount of music that qualifies as good jazz for listening at any time of the year, such as a roaring big-band "Jingle Bells" by Benny Goodman, a high-energy "Swingin' Them Jingle Bells" by Fats Waller, a shouting "Santa Claus Is Coming To Town" by Woody Herman, and "I Want You For Christmas" by Dick Robertson and his Orchestra (a Bob Crosbyish combo that features some marvelous Bobby Hackett cornet).

Moreover, only a grinch would complain about the throwaway numbers. Big Tea's warm vocalizing is perfect for his dance version of "The Christmas Song". Ella's crystal-clarity may be wasted on "Santa Claus Got Stuck In My Chimney," but it sounds as great as ever. Louis Prima's typical outgoing jive spreads its usual good cheer on "What Will Santa Claus Say (When He Finds Everybody Swingin'?)" And any recording that includes Louis on six cuts has to have something going for it. (Frankly, the closing track, on which Pops, nearly at the end of his life, reads "The Night Before Christmas," infusing it with childlike innocence and love of humanity, gets me misty-eyed even before his poignant closing insertion: "... a very good night. And that goes for Satchmo, too. Heh, heh.")

The CD is a gap-filler, uneven in spots, but as a Christmas entry, it gets its job done. Judged as a jazz record in my "This Month's Records" column, I'd give it three stars out of a possible five. It's $15.00 plus the shipping charges mentioned below from Stash Records, 611 Broadway - Suite #411, New York, New York 10012. Shipping: Domestic - $3.00; Canada & Mexico - $4.50; Overseas - $5.50. New York residents add 8% sales tax. Charge customers may phone Tues-Thurs 10-5 to (800) 666-5277.

Now for the rest of the ten albums. I have not done the concentrated re-listening to these that I would do if I were giving them a formal review, but what the heck, it's Christmas we're talking here, right?

I think that most of them are still available, but rather than fill up this page with addresses, I'll include the phone number of each producer at the end of this column (except for Parkwood, for which I have only the address). You take it from there.

Christmas Records

Unquestionably the rarest recording to be discussed today is <u>Merry Makers SC-1001</u> "Songs of Christmas" by Turk Murphy's San Francisco Jazz Band. Turk is one of my all-time favorite musicians, and hearing his band play Christmas music does wonders for the elevation of my Christmas spirit. Even so, I have to acknowledge that <u>SC-1001</u> is excessively burdened with lightweight material and is hardly one of the great man's stronger entries. On the other hand, it is a particularly choice acquisition for a Murphyphile because it has not, at this writing, ever been issued commercially, having appeared only as part of a special Christmas promotion for See's Candies.

Fans of Murphyesque West Coast revival Dixieland will have an easier time locating <u>Uptown Lowdown Jazz Band BDR-2</u>, "Jingle Jazz" by the Uptown Lowdown Jazz Band, produced by Dan Polin. It's an amiable run-through of mostly pop tunes about Christmas, done with the ULJB's characteristic brassy two-beat. Special aficionados of this fine octet will relish the fact that each sideman gets a track where he (or she) is prominently featured.

Speaking of "uptown," if your tastes run to uptown-style New Orleans jazz, you'll be interested in <u>G.H.B.-209</u>, "A New Orleans Christmas With Sammy Rimington." This outstanding post-George Lewis clarinetist here does, with a gently-swinging rhythm section, what Lewis himself did for conventional church music in his excellent "George Lewis Plays Hymns" album. That is, Rimington delivers unembroidered melody on the selections, albeit with a jazzman's phrasing, attack and tone, plus some phrase-end fills, with all of the heartfelt conviction and emotion characteristic of this branch of Dixieland.

Chicago-style fans will perk up their ears at <u>World Jazz WJLP-5</u>, "Hark The Herald Angels Swing" by The World's Greatest Jazz Band of Yank Lawson & Bob Haggart. The running time on this platter is a little light, and the band is not overexerting itself, but its star-studded lineup of top Chicagoans is one that was unparalleled for its day. Because death or infirmity has stilled the voices of some of the personnel, the album has an added attraction that it did not have at the time of its release.

One of the quintessential Chicago players, and currently my favorite living musician, offers the only solo session on this list, <u>Parkwood Records 108</u>, "Joy To The Jazz World" by Art Hodes. Hodes' supremely righteous piano gently but firmly manages the seemingly impossible task of making blues-drenched performances into communications that uplift and affirm the seasonal message of good will.

For sheer through-the-lineup virtuoso technical ability, combined with a broad-based grounding in all aspects of pre-swing jazz, The Jim Cullum Jazz Band is probably the leading contender for the title of best organized Dixieland band in the country, <u>World Jazz WJLP S-21</u>, "'Tis The Season To Be Jammin'", presents the Cullums exercising their usual good taste, imaginative structuring and superlative musicianship on a program of Yuletide music.

If you're willing to try something off the beaten track, you won't go wrong with <u>The Place for Jazz PPJ-111</u>, "The Unidentical Jazz Twins' (Plus Hank Bredenberg) Christmas Album". This collection of trio performances by, of all things, trombone, electric guitar and electric bass, is (obviously) not a Dixieland platter, but it is very accessible and consistently creative in deploying the resources at hand. Nancy would have preferred a little less electronics, but I rate this one very highly in terms of what it accomplishes.

| TEXAS SHOUT: HOW DIXIELAND JAZZ WORKS |

Ideally, a Christmas Dixieland jazz recording would be one that was so satisfying from a jazz viewpoint that it could be enjoyed for that reason alone, at any time of the year, quite apart from the extra lift it gets from being played at Christmas. Some of the albums discussed above meet or come close enough to that target, but I have saved for last the one that is a winner any way you want to look at it.

Sackville 3038, "The Sackville All Star Christmas Record", by The Sackville All Stars (consisting of Jim Galloway, Ralph Sutton, Milt Hinton and Gus Johnson), is a magnificent job of turning seasonal songs (including such unlikely starters as "Silent Night") into inventive, satisfying jazz while still retaining the reverential aspects of the more religiously-leaning works. These four giants of the idiom never once put a foot wrong throughout the date. If you are only going to get one of the albums discussed in this column, this one is the clear winner.

Here are the telephone numbers/address promised above: G.H.B./Jazzology - (504)525-1776, Merry Makers - (415) 383-6608. Parkwood Records - Box 174, Windsor, Ontario, Canada N9A 4HO. The Place For Jazz - (305) 945-0494. Dan Polin - (206) 546-1498. Sackville (Coda Publications) - (416) 593-7230. World Jazz - (602) 840-3200.

No doubt many of you know of other Christmas productions that would be suitable for *WCR* readers. However, the library covered today will certainly get you started.

Moreover, as indicated, it touches on several branches of our music. Perhaps the holiday season, with its spirit of tolerance toward all, is just the time for those of you who have concentrated so far on just one or two Dixieland styles to sample the delights of some others. Merry Christmas to all, and to all a good night.

Christmas Record
Artwork Lenora Caddy

CHAPTER 19   DIXIELAND vs. RAGTIME

I not only love both ragtime and Dixieland jazz, but I love both of them equally. Thus, although I've followed both for decades, I never saw much need to focus closely on the precise differences between them.

That situation changed when Dick Zimmerman and I were invited to conduct a seminar on ragtime and Dixieland as part of the 1990 West Coast Ragtime Festival in Fresno. I realized that, if I was supposed to be an expert on these musics, at the very least I ought to be able to articulate the unique properties of each.

Both have a number of fairly obvious similarities. Both, for example, use the same kind of basic circle-of-fifths harmonies. Both have four beats in each measure (disregarding, for this purpose, questions as to whether those four beats are played with a two-beat feeling or a four-beat feeling). Both typically use melodic phrases that are either two or four bars long.

Actually, it is not surprising that ragtime and Dixieland use essentially the same musical vocabulary. Both developed during the 1890s out of the same musical sources. Both developed in response to a need, in the saloons, dance halls, gambling rooms and sporting houses of large cities, for functional, outgoing, accessible, danceable music that would put patrons in a mood to spend money on the products offered by the establishment.

In fact, because ragtime and Dixieland have so many similarities, an unsophisticated listener might conclude, on a superficial listening, that they sound the same (if the same instrumentation was used for the comparison). Nevertheless, each is a distinct style of playing. My task was to figure out what is the definitive characteristic (or characteristics) of each style so that I could discuss them intelligently at the seminar.

I started out examining some of the more common generalizations I've seen over the years in the literature of ragtime and early jazz. It turned out that a number of them did not stand up to rigorous analysis.

To illustrate: I've often heard it said that ragtime is supposed to be played as written while Dixieland is supposed to be improvised. While it may be true that ragtime often is played as written while Dixieland often is improvised, this rule of thumb is not sufficient to distinguish the two.

Hot dance-style Dixieland, for example, is heavily scored, yet its jazz content is not diminished thereby. Similarly, transcriptions of famous Dixieland performances, if played with the right attack and feeling, are effective and jazzy re-creations of their sources.

By contrast ragtime is a style of playing that can be applied not just to rags, but to popular songs, classical themes, marches, etc. The early ragtimers freely improvised on such material using the then-new ragtime licks. Indeed, Scott Joplin himself improvised on his own scores, as demonstrated by his surviving hand-played piano rolls. Many ragtimers (including myself) still regularly improvise in the style.

It has often been said that ragtime is primarily a vehicle for solo piano, while Dixieland is oriented toward group playing. Certainly much of ragtime is rendered as piano solos, while Dixieland is most commonly found in band performances. However, it doesn't take much thought to realize that this generalization doesn't hold up either.

During the ragtime years, ragtime was played by every conceivable combination of instruments, including military bands, hotel orchestras and saxophone ensembles. By contrast, any intelligently-compiled list of great Dixieland performances would include quite a few solo recordings, mostly on piano but probably also including solos by guitar or banjo.

So the written/improvised distinction doesn't answer the question. Neither does the solo/group distinction. Nor did any of the other common generalizations I explored. I could always find exceptions to them.

By this time in my thought process, I had seemingly covered everything - instrumentation, examination of the published music, whatever. All of the concrete components, and of elements capable of being notated musically, of ragtime could also be found in Dixieland. Nothing that I could lay my hands on told me how to distinguish between them. Yet, the two musics are different. What was left?

Having eliminated everything else, I was able to focus more clearly on an elusive and intangible notion that, after reflection, does explain to me the difference between ragtime and Dixieland. Morever, as the idea began to take shape in my mind, it explained a few other things, too, as I'll set forth below.

The difference, I decided, is entirely in the rhythmic feeling generated by the music. Ragtime gets its rhythmic excitement in a vertical way, via the interplay of its oom-pah bass line with its constantly syncopated melody. Dixieland gets its rhythmic excitement in a horizontal way, via its distinctive forward-thrusting momentum - the quality referred to when jazzmen say a band is "swinging".

Once you have this thought in focus, you can fairly easily test the part relating to ragtime. If you play a ragtime passage but straighten out the syncopations so that the melody is unsyncopated, it quickly and obviously loses its special rag flavor.

The same thing is true of ragtime's oom-pah (or two-beat) bass rhythm. Many rags have short passages of suspended rhythm, or of four- beat block chords in the bass line. However, when such devices are employed for more than a few consecutive bars, the music (to my ears at least) starts to sound a lot less raggy. You need the interplay of the syncopated melody and the oom-pah bass to generate the giddy, jingling rhythmic effect that gives ragtime its special excitement.

(Syncopation, for the uninitiated, is the setting of a rhythmic accent in an unexpected place. Doing so elevates the rhythmic excitement of the passage. In ragtime, the effect is most commonly achieved by putting a strong melodic emphasis on a normally weak beat or between the beats, or by creating a melody line in which strong accents regularly recur in a manner that is out of phase with the rhythm, e.g., successive figures of three eighth notes against a 4/4 beat.)

Dixieland vs. Ragtime

There is no simple comparable test for "swinging." You won't find "swing" in printed scores available to any skilled sight-reader.

Thus, the ragtime-Dixieland difference is not in the construction of the music. The difference results entirely from the way the musician articulates the notes. The jazzman articulates them with that special forward motion described above, while the ragtimer does not.

Wait a minute, one might say. Tex, you're oversimplifying the situation, because all cohesive music will have a certain forward movement - ragtime, Viennese waltzes, marches, hoedowns, etc. That's what makes it hang together.

The point is well taken. However, other types of music do not have, as a part of their forward movement, a particular type of urgency in feeling, one that seems almost to grab you and drag you forward. I hear that urgency only in jazz, and believe it is the unique quality that makes jazz "hot."

Note that I am not saying that jazz needs to be fast or loud to be "hot." I am saying that it needs to communicate an urgency, a sense of passionate commitment, that is reflected in its rhythmic feeling, and that this element has, for better or worse, come to be referred to by many branches of jazz (especially the older ones) as "hot" playing.

The nature of "hot, swinging" rhythm is not easily captured in words (as anyone who has waded through the above paragraphs will already have discerned). In fact, many better jazz writers than I have wrestled with describing the concept, usually emerging with mixed results at best.

(I have sometimes seen the notion referred to as use of dotted-eighth phrasing or playing with "swing eighths". While both characterisations are on the right track, neither - for me, at least - fully captures "swinging" in words.)

This difficulty in describing jazz rhythm reflects and explains the fact, one which most jazz fans instinctively understand, that jazz must be heard for its unique qualities to be appreciated. A trained pianist can, without any previous exposure to ragtime, sight-read a ragtime manuscript and achieve a ragged effect. However, even though the first jazzmen must have evolved their music in some spontaneous way from non-jazz sources, it is virtually impossible today for anyone to learn to play jazz without first being able to hear it.

To underscore this point, note that the jazz age did not begin until jazz found its way onto records in 1917. Jazz had been played in New Orleans for some twenty years prior to that time, and a few jazz combos had toured the country. Nevertheless, the boom did not get under way until jazz reached an aural mass media. Ragtime, on the other hand, had taken the U. S. by storm simply by reaching a written mass media (published sheet music) in the late 1890s.

In short, having thought my way through the ragtime-Dixieland difference, I wound up essentially where Duke Ellington was decades ago. That is, when you're talking about jazz, it doesn't mean a thing if it ain't got that swing.

| TEXAS SHOUT: HOW DIXIELAND JAZZ WORKS |

At this point, I had concluded that the distinguishing feature between ragtime and Dixieland jazz is that jazz is played with a certain urgent type of forward movement, known to Dixielanders as "hot" or "swinging" rhythm, while ragtime is not. My next move, in preparing for the ragtime-Dixieland seminar I was to conduct with Dick Zimmerman at Fresno's West Coast Ragtime Festival, was to test that conclusion against the variety of music that would be heard at Fresno during that weekend.

Most of the music seemed to pass this test, but two types did not. Typically, at ragtime weekends, there is a certain amount of Jelly Roll Morton-style and Harlem stride piano played.

Unlike ragtime styles, stride and Morton have the forward movement I had identified as belonging to jazz. Although some ragtime authorities consider stride and Morton to be ragtime styles, my analysis was suggesting that these authorities are mistaken and that both are truly classifiable as jazz styles.

Liking both ragtime and Dixieland, including stride and Morton, I had never particularly given the subject of their precise categorization much thought. However, considering stride and Morton as jazz styles seemed to explain a few things.

First of all, that view is consistent with virtually all writing about jazz. To the the best of my recollection, every comprehensive treatise I've seen that deals with pre-swing jazz but not with ragtime will include stride and Morton on the jazz side of the fence. It is only the authorities who try to deal with ragtime, or with ragtime and Dixieland, who express conflicting views on the topic.

Second, my observation is that ragtime buffs who do not like Dixieland jazz often do not care much for stride or for Morton, while Dixieland fans who say they don't like ragtime usually do enjoy stride and Morton. If both stride and Morton actually are on the jazz side of the line, this divergence of opinions makes perfect sense.

There is another convincing argument telling us that stride and Morton are jazz and not ragtime. If you request a rendition of, say, "Carolina Shout" from a ragtime pianist who does not play jazz, the result will not sound like a Harlem stride number but will sound like a novelty rag. Conversely, if you want a Missouri Valley classic rag from a stride pianist who does not play the common ragtime styles, the result will swing (see, for example, Raltph Sutton's wonderful 1949 <u>Backroom Piano</u> session -- <u>Verve MGV 1004</u>). The stride pianist plays the notes on the score with jazz's unique momentum, but the ragtimer does not give those same notes the same feeling.

If stride and Morton are not ragtime styles, why are they commonly heard at ragtime festivals? I can think of three reasons.

Many ragtime fans, like myself, also like Dixieland jazz. They're perfectly happy to come to a "ragtime" weekend and listen to music they enjoy, even if it isn't always strictly ragtime. We see the same thing at many of today's "Dixieland" festivals where, as I have previously pointed out in these pages, some of the most popular bands are playing non-genre music, i.e., music which makes no claim to be Dixieland.

Dixieland vs. Ragtime

Further, stride and Morton came directly out of the ragtime years. There is a lot of ragtime that informs both styles. Despite the difference in rhythmic movement between ragtime and jazz, there is much in stride and Morton that a ragtimer will recognize and be comfortable with.

Third, most ragtimers are quick to appreciate a high level of technical keyboard accomplishment. Stride piano, in my view, is the most difficult non-classical piano style there is. For his part, Morton was one of the finest pianists of his day from the point of view of sheer keyboard mastery. A tickler who is able to execute a flawless rendition of "Carolina Shout" or "Shreveport Stomp" is, for that reason alone, sure to get attention, and a warm round of applause, from a room full of ragtime fans.

So far, I'd concluded that ragtime and jazz differ only in their rhythmic feeling, and that Harlem stride and Morton-style piano were properly classifiable as jazz and not as ragtime. Nothing extraodinary there. I'd merely clarified in my own mind a couple of points that are commonly made in jazz literature.

However, I wouldn't let the subject alone. Having concluded that stride wasn't ragtime, I decided to see what other differences there might be between stride and ragtime. That line of investigation produced a result that still surprises me.

Stride piano makes heavy use of riffs, i.e., short repeated phrases that develop emotional intensity through repetition. As I began examining the common stride riffs - the licks that stride pianists most frequently toss in as fills while they're thinking through their next moves -, I realized, to my astonishment, that none of them are syncopated!

Take, for example, what is probably the most commonly-used stride fill, a right-hand four-note broken arpeggio. This figure plays the four notes in the following order: top note, next-to-the top note, bottom note, next-to-the bottom note. In 4/4 time, they are played as eighth notes. As explained below, the first note is struck a half-beat ahead of the down beat. This lick is usually repeated a few times without a break, that is, it becomes a string of unsyncopated eighth notes.

Without taking you through a dry musical analysis of each riff, I could say the same about all of the other common stride licks, such as the triplet-based figure Fats Waller uses at the beginning of "Valentine Stomp" - they aren't syncopated. However, they all are very "pushy." That is, they all have a built-in drive that whips the music ahead.

A stride lick achieves this pushy effect because its first note is usually an eighth-note pickup that slams the lick into the downbeat. In fact, if you play the lick without this pickup, the treble line suddenly becomes stiff and unswinging.

By taking this reasoning to its logical extreme, a pianist could put together a stride chorus of hot licks that builds, is logically constructed, but is entirely unsyncopated. The conclusion to be derived from such an exercise, one that amazed me, is that it is not essential for jazz to be syncopated! As long as the notes are articulated using jazz's unique forward motion, the music will be hot and will swing, without regard to whether the lines happen to be syncopated at the time.

As far as I know, the notion of unsyncopated jazz has never before appeared in print. (I'll probably get my head handed to me in future "Letter Drop" submissions for suggesting it.)

TEXAS SHOUT: HOW DIXIELAND JAZZ WORKS

The conventional wisdom says that ragtime conditioned the general public to syncopated music and that jazz built on this foundation to incorporate much more sophisticated syncopation than ragtime has. It is certainly true that syncopation has always been part of the normal vocabulary of jazz; there was no reason for it to be otherwise, once syncopation had become so pervasive via ragtime's popularity. Also, any time you have seven or so musicians improvising at once, you will encounter an extremely complex and sophisticted pattern of syncopations.

However, I now believe that, while such syncopations heighten the interest of jazz music, they are not a sine qua non of jazz. To draw an analogy: Whenever I have a hot dog, I always pile on catsup, mustard, relish, hot peppers, and (depending on the situation) maybe sauerkraut, chili and/or cheese. Those condiments add tang and spice to the meal. If I remove them, the hot dog will not be so flavorful, but it will still be a hot dog. So it is with jazz and syncopation.

One can see this distinction more clearly by studying the basic jazz piano style of the thirties, which typically includes lots of long unsyncopated eighth-note runs. When you listen to Teddy Wilson or Art Tatum play, and they go into these glistening runs, you don't feel any sense of the performance becoming any less jazzy at those points. That's because these artists continue to articulate the notes, syncopated or not, in a jazzy, swinging way.

When I told my lovely bride Nancy that I was going to write an article in which I would say that jazz does not need to be syncopated, she perceptively replied: "If you make such a radical statement, shouldn't you be able to back it up by citing at least one jazz performance that isn't syncopated?" That's a tall order. As I mentioned above, there is no reason for jazzmen to try to avoid syncopation, especially when it adds so much flavor to the results.

However, Nancy came to my rescue by recalling what might just be the only album in our 5000-record collection that contains some unsyncopated jazz renditions. She remembered it because I had cited it (for another reason) in a review a few years ago, and the cite had prompted a letter to the editor from a reader who took strong issue with what I'd said about it. As a result, Nancy and I had discussed the philosophy of that record, and of my interpretation of it, a few times.

"George Lewis Plays Hymns" is one of the great clarinetist's best and most beloved albums. It is a trio session in which, accompanied by bass and piano, Lewis plays unsyncopated sacred music, adding a few fills but without really attempting to improvise on most of the melodies.

I have always enjoyed it. Until recently, though, I believed that it did not qualify as a jazz record because most cuts contained neither improvisation nor syncopation. I felt its success was due to the sincerity and passion of Lewis's playing, not to its jazz content.

Nevertheless, much of it swings. It's a tough call, but I may be changing my mind about "George Lewis Plays Hymns". At least for the tunes that aren't in 3/4 time, I am now willing to consider that several of its performances may be jazz. Lewis and his sidemen, being people who never (to my knowledge) played anything else but jazz, automatically brought a jazzman's attack to any material they played, thereby usually turning it into jazz.

Dixieland vs. Ragtime

(By the way, this change of mind does not mean that I agree with the reader who took me to task. Actually, I think we were both wrong about the point then at issue, but I believe now that he was closer to the right answer than I was .)

This conclusion explains why, in quite a few recordings where classical, dance or other non-jazz musicians have assayed transcriptions of jazz charts, the notes are right but the feeling isn't. These players don't know how to articulate notes and phrases like jazzmen.

On the other hand, even the relatively commercial sides by no-nonsense jazz units like Basie, Ellington, Goodman (in his heyday), etc., often have a buoyant, propulsive feeling that recommends them to jazz fans. Such jazzmen naturally swung everything they approached.

The sort of definition and categorization that has been outlined above is useful, despite the understandable reluctance of many musicians to be categorized. If we understand how our music works, and what its essential characteristics are, we're better able to appreciate it, to concentrate on the best it has to offer, and to act in a constructive way to encourage its general improvement as an art form.

At the same time, we must not lose sight of two points: We are talking here about a branch of popular culture, where it is not always possible to draw bright lines. Also, we should never use categories and definitions in a manner that limits our own horizons with respect to enjoying the music.

On the first point, while we may be able to define the differences between ragtime and Dixieland, or between styles of Dixieland, there will always be artists who sometimes operate at the borders thereof, perhaps - like the <u>George Lewis Plays Hymns</u> LP - with one foot on each side. Wally Rose, for example, one of my all-time favorite pianists and a major early influence on my own playing, performs classic rags in a particularly propulsive and forceful way. Are these renditions jazz or ragtime?

Similarly, while I have concurred above with the general view that Jelly Roll Morton is a jazz pianist, it is clear that there is much more ragtime in Jelly's playing than, say, James P. Johnson's or Fats Waller's. I believe that this situation has caused certain critics, usually ones who prefer more advanced jazz forms, to say that Jelly is "old-fashioned" or "dated" when compared to the stride greats.

The correct approach to such hair-splitting is to think about it, but don't let it bog you down. If you like ragtime, or Dixieland jazz, and you find enough of your preferences in the performance of an artist to satisfy you, relax and enjoy the music without regard to what someone may wish to call the style.

In fact, eclectic performers, who are able to understand a variety of musics, picking and choosing elements of each, forging them into a coherent whole, are often the most interesting and unpredictable ones on the bill. Dick Wellstood, one of the latter-day greats of vintage jazz, was a master at doing so, thereby infusing his tickling with endless surprising delights.

However, if you do your listening with an awareness of stylistic borders, and of the factors that characterize the music on each side of them, you'll find your own appreciation of the performances considerably increased. Further, I'll bet that you'll find yourself enjoying some styles that you hadn't previously cared for all that much.

TEXAS SHOUT: HOW DIXIELAND JAZZ WORKS

That's what this somewhat lengthy and academic musical discussion of ragtime, Dixieland, syncopation and rhythmic feeling has been designed to stimulate. If you've read through this far, I hope your reward will be that these thoughts may go some way toward making the future good times you're going to have with our music into even better ones.

Scott Joplin 1900s
Photographer Unknown

Jelly Roll Morton 1924
Photo by George Hoefer

Original Dixieland Jazz Band 1919
Photo by George Hoefer

Dixieland vs. Ragtime

Fats Waller 1930s
Photographer Unknown

Teddy Wilson & Benny Goodman
1930s *Photographer Unknown*

Art Tatum 1930s
Photo by Jack Bradley

George Lewis 1940s
Photographer Unknown

Wally Rose 1940s
From the collection of Ed Lawless

CHAPTER 20   POPULAR HISTORIES

I once read a Sunday-supplement article (I wish I'd saved it) that contained, among other lists, a ranking of the subjects about which the most bad books had been written. I don't remember which was which, but Jazz and Movies were ranked in the first and third slots.

As someone deeply interested in both, I can testify that there is a lot of truth in that list. With respect to movies, it seems that anyone with a reasonable collection of stills can get a book published displaying them, frequently mislabeled, replete with a text suffused with all kinds of unverifiable gossip, speculation and outright misstatements. Similarly, books about jazz regularly appear that offer opinion or guesswork as fact, refer to long-discredited research and set forth first-hand "recollections" that are easily disprovable via a glance through the standard references.

Nevertheless, if you're a novice at a topic and you want to get oriented toward it, the best way to do so is to read general surveys and popular histories of the field. That's what I did for both jazz and movies.

When my long-standing love affair with movies began to crystallize into a serious pursuit - as the result of a wonderful book on silent films that my first wife happened to see on a sale stand and thought I might enjoy - I started compiling a shelf of references which includes, as I later learned, volumes so useless that I doubt I'll ever get around to reading them. Similarly, because I lacked any mentor to guide me, as a teenager I waded through my local library's jazz collection, picking up classics as well as hopelessly biased and/or dated material that, had I allowed it to do so, could have severely narrowed both my outlook toward and enjoyment of this music.

Unless the book contains discographical data or musical analysis that can be applied to my record or sheet music collection, I rarely read jazz books anymore. I haven't felt the need to do so because, fortuitously, I started collecting records at the beginning of the LP era.

12" LPs, with their sizeable back sleeves allowing for a fairly ample text, proved to be a painless way to learn about Dixieland in depth. The sleeve notes weren't all that long, and were focused precisely on the specific tunes and artists I was about to enjoy. Reading them at time of purchase, when I was first listening to the record, helped fix the comments in my mind, enabling me to associate them with the tunes so closely that I can still, decades later, easily recall them when discussing jazz or announcing from the bandstand.

Unfortunately, today's listeners do not have this opportunity because LPs have all but disappeared from the market. Judged by the volume of sales, the format preferred by today's buyer is the audiocassette.

TEXAS SHOUT: HOW DIXIELAND JAZZ WORKS

For casual listening in the car, as an escape from the noise clogging the radio waves and to make the miles pass more swiftly, audiocassettes are hard to beat. However, they are an inferior collector's medium.

Even the best cassettes are still made of flimsy materials, more easily given to wearing out than were LPs or 78s, and subject to the occasional jam or tangle that requires junking the whole album (if you scratch part of an LP, you can still listen to the rest of it). Further, cassettes can't be programmed for listening to selected tracks.

The chief weakness of cassettes, from the viewpoint of today's column, however, is the inadequacy or outright nonexistence of liner notes in the typical tape package. To be sure, there is little enough space for any, unless the producer goes for the additional expense of a multi-fold insert. However, I see far too many cassettes in which the available space on the reverse of the insert is left blank, thereby abandoning any effort to include even those few words that might involve the listener more deeply with the music.

That's really too bad. Older-style jazz isn't so commercially healthy that it can afford to pass up the chance to help people enjoy it. Maybe CDs, with their accompanying booklets, will take up the slack, but I think the jury's still out on that point.

In the meantime, we're back to Square One. If you want to orient yourself to Dixieland, ragtime and related music, your best bet is to read a book on it, hoping, despite all the dreck on the market, that you'll pick a good one.

I'm going to use the rest of this column to try to give you a leg up. Although I haven't read some of these books for decades, the good ones in the field stand so far above the pack that it's easy to recall them.

All of the titles mentioned below can be read and enjoyed by someone who is not a musician. They supply background against which to appreciate our music, and will point you in the direction of worthwhile artists who've recorded it.

Far and away the best popular history ever written about music within *West Coast Rag's* main area of interest is *They All Played Ragtime*, by Rudi Blesh and Harriet Janis. Ms. Janis's meticulous research, done at a time when many important ragtimers were still on the scene to be interviewed, provided the perfect platform for Rudi's articulate, romantic, fan-oriented, highly readable prose. This remarkable work has, understandably, been reprinted several times and has inspired many people, including this writer, to become ragtimers.

Further, for a pioneering volume - the first book ever written about ragtime - it stands up amazingly well over the decades. I am not aware that any of its factual research has ever been disproved in a significant respect. Further, its value judgements made are still sound, with the following exception:

TAPR, as it is affectionately known in the ragtime community, focuses primarily on Scott Joplin and the other Missouri valley ragtime composers. In doing so, it tends to dismiss the white ragtime composers of Tin Pan Alley and of novelty ragtime. Eventually, Rudi acknowledged that, although these ragtime branches did produce works of insufficient merit to justify resurrection, they also produced a substantial body of worthwhile material, including some masterpieces. In fact, the same statement can be made of the other ragtime styles, and indeed of all segments of popular culture.

Popular Histories

If Dixieland, and not ragtime is your thing, seek out *Mr. Jelly Roll*, by Alan Lomax. Lomax cuts back and forth from Jelly's story, told in Morton's own colorful words, to independent research about the period and place under discussion, providing the appropriate setting (and sometimes some corrections) to Morton's narrative. It is a compelling tale, luxuriant in detail, of triumphs and setbacks, ending with Jelly's last struggling years, covered so poignantly that I got misty-eyed as I read of his trek West over snow-covered mountain roads with his two aging automobiles chained together.

One of the wittiest of the jazzmen/writers was archetypical Chicago guitarist Eddie Condon. All of his books are brim-full of engaging anecdotes about his free-wheeling and usually famous cohorts. *We Called It Music*, by Eddie Condon and Thomas Sugrue, did much to point me toward the right Chicago musicians, even while I was splitting my sides laughing at such stories as the one where, as an audition tune for a gig at a sedate hotel, Condon's youthful jazz combo ripped through "Meet Me Tonight In Dreamland," only to have the manager ask, at the conclusion ... but, no, I really should let Condon tell it as only he can.

Bits and pieces of interviews with great jazzmen are broken down and reassembled into chapters on specific topics or scenes in *Hear Me Talkin' To Ya*, edited by Nat Shapiro and Nat Hentoff. This entertaining book will introduce you to a lot of famous players, making you feel like they're sitting at your table over a beer, chatting just for your ears alone.

The bio-discography is a type of jazz volume that usually focusses on an artist's records, interspersing the analysis thereof with sketchy information about the person. Such books are quite specialized, and really ought to be discussed in a separate column (which I'll probably write some day) dealing with jazz reference material.

One work, though, that splendidly transcends the limitations of the bio-discography is *Bix: Man And Legend*, by Richard Sudhalter, with Philip Evans. Sudhalter, a fine Bix-influenced trumpeter and a first-rate writer, built an astonishingly complete biographical text out of Evans' painstaking research, including appendices that contain a definitive Bix discography and itinerary. This is one of the few cases where the author was able to capture the flavor of a jazzman who had died decades before in a way that brings him vividly to life for the reader.

Those specifically interested in the earliest days of jazz won't go wrong with *In Search Of Buddy Bolden, First Man Of Jazz*, by Don Marquis. Marquis unearthed an incredible amount of information about a topic one would have thought was barely documented, the New Orleans Black life at the turn of the century, writing it up in a way that causes the whole sprawling scene to jump right out of the pages.

The immortal stride pianist Willie "The Lion" Smith does the same thing for the barrelhouses of Harlem in his rich autobiography *Music On My Mind*. You don't know what a lowlife bar is until The Lion takes you to the ones he worked, where waitresses and female entertainers could pick up additional tips from the tables by doing the "ups," a calisthenic that you won't be taught in your aerobics class.

More recently-written jazz volumes suffer a bit because there are so few of the original participants left to be interviewed. Thus, the tone tends to be a bit more academic, and the players a bit more remote - not an ideal state for a book about a music that depends so much on the emotional response it evokes in its listeners. On the other hand, the distance lets the author see his subject in perspective, enabling him to produce helpful commentary on the nature of an artist's overall output.

These strengths and weaknesses can be found in three excellent volumes, *A Left Hand Like God*, by Peter Silvester (the only full-length work to date devoted entirely to boogie-woogie piano); *Louis Armstrong, An American Genius*, by James Lincoln Collier, and *Sidney Bechet, Wizard Of Jazz*, by John Chilton. However, for maximum benefit, readers thereof should, I think, have some prior familiarity via recordings with the artists being discussed.

Concentrating as I have on LP liner notes, I have not read some very highly-regarded books about our music, such as the reminiscences of Danny Barker and Bud Freeman. Similarly, because I am not that interested in reading books that spend too much (for me) time on swing, I have not read Warren Vaché, Sr's editing of the memoirs of Pee Wee Erwin, nor the recent volumes by Chip Deffea. I'll mention them, though, because they have received so much praise from so many reviewers that I'm sure they will reward reading by anyone interested in the artists being discussed therein.

Finally, without wanting to cast gratuitous brickbats, I would classify *Shining Trumpets*, by Rudi Blesh, which is somewhat dated and overly opinionated, and *Blues People*, by LeRoi Jones, which is badly biased, as tomes that have outlived whatever use to jazz researchers, they may once have had. I mention these volumes because they are still frequently cited in jazz bibliographies. I would recommend that, if you want to investigate either of them, you postpone doing so until you are firmly enough based in the music to be able to discount for their deficiencies.

What about other big names, such as Bessie Smith, The Original Dixieland Jazz Band, Ma Rainey and Fats Waller? Of course, there are books about them and virtually every other well-known jazzman, as well as lesser names. With respect to the three just mentioned, I've read several, some with special merits, but none which satisfies me enough to recommend it here. However, for useful treatments of important figures at less than book length, try *Jazz Masters Of The 20's*, by Richard Hadlock.

I have suggested eleven books, plus a few I haven't gotten around to as yet. That ought to be enough to get you started. Each will provide you with enjoyable reading as well as sound additional grounding in our music. Once you've gotten your arms around everything that's in them, you should be in a good position to find your way unescorted. Happy reading.

CHAPTER 21   ECONOMICS OF DIXIELAND

In the mid-1980s, I had a chance to talk about the economics of the tavern/restaurant business with the manager of a room that regularly hired musical entertainment. What he told me made sense to me. I suppose that it is still true in its general aspects.

Moreover, the information told me a lot about why the Dixieland club scene, and indeed the broader Dixieland world, is the way it is. Thus, I thought you might find it interesting as well.

The information consisted of two rules of thumb. First, the margin on drinks is 50% and on food is 10%. Second, in order to sustain live entertainment, the room needs to be able to sell at the bar a total of three times whatever the entertainment costs.

Note that the gross sales requirement only applies to sales at the bar. The margin on food is too small to be worth bothering with in a typical club. (This situation may not be true if the establishment is primarily a restaurant; however, such venues are not as likely candidates to hire Dixieland bands as are taverns that also serve a light menu.)

Checking to see if the rule of thumb made sense, I postulated hiring live entertainment for, say, $500 for the evening. That means the club needs to sell $1,500 at the bar, on which it realizes a margin of $750. However, it has to pay the act $500, leaving a before-tax profit of $250, and an after-tax profit of about $160.

Now if the room would typically sell $500 at the bar anyway, it can get that same $160 by having no entertainment at all. (Again, food doesn't enter into the equation, because even another $1,500 of food sales would only add about $100 after tax to the take.)

Perhaps someone out there will confirm whether these calculations are in the ballpark, but they seem plausible enough to me. Whatever the right figures are, a clubowner probably isn't going to go to all the hassle to hire live entertainment, set up extra tables, etc., unless he has reason to think that he will do significantly better financially than he will if he doesn't hire live entertainment.

Let's assume that these rules of thumb are generally accurate and see how they might apply to hiring a Dixieland band. Just to put things on the low side, we'll postulate that we have a six-piece band (not the typical seven, or the eight that go with the two-trumpet sound), that the musicians get $50 apiece for the evening (pretty much a minimum), and that there is no additional charge for a leader's fee.

In that case, it costs at least $300 to hire the band, so the audience needs to drink $900 worth to even begin to make the date worthwhile for the club. That $900 will be spread over the patronage for the evening.

TEXAS SHOUT: HOW DIXIELAND JAZZ WORKS

How many customers can we handle? It's pretty common for taverns to have less than 100 seats commanding an uninterrupted view of the bandstand. However, even at 100 seats, and a reasonable assumption on drink prices, our audience needs to drink about two drinks per person during the evening just to get things to the breakeven point.

Well, two drinks doesn't seem all that much, you say. Besides, audience turnover during the evening hasn't been taken into account. Normally, I'd agree with you, but not with respect to the Dixieland market which, for reasons I've previously discussed in this column, currently is almost exclusively confined to senior citizens.

Older folks don't drink as much as younger folks. Perhaps it's because many of them are on fixed incomes, perhaps they are intrinsically more conservative in looking out for themselves, perhaps they pay more attention to the recent focus on drunken driving, or some combination thereof. (Maybe more of the really heavy drinkers kill themselves off before reaching senior citizen status.)

Also, older folks don't stay out as late as younger folks, a fact which reduces turnover at Dixieland night clubs nearly to zero. (In fact, as this column was in process, I received a Dixieland jazz club newsletter saying that, in response to members' expressed desires, meeting times have been moved up to 1:30-4:30 p.m. on Sunday afternoons!)

Recently I worked a 9:00 p.m.-1:00 a.m. Saturday night Dixieland gig that invariably opened to a packed house which dwindled down into a ghost town after midnight. Moving the starting time back to 8:00 p.m. didn't really cure the problem of playing the last set to a pretty thin audience.

As it happened, the club was one that normally stayed open until 2:00 a.m. on Saturdays. When we weren't playing, it usually presented music that appealed to a younger crowd.

The manager couldn't help noting that, even though the place was packed when the Dixieland band began playing, his Dixieland Saturdays were always his financially least successful. Not only did the older Dixieland audience drink less per person, but the club lost the two hours of business between midnight and 2:00 a.m. when a younger crowd would still be on hand spending money.

To return to our example, it's really not all that easy to get an older group to spend the required $900 on drinks in a typical small-to-moderate sized neighborhood tavern. And remember, every extra dollar spent - to hire an extra musician or an extra waitress, to pay for advertising, to tune the piano - requires an additional three dollars at the bar to get the club back to Square One.

The foregoing discussion, I believe, fairly represents the economics of today's Dixieland band tavern scene. It explains a number of things about what confronts us when we get the urge to go out for an evening and hear some older-style jazz.

It explains, for example, why it's so hard to find any. When I first became interested in the music, in the 1950s, just about every big city had a club where you could hear Dixieland played, at least on weekends but usually nightly, often by full-time profesionals. Now, even in our largest metropolitan areas, you can't be sure of finding a Dixieland band at all, let alone one of sufficient quality to justify the time and expense of going out to hear it.

Economics of Dixieland

There are two notable exceptions to that statement, however. In New Orleans, where Dixieland is a well-known part of the cultural heritage and a prime tourist attraction, you'll find clubs which regularly feature Dixieland combos, and there are a number of full-time musicians making their living playing Dixieland. Similarly, in the Orlando area, where Walt Disney's operations have established nostalgic entertainment as a key part of the atmosphere, Dixieland is sustained on a steady and visible level.

For the rest of the U. S., you can probably count on your fingers the number of full-time organized Dixieland combos. By that term I mean bands that do not play other styles of music than Dixieland and are made up of musicians who derive all of their income from playing Dixieland music, not significantly supplementing it with such things as teaching music, studio and dance work or part-time non-musical activities. The most prominent example thereof is probably Jim Cullum's excellent septet in San Antonio. Is there another one of comparable stature?

Sadly but truly, Dixieland jazz doesn't come anywhere near paying its way these days. In fact, this situation exists not only in the nightclub scene, but everywhere else in the field.

Dixieland festivals, for example, dot the landscape, particularly on the West Coast. Some of them are regarded as profitable, reporting significant earnings to further the cause of our music.

However, every festival I know of is critically dependent on the efforts of dozens, sometimes hundreds or thousands, of unpaid volunteers in order to function as it currently does. I feel sure that, if every such volunteer were paid the minimum wage for each hour spent in festival work, the festival scene would sink beneath a sea of red ink.

The same thing is true of recordings. The vast majority of recorded Dixieland released today is financed by the artists themselves (sometimes for vanity reasons), partly because independent production of such records is a weak competitor for investment money. In most cases, a person thinking of producing a Dixieland album could save himself a lot of time and effort, and easily do better financially, by putting his funds into a long-term high-quality bond.

Indeed, of the very few record producers who have committed themselves to Dixieland in a major way during recent years, all the ones I know are lifelong fans motivated essentially by artistic reasons in their recording projects. While they are not trying to lose money, earnings are a secondary consideration. Frequently, they plow all of whatever profits they do make into the production of additional recordings.

Well, thank Heaven for such people, and for the wonderful folks who act as volunteers at festivals. Without them, we would all be much the poorer, not only in terms of opportunities to hear our favorite music but of opportunities to meet some of the friendliest, most warm-hearted and generous human beings on the planet.

The fact that Dixieland jazz is not commercially viable also provides, to me, a simple, logical answer to a question that I've frequently encountered, namely "Why aren't more Black musicians playing Dixieland?". Given that (1) most Dixieland performers these days are hobbyists, (2) playing an instrument at a level required to execute Dixieland effectively calls for a very substantial investment of time in both

TEXAS SHOUT: HOW DIXIELAND JAZZ WORKS

practicing and in understanding the idiom, (3) the proportion of the white population involved in Dixieland today is minuscule and (4) anyone deciding to learn to play Dixieland will be doing so with full knowledge that he is unlikely to be compensated for putting in that time in an amount anywhere near what his time is worth - given all those things, is it surprising that few Blacks elect to become Dixielanders?

To put it another way, in order to choose to play Dixieland anymore, a person will usually have achieved a sufficient level of affluence to be able to indulge a very time-consuming hobby. Proportionately, far fewer Blacks than whites have achieved such a level of affluence. If you calculate the number of whites who play Dixieland as a percentage of whites in the general population who live above the poverty level, and if you apply that same percentage to the number of Blacks in the population who live above the poverty level, how many Black Dixielanders would you expect to come up with?

I've often read that there are sociological reasons discouraging today's Blacks from playing Dixieland - that the music carries a cachet of Uncle Tomism, that subtle social pressures prevent Blacks from entering what has now become a Dixieland environment that is all white, etc. I'm not a sociologist and would not attempt to speak to such points. I suppose, though, that there is some merit to those ideas.

However, I can't help noticing that, at least in New Orleans where the scene is commercially viable, there are Black musicians (and some younger ones, too) playing Dixieland. Thus, when I see the question "Why aren't more Blacks playing Dixieland?" I mentally say to myself "I'll bet that relatively few can afford to do so."

At any rate, whether for Blacks or whites, for festival volunteers or record producers, or anyone else, Dixieland jazz is overwhelmingly a hobby music these days. This is hardly a startling conclusion - anyone with two eyes can see that it is so -, but the foregoing comments about the economics of hiring a band for a commercial club gig do place in perspective just how precarious the situation really is. Further, this situation has had a noticeable effect on both the music itself and on how it is perceived by what public it has.

In our example, we postulated hiring a sextet at $50 per musician for the evening. We can find bands that, will play regular club gigs for less, sometimes for not much more than drinks, but if you tell yourself you're playing it for pay, $50 is pretty much a going minimum.

Unfortunately, it was also pretty much a going minimum thirty years ago when I started playing Dixieland in night spots. Think about how much inflation we've experienced in thirty years, while the going nightly rate for Dixielanders remained in the $50-$75 range, and you'll quickly see why professional Dixieland players are a disappearing breed.

If the older-style jazz musicians of today are mostly hobbyists, they have the benefit (not one to be treated lightly) of being able to perform reasonably free from the constraints of that dreaded word "commerciality". However, like everything in the real world, there are both pluses and minuses to this situation.

Economics of Dixieland

"Practice makes perfect" is an old saw, but it is certainly true when it comes to playing music. It hardly needs to be said that the full-time professional who plays a four-hour Dixieland gig each night, and who has additional practice time available during the day, ought to be better at doing so than a hobbyist musician who plays one or two gigs a week and catches what practice time he can in the evenings.

Moreover, if you are a person who values imagination and creativity in jazz solos, you can hardly fail to notice the appreciable amount of chord-running and favorite licks that emanate from festival stages these days, even from the most prestigious events and best-known bands. You must have observed that the individual Dixielanders who most often surprise you, the ones who best blend innovative ideas with the ability to execute those ideas, are, with few exceptions, artists who make a full-time living out of music (not necessarily 100% Dixieland), or have spent an appreciable part of their careers as full-timers, or are doing so much playing that they are virtually full-timers.

Clearly, at least if you compare today's Dixieland with records from 20-30 years ago, something has markedly changed in the soloing arena. I believe that the relative dearth of professionals in the ranks is a significant factor behind that change.

Actually, the effect of hobbyism on the quality of today's Dixieland music is a subject that deserves a column all its own. I'll write one for you some day.

Apart from the effect of hobbyism on the music itself, I think that whenever a product becomes exempt from the commercial demands of the marketplace, when it is no longer seen as being required to pay its own way, it is in danger of losing something important. Specifically, it may lose a common basis for judging what its standards are.

For example, I see a slackening of standards with respect to what constitutes a record review worthy of publication. In the periodicals I read, there seem to be more and more reviewers who are all too willing to write a review that consists of announcing that a record has been made and then praising it to the skies in general terms.

Some of these reviews contain little or no useful information to a reader contemplating purchase of the album. Such information might include the style of Dixieland being played (I wonder if some of the current crop of reviewers are fully aware of the variety of Dixieland styles?), the instrumentation, the quality of the fidelity, and how to order a copy by mail.

Similarly, as I have previously noted in this column, the Dixieland scene is being increasingly populated, for understandable reasons, by an audience not primarily motivated by a desire to hear good Dixieland jazz. They'd really rather hear country, Latin, swing, pop or whatever.

There are some compelling non-economic factors contributing to this change. Still, if pure Dixieland were better able to pay its own way, I feel sure we'd see a much smaller proportion of non-genre music in the current Dixieland scene.

We pay serious attention to Dixieland jazz, we write articles about it, because we believe that our music is an art form, one which remains capable of creative expression, of speaking to us on a level deeper than its surface characteristics. If we are not going to try to maintain that view of the music in the face of the many pressures leading us to do otherwise, then we might as well open our Dixieland festival stages to anything that will provide a few laughs and a danceable beat; we might as well open *WCR's* pages to listings for ice cream tastings and balloon ascensions.

In short, standards are important. If Dixieland is a valid art form, we ought to be able to recognize what is Dixieland and what isn't. We ought to know how to tell good Dixieland from the not-as-good, and we should strive to seek out the best quality available within the limitations of our individual budgets, travel ranges, etc.

How can we each play a part in the effort to maintain standards and still enjoy the things about the scene that we're enjoying now? I can think of one way, taking off from my deeply-held belief that the more you know about something, the more you're likely to get out of it and the more fun you're likely to have with it.

Why not take a little time to focus your thinking on just what it is you like about the music and why? Why do you prefer this band, or this clarinetist, or this vocalist, or this tune, over that one? See if you can refine your own criteria for understanding and liking Dixieland in a way that will help you locate what you believe are the better elements of it.

That's an effort which costs you nothing and which you can make while you're on the scene having a good time. After you've started along that path, then do one more thing - discuss the subject with your friends and fellow fans, and try to get them started along the same trail.

The goal here, of course, is to heighten your awareness of Dixieland as an art form, to get you to gravitate toward the better music without giving up the things you already enjoy about it. If you want to see bands with good-looking female singers, fine, but why not learn to find the one who's just as good-looking but a better vocalist, or who has a better band backing her up? If your real desire is to hear the bandleader tell jokes, no problem, but why not spend your time with the band that has both good jokes and good music? Let's dance to Dixieland by all means, but why not choose the band that's not only danceble but listenable when you decide to sit one out?

If we can try to keep the music a little more in focus, perhaps we can get our crowds moving toward the stages which not only entertain us but also are producing a higher level of artistic accomplishment. If that movement takes place, the bands left behind will be under pressure to improve their artistic content as well. Then we'll all be better off.

Personally, while I love Dixielanders, the fans, the scene, the performing, etc., I also love this music for itself alone. I enjoy sharing the high it gives me and have tried over the years, via such things as this column, record reviews, liner notes and live presentations, to get you thinking about how the music works, what separates the best from the rest, and how to derive as much pleasure from it as I do.

In fact, in recent years, I've been involved in presenting three special shows on the festival circuit designed (hopefully in an entertaining way) to heighten the audience's ability to appreciate our music. Judging from the way these shows have been received, I'd say there is a high degree of interest out there in this topic.

I don't expect that you all will agree with my views (nor would I prefer it that way), but I would like to get everyone reading these words to think more about the

Economics of Dixieland

subject. Some of you have told me that my activities have helped expand your jazz horizons, so I know the process works; I know you can get involved in it without too much effort and can lead others to do so.

There is also a way you can help deal with the economic problems mentioned at the start of this column. It will take a little more time and money, but the rewards justify the expenditure.

Why not decide, once you've started to crystallize your ideas on the type of Dixieland you prefer, that during the next year you'll go out to hear it live just a few more times? Attendance by each of us at, say, three or four more club gigs, or jazz society meetings, or anywhere that Dixieland is played, would go a long way toward making our music more viable in the market, and it wouldn't cost any of us all that much individually.

Nancy and I made that decision about two years ago. There are four older-style jazz societies around Wilmington, Delaware that we have long supported via membership, but none are close enough to attend conveniently. Moreover, there are no night spots in our area regularly presenting Dixieland.

However, when we started to read, in the club publications, that attendance was dwindling at their regular presentations, we figured it was time to put our money where our hearts were. We picked one of the clubs and decided, though it is a two-hour drive each way, that we'd try to get to as many functions as we could.

My playing and travel schedules still keep us from making the trip more than about three times a year, but it's been well worth the effort. We've met some great people, bought some fine recordings at the record bar that aren't available in my local stores, taken advantage of the opportunity to dance (obviously not an option at my own gigs) and heard some terrific music. We got to know some musicians a little better, including the excellent banjoist Cynthia Sayer who, shortly after our jazz society conversation, became a member of The Rent Party Revellers.

Even though the current economics of Dixieland are discouraging, we can all, without sacrificing any of our pleasure, and without putting in much more time and money, do something to help insure the standards of the music are maintained and that the demands of the commercial market place are satisified. For me, the alternatives are too bleak to contemplate.

TEXAS SHOUT: HOW DIXIELAND JAZZ WORKS

The Jim Cullum Jazz Band
Courtesy of Jim Cullum   Photographer Unknown

CHAPTER 22   NJJS HALL OF FAME

In the May 1991 issue of *Jersey Jazz*, a periodical published by the New Jersey Jazz Society, its excellent editor Warren Vaché, Sr. (also a fine string bass player) authored one of his typically thoughtful and provocative essays, this one dealing with the selection procedures for a Jazz Hall Of Fame that had been established some years before by the Society. Warren particularly lamented that a number of worthy players from jazz's earliest years had not yet been enshrined, his selected list of nominees including trumpeters Nick La Rocca and Manny Klein.

I sent in some comments on the matters raised by Warren, which he published in the next issue of *Jersey Jazz*. Upon re-reading my submission, I think that it stands pretty much on its own apart from Warren's article and that it contains some thoughts which might interest *WCR* readers. Accordingly, the balance of this month's "Texas Shout" consists of a reproduction of the text of my letter.

◊ ◊ ◊ ◊ ◊ ◊ ◊ ◊ ◊ ◊ ◊ ◊ ◊

I read with great interest your thoughts in the May 1991 *Jersey Jazz* regarding the nominating procedures for the Jazz Hall Of Fame. I agree that, comparing the names on your list of candidates with the names that have been selected to date, it appears that the nominators do not have a broad-based view of jazz history.

I think this deficiency is unfortunate. However, it is understandable if one keeps in mind the wrenching changes that jazz has undergone in its brief lifetime.

All styles of jazz require players to have ensemble skills (the ability to improvise meaningfully with other improvising jazzmen) as well as solo skills. However, the emphasis on these skills, as well as the musical vocabulary used for them, has changed drastically over the years.

I have been able to identify seven different pre-swing styles of jazz, each with its own objectives and approaches: the white New Orleans style sometimes confusingly referred to as the "Dixieland" style, pioneered by the Original Dixieland Jazz Band and carried forward through such combos as the Original Memphis Five and the various Red Nichols groups of the twenties; the downtown black New Orleans style (exemplified by most of the recordings made in the twenties by Black New Orleans musicians, such as King Oliver, Jelly Roll Morton, Louis Armstrong and Sidney Bechet); Chicago style; hot dance; uptown New Orleans (exemplified these days by The Preservation Hall Jazz Band); West Coast revival; and British trad.

The latter three are revival-period styles. West Coast revival and uptown New Orleans first attracted major attention in the early 1940s, while British trad came along in the late 1950s.

TEXAS SHOUT: HOW DIXIELAND JAZZ WORKS

Of these seven styles, six put a higher value on ensemble skills than on solo skills. Only the Chicago style puts a higher value on solo skills than on ensemble skills. (Note again that both skills are always regarded as important - it is the relative emphasis that makes the difference.)

By contrast <u>all</u> of the other, so-called "advanced" styles of jazz - swing, mainstream (improvised small-band jazz played by swing musicians), progressive, bop, etc. - put a higher value on solo skills than on ensemble skills. Further, while the onset of swing changed this emphasis, the development of bop, with its deliberate rejection of much of the preceding vocabulary of jazz, introduced a further radical change in emphasis - the reharmonization of tunes to use higher chords, the utilization of step-wise chord progressions vs. the more typical circle-of-fifths, the superimposition of jagged melodic phrases above the the normal four-bar phrase length and the like.

The effect of these changes is that jazz has been divided into three fairly large bodies, each with its own rules. As you move from pre-swing styles into swing-era styles, you need to adjust your values from ensemble orientation to solo orientation, and as you move beyond swing into the "modern" styles, you need to make an adjustment to your ears to accommodate the very different sounds you'll encounter.

Most people either can't or won't make these adjustments. Very, very few jazz fans are able to say honestly that they appreciate Dixieland, swing and bop in equal measure.

That, I think, is the difficulty with having one panel of experts to nominate names for a Hall of Fame. If you believe that jazz really started with Charlie Parker, you are very likely to consider jazz based on a Dixieland vocabulary as being simplistic, dated, crude and noisy. Conversely, if you believe that, after Jelly Roll Morton, jazz degenerated into a bunch of soloists playing as high and as fast as possible, you will probably think that Dizzy Gillespie belongs in a Hall of Infamy rather than the reverse.

I am not surprised that the Hall of Fame sponsored by the New Jersey Jazz Society contains musicians who, by and large, reflect the general Chicago/mainstream/swing taste of the society's membership and officials. However, if a truly balanced Hall of Fame were desired, you might be more likely to get it by having three different panels make the nominations.

One panel would be comprised of "experts" whose main area of interest was in jazz styles based on the twenties styles, including revival styles thereof. The second would deal with musicians of a post-twenties, pre-bop persuasion, covering swing, mainstream, jump and, maybe, progressive. The third would cover bop, free and other styles of "modern" jazz. Anyone qualified in more than one area, of course, could serve on more than one panel.

In that manner, names of musicians such as the ones nominated in your article could get consideration by experts who understand them, and so could such equally worthy names as Lu Watters and Thelonious Monk. As things now stand, I think it would be nearly impossible to assemble a panel of jazz experts that would be likely to vote in the same year to place, say, a Miles Davis, a Nick La Rocca and a Manny Klein into a Jazz Hall of Fame.

NJJS Hall Of Fame

As a related point, many of the "experts" involved in making such selections tend to see jazz as always moving forward. For that reason, they are inclined to downplay major changes in the field that occur in older styles of jazz.

If, however, changing the course of a given stream of jazz qualifies you for consideration in a Hall of Fame, as I think it should, then musicians who choose to work in older styles should be recognized for such accomplishments. The same statement can be made of musicians who have exerted a wide influence on the playing of other musicians.

As a case in point, the two most widely imitated clarinetists in all of jazz today have to be Benny Goodman and George Lewis. Partly because Goodman was on the leading edge of jazz in his day, everyone is willing to rush him into his deserved place in the jazz pantheon. However, Lewis began recording during the revival period of Dixieland, a factor which, in some people's minds, diminishes his claim to the same honor.

Similarly, the three most widely imitated trombonists in pre-swing jazz are, virtually beyond question, Jack Teagarden, Jim Robinson and Turk Murphy[*]. With so many musicians all around the world trying as hard as they can to imitate them, Robinson's and Murphy's influence continues in a measure well beyond that of many musicians routinely put forward as potential immortals. Whether one prefers their styles or not, Robinson and Murphy left their marks in a way that few jazzmen did. They deserve recognition for that very significant accomplishment.

How many jazzmen have, virtually single-handedly, created styles of jazz that took hold and inspired disciples who preach their gospels decades later? Lu Watters did, founding the West Cost revival style of Dixieland. So did Ken Colyer, working in tandem with Chris Barber regarding British trad.

Personally, in addition to the names you list, I can think of seven revival period musicians whose impact on jazz was so powerful that, under any reasonable criteria for selection, each ought to be in a Jazz Hall Of Fame: Bunk Johnson, George Lewis, Jim Robinson, Lu Watters, Turk Murphy, Ken Colyer and Chris Barber. I would think that a jazz buff who has devoted as much time to swing styles, or "modern" styles, as I have to Dixieland styles would be able to come up with a comparable list of names in those styles that cry out to be enshrined.

I doubt that the present procedure has a chance of giving balanced consideration to many such jazzmen. However, as I've said before it's NJJS's Hall, so NJJS and its members are really the only ones that need to be happy with the selections. If I ever open my own Hall, though, Turk will be in it and (much as I dislike "modern" jazz) so, probably, will Ornette Coleman.

[*] Warren added an Editor's Note to my letter, observing that many other trombonists have been highly influential on their successors, that all jazzmen borrow from each other, and that most players, quite properly, avoid deliberate imitation in favor of selectivity from various available sources. I couldn't agree more. I believe

that deliberate imitation is a musical dead end and that the better players recognize a need to go beyond mere imitation.

Nevertheless, there is a certain amount of imitation in jazz. With regard to Dixieland trombone, I see Turk, Big Jim and Tea clearly leading the pack in terms of numbers of conscious out-and-out imitators. Whether imitation is desirable or not, if a musician does inspire a significant group of imitators, that factor tells me that he is impacting the music to a degree that his name ought to be considered when Hall of Fame nominations are being discussed.

Benny Goodman   1940s
Photo Courtesy of Capital Records

Jack Teagarden
Photo by Nossett   Courtesy of Duncan Schiedt

CHAPTER 23   PICKING TUNES YOU CAN SWING

Not long ago, I was having dinner at a festival with another bandleader. I said something about leaders being on the lookout for good tunes to play. My friend's response caught me off guard.

He said, "Why do I need to look for good tunes? I already know lots of good tunes."

Personally, I am a bandleader who pays a lot of attention to repertoire. Not having given the subject all that much thought, I assumed that other bandleaders also spent some time in selecting material for their combos to learn and that, in connection with this activity, they would have a heightened sense of awareness with respect to locating the best jazz vehicles.

However, having a lot of respect for my friend as a bandleader and Dixieland musician, I tried to put myself in his position. I realized that, if you look at our music from a certain viewpoint, his remarks make a lot of sense.

To see the issue in perspective, we need to remind ourselves of what Dixieland jazz is all about. The factor that distinguishes jazz from other types of music is its rhythmic feeling, the buoyant, propulsive, infectious type of beat that jazz buffs refer to as "swing" (not "Swing," the jazz style of the thirties, but rhythm that "swings") played with a feeling that communicates the passion and personal involvement of the musician, the feeling that jazz buffs refer to as "heat."

If music isn't hot or doesn't swing, in the senses just mentioned, then it isn't jazz. Note that "swinging" and "playing hot" doesn't mean music that is fast and loud - it means music played with the type of beat and feeling described above, whether fast or slow, loud or soft, restrained or boisterous.

Moreover, you can't have too much swing and heat. The more you have, the jazzier a performance will be.

Further, if you want your performance to be judged as jazz, you must recognize that there is no substitute for swing and heat. You can't make up for the lack of swing and heat via a well-organized presentation. You can't compensate for that lack via clean execution, pure tone, or any other technical accomplishment. You can't gain points over jazzier bands by one-upping them on repertoire.

Put another way, a hot, swinging performance of the most overplayed Dixieland tune in the world (whatever that may be) is more successful as jazz, more deserving of the attention of jazz fans, than a slightly less hot, slightly less swinging performance of the least-heard selection that can be unearthed. I have a lot of tolerance (even preference) for diversity in the jazz community, but in this instance I would go so far as to say that any person who has trouble accepting the truth of the preceding statement does not fully understand what makes jazz the unique music that it is.

TEXAS SHOUT: HOW DIXIELAND JAZZ WORKS

Now let's go back to my dinnertable conversation. What my friend was saying, I think, is that he, like any seasoned Dixieland musician, has become familiar over the years with dozens, hundreds, perhaps thousands, of tunes which, in the hands of a musician who knows how to play Dixieland, can, without much trouble, be made to swing with heat. Because swinging with heat is the heart and soul of playing our music, he can call up any of those titles with a basis for believing that the resulting performance will pass muster as jazz.

That is a perfectly valid way to look at programming. Many bands do quite well by operating in such a manner, providing sound, worthwhile (and sometimes much better) jazz for their fans.

I'm not saying that leaders shouldn't seek out worthy but neglected material for their sidemen. There is a decided value in doing so. Because I put a high value on exposing audiences to the almost limitless breadth of Dixieland jazz, finding underplayed quality material is an activity that occupies a significant portion of my own bandleading agenda. I am simply saying that, if you and your sidemen know how to play Dixieland properly, you can get the job done without doing so if that is your wont.

However, all bandleaders do, by some process, choose a repertoire for their combos, even if that process involves a spur-of-the-moment onstage inspiration as to what the next tune ought to be. The foregoing points suggest to me a simple practice to be followed in the tune selection process, perhaps an obvious one, but one that seems to me to be overlooked more than it should be.

Namely, keeping in mind the abilities of his sidemen, and of his ensemble collectively, a leader should not decide to present a tune to his audience, either live or on record, unless he has a high degree of confidence that his band will be able to deliver a rendition of it that swings with heat - at least, not if he wants the performance to be regarded as jazz.

I can understand why a band may particularly wish to show the audience the difficult arrangement it has mastered. Similarly, no one knows better than I the joys of exposing the crowd to a quality tune that will be new to most of the listeners. However, if a rendition isn't going to be hot and swinging, a band shouldn't be surprised if the knowledgeable jazz fans, the peers that it may want to impress the most, are somewhat turned off by its version and say, as my good friend Anna Wahler occasionally would, that the ride is STAD (see *WCR's* "Letter Drop" column of April 1991 for a full translation of this unfavorable assessment).

Let me give you a concrete illustration of this point. Not long ago, I reviewed (and recommended to you) an enjoyable audiocassette by Denver's Queen City Jazz Band (<u>Happy</u> <u>Hairy</u> <u>Zeno</u> <u>HHZ 118</u>, "We Came To Play"). Included in the program is Wilbur De Paris' composition "Wrought Iron Rag." In his liner notes to the album, QCJB leader Bill Clark says "This is the hardest song in the world."

In addition to being a fine musician (and teacher of jazz), Bill is a most articulate person, fully capable of speaking for himself. I do not purport in any way to be putting words in Bill's mouth, but I would like to speculate a bit about exactly what he meant by the above-quoted sentence.

I don't hear him saying that the notes and melodic lines which the musicians have to play to execute "Wrought Iron Rag" are particularly difficult - certainly not for a septet that has the QCJB's musicianship. "Wrought Iron Rag" does not call for

Picking Tunes You Can Swing

for a septet that has the QCJB's musicianship. "Wrought Iron Rag" does not call for any instrument to move outside of its normal range, or in exceptionally dense flurries, or with unusual leaps and twists.

What I think Bill meant was that, looked at from the viewpoint of a Dixieland jazzman, "Wrought Iron Rag" is put together in a fashion that Dixielanders do not find comfortable. Said another way, the hardest assignment in the world for a Dixielander may be getting "Wrought Iron Rag" to swing with heat.

If so, I see exactly where he's coming from. I have heard many recordings of "Wrought Iron Rag," quite a few of them by highly-regarded combos, including De Paris' own. As best I can recall, the tune has, to a greater or lesser degree, defeated all comers with respect to (what I assume is) their goal of creating a fully successful jazz rendition.

Although I have never bothered to learn "Wrought Iron Rag," I have played along with records of it on many occasions. It is a long, extremely complex piece with roadblocks in virtually every bar - that is, the musician is constantly encountering melodies that don't go where normal Dixieland melodies go, harmonies that don't progress as do typical Dixieland tunes, sudden tempo changes in unexpected places, and passages that call for tight, intricate voicing instead of the familiar Dixieland polyphony. As a result, the artist never gets to relax and concentrate on the thing he's supposed to be doing - playing hot and swinging. Consequently, the rendition, at some point (and maybe at several) fails to swing with heat and loses some of its jazziness.

I do not denigrate distinctive melodies, novel harmonies and creative routines. Quite the contrary; I avidly seek them out. However, like everything else, these virtues have their limitations as well. When those limitations are exceeded, as I think they are in "Wrought Iron Rag," they become crippling handicaps.

Personally, I have been ready for years to see the jazz community give up trying to overcome "Wrought Iron Rag." I believe it is a thoroughly misconceived, unplayable (as jazz) monstrosity that should be consigned to the scrap heap.

However, I know there are readers out there who've enjoyed hearing "Wrought Iron Rag." Fine - I'm happy to see them having a good time. I can also understand why bands keep launching kamikaze assaults on this tune, just as Sir Edmund Hilary insisted on trying to scale unclimbable heights, just because they were there.

My point is, if you want to woodshed a piece as a way of disciplining and challenging your band, great. If you want to include it in your show to demonstrate to us all that you can negotiate it without any obvious clams, no problem. However, if you can't get it to swing with heat, don't expect to be given passing grades on the jazz scale.

I have picked on "Wrought Iron Rag" partly because Bill's "hardest tune ..." comment suggested to me that another informed writer may share my view of the problems it poses opposite swinging with heat. If I've misrepresented Bill, I apologize. And his album is a good one, anyway.

But the larger point is valid, I think. If your band hasn't reached the stage where it can get, say, multi-theme pieces off the ground, leave them out of your show and records until it does. After all, many combos (particularly ones who play strict uptown New Orleans style) create wonderful jazz using not much more than a repertoire of one-strain tunes with spare melodies and common chord patterns, played in standard keys. Loads of blues singers in the twenties created bodies of recordings - performances now venerated around the world - built on not much more than one 12-bar blues foundation with little or no variation from tune to tune in melody, harmony or even key. Remember, it don't mean a thing to a jazz fan, not a thing, if it ain't got that swing.

Having said that, I should emphasize that the degree of simplicity or complexity in a tune's construction is not necessarily a good barometer of whether the number is easily swingable. As I have previously remarked in these pages, tunes like "Tiger Rag", "That's A' Plenty" and "Eccentric" are quite intricate pieces that have nevertheless become part of the standard repertoire for most Dixielanders. Conversely, lots of pop tunes from the twenties of fairly common construction, including quite a few hits, don't seem to be particularly receptive vehicles for Dixieland units.

As additional examples, many of the works of Jelly Roll Morton, and the titles recorded by the Original Dixieland Jazz Band and King Oliver's Creole Jazz Band, are well above average in complexity, yet they swing like crazy once you've learned them. A composition in this category that readily occurs to me is Turk Murphy's "Duff Campbell's Revenge."

Turk was one of Dixieland's finest composers. He had a remarkable gift for melody, his sizeable body of originals being abundantly decorated with singable lines that linger in the mind. He had the knack for finding distinctive harmonies for these melodies, harmonies that seem strange at first but are very comfortable when you get used to them.

Thus, "Duff Campbell's Revenge," a first-rate selection with a truly daunting chord pattern, isn't something that you can just "ear in" after a couple of run-throughs. However, most bands who've done the work to get it under control haven't had any particular trouble getting it to swing - and that includes a couple of Chicago-styled combos (bands whose normal approach to Dixieland is at the opposite end of the jazz spectrum from Turk's): Eddie Condon's aggregation and Parke Frankfield's Swing 'N Dixie.

In sum, keep on trying to stretch your abilities and those of your sidemen. Keep rehearsing those toughies that have resisted you so far, but which you're sure can be conquered (and have the perception to forget those that can't). However, when you get out in front of us, and you want to give us our best blast for the buck jazz-wise, make sure your reach stays within your grasp.

If you do, when you look around, I'll bet you'll be able to locate fairly easily more than enough tunes that you can swing with heat and thereby get us goin'. Believe me, we'll come back for more.

July 1992 West Coast Rag

CHAPTER 24

CREATIVITY/REPERTORY BANDS/IMAGINATION

In the previous "Texas Shout," I expressed my view that the heart and soul of Dixieland jazz is playing so that the music swings with heat. I suggested that each bandleader remember to choose a repertoire that gives his lineup, in light of its overall capabilities, the best chance of achieving this objective.

Let's suppose that you're a bandleader who is blessed with a band that knows how to swing with heat - no small achievement in a field that currently contains a discouragingly large number of combos which apparently have not yet grasped that, without those two elements, they can't be considered to be playing jazz. Now that you've put your group solidly onto the level occupied only by jazz bands, how do you work your way up out of the crowd?

That one's easy. You use imagination - creativity - in your performances. You put as many elements into your music, and its setting, as possible that will distinguish it from the other contenders without diminishing its jazz content.

There are plenty of bands out there that are not bothering to be imaginative. All of the greats of Dixieland have their imitators. Devotees of Turk Murphy are everywhere, replicating Turk's recordings and/or solos. The same can be said of George Lewis, Lu Watters, King Oliver, and a host of immortal names.

There is nothing wrong with doing so. On the other hand, as I will amplify below, trying to replicate what someone else has already done adds nothing significant to the already existing body of Dixieland jazz.

If you want to be remembered as a superior practitioner of any art form, you must find your own voice within it. Everybody knows who painted the original Mona Lisa, but can any of you name a single one of the thousands of artists who have made copies of it? Dixieland jazz works exactly the same way.

The elements of a performance are (1) presentation (if you're appearing live), (2) the tunes that are played and (3) the way those tunes are rendered. Each of these elements can be handled creatively.

With respect to the non-musical aspects of a presentation, I have already written (see "Texas Shout" for August 1990) that a band can help its musical show considerably by paying attention to the setting in which the music appears, by finding a way to keep the audience entertained. I won't elaborate on this topic again, but will note that, given two bands whose musical products are identical, I will certainly choose to go to see the one that has the more colorful and engaging presentation of that music.

However, because I am principally attracted to Dixieland as an art form, I will always prefer to see a band that plays better jazz, even if its presentation is less enticing. I would hope that Dixieland fans, as they develop experience with the music and a heightened awareness of its many rewards, would over the long haul tend to agree with that viewpoint. Thus, let's talk for the rest of this column about increasing creativity within the music.

Of the two remaining elements, repertoire and performance, performance is beyond question the most important. To illustrate what I mean, let's consider four bands, each with identical abilities to swing with heat.

At the bottom of the ranking will be the band that plays the same old tunes the same old way. Just above the bottom will be the band that plays a highly imaginative, well-chosen repertoire, but plays it the same old way - running changes, using a limited palette of sound textures, giving us the same things we've heard thousands of times but on somewhat different melodies and chord patterns.

Ahead of that band, nearing the top of the heap, will be the combo that plays the same old tunes, but in a highly imaginative way - giving us fresh ideas from the soloists, novel voicings and different instrumental textures, causing the seemingly familiar numbers to emerge in brand new costumes. To underscore that point, and to state precisely what's meant here, a fresh, varied ride, with fertile solos, empathetic interplay among the sidemen, and distinctive ensemble effects on, say, "When The Saints Go Marching In", is a superior work of art within the idiom than a rendition of "Elephant Wobble" in which the soloists, playing in their usual sequence, trot out once again their favorite licks.

At the top of the pile, of course, is the group that does both. This will be a combo that looks for worthwhile but underplayed material, but which always remembers to approach every selection, whether familiar or not, as a challenge for finding something musically new and valid to say.

This ranking reflects a point I have made from time to time in various editions of "Texas Shout", but it is one that we shouldn't forget if we care about Dixieland as an art form. Namely, from an artistic viewpoint, the musical performance is everything.

Tunes are inanimate collections of notes. They do not know whether they have already been played thousands of times by Dixielanders, or whether they have just been rediscovered.

Despite what many players and fans think, tunes do not become "exhausted" through being played frequently. A piece that was a superior vehicle for Dixieland in the twenties or thirties is just as superior now, provided we remember to bring to it an imaginative, searching spirit.

Said another way, a mediocre ride is mediocre no matter how you slice it. It does not become less mediocre because the vehicle chosen is a newly resurrected, underplayed gem of a composition. Similarly, a hot, swinging, imaginative ride does not become less interesting artistically because the vehicle chosen has been played and recorded many times in the past.

How does a bandleader go about fostering creativity? With respect to soloing, there's not much you can do directly. You're ultimately dependent on the degree to which your individual sidemen are willing to stretch themselves in order to find new things to say and avoid favorite licks.

Creativity/Repertory Bands/Imagination

However, you can do some things that will stimulate the juices within the ranks. Vary the tempos and keys from tune to tune. Call the solos in a different order. Try part-chorus solos occasionally.

With respect to harmonies, Dixieland is fairly basic in that respect and you can't do very much modification without moving into advanced jazz forms. However, you can look for more interesting voicings of your horn passages, perhaps by assigning the melody to some instrument other than the usual cornet lead.

Dynamics is an overlooked area for creativity. The imaginative juxtaposition of loud and soft passages can be a sure-fire ear-catcher for the audience.

In routines though, the field is wide open. Must the strains always be played in the usual order on this title? Does it offer an opportunity for a subunit? Does the tune have several strains that are suitable solo platforms, so that you can have some solos on one and then move to another for the remainder? Can you find new places for breaks, stop-time passages, key changes, special interludes, arranged effects and the like? Does the song have a good but underutilized lyric? Can you develop a special introduction and/or tag for it?

Let me mention two examples I've noticed where, I think, it's time for a little more creativity to appear on our stages: Duke Ellington's "The Mooche" and Lu Watters' "Doin' The Hambone".

"The Mooche" is one of the all-time-great mood pieces of Dixieland exotica. I'm not at all surprised that so many combos have been attracted to it.

However, and I'm speaking as one who has reviewed many renditions of this selection, virtually everybody delivers the Ellington chart nearly verbatim when they get around to executing "The Mooche". Did Ellington really say, over sixty years ago, everything that could possibly be said about this tune, leaving us with nothing to do through the following decades but regurgitate his effort?

Frankly, I've heard so many Ellington clones on "The Mooche" that I have to struggle to pay attention and take notes on the review copies. Once that "dum-da-da-da-dum" tom-tom starts, I can tell myself that I know exactly what's going to happen for the next three or four minutes, and I'm almost always right. Same problem with the few combos I've played with that perform "The Mooche" - their charts are so firmly locked into Ellington, so lacking in novelty, that it's all I can do to keep from going to sleep at the keyboard.

I don't know about the rest of the audience, but your band could sure hold my attention if you, say, opened "The Mooche" with a duet on the minor blues strain, added instruments for a couple of choruses as you build up to a full ensemble for the descending C-minor strain, took a few more choruses on the major blues strain, and ended with the major blues riff strain, closing with a clarinet cadenza into a sustained minor chord. How would that rendition work? Darned if I know, but it would be thought-provoking and <u>your</u> version instead of Ellington's.

"Doin' The Hambone" has not been as widely waxed, probably because it is not one of Watters' best compositions, ranking well below his three masterpieces, "Emperor Norton's Hunch", "Big Bear Stomp" and the underplayed "Antigua Blues". Still, Watters' rendition chugs along well enough, and I can see why his disciples keep it alive.

TEXAS SHOUT: HOW DIXIELAND JAZZ WORKS

However, in "Doin' The Hambone", Watters did not write a tune; he wrote a routine. There is very little melody to the number, which consists primarily of a series of themes in which stop-time licks occur in varied spots.

As best I can recall, all of the post-Watters recordings I've encountered of "Doin' The Hambone" render the tune exactly per the Watters original, even to the point of having the one solo played on the piano. Couldn't one of the stop-time strains be smoothed out for a solo? What would happen if some breaks were put into the main strain instead of the later ones? Could any theme be made more effective if it were played at a volume significantly below the quadruple forte heard on all of Watters' sides? So far, it appears that we aren't going to be given the opportunity to find out.

In effect, the renditions we're hearing of these numbers are not those of the band playing them. We're hearing Ellington's and Watters' renditions. These tunes are being used almost exclusively as repertory numbers.

Repertory is a special concept within Dixieland that is exempt from the creativity requirement. It consists of a more or less conscious effort to duplicate a performance that appears on a previous recording. Creativity in a repertory performance defeats its purpose.

I can see some value in repertory Dixieland. If Oliver, Bix Louis, Turk, Bunk, Wild Bill and the others are no longer around to play their great creations for us, and if their creations are truly the immortal performances we know them to be, there is something to be said for scoring them in a way that will let today's audiences hear them live.

Repertory can be a valuable teaching tool, providing your sidemen, and others new to our music, with an accessible way of listening to acknowledged masterpieces of the idiom. It avoids the somewhat less immediate, colder activity of listening to records.

Also, many musicians derive satisfaction from executing someone else's magnificent conceptions. As you have doubtless gathered, I am not a musician who personally prefers to play in that manner. However, this is strictly a question of taste, and I recognize that doing so constitutes a perfectly valid way to enjoy performing music.

Even so, executing repertory Dixieland is an artistically empty endeavor. If you can't have the original Mona Lisa in your home, you may well be quite satisfied to appreciate a photograph of it, but nobody pretends that the photograph, in and of itself, has much artistic value.

When repertory Dixieland bands produce records, this problem becomes especially focused. Granted, there may be some marginal benefits in hearing the music in present-day fidelity (although the miracles of modern sound techniques for cleaning up old records are making serious inroads into that advantage).

However, most of the great recordings in Dixieland are reissued with satisfying frequency. If I'm going to take a record off the shelf, I can't really see why I'm going to select one by The Dixieland Repertory All-Stars that tries to sound like one by Turk Murphy, or King Oliver, or Jelly Roll Morton, or George Lewis, or Lu Watters, etc., when I can choose the original instead.

Creativity/Repertory Bands/Imagination

Much the same thing is true of live performances. If your band is one that does not try to be creative, that is content to duplicate essentially what you've heard on your favorite records, why should we get dressed up, go out of the house, and pony up the admission to listen to you when we can stay home, save ourselves the time and money, and hear the records you're copying in the comfort of our living rooms?

The practitioners of the more advanced forms of jazz typically look down on today's Dixieland community, calling it a group of hobbyists who have nothing of value to add to jazz. Although, as with most generalizations, this one is probably a bit too sweeping, there is a measure of truth in that accusation.

However, things don't have to be that way. Dixieland is the same as it always was, an idiom that has plenty of room for timeless music.

Your band can get its head up above the pack by deciding to take a chance, to get imaginative, to try to create some of that timeless music instead of playing it safe. The rest of us can help by insisting on and applauding such efforts, and by applauding even louder when those efforts succeed.

Otherwise, we might as well concede that our critics are right, and Dixieland is just a sterile playground for hobbyists determined to recreate the past. I know which route I prefer.

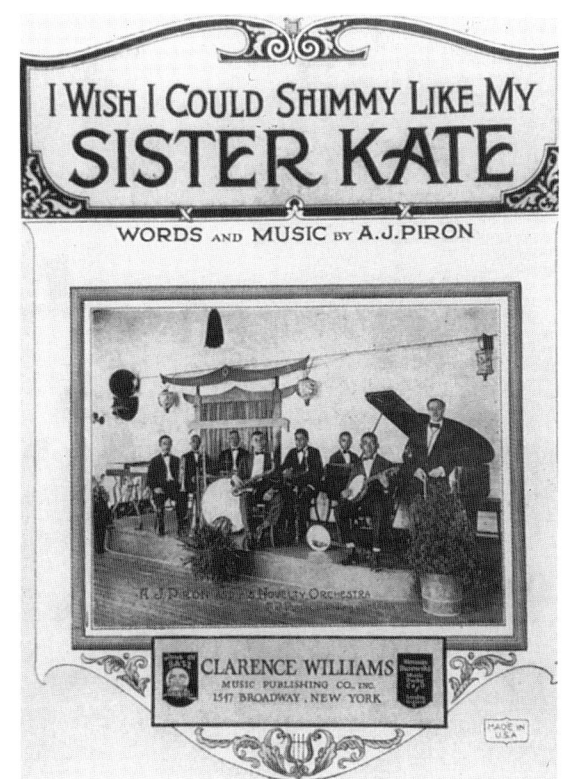

A.J. Piron & His Novelty Orchestra
1923
Photo by George Hoefer

TEXAS SHOUT: HOW DIXIELAND JAZZ WORKS

Those Draftin' Blues Sheet Music
Courtesy of Tex Wyndham

CHAPTER 25   "STORYVILLE BLUES"

One of the most important recording dates of the Dixieland revival, the session which first focused widespread critical attention on the uptown New Orleans style, took place on June 11, 1942 in the third-floor piano storeroom of Grunewald's Music Store in New Orleans. It marked the recording debut of veteran trumpeter Bunk Johnson, backed by a band which, in the 1950s under the leadership of its clarinetist George Lewis, went on to achieve worldwide popularity and lasting influence.

One of the numbers recorded by Johnson on that historic occasion was an old pop tune that has gone on to be a great favorite of West Coast revival-style combos. In attendance was David Stuart who, in the liner notes to a 1962 reissue of these sides, Good Time Jazz M12048, said of this particular selection:

> "Storyville Blues" was the third number. The tune has been recorded since under several titles. "Storyville" was chosen because it's a good honest word and as far as I know hadn't before been used as a song title.

Thus, we know that the piece now widely played under the title "Storyville Blues" did not start out with that appellation. For those who are interested, I'd like to spend the balance of this column sharing with you such information as I've been able to gather regarding the origins of this now-familiar anthem.

Acting on a tip I got years ago, from (if memory serves) sheet music collector and piano-roll expert Mike Montgomery (but it might have been Thornton "Tony" Hagert) at a Ragtime Society Bash in Toronto, I went looking for a piece of sheet music called "Those Draftin' Blues". The cover and both pages of the music are reproduced alongside this column.

Examination of this material shows beyond any reasonable question that it is indeed "Storyville Blues". The differences between "Those Draftin' Blues" and the customary way of playing "Storyville Blues" are so trivial as to be insignificant - easily attributable to lapses in Bunk Johnson's memory (which subsequent research has shown to be highly suspect in a number of respects).

The song sheet credits the 1918 tune to Maceo Pinkard, a successful Tin Pan Alley denizen whose works are still heard on the jazz scene. He is the composer or co-composer, for example, of such standard Dixieland tunes as "Sweet Georgia Brown", "Sugar", "(I'll Be a Friend) With Pleasure" and "Them There Eyes".

It wasn't easy to turn up a copy of "Those Draftin' Blues". The song is not a common item to find on music dealers' lists, a fact which implies that it was not popular and did not sell in large numbers.

An analysis of the sheet music reveals why the tune might not have been a hit. To be popular, a song has to contain an effective combination of lyric and melody. The lyric to "Those Draftin' Blues", even after allowing for the heated patriotism found in many ditties from the World War I days, is rather downbeat and somewhat maudlin. Moreover, its melody, consisting in large part of long notes within the chords, mounted on a plain-vanilla chord progression, can hardly be called inspired.

I make the foregoing points not to disparage "Those Draftin' Blues" as a jazz tune. The qualifications for a composition to be a good jazz vehicle do not coincide with the requirements for success as a pop tune.

(As an aside, quite a few tunes that we regard today as staples of the jazz repertoire did not make it in the popular market. One such title that comes readily to mind is "China Boy". The reprint copy in my collection suggests that "China Boy" was originally a pseudo-oriental lullaby, meant to be played slowly. In fact, it's never-heard verse couldn't breathe if played at the heady pace typically used for "China Boy" today.

It seems unlikely that "China Boy" was a commercial success as a pop song. Copies are so rare that, in thirty years of collecting sheet music, I have never seen an original edition of it, nor has an original ever turned up on any of the lists regularly sent to me by dealers. Yet, I doubt that there is a sizeable Dixieland festival that takes place in the U. S. today at which "China Boy" isn't played at least once.)

My reason for observing that "Those Draftin' Blues" is not a remarkable piece of composition relates to the effort to trace the tune to its roots. Once we've located its first publication, we can ask ourselves if there is anything that precedes the song sheet - that is, did Maceo Pinkard write this tune, or does it have some pre-existing life that Pinkard appropriated, much as W. C. Handy (as Handy freely admitted) adopted melodies he heard from itinerant singers into his world-famous blues?

Because "Those Draftin' Blues" is a relatively ordinary work from the viewpoint of musical structure, and because Pinkard is known to have composed several other more successful and imaginative numbers, I have no trouble reaching the following conclusions: (1) Pinkard had no need to "steal" this fairly commonplace idea. (2) He was certainly capable of writing something at or above the level of inspiration found in "Those Draftin' Blues". (3) The composition does, most likely, start with him.

Having formed those views, I'll turn to the persistent rumor, which I've seen from time to time (most recently in an article in the June 1991 *West Coast Rag*), that the "Storyville Blues" theme can be traced back to 1897, that it originated in New Orleans, and that it is attributable to Tom Turpin, the great ragtime pianist from St. Louis. Personally, I have never believed the Turpin attribution - the musical structure of "Storyville Blues" is totally unlike any portion of Turpin's authenticated compositions of which I'm aware.

However, to dispose of this question, I called my friend Trebor Tichenor, a world-class expert on piano rolls and ragtime sheet music, the excellent pianist for the St. Louis Ragtimers, and probably the foremost authority on the activities of St. Louis-based turn-of-the-century ragtimers. I called Treb at the right time, because he was just putting to bed a book on Turpin, projected for eventual publication by the Smithsonian.

"Storyville Blues"

Treb had also heard that Turpin has been put forth as having written the "Storyville Blues" theme, but he does not believe this claim. Treb has never found any evidence tending to substantiate Turpin's authorship. Further, Treb agrees with me that the tune is stylistically at odds with the musical portrait of Turpin emerging from Turpin's other established works. In the absence of concrete evidence to the contrary, Treb's opinion on this point is good enough for me.

With regard to the alleged New Orleans origins of the "Storyville Blues" theme, I called another friend, Al Rose, author of several major volumes of jazz lore and probably the definitive voice on early Crescent City jazz tunes. Al said that, to his knowledge, the tune has no New Orleans connection and that he knows of no reason why it should not be thought of as having been written by Maceo Pinkard at the time of its publication in 1918. Again, unless someone comes up with something more solid than hearsay and speculation, Al's pronouncement on this matter ends the discussion as far as I'm concerned.

At this point, we've concluded that the correct title for "Storyville Blues" is "Those Draftin' Blues" (and I think it should be played under that title going forward), that it was not written by Tom Turpin, and that it was written by Maceo Pinkard for publication in the song sheet that illustrates this column. Having done so, we need to examine another loose end about the tune.

Most contemporary renditions of the number end with a variation on the chorus that begins each phrase with a series of ascending half-notes played in a crescendo. This chorus does not appear in the original sheet music (nor, Trebor informs me, in Maceo Pinkard's piano roll of "Those Draftin' Blues"). Where did this chorus come from?

Oddly enough, the general genre discographies are not usually indexed by song title. However, my examination of three references that are, Roger Kinkle's *The Complete Encyclopedia Of Popular Music 1900-1950* and Brian Rust's discographies of jazz records and of British dance bands, produces only two citations to issued vintage-period records of "Those Draftin' Blues". The first is a 1918 side by Wilbur Sweatman and the second is a 1940 rendition by Skeets Tolbert. I have not heard them, so I don't know if either contains the crescendo chorus.[*]

Although I can't be certain that there are no others, I believe the next three recordings of this theme are Johnson's 1942 version; Lu Watters' Yerba Buena Jazz Band's 1946 version (which was titled, for reasons discussed below, "Bienville Blues"); and Turk Murphy's Jazz Band's 1950 version (reissued on <u>Good Time Jazz L-12027</u>). I have all three in my collection. The first two do not contain the crescendo chorus, but Turk's does.

I have seen it said somewhere, although I can't recall the reference (but I do remember that no supporting evidence was given for the statement), that Turk Murphy wrote the crescendo chorus. In an attempt to nail this point down, with the generous assistance of clarinetist (and leader of the Zenith Jazz Band) Earl Scheelar,

---

[*Author's note: After this column was published, I received communications from two generous readers, Pete Pepke and Don McGrath, confirming that the crescendo chorus does not appear on either the Sweatman or the Tolbert 78.]

| TEXAS SHOUT: HOW DIXIELAND JAZZ WORKS |

I put the question to Turk's widow, Harriet, and the following alumni of Turk's combo: Bob Helm, Wally Rose, Pete Clute, Bill Carroll, Bill Armstrong and Jim Maihack.

Of those who had any opinion on the subject, all believed that Turk wrote the crescendo chorus. However, as reported below, only Jim Maihack was able to cite an instance in support of that view from his own first-hand knowledge. (To be precise, Bob Helm was uncertain when first asked - by Earl -, but when I asked him again a few weeks later, Bob was willing to say definitely that Turk wrote the crescendo chorus. I'm not sure, in light of the sequence of events, how much weight to give Bob's second try.)

Jim told me of one occasion when Turk described a conversation some years ago between himself (Turk) and Ward Kimball, trombonist/leader of the Firehouse Five Plus Two. In that discussion, Kimball told Turk that the FH5 had recently waxed an album made up entirely of traditional material. Turk concluded his story by saying to Jim words to the following effect: "I didn't have the heart to tell Ward that I had written that one part of 'Storyville Blues' myself". (Incidentally, the recording Kimball referred to was released as Good Time Jazz M12040, entitled "Dixieland Favorites"; it includes a 3/21/60 performance of "Storyville Blues" played with the crescendo chorus.)

Even without regard to the foregoing anecdote, looking at the question from a purely musical viewpoint, I am prepared to believe that Turk is the composer of the crescendo chorus. At the same 5/8/50 session at which his band first waxed "Storyville Blues", Turk also recorded "By And By". On the latter number, the band plays an eight-bar interlude in which the horns are voiced in whole and half notes, much like the crescendo chorus of "Storyville Blues". This eight-bar interlude does not appear in my two hymn-book editions of the music to "By and By" (which are titled "When Morning Comes" and "When The Morning Comes"). These circumstances suggest to me that Turk wrote the eight-bar interlude, and that he did the same sort of thing for its session-mate, "Storyville Blues".

For whatever it's worth, the rideout on Turk's performance of "See, See, Rider" on Columbia CL 650 is a variation which, as far as I know, had not appeared in any previously recorded version of the tune. It is a chorus in which the horns play a climbing figure in harmony. To me, this "See, See, Rider" finale, which I'd guess that Turk wrote, bears stylistic similarities to the crescendo chorus of "Storyville Blues". Thus, I'm satisfied to credit the evidence supplied by Jim Maihack and to attribute the "Storyville" crescendo to Turk.

As a postscript, I asked Helm and Rose, who were on the Watters 78, how Watters came to play the number under the title "Bienville Blues". Both were sure that Turk had picked the title, but neither could recall why.

Jim Maihack also supplied that missing piece. Turk told Jim that he (Turk) picked the title from a map of New Orleans' French Quarter and used it on a whim to see what would happen. He (Turk) added that, sure enough a few years later another band did record the tune as "Bienville Blues".

What questions remain? Well, I am a bit puzzled by Stuart's 1962 comment, quoted above, that, since Johnson's 1942 recording "the tune has since been recorded under several titles" (emphasis added). Between 1942 and 1962, to my knowledge, it was recorded under only two titles, "Storyville Blues" and "Bienville

"Storyville Blues"

Blues". I wouldn't think that two instances are enough to constitute "several", but maybe I'm being too picky over Stuart's phrasing.

Anyway, if you're still awake, you now know as much as I do about "Those Draftin' Blues/Storyville Blues/Bienville Blues". I would be very interested in knowing if there is any additional reliable first-hand or documentary evidence on this subject.

TEXAS SHOUT: HOW DIXIELAND JAZZ WORKS

Original Memphis Five   1920s
Photo from The Record Changer

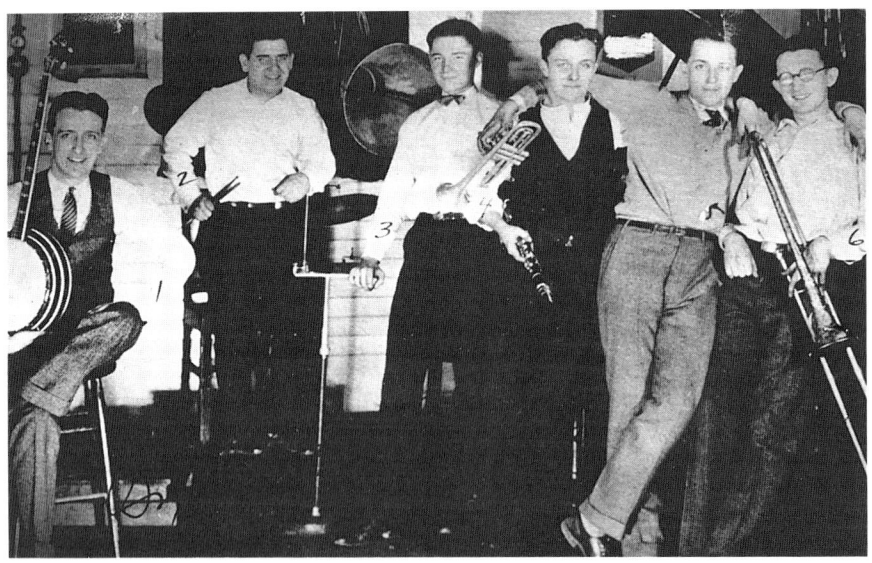

Bix and his Rhythm Jugglers   1925
Photo from Downbeat

CHAPTER 26   WHITE NEW ORLEANS

In New Orleans, as jazz was being developed, there were three fairly distinct styles of Dixieland. Two were played principally by Black musicians, one by whites.

The "downtown" Blacks, including many Creoles, played a schooled, technically accomplished type of jazz that is heard on almost all of the recordings made during the 1920s by Black musicians from the Crescent City - Oliver, Bechet, Armstrong, Ory, Noone, Morton, Dodds, etc. The "uptown" Blacks played a more functional, direct, dance-hall style that did not achieve much critical notice until the revival of the early 1940s, when it was heard on the records of Bunk Johnson.

The jazz style of the early white New Orleans musicians was once the most famous style of jazz in the world. It was the first kind of jazz to appear on record, bursting on the scene in 1917 via tremendously successful 78s by the Original Dixieland Jazz Band.

Today this style, which I call "white New Orleans", has virtually disappeared from the face of the earth. I think that's too bad. I'd like to devote the remainder of this column to describing the characteristics of white New Orleans, to offering my views as to the reason for its neglect in the Dixieland community, and, I hope, to pique your curiosity about it to the point where you will seek out some recordings of it.

Because the ODJB's records sold so well, because these were pioneering sides that let the general public hear jazz for the first time, and also because the band was a wonderful band whose recordings still retain the power to exhilarate the listener, it was an extremely influential band, perhaps the most influential of its day. Other budding jazzmen in New York, where the ODJB's first sides were made, obviously paid close attention - the white New Orleans style is clearly carried forward in the various New York-based Phil Napoleon units (such as the Original Memphis Five and Ladd's Black Aces) and those featuring the prolifically recorded cornetist Red Nichols. The first great white jazz soloist, cornetist Bix Beiderbecke, learned the white New Orleans style from playing along with the ODJB's recordings (and, indeed, continued to record tunes from the ODJB's discography throughout his career).

Moreover, the white New Orleans style exerted a lasting effect on the Dixieland repertoire that continues down to the present day. Even allowing for the fact that there seems to have been a common body of themes floating around New Orleans, and that the various musicians in town felt free to draw from these themes and claim composer credit therefor, the ODJB's compositions still form an impressive part of the body of standards that every Dixieland musician knows - "At The Jazz Band Ball", "Tiger Rag", "Original Dixieland One-Step", Fidgety Feet", "Clarinet Marmalade" and "Margie" fall in that category.

TEXAS SHOUT: HOW DIXIELAND JAZZ WORKS

Further, evergreens like "(Back Home In) Indiana", "The Darktown Strutters' Ball", "Jazz Me Blues", "Royal Garden Blues", "Alice Blue Gown" and "St. Louis Blues" undoubtedly can thank the ODJB's groundbreaking recordings thereof for giving them a running start in becoming the jazz standards that they are. Actually, the ODJB had a virtually flawless ear for picking tunes. A 1990s combo that decides to learn titles at random from the ODJB's list will run across winners almost every time - "Dolly, I Love You", "'Lasses Candy", "Broadway Rose", "Home Again Blues", "My Baby's Arms", "Mammy O'Mine" and so on. As a personal note, the very first number I recorded as a soloist, and still one of my most sure-fire audience-pleasers today two decades later, was one to which I was introduced by the ODJB, Irving Berlin's great post-World War I comedy song, "I've Got My Captain Working For Me Now".

The Original Dixieland Jazz Band's shadow was so far-reaching that, from time to time, I have heard the style of Dixieland that the ODJB played referred to as the "Dixieland" style. However, I find it confusing to use the word "Dixieland" that way.

First of all, such use is not commonly accepted throughout the Dixieland community - in fact, the white New Orleans style is so invisible on the current scene that some commentators seem to be unaware that it exists as a separate Dixieland style. Second, as I said in my very first "Texas Shout" column in the November-December 1989 *WCR*, I believe the name "Dixieland" should be reserved as an umbrella term to describe all pre-swing jazz styles (including revivalist styles thereof).

For those reasons, I am suggesting the term "white New Orleans" to describe the style of Dixieland music being discussed in today's column. You will not see that phrase so employed in much other critical writing about jazz, but "white New Orleans" is sufficiently descriptive that, if you use it going forward, I think your listeners will readily understand what you mean.

Who played white New Orleans? In addition to the ODJB and the others mentioned above, some of the best-remembered names include the Chicago-based New Orleans Rhythm Kings and a number of fine bands that recorded during the twenties in the Crescent City, such as the New Orleans Owls and one of my all-time favorite combos, the Halfway House Orchestra.

What are the distinguishing characteristics of white New Orleans? You can't tell it by the feeling of the rhythm, which may be either two-beat or four-beat. However, there are three factors for which you should listen.

First, like most of the Dixieland styles (hot dance and Chicago being the exceptions), white New Orleans is an ensemble-oriented style - that is, the ability to improvise effectively in an ensemble context is more highly valued than solo skill or reading skill. Second, the musicians tend to play with a reasonably "legitimate" tone and attack within a context of cleanly executed routines (sharp-edged breaks or stoptimes, crisp beginnings and endings, etc.). Third, and this is the most critical factor, the white New Orleans style has no significant blues content; it tends to stay within a more narrow emotional pitch, one of optimism, generating an outgoing, breezy, atmosphere.

It is that latter factor, I think, that has caused white New Orleans to be dismissed by many jazz critics and to be neglected by today's Dixielanders. When

White New Orleans

the Black New Orleans jazzmen started to record in 1922 and 1923, one could easily hear the higher blues content in their playing - the growls, smears and gutbucket timbres emanating from the phonograph. It was obvious that this music had a broader emotional spectrum than the type of jazz that had been recorded up to that time. Anyone who is going to listen to a series of consecutive Dixieland performances will find the experience more satisfying if the emotional range varies along the way.

As a result, I believe that the white New Orleans players are often viewed as one-dimensional performers who "can't" play the blues. Moreover, because they tend to exhibit a high degree of precision, and to play with fairly legitimate tone and attack, white New Orleans bands are regarded in some circles as generic, good-time Dixieland units whose music is on the shallow side.

Shortly before writing this column, for example, I read a review of a Red Nichols reissue album in which the critic, although recommending the album, nevertheless noted that Nichols' other virtues overcame his inability to play the blues. Along the same lines, in his excellent survey of twenties jazz, *Early Jazz*, Gunther Schuller simply forgot to include a chapter on Nichols (one of the most widely recorded of twenties jazzmen), somewhat shamefacedly repairing the omission via a catch-up chapter in his next volume, dealing with the swing years.

I collected albums voraciously throughout the entire 12-inch LP era. Yet, as far as I know, no U. S. producer - even including the tiny completist/collector labels - ever released an entire LP devoted to reissues of sides by the Halfway House Orchestra or the New Orleans Owls or the twenties cuts by the original Memphis Five.

About the only artists playing the white New Orleans style who have not been overlooked, or damned by faint praise by the critical majority, are the New Orleans Rhythm Kings and Bix Beiderbecke. I'd guess that the NORK's reputation survives not only because it was a good band, but also because its records were the primary ones listened to by Eddie Condon and the other artists who created Chicago style, a Dixieland branch that is still going strong and is widely admired, one which incorporates many tunes waxed by the NORK as staples of its repertoire. Bix's records, of course, reveal a tone of exceptional loveliness and a gift for shaping melodic lines of such originality and beauty that, without need for blues content, they display a gem-like perfection.

The ODJB's 78s are regularly reissued, but many critics believe that band to be mainly of historical interest. I am not one of them; as you can gather from the above remarks, I love the ODJB.

I believe that white New Orleans Dixieland jazz is generally misunderstood, too often judged by the wrong criteria. In my view, you can see white New Orleans players and bands in proper perspective more easily if you remember that they are working within a distinctive Dixieland style, one that maintains an upbeat mood and does not have significant blues content or other emotions. If you do so, you are less

TEXAS SHOUT: HOW DIXIELAND JAZZ WORKS

likely to criticize its musicians for failing to do something that they are not trying to do in the first place, and you are more likely to judge the music for its strengths, which are considerable.

It helps that process if you step back a pace or two and remember what jazz is all about. As I discussed in "Texas Shout" in November and December of 1991, I believe the distinguishing characteristic of jazz, the one thing that sets it apart from other musics, is its feeling of compelling and passionate forward momentum, often referred to as "hot and swinging" jazz.

Note that this distinction has nothing to do with emotional range or with improvisation. Although I have often seen it said that jazz goes hand in hand with blues content and with improvisation, I personally believe that neither characteristic is essential to a jazz performance and that neither characteristic is unique to jazz.

I don't want to beat this subject to death again in today's column, but with respect to emotional range, you can find the complete range of emotion in many types of non-jazz music, such as grand opera, ordinary American popular music of 1900-1950, country, folk and ragtime. You don't need to go to jazz to hear music that is blue, happy, nostalgic, humorous, wistful or any other emotion you wish to choose.

Similarly, improvisation - the extemporaneous rendition of musical passages during a performance - is a regular, accepted part of many non-jazz musics, e.g., blues & gospel, country & western, rock 'n roll, ethnic (the raga music of India, among others), folk and, yes, even ragtime (notwithstanding the opinion of some ragtimers that the only worthwhile ragtime is composed in advance and executed as written). Improvisation, in and of itself, doesn't constitute "jazzing up" a piece of music nor is improvisation essential to jazz. It's not too difficult, for example, to find hot dance jazz rides from the twenties, swing from the thirties, progressive or bop from the forties, that contain no improvisation whatever and are as hot and swinging as any jazz fan could want.

The quality that sets jazz apart from other music is that its players articulate the notes, whether blue notes or non-blue, written or improvised, in a way that is hot and swinging. One could conclude from that statement that the hotter and swingier a jazz performance is, the jazzier it is.

Said another way, a hot swinging jazz performance which displays only one emotion is jazzier, more worthy of a higher ranking on the jazz scale of artistic merit, than a slightly less hot, slightly swinging performance which contains a wide range of blues and other emotions. That is the conclusion I've reached after much thought on the subject, but I will warn you that the majority of jazz criticism I've seen does not agree with me.

I believe most critics would say that, at least to some degree, a jazzman may (and should, if the goal can't be attained any other way) cut back on swing and heat in order to achieve a broad range of emotional expression. Doing so may well produce a satisfying overall result. I might even prefer to listen to it under some circumstances. However, in my opinion, a jazzman who follows that approach winds up with a product that may be more well-rounded, but is also less jazzy.

At any rate, if you adopt my view of the matter, the work of the white New Orleans Dixielanders gets a new lease on life. If you're looking for flat-out heat and

White New Orleans

drive, I'll match the blistering 1/27/27 Columbia version of "After You've Gone" by the Charleston Chasers with just about anything you want to name. For sheer effortless straight-ahead steadily building momentum, Albert Brunies' incredible Halfway House Orchestra was the equal of any group that recorded in the twenties.

If you don't knock musicians for failing to play blues, you're much more likely to be able to appreciate the talents of Red Nichols, one of the most technically gifted cornetists who ever played our music. He had a big round brassy tone, an authoritative attack, the ability to hit pitch dead center across the full range of his instrument and a flexibility which enabled him to execute acrobatics on his horn that would eviscerate most cornetists. Moreover, Nichols' exceptional skills stayed with him throughout a long and productive career, his latter-day Five Pennies unit being one of the best Dixieland bands of its day, its 1958 Marineland concert on Capital ranking as a classic of the revival period.

There are those who seem to feel that, by praising someone, you are somehow denigrating or downgrading someone else. Let me say, then, that by trying to raise your consciousness towards the merits of the white New Orleans Dixielanders, I am most emphatically not saying that their accomplishments in any way diminish the work of such immortals as Oliver, Morton, Dodds, Armstrong, Teagarden, Hines and all the others on your list and mine of all-time greats of our music.

I am saying, however, that the white New Orleans material remains thoroughly satisfying when heard today, that some of it deserves to rank alongside the best Dixieland jazz ever waxed, that it should be recognized as part of a distinctive and valid Dixieland style having objectives and standards somewhat different than those of the Black New Orleans musicians, and that its musicians should be judged according to how well they met their objectives and standards. And, I submit, if their music is viewed in that light, it deserves a place on our stages and in the record bins that is larger than the zero it gets now.

Fine, you say, I'm sold, Tex. Now where can I hear some of this great music?

Well, that's a tough question. As I've said, the records haven't been easy to come by. However, now that the CD era is upon us, I seem to be seeing more archival CD sets that present complete recordings of given artists or bands. Perhaps we're due for some reissues of the New Orleans white bands of the twenties, Phil Napoleon, Red Nichols, Miff Mole, etc.

European labels have been quicker to recognize the value of the white New Orleans style. Most of the recordings I own of white New Orleans are imports obtained directly from England or through domestic specialty dealers.

It takes a bit of digging to find the right stores or dealers, but if you keep your eyes open reading the Dixieland press, you'll run across some. I subscribe to a couple of British jazz magazines, keeping a want list culled from records covered in the reviews or ads - sooner or later I'll discover the albums on a dealer's flyer or in the rack of some big-city specialty store.

Where can you hear the white New Orleans style at a festival? Beats me. Because the records haven't been around, today's bands have had no chance to pick up any significant influence from the white New Orleans musicians. As a result, you can discern only occasional flashes of the style in a musician here and there or in portions of the music of a band that mostly plays some other style.

| TEXAS SHOUT: HOW DIXIELAND JAZZ WORKS |

For example, I hear some white New Orleans surface from time to time when listening to the Hot Frogs, a band that plays a variety of Dixieland from funky New Orleans-ish four-beat to good-natured West Coast revival. The presence is doubtlessly attributable to trumpeter Mike Silverman's acknowledged appreciation of Red Nichols.

Some of the early Buck Creek recordings contained an element of white New Orleans. This was surely a coincidence because, to my knowledge (and I've played a number of gigs with the band), none of the Buck Creekers pays much (if any) attention to the early white New Orleans style bands. At any rate, that flavor isn't as strong as it used to be, Buck Creek apparently having elected to move closer to Black New Orleans as filtered through the influence of the New Black Eagles.

However, this column was inspired by the arrival on my doorstep of a review copy of JSC 001, "Premiere", the debut recording of the Jazz Salvation Company, a contemporary sextet displaying a light-footed bouncing two-beat, a well-knit ensemble that pays attention to dynamics, and an outgoing, easy-to-like presentation. As I listened through the tape's 55 minutes, I realized that, in spirit and general approach, the Salvations could well have handled the gig at the Halfway House on Albert Brunies' night off.

After taking notes on the dozen rides, I concluded that the Jazz Salvation routines were imaginative, varied and comfortably executed, displaying engaging rhythm, intelligent use of subunits, preferred space for the team's two best soloists (clarinetist Duane Ewing and pianist Red Thomas) and the good sense to concentrate on the band's strongest features. Despite the fact that a few cuts continued after inspiration had run dry, and the other soloists (though idiomatic) had little to say, I ranked the cassette as an above-average release that had its own personality. I'd give it four stars (out of a possible five) if I were covering it in "This Month's Records".

However, I decided to talk about it here as a way of telling you about a style that I personally enjoy very much. (I've already told you in these pages that my Halfway House album is my desert island record.) I'd like to alert you to the fact that the white New Orleans musicians did have their own way of playing Dixieland, a worthwhile way which is not, as some writers seem to believe, some kind of flawed imitation of the Black New Orleans approach.

And if all else fails in the record stores, you can get a fairly representative snapshot of the way the style operates by picking up the Jazz Salvation Company's audiocassette. It's $11.00 postpaid from Jazz Salvation Company, 5330 Winter Creek Road, Santa Rosa, California 95404.

White New Orleans

New Orleans Rhythm Kings   1922   *Photo by Bloom-Chicago*

Original New Orleans Owls   1924   *Photo by Rene Gelpi*

Charleston Chasers   1928   *Photo by George Hoefer*

The Jazz Salvation Company   *Photographer Unknown*

Hot Frogs Jumping Jazz Band   *Photo by E. J. McNicol*

CHAPTER 27   WEST COAST REVIVAL

Through the years, there have been many enormously influential Dixieland bands. However, only one combo has ever singlehandedly created a new style of Dixieland. The band is Lu Watters' Yerba Buena Jazz Band and the style is called West Coast revival (sometimes known as San Francisco style).

I'd like to use today's column to discuss the characteristics of the West Coast revival style. Along the way, I'll toss in some thoughts regarding what I believe to be misconceptions about it in certain areas of the Dixieland community.

Trumpeter Watters and his sidemen were professional musicians making a living playing the prevailing popular and jazz styles of the late 1930s, essentially swing and big-band dance. At that time, the most common form of Dixieland was Chicago style, the Dixieland style that best fits the general solo orientation of swing musicians.

Watters and his colleagues had been listening to small-band jazz recordings of the 1920s, particularly the downtown New Orleans style 78s of King Oliver, Jelly Roll Morton and Louis Armstrong. Hearing an approach to the music that was hardly to be found at all any more; in instrumentation employing two-beat rhythm, banjo and tuba, all musical devices not employed by swing musicians; and some worthwhile tunes that had been totally forgotten, they decided to get together after hours to revive this instrumentation and repertoire.

After some jam sessions at the Bay Area's Big Bear Tavern, the band went into the studio on December 19, 1941 to wax eight sides which were released on the Jazz Man label. The lineup was Lu Watters, Bob Scobey, cornets; Ellis Horne, clarinet; Turk Murphy, trombone; Wally Rose, piano; Clancy Hayes, Russ Bennett, banjos; Dick Lammi, tuba; and Bill Dart, drums.

The YBJB's sound resembled nothing previously heard on the Dixieland scene. It touched off a storm of controversy between the band's supporters and detractors involving, in my view, a degree of misunderstanding on both sides that continues down to the present day.

Life is often a series of trade-offs. One gives up something in order to get more of something else.

Up until the YBJB's recordings, jazzmen had chosen to go for as much buoyancy as possible, to get the sound "off the ground", to achieve the springy effect that was considered to epitomize "swinging". In order to do so, one must typically give up a measure of volume, a tradeoff which also involves some relaxation of punch. Said another way, few instrumentalists are able to maintain a feeling of buoyancy, of floating on the beat, while simultaneously playing loudly and with lots of muscle.

The Yerba Buena Jazz Band, judging from the music it produced, made (consciously or not) the opposite choice. It elected to go for power, and to give up both dynamics and buoyancy to get the maximum amount of power.

| TEXAS SHOUT: HOW DIXIELAND JAZZ WORKS |

Thus, the most easily identifiable characteristic of West Coast revival is its brassy, full-throated, forceful ensemble sound. It comes at you like a steamroller. Instead of inviting you to lift your feet and soar over the dance floor, it demands that you strut across it in much the same way that a military band stirs you to "second line" by marching nearby down the sidewalk.

The YBJB's ensemble was totally devoid of dynamics. It played at top volume all the time, on every recording Watters ever made, generating about the loudest sound ever heard from a jazz band of its size - an aggressive, outgoing, pile-driving sound that grabs you by the shirt front and drags you along with it.

Its rhythm, instead of following the prevailing trend toward lightness, was the heavyweight champion of jazz. Lammi's groaning tuba came down on the beat like a ton of bricks, the two banjos and Dart's metronomic wood blocks set up a beat that would penetrate the tinnest ear, and Rose's two-fisted piano kept going throughout the sides, rolling up and down the keyboard behind both solos and ensembles.

The jazz world hardly knew what to make of the YBJB. Pianists of the thirties had followed Earl Hines' lead toward spare, single-note treble lines, spiced by left-hand jabs, letting the bass, drums and (if there was a stringed instrument) guitar deliver the expressed beat formerly handled by the left hand - all while staying out of the soloists' way. Drummers had been moving away from the steady, booming bass drum, heading for the lighter sounds on their kits - the snare, the ride cymbal, the closed hi-hat, the brushes. Softer-edged instruments, such as string bass and guitar, were typical, setting up less likelihood of clashing with the relatively dense lines employed by swing soloists vs. the preceding generation of Dixielanders. The Yerba Buenans turned their backs on all of these developments.

Not surprisingly, many members of the jazz community did not respond well to such rejection of their values. It was commonly asserted, and still is in some places, that Watters had set jazz back twenty years and that his music did not swing. Actually, neither accusation is justified.

Although the YBJB's rhythmic feeling has more in common with a brass band than a 1930s swing band, it clearly swings. The YBJB has a wonderful cohesion, and all of its sidemen play with a jazz feeling. Compare the Yerba Buena Jazz Band with, for example, a circus band or a military band, and you will recognize right away that the YBJB is indeed playing jazz, that it generates a heat and drive that these other, somewhat similar, units lack.

As for setting jazz back in time, quite the reverse is true. The YBJB's sound was so new and different that it inspired disciples who maintained its approach as a separate Dixieland style.

I have occasionally seen it said that Watters was trying to imitate King Oliver's Creole Jazz Band. Perhaps the surviving members of the YBJB can say definitively whether such was the case, but based on what I hear on the records, I can't go along with that statement.

Watters may have gotten the idea for a two-trumpet front line from hearing Oliver's discs, but even a casual listener comparing the records should be able to recognize within the first few bars that the Yerba Buena Jazz Band sounds nothing at all like the Creole Jazz Band. Watters and his men, as I've said, were accomplished professional musicians who were perfectly capable of recreating the twenties recordings note-for-note, with the proper timbre and inflections, if they wanted to do so. If they had been trying to imitate Oliver, or any other 1920s jazzman, it's hard for me to believe that they would have missed this goal so completely.

What Watters did was what all good jazzmen should do. He got under the skin of the music, came to understand it fully, and played it his way. He found a way to make a distinctive and personal statement within the basic Dixieland framework.

Indeed, it was because the YBJB didn't sound like any other band that it was able to create a new Dixieland style. If it had sounded like the Creole Jazz Band, or the Hot Five, or the Red Hot Peppers, I doubt that anyone would have remembered Watters for long. Offhand, I can't think of any jazzman who's attained a truly lasting reputation by imitating some other jazzman.

Because most jazz critics know that it was Watters who brought the banjo and tuba back to Dixieland, it seems to me that many of them are too quick to conclude that any banjo-tuba Dixieland band is automatically a West Coast revival unit. Such a conclusion ignores the fact that, prior to the wide adoption of electrical recording around 1925, just about all jazz bands with string and bass instruments utilized tuba and banjo, which better fitted the older acoustic recording techniques than guitar and string bass.

There were already five Dixieland styles up and running before the YBJB came along - white New Orleans, hot dance, uptown New Orleans, Chicago and downtown New Orleans. All of these recorded with tuba and banjo on occasion. The presence of a tuba and banjo does not necessarily mean that a band is a West Coast revival band; regardless of its instrumentation, and regardless of whether it plays with a two-beat or four-beat pulse, a combo has to generate that feeling of going for substantial power to be a post-Watters unit.

What are the other distinguishing characteristics of West Coast revival Dixieland? The striving for power is the easiest one to hear, but there are a few others. They all result from the fact that the style itself traces back to one small group of specific musicians, i.e., the customary way of playing a given instrument in West Coast revival style depends in large part on the way a specific Yerba Buenan executed his assignment.

For example, as noted above, the pianist tends to have a decided streak of ragtime in his playing, and to play in a strong two-handed way throughout the performance, just as Wally Rose did (and still does). I cut my jazz piano teeth on Rose's playing as recorded with Watters and Murphy. I didn't fully realize how different this approach was, opposite some other Dixieland styles, until the time years ago when I was hired for a gig with a band that proved to be a Chicago-style band; I played so many notes that I just about drove the clarinetist crazy (the leader and I got things straightened out at the first break).

Similarly, the West Coast revival style has an outgoing spirit tempered by only a moderate blues content. Some of this blues element came from Bob Scobey, whose distinctive, incisive trumpet reflected a blend of Armstrong and the straight-ahead Chicago lead tradition. Most of the blues feeling, however, came from the two Yerba Buenans who had the largest degree of blues in their sounds - trombonist Turk Murphy, whose rasping timbre and sure-footed counterlines showed the attention he'd paid to lowdown sliphornists like Roy Palmer and Kid Ory, and clarinetist Bob Helm (not on the initial YBJB session, but the definitive YBJB stickman), whose thick, slurry lines were about the only ones in the 1940s electing to follow Johnny Dodds' path (while everyone else was trying in vain to catch Goodman).

Despite all the controversy, Watters lived to have the last laugh. He saw the West Coast revival style spread throughout the world, as bands from Europe to Japan unabashedly generate the YBJB's sound.

Further, Watters saw how common his style became on the U. S. festival scene. Take a typical lineup for a Dixieland festival that hires organized bands. Subtract out the names that don't really play Dixieland - the big swing bands, the ragtime orchestras, the country units, the blues bands, the pop orchestras, the Latin combos, etc. If you sort the remaining Dixieland outfits into the seven Dixieland styles, I'll bet that, at many festivals, you'll find more these days in the West Coast revival category than any other.

I was introduced to Dixieland jazz via the West Coast revival style, first through the Firehouse Five Plus Two and then Turk Murphy and Lu Watters. Turk is, as many of you know, my all-time favorite musician. Although I have come to enjoy all seven styles of Dixieland, plus certain closely-related music, I still feel a special response to a Yerba Buena-ish combo in full cry or a rusty-gate Murphy-ish trombone solo.

Even so, from time to time in this column, I've done a little scolding of certain elements of the Dixieland community that has probably fallen most heavily on West Coast revivalists. I've done so because there is a pernicious type of archivalist mentality afoot among Dixielanders that, without meaning to do so, actively works to stop the music dead in its tracks and turn it into a museum piece - and this attitude is more apparent among West Coast revival musicians and their fans than in other styles.

I know whereof I speak. Coming to the music through Turk, as I did, I couldn't help but admire his dedication to digging out underplayed items and presenting them with obvious respect for their sources.

I strove to follow what I interpreted as Turk's lead. In chording numbers for my Red Lion Jazz Band, I always tried to get the original sheet music, faithfully setting down each passing chord for the band exactly as it was in the piano score. I always tried to check out the "original" recording, to see if it contained special strains or features that I needed to include to "legitimize" the Red Lions' presentation.

However, two things happened that helped me put such research and effort into a different perspective. One was my increasing involvement in reviewing all kinds of Dixieland records and the other was recurrent conflicts among (1) the sheet music scores, (2) the vintage recording(s), and, sometimes, (3) my own musical instincts.

West Coast Revival

As I did more record reviewing, a broad range of review copies began arriving at my door, some of which were in styles of Dixieland that I hadn't initially preferred or to which I'd paid little attention. Wanting to be as fair and objective as possible in assessing each one, even if it was a recording that I might not have purchased for myself, I tried to review the record from the point of view of the artist - to determine what his objectives were, how well he'd achieved them and, along the way, whether I thought the objectives were worthy ones.

I found myself discovering new elements of the music, ones that were not emphasized as much in West Coast revival Dixieland, but ones which were enjoyable and valid on their own terms. I came to recognize that the common elements among all styles of Dixieland (in addition to the basic musical vocabulary) are heat and swing, and that a lack of these two elements cannot be compensated for via obscure repertoire, ingenious arrangements or anything else.

As dozens of albums flowed in each year, I also came to put a premium on creativity within the idiom. I received lots of competent, swinging, enjoyable discs by bands that were happy to walk the middle of the road, to play the standard tunes typically utilized within their particular branches of Dixieland, and to play them the customary way. I could, and still do, give these recordings a recommendation that tells the reader they're worth their cost (the equivalent of a "three stars out of five", or an average, rating in my "This Month's Records" column for *WCR)*. However, when you've heard as many records as I have, and if you believe (as I do) that Dixieland is an art form and not just background music for good times, you are going to save your highest ratings for musicians and bands having something original to say.

One of the conflicts referred to above occurred whenever I noticed that the original sheet music might have a passage that would be very interesting when rendered by a solo piano (song sheets are typically scored for voice and solo piano), but would be awkward for a full band to handle smoothly. Sometimes, while working over the tune at the keyboard, my hands and mind would want to skip past a passing chord in the music to get a stronger feeling of forward momentum. Should I follow my instincts and chart the swinging chord pattern, or should I force the Red Lions to fight their way through the "right" one?

Other conflicts occurred between the sheet music and the recordings with respect to melody line or chords. Which was "right"?

Moreover, as my LP collection expanded, I realized that there were several vintage recordings of certain tunes, each of which could be considered an "original" recording. Which of those was "right"? Bix's 78 of "Rhythm King" opens with a horns-only introduction, while the Coon-Sanders Nighthawks begin with a scored Charleston-like stoptime figure. Why was Bix's version always turning out to be the one everybody played?

Contemplating these questions, I decided to resolve such conflicts by making the choice that I thought would lead to the greatest amount of heat and swing in the Red Lions' performance of the tune. As I became more and more convinced that this was the correct way to go, I began to re-examine some of the premises I'd been following, and had been discussing with other West Coast revival disciples. I decided that too many of us were misreading the scriptures as laid down by Watters and Murphy.

TEXAS SHOUT: HOW DIXIELAND JAZZ WORKS

Because the Yerba Buenans were reacting against the prevalence of Chicago style jazz in 1940, its devotees have sometimes read the movement as one in which anything that smacks too much of Chicago is to be avoided at all costs. They won't perform tunes the Chicagoans typically play, no matter how good those selections are. They'll avoid any musical devices normally employed by Chicagoans, even if those devices help get the tune to heat up and swing harder.

Because the Yerba Buenans sought out underplayed tunes, its disciples have sometimes read the movement as demanding that obscure tunes be played - the more obscure the better, regardless of the quality of the tune as a vehicle for swinging jazz. You can, they say, make up for a diminution of swing and heat by playing numbers most people haven't heard before, and the more unknown a title is, the less swing and heat you need to generate to justify playing it.

(Personally, I think that any musician who tells you that a tune like, say, "Royal Garden Blues" is "exhausted" is copping out. He's in effect admitting that he has so little imagination and creativity that he needs the help of a tune you don't know in order to show you something you haven't heard before.)

Because the Yerba Buenans were record collectors, its disciples have sometimes read the movement as one that insists upon replicating licks from old records as a way of playing the number "correctly". This reading has been carried to an extreme by bands that today will deliver, virtually note for note, exact renditions of performances by Lu Watters' Yerba Buena Jazz Band and Turk Murphy's San Francisco Jazz Band, even though those records were recorded in perfectly acceptable fidelity and are readily available at festival counters and well-stocked record stores. Moreover, fans of these clone bands apparently can't get enough of hearing these same renditions played over and over.

After a quarter-century of reviewing hundreds of records, I have little patience with musicians who deliberately avoid creativity and try to justify such action by citing what some jazzman in the past has done. All of the vintage jazzmen revered by today's copyists were themselves originals. I defy you to find a Lu Watters record that sounds anything like any previous waxing of the same tune. Furthermore, Watters and Murphy made no attempt to avoid worthwhile tunes whatever their source.

In short, the original West Coast revivalists were exceptionally creative people. Imitating their work may be well-intentioned, but it is not really going to keep vitality in the style. To pay tribute to Watters and Murphy in the proper way, a musician should get under the skin of their style, get below the mere notes played on the records and understand the approach so well that he plays it as naturally as breathing. Then he should do what the Yerba Buenans did - play West Coast revival, but with his own distinctive stamp.

I have preached this sermon before in this column. However, it is an important one to hear, I think, if you want the style to live, to grow beyond regurgitation of past triumphs.

I was inspired to go through this diatribe once again by the arrival at my home of review copies of two albums by a band that plays West Coast revival the right way, Seattle's Uptown Lowdown Jazz Band. One is a 57-minute tape, recorded live on a cruise, entitled "Cruisin' Avalon" and the other is a 68-minute studio session entitled "Business in F".

West Coast Revival

Throw on either one and you'll realize right away that this is a West Coast revival band, a brassy, two-cornet two-beat outfit that traces its heritage back to Watters and Murphy. After just a few more bars, you'll also realize that the ULJB has found its own voice within the style, a distinctive, instantly recognizable one.

The presence of the superb Paul Woltz as a sort of utility infielder, going from bass saxophone to alto saxophone (sometimes replacing the tuba), gives the band a distinctive, thicker sound that is, as far as I know, different from that of any other West Coast revival band. However, the ULJB doesn't stop there in terms of carrying West Coast revival in imaginative directions.

While they can blast out a rideout with as much volume as any two-trumpet band on the circuit, the Uptowners keep a remarkable balance in their rides via an intelligent use of dynamics. The softer passages put an extra control on the emotional pitch of the performances, making them more satisfactory than the efforts of certain bands I've heard (including some popular ones) which, in their efforts to duplicate Watters' and Murphy's full-volume approach, only succeed in getting noisy and in reaching the out chorus with nowhere to go in terms of building a big finale.

Further, leader Bert Barr's well-wrought arrangements for Uptown Lowdown are starting, in these more recent releases, to make more use of sub-units within a given selection, not only adding another measure of variety, but also making wider use of the high quality of the talent available within the ranks of this full-time professional unit. And, while these albums contain plenty of West Coast revival standbys and tasty obscurities, you'll also hear Uptown's own spin on such Chicago standbys as "Dinah" (red-hot jam spotlighting Woltz) and "Avalon" (juicy small combo).

The cruise album, in audiocassette format only, being an in-person date, has a few uneven tracks and some indifferent acoustics, but it's still a good buy. The band is relaxed, playing a relatively conventional post-Watters/Muphy program. I'd give it four stars in "This Month's Records".

"Business In F", available in CD or audiocassete, is another story, a highly imaginative, skillfully executed album that contains everything but the kitchen sink and yet never once puts a foot wrong. Its charts invariably bring out the best aspects of both the tunes and the players, including featured spots for most sidemen. This five-star item is probably Uptown's best release to date and one of the more original West Coast revival discs currently on the market.

ULJB CDs are $17, cassettes $12, plus $1 for shipping (1 or 2 units), from Uptown Lowdown Jazz Band, 2836 140th Avenue N. E., Bellevue, Washington 98005. Washington residents add 8.2% sales tax.

Today's column really ends here but I'd like to add one footnote before we leave the ULJB. Its devotees have dubbed the band's sound "Seattle style", which probably serves it well as a marketing gimmick. However, don't be seduced into thinking that Uptown plays a new "style" of Dixieland jazz.

Actually, Dixielanders use the word "style" in two senses. In the smaller sense, each player and band has its own way of playing Dixieland, its own "style" if you will. However, in the larger sense, there are, so far, only seven basic Dixieland styles: white New Orleans, downtown New Orleans, uptown New Orleans, hot dance, Chicago, West Coast revival and British trad. Everyone I've heard either fits dance, Chicago, West Coast revival and British trad. Everyone I've heard either fits into one of these categories or operates around the common borderlines between them.

To illustrate: Cornetists Bobby Hackett and Wild Bill Davison did not sound anything like each other. Each had his own instantly recognizable tone - Hackett's clear and warm, Davison's tart and saucy. Each had his own "style" of phrasing as well.

However, each was basically a Chicago style Dixielander. Both played regularly with Eddie Condon. Even though their sounds were different, you could replace one with the other in a typical Condon unit and none of the other players would have had to make any significant adjustment to accommodate the change. The basic rules and objectives would remain the same.

So, while one could say that Hackett and Davison each had his own "style", each operated squarely within Chicago style. So it is with Uptown Lowdown's "Seattle style", which is squarely within West Coast revival.

Lu Watters   1949   *Photo by Ed Lawless*

West Coast Revival

Lu Watters Yerba Buena Jazz Band   1940s
Photo from The Record Changer

Yerba Buena Brass - Turk Murphy, Lu Watters, Bob Scobey   1940s
Photo from The Record Changer

TEXAS SHOUT: HOW DIXIELAND JAZZ WORKS

South Frisco Jazz Band 1990s
Photo by Dan Polin

Uptown Lowdown Jazz Band 1980s
Photo by Dan Polin

Feb. 1993 West Coast Rag

CHAPTER 28   PERIODICALS

In "Texas Shout" for February 1991 and February 1992, I suggested some books about older-style jazz and ragtime. Today, for those interested in regular reading at less than book length, I'd like to discuss some periodicals.

I'll list addresses and subscription rates as I now have them. However, keep in mind that I am writing several months before these words will be published and that prices for small-circulation periodicals don't usually remain constant for too long.

If you're only interested in ragtime, the choice is fairly easy. The longest established and best U.S. ragtime periodical, containing both current news and historical articles, is *Rag Times*, which is sent every two months to members of The Maple Leaf Club. To join, send $10.00 for U.S. and Canadian residents, $13.00 elsewhere, to The Maple Leaf Club, 15522 Ricky Court, Grass Valley, California 95949.

The two widest-read independent U.S. periodicals concentrating exclusively on older-style jazz and ragtime are *West Coast Rag* (referred to hereinafter as *WCR*) and *The Mississippi Rag* (*MR*). *WCR* devotes more space to activity in the Western U. S. than does *MR*, while *MR* gives somewhat more coverage to swing and mainstream jazz than does *WCR*. Both contain festival listings that mention dates, contacts and principal artists, and both have about the same lineup of major advertisers.

However, each publication is the mirror image of the other with respect to emphasis. For that reason, I consider them complementary, not competitive. Someone desiring to have a current and comprehensive picture of the scene really should read both. My experience is that the texts have virtually no duplication of coverage.

WCR's primary function is to act as a social calendar of the festival scene. Its principal articles look toward the future, to upcoming festivals. One reads *WCR* to find out who's playing where, how to get tickets, what they cost, whether no-smoking venues are available, whether dancing is permitted, etc.

In that sense, *WCR* is like the shopper's guide that is sometimes handed to you as you enter the supermarket or the shopping mall, listing the day's specials. It's of keen interest while you're there, but once the day has ended, it has little lingering value.

WCR supplements its festival coverage with profiles of musicians who appear thereat, reviews of their records, general columns about the music (like "Texas Shout"), etc., which would be useful if saved for future reference. Nevertheless, most of what's in a typical issue of *WCR* is obsolete once the next issue appears.

In keeping with the ephemeral nature of much of its coverage, *WCR* is often irreverent and breezy. It regularly contains humor, sometimes sophomoric, that has nothing whatsoever to do with music.

| TEXAS SHOUT: HOW DIXIELAND JAZZ WORKS |

MR, by contrast, is essentially a news magazine. Except for fleeting mentions once in a while by its regular columnists, *MR*'s text never deals with upcoming events nor with non-musical subjects. Everything it covers - historical articles; festival, record and book reviews; profiles of current musicians and bands; etc. - deal with something that has already happened. Very little of *MR*'s text goes out of date, so that older issues are highly useful for later reference.

WCR, then, looks ahead while *MR* looks back. This fundamental difference in emphasis is best exemplified by the headline articles. In *WCR*, the principal front-page story is usually a descriptive roundup of the jazz festivals scheduled for the current month. In *MR*, the lead article is almost always a lengthy historical essay, typically a profile of an individual musician.

Personally, I wouldn't be without either *WCR* or *MR*. *WCR*'s subscription rates and address are set forth elsewhere in this issue. *MR* is $18/year in the U.S., $20 elsewhere, from *The Mississippi Rag*, P. O. Box 19068, Minneapolis, Minnesota 55419.

I have previously commented herein on the currently uneven state of U.S. record reviewing. I regularly receive a fair number of domestic jazz and ragtime periodicals. Unfortunately, in my opinion, not one of them has a record reviewing staff that, throughout the lineup, is so knowledgeable and reliable that I will put a record on my want list solely because it has received a favorable review in the publication. To reach that level of confidence, I have to go overseas.

Although it is not exclusively devoted to older-style jazz, I consider the best all-around jazz magazine in the world to be *Jazz Journal International* (*JJI*). Currently in its 46th year of publication, it is a slick-paper monthly that is occasionally found on exceptionally well-stocked newsstands. It treats all types of jazz (except, perhaps, for the most anarchic, free-form styles) with an impressively even-handed, respectful and informed manner.

I don't read all of the articles in *JJI*, but I consider it an extremely valuable source, in both ads and record reviews, for references to good recordings produced outside the U.S. that I might be able to track down from specialty dealers. About half of each issue consists of its excellent, concise record reviews, which typically set forth running time, dates and personnel. Assuming that I like the style of jazz being reviewed, I will go looking for an album, even if I've never heard of the artist, if it is favorably reviewed by any of *JJI*'s reviewers; I have rarely been disappointed by purchasing such recordings.

Importing *JJI* from England is costly. It is the most expensive periodical I buy. Each year at renewal time, I wonder if I should be spending this much, but I always decide to continue, and I haven't been sorry yet. A year's subscription is currently $55, from *Jazz Journal International,* 1/5 Clerkenwell Road, London, England EC1M 5PA.

While we're on British magazines, let me recommend to discographically-minded readers a small digest-sized every-other-monthly called *Storyville*. It concentrates on nailing down discographical details of the lives of jazz musicians who played in the 1920s, i.e., who played where, on which days, with which other musicians, at which clubs or on which records, etc.

Periodicals

Though *Storyville*'s articles and pictures are oriented in that direction, and though they can sometimes involve listings of minutiae that only a librarian could love, much of what it contains can't be found elsewhere and is of decided interest to a serious Dixielandphile. It has a few pages of record reviews, equal in quality to *JJI*'s. Six issues of *Storyville* may be ordered by U.S. subscribers for $20 from Storyville Publications and Co., Ltd., 66 Fairview Drive, Chigwell, Essex, England IG7 6HS.

Over the years, when I've been hired to play at a Dixieland festival, I've typically signed up for a year's membership in the local jazz society (if there is one). It's a way of trying to support people who support me, and also give me some flavor, before I arrive, of what sort of entertainment the locals prefer.

Of course, I've belonged for years to the four older-style jazz societies that function in this general area (none of them, unfortunately, conveniently close to my home). Frankly, I can't begin to comprehend the mentality of Dixieland musicians who don't bother to join their local Dixieland clubs, but that is a subject for another day.

As a result, I've seen lots of jazz club newsletters. They vary widely in quality and in appearance. Most of them are of strictly local interest, but there are two that I believe might justify reading by someone not living close enough to attend the club's functions.

At present, the best jazz club publication I know of is *Jersey Jazz*, the monthly (except August) magazine of the New Jersey Jazz Society. A few of its columnists reflect the somewhat limited view (and the Society's general orientation) that, of the seven Dixieland styles, only Chicago style (and, maybe, once in a while, hot dance) has anything of value to offer today's discriminating listener.

I have often pondered whether the more-or-less steady repetition of text that casually dismisses several Dixieland styles is appropriate or healthy for a club publication that purports to support all older-style jazz. However, I wince my way through these passages because there is a lot of red meat in *Jersey Jazz*, and the writing is consistently a cut or two above that of most jazz club publications.

Its quality is 100% attributable to the excellent work of the only editor *Jersey Jazz* had throughout its first twenty years, Warren Vaché, Sr., a skilled bassist and father of two well-known jazzmen, clarinetist Allan and cornetist Warren, Jr. Warren's own curmudgeonly editorials are consistently thought-provoking. Moreover, the Society's proximity to New York City where, despite the current low incidence of Dixieland in Gotham night spots, quite a few of the country's top Dixielanders are located, gives the club a steady source of material of more than local interest.

Last summer, Warren requested that he be replaced as *Jersey Jazz*'s editor, effective at year-end 1992. He will be an impossible act to follow, but the publication does have a seasoned list of capable contributors. Moreover, the new editor, Don Robertson, has a distinguished record of service to jazz. Membership in the New Jersey Jazz Society is $25/year from Mrs. Shirley Klinger, 142 Tappan Avenue, North Plainfield, New Jersey 07060.

The Second Line (*SL*), a digest-sized quarterly that comes with membership in the New Orleans Jazz Club, is I think, the world's longest continuous jazz club magazine. It concerns itself totally with Dixieland jazz that has a close relationship to the Crescent City, both today and in years gone by.

Reflecting a declining club membership during the 1980s, *SL* is somewhat thinner than it used to be. It recently changed editors, the superb Don Marquis having performed yeoman service for years and turning the reins over to Carolyn Stafford and John Pult (but remaining on the scene as a consultant).

Some of *SL*'s articles are sincerely but amateurishly written. Further, recent issues have relied somewhat heavily on material by Floyd Levin that had previously been published in *West Coast Rag, Jersey Jazz* and/or the various other publications in which Floyd's byline appears from time to time.

Nevertheless, several of the favorite names on today's festival circuit now live in New Orleans; their activities would be of interest to some *WCR* readers. Further, *SL* occasionally runs articles of scholarly research on veteran New Orleans musicians, or on aspects of turn-of-the-century life therein, that students of our music's roots will find invaluable. Corresponding (non-resident) membership in the New Orleans Jazz Club is $25/year from the club at Suite 265, 828 Royal Street, New Orleans, Louisiana 70116.

There are many more periodicals in the semi-underground world of Dixieland jazz and ragtime. Some, like the now-defunct *TJ Today*, which was essentially an index of contacts for musicians, jazz clubs and current gigs, are extremely specialized.

However, the ones described above will keep you well enough informed about the scene so that (1) you won't miss anything big, (2) your own enjoyment of the music will be enhanced and (3) you'll be one up on most of the people around you at the next concert you attend. Besides, subscribing to jazz and ragtime magazines is a relatively inexpensive and fun way to help support the music. Think it over.

The American Rag

Formerly WEST COAST RAG
News You Can Use About Traditional Jazz and Ragtime

Vol. 8, No. 11   Fresno, CA 93711 $2.00   December 1996

The American Rag (formerly West Coast Rag) Holiday 1996 Issue   *Artwork© by Robert Butler*

Don Jones, Publ./Editor The American Rag

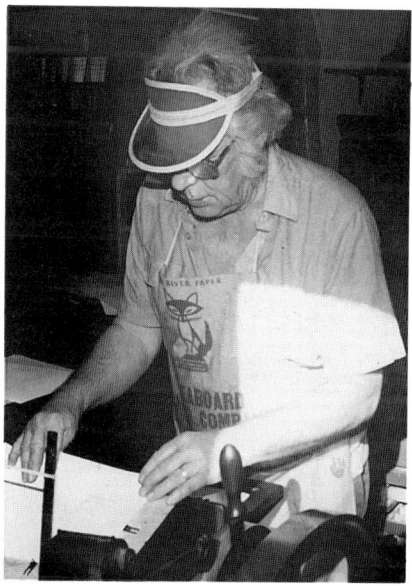

Woody Laughnan, Publ./ Editor, West Coast Rag

TEXAS SHOUT: HOW DIXIELAND JAZZ WORKS

The Mississippi Rag®

THE VOICE OF TRADITIONAL JAZZ AND RAGTIME

MSB Center
1401 W. 76th St., #250
Minneapolis, MN 55423

Established 1973

Phone: (612) 861-2446
FAX: (612) 861-4621

Leslie Johnson, Publ/Editor, The Mississippi Rag
Photo by Dennis Johnson

CHAPTER 29   ENSEMBLE SKILLS

To play Dixieland jazz effectively, an instrumentalist must attain at least a minimum level of competence in three general areas. I have referred to them in prior columns as "reading skill", "solo skill" and "ensemble skill".

Each of the seven styles of Dixieland uses all three skills. However, the degree of importance assigned to a given skill differs depending on the style being played.

"Reading skill" is the ability to execute pre-planned notes (whether written down or as part of memorized "head" arrangements) with a jazz feeling so that they sound spontaneous and blend properly with the other instruments. The hot dance Dixieland style (see "Texas Shout", February 1990), places its highest values on this skill.

"Solo skill" is the ability to play jazz solos that are creative, presenting a distinctive, personal and fresh vision of the selection. Chicago style, the only solo-oriented Dixieland style (see "Texas Shout", July-August-September 1991), considers this skill the most important of the three.

The other five Dixieland styles - white New Orleans, downtown New Orleans, uptown New Orleans, West Coast revival, and British trad - rank ensemble skill highest. With the majority of the bands at most of today's festivals probably being uptown New Orleans, West Coast revival or British trad, ensemble skill thus becomes, at many weekends, the most critical one on the scene. However, for reasons explained below, it often goes unrecognized and unrewarded by audiences, and sometimes even by musicians.

That's because ensemble skill is an invisible skill. Success at ensemble playing requires complete selflessness, performance at all times solely for the benefit of the band without unduly calling attention to one's self.

I'd like to use the balance of this column to try to make this important ability a little more visible, to draw your attention to it and give you some idea of how you can go about recognizing it. Let's start by defining it more precisely: "Ensemble skill" is the ability to listen simultaneously to as many as seven other musicians all improvising around you, to assimilate these seven lines, and to concurrently improvise exactly those notes that will complement and enhance their work, thus making the whole greater than the sum of its parts - while also making your own personal and original statement within the overall picture.

Sounds difficult, doesn't it? You better believe it. Ensemble skill is an ability one acquires only via steady, dedicated playing with other improvising musicians, both live and - to experience the challenge of working with different approaches and the best jazzmen - along with recordings.

The high value placed on ensemble skill in five Dixieland styles explains why a bandleader in one of those styles typically makes the seemingly odd, but usually

TEXAS SHOUT: HOW DIXIELAND JAZZ WORKS

correct, decision to fill a vacancy with an instrumentalist who is deeply committed to the style vs. a more technically accomplished but less devoted performer. Great technical skill is not normally required for effective Dixieland ensemble playing.

Dixieland is the branch of jazz in which the largest number of musicians can be improvising at once without need for any sort of written charts. In swing, bop and more advanced styles, with their busy lines and complex chords, an arrangement is needed to keep ensembles from being too cluttered if you have more than about five players on stage. With Dixieland, you can have as many as eight before charts are needed.

However, with eight improvising Dixielanders, no one player has a lot of room in which to operate. The role of each instrument in a Dixieland ensemble is very specifically defined. A player who steps out of this role, by going too far outside the normal range of his instrument, or by playing too many notes, will invade territory belonging to another player and upset the balance of the ensemble.

For that reason, virtuoso technique, though not to be denigrated, does not necessarily increase one's ability to play ensemble Dixieland. Playing the right notes is what matters, and those notes may turn out to be a few easy-to-play notes in the mid-range.

For example, the great trombonist Jim Robinson had a fairly limited vocabulary of favorite licks and a technique within the grasp of an average junior high school sliphornist. However, Big Jim's propulsive effect on ensembles, and his expressive use of those licks, was such that he is, beyond question, the most imitated uptown New Orleans trombone player.

Why is ensemble skill unrecognized by audiences? Well, think about what happens when you're watching a Dixieland band.

You'll hear the band execute ensemble passages; during the performances, some of the sidemen will solo - usually the front line horns and pianist, maybe the banjo/guitarist, sometimes the bassist or, more seldom, the percussionist. While the solos are going on, you're paying attention to the soloists. A flashy solo will inevitably be rewarded with applause and, if the audience has enough seasoned listeners, a good solo (flashy or not) will achieve the same result.

After the set, and perhaps long after the festival, you will be likely to remember the names of the soloists who got such favorable audience response. You are less likely to remember the names of the artists who didn't solo. (Think of as many bands as you can in which you know the name of the cornetist/trumpeter; now go back through the list of bands and see how many of the drummers you can name.)

Similarly, if a soloist did not get a favorable audience response, or did not play good solos, you are not as likely to remember him. Indeed, you may conclude that he is not as capable a musician as the soloists who got louder applause - and you may well reach that conclusion without considering whether that musician was actually supplying one of the key ingredients that caused the band as a whole to be successful in ensemble passages. The musician's ensemble skill has been, except for the most discerning and knowledgeable listeners, invisible.

Ensemble Skills

Musicians, though perhaps more knowledgeable as a group then a general audience, may well make the same mistakes as spectators. As a rule, though, they are quicker to recognize ensemble skill when they're on stage with a talented ensemble player, particularly if the player performs on a rhythm instrument. Still, even in the five ensemble-oriented styles of Dixieland, an artist who plays an instrument that normally solos, and who is a below-average soloist, risks having his ensemble skills go unrecognized by his colleagues.

O. K., you say, how do I identify these wonderful ensemble players? It's sort of a process of elimination, actually.

First off, if a band really cooks, if it swings hard during the ensembles, you can feel reasonably confident that each member is a competent ensemble player. Even one weak link in that respect usually prevents the combo from achieving that seemingly effortless feeling of buoyancy and momentum that characterizes hot jazz. Remember each name in the lineup when you see such a hot outfit.

If you do so often enough, you will eventually come to realize that there are certain musicians whose presence onstage seems to insure that the band is going to cohere. You seldom see them working in a situation that produces below-average heat. These are the outstanding ensemble musicians, the ones who find those right notes to play that encourage their colleagues to perform at peak and which knit the group into a swinging unit.

Names? Many of them are good soloists as well, and today's column is not really designed to give soloists more publicity. As for the good ensemble players who are below-average soloists, I'd just as soon not single out any contemporary musicians for that type of two-faced distinction. You can find them for yourself using the above-described procedure.

Two names on the current scene come to mind, however, relating to jazzmen who almost never take solos, who've concentrated on developing themselves as bandsmen. Both have done a superb job in that respect.

Tubaist Bob Rann's fruity sound and percussive attack play a pivotal role in defining the powerful beat of the South Frisco Jazz Band. Up to the date of the 1989 South Coast Metro Festival in Costa Mesa, I don't think I'd ever heard Bob play any other way.

At the start of one of The Rent Party Revellers' sets at that event, Chuck Stewart suffered a mishap to his tuba that required an immediate repair. We kicked off without a bass, while I dispatched Nancy to comb the vicinity for itinerant tubaists. A few tunes later, she showed up with Bob Rann in tow, who was rushed onstage and confronted with our usual list of nearly forgotten numbers, many of which had to be new ones for Bob.

I may be too close to it to judge, but I think our rent party approach to rhythm is some distance along the spectrum from South Frisco's. Bob, however, needed no adjustment at all and fit in as if he'd been a Reveller all his life. There's a musician who can really play ensemble.

Over the years, I've reviewed a lot of recordings that include British drummer, now transplanted to New Orleans, Barry Martyn in the rhythm section. Martyn doesn't solo, but thoroughly understands the function of the drums in uptown New

TEXAS SHOUT: HOW DIXIELAND JAZZ WORKS

Orleans style - that is, the drums supply the color, acting as the link between the front line and the rhythm section, while the other rhythm instruments play a functional beat. (In the other styles of Dixieland, this role is usually taken by the pianist.)

Eventually, I came to realize that I was giving favorable reviews to records including Martyn, whether he was leader or sideman, whether the combo was large or small, in circumstances involving a wide variety of other sidemen. Therefore, he has the ability to play in a manner that pulls the band together and gets it off the ground, a first-rate ensemble musician.

To give you a more concrete example, I tried to think of a vintage-period jazzman who is regarded as an indifferent soloist but a fine ensemble player. This is not an easy task, as we all differ in our assessments of any given artist's solo talents.

Left to myself, I would nominate trombonist Jimmy Archey for that category. I've always enjoyed my recordings on which he played, although his solo style usually strikes me as limited and monotonous.

However, my view of Archey is hardly the universal one. The eminent critic Rudi Blesh regularly included Archey on his historic "This Is Jazz" broadcasts, something he would not have done (given the wide selection of jazz talent available to Rudi in New York City) if he had thought Archey to be deficient in any respect. Moreover, in his recent book *The Jazz Crusade,* author Bill Bissonnette lavishes special praise on Archey's soloing.

There is one name, though, that provides, for me, the perfect illustration of the point being made in this column. The individual in question appeared on literally hundreds of vintage jazz recordings, including many of the greatest classics in the field, often in the company of such immortals as Louis Armstrong, Sidney Bechet, Bessie Smith, King Oliver, James P. Johnson, and Willie "The Lion" Smith. He was, among other things, a singer, bandleader, jug player, and composer or co-composer of some of the most beloved tunes in the idiom. His main instrument was the piano; when commenting on his pianistics, the virtually unanimous critical assessment has been that his tickling was, at best, bland and competent - however, I do not recall reading any critical comment that addressed his abilities as an ensemble player.

I am speaking, of course, of Clarence Williams. Recordings on which Williams performs are constantly being reissued, invariably to favorable reviews. Personally, I've never heard a record including Williams that I felt wasn't worth hearing. While Williams may not have been an arresting soloist, no one could possibly have made so many good recordings, in such a variety of combinations and contexts, unless he was an exceptional ensemble musician.

One could argue, I suppose, that Williams was a bandleader and that his beneficial effect on his cohorts was primarily due to his leadership skills rather than his ensemble skills. There may be some merit to that position, but I am not persuaded by it.

Williams' discography embraces sessions with musicians who were themselves forceful personalities, people who knew what they wanted, and who were in many cases the leaders on the dates - Oliver and Bessie, for example. Even when they were sidemen, individuals like Bechet and The Lion were not given to letting themselves be pushed around.

Still, once the studio light was on, with Williams in the band, they turned out jazz that still connects after all these decades. Something about Williams' playing had to be a significant factor in bringing about that result. He and others like him deserve to be recognized for that achievement.

Thus, let's be more alert to giving credit where credit is due. The next time you see a combo that's hitting on all cylinders, that's turning out a swinging beat that compels you to respond and which lifts your emotions, remember that every jazzman (or woman) onstage, not just the soloists, is a vital cog in producing that result. Each has mastered a difficult and important - perhaps the most important - skill in his branch of Dixieland.

Remember their names. When you want more of the same, look for other bands that include some of those names in the personnel. If you do so, I predict that you'll come to a deeper understanding of our music, and spend higher-quality time enjoying it.

Big Jim Robinson 1960s *Photo by Andrew Wittenborn*

TEXAS SHOUT: HOW DIXIELAND JAZZ WORKS

Barry Martyn 1972 *Photo by Ed Lawless*

Bob Rann 1980s *Photo by Dan Polin*

CHAPTER 30   JAZZ SINGERS

I recently read a record review in a respected jazz periodical in which the reviewer, discussing a singer whom I will refer to as "X", said: "X ... was not a jazz singer, X was not a dynamic improvisor. ... X was a practitioner of crooning ..."

By contrast, in *Jazz Singing*, the only book-length treatment to date of the subject, author Will Friedwald states: "Louis Armstrong and X [are] the two most important figures in jazz-derived popular singing. ... X's greatest accomplishment ... was the application of jazz to the music of Tin Pan Alley."

These diametrically opposed assessments are characteristic of the confusion that exists among the jazz community whenever the question of jazz singing is discussed. This confusion, in my opinion, results because some jazz commentators are not comfortable viewing a singer as a musician whose instrument happens to be his/her own voice instead of a trumpet, trombone, piano, etc.

However, if you look at singers that way, you'll have no trouble discerning which ones have the ability to sing jazz. You'll do so simply by applying the same rules you'd use to determine whether any other instrumentalist has that talent.

First, let's dismiss some red herrings. We'll start with the "crooning" point raised above. The reviewer seemed to feel that X's skills as a crooner could be offered as evidence that X could not sing jazz.

Well, Tommy Dorsey could produce one of the creamiest, most sensual tones ever heard from a trombone. He used that skill to great advantage on many successful non-jazz pop recordings. However, I've never heard anyone suggest that doing so somehow diminished his considerable talent as a jazz trombonist.

Benny Goodman not only deployed his singing clarinet on many romantic non-jazz dance sides, but also was, I understand a creditable classical clarinetist. Anyone who used those facts to try to prove that Goodman was not also a jazzman would be laughed out of the room.

A singer may be able to croon, yodel or hum, and may attain an enviable reputation in the pop market by doing so. However, that statement tells you absolutely nothing about whether that singer also has the ability, when called for, to sing jazz. Just because you can do one thing well doesn't mean you can't also do something else well in the bargain.

Probably because the great Nat "King" Cole emerged from the jazz community in the first place, and was in fact one of the best jazz pianists of his day, he has always been universally acknowledged, and rightly so, to be a great jazz singer as well. However, Cole was also a "crooner' if there ever was one, achieving his greatest fame and success via his distinctive, smooth, intimate vocalizing on ordinary pop ballads.

TEXAS SHOUT: HOW DIXIELAND JAZZ WORKS

For a second red herring, the above-quoted reviewer also seemed to feel that one could not be a jazz singer unless one was a "dynamic improvisor". This conclusion reflects the commonly-held notion that improvisation is a sine qua non of jazz.

I have addressed this notion several times in previous "Texas Shout" columns. I don't want to go through the reasoning again in detail today, but if you've been a steady reader you will be familiar with my view that improvisation, though typically a predominant part of most jazz performances, is not essential to jazz. There are many well-known hot dance sides from the twenties, swing-band 78s from the thirties, progressive and bop rides from the forties, etc., which are fully scored from beginning to end and which are recognized by all and sundry to be jazz renditions.

The distinguishing feature of jazz, as I have often stated in these pages, is its unique rhythmic feeling, the characteristic that most jazzmen refer to as "hot, swinging" rhythm. An instrumentalist who can play music with that feeling has the ability to play jazz, without regard to whether the notes are improvised or scored, or to whether they are played with a tart tone or a velvety "croony" timbre.

In short, if an artist can be hot and swinging when required, then he/she can play jazz. That's the rule you apply to trumpeters, trombonists, pianists, etc., and it's the same rule you apply to vocalists.

By that rule, we recognize that Ella Fitzgerald, who often improvises wildly adventurous melodic lines is a jazz singer, but so is the wonderful Maxine Sullivan who swung effortlessly and naturally while rarely deviating much from the melody lines written by the composers.

By that same rule, we can see that many successful singers, some of whom had excellent voices, did not possess the ability to sing jazz. Al Jolson, one of the most dynamic and popular entertainers of all time, who had a full, rich voice and impeccable timing and pitch, apparently could not swing, or at least if he could, he never did so on record. History, then, does not include Jolson in its list of jazz singers, nor Eddie Cantor, nor Sophie Tucker, nor Gene Austin (one of the twenties' most popular singers, now mostly forgotten).

You'll be able to use this rule to find out which of the singers you encounter belong on your list of jazz singers. For the benefit of those who might like to investigate the subject a bit more, I'd like to use the balance of this column to mention some vintage-period jazz vocalists whom I have particularly enjoyed over the years.

I do not intend to be exhaustive in naming individuals. The omission of your particular favorite - maybe Sinatra or Calloway - is in no way intended as a slight or a denigration of that person's skill. If you want to add some names to the ones mentioned herein, I'd probably go along with most of them.

Number One for me, and probably for many others, is Bessie Smith. The majesty and power of that great big voice are simply galvanizing, triumphing not only over sometimes inferior material but also over her somewhat limited range, to the point that there are no bad Bessie Smith records. Fortunately, her recordings are almost constantly in print. If you have never heard any of them, you're really missing something.

Jazz Singers

The only other black female of the twenties who can be mentioned in the same breath with Bessie is, of course, Ma Rainey, whose rich voice adorns a wide variety of material from vaudeville songs to jug band ditties. I also have a soft spot for Clara Smith, whose heavy, dark tones were particularly effective on very slow, sombre tunes. Ma Rainey's recordings will be at nearly any large record store with an extensive blues section, but Clara Smith's sides, if available at all, will only be found from specialty dealers.

You'll also have to dig to find recordings by the white jazz thrush who stood head and shoulders above her competition in the 1920s, the irresistible Annette Hanshaw. Discovered as a teenager singing at a party, she became a big star even though she didn't care much for show business and got out of it after a relatively few years. Her clear-toned, unaffected singing, sometimes accompanied by her own piano or ukulele, sometimes by the best of New York's white jazzmen, sounds as fresh and appealing today as when it was recorded decades ago.

Before we turn to the male singers, I'll toss in the name of one little-known sleeper, the ill-starred vaudevillian Jane Green, who waxed about twenty sides in the mid-1920s. A dozen of them were collected in 1989 on <u>Superbatone 732</u>. Superbatone Records, P.O. Box 1146, Venice, California 90291 may have some copies of this LP left in stock; if you can unearth one, I'll bet you won't be sorry.

Among the 1920s males, the list starts with Louis Armstrong, the person who virtually defined jazz singing (along with many other things in the jazz vocabulary). The next name is that of X in the example that opened this column, Bing Crosby.

Friedwald's above-quoted assessment of Armstrong and Crosby ought to be beyond dispute. From Crosby's earliest recordings with Bix, The Rhythm Boys and various Whiteman sidemen right through his swinging LP with Bob Scobey's band, Der Bingle obviously could get hot when he had a mind to do so. If you ask me, anyone who really believes Crosby couldn't sing jazz ought to turn in his critic's badge.

I don't listen as much to reissues from the thirties as those from the twenties. However, I'll listen to Mildred Bailey any time. The warmth of her voice and the comfortable feeling of her delivery put her at the top of my thirties list, closely followed by Lee Wiley and Maxine Sullivan.

Ms. Wiley's singing combines a fun-loving wholesomeness with a faint but definite seductiveness in a way that I've never heard equalled. Ms. Sullivan, as mentioned, stuck to business, blending her smooth pipes, crystal-clear enunciation and dead-center pitch into an understated style that, in its subtle fashion, swung like mad.

On the male side, Jack Teagarden first appeared in the twenties, as did Ms. Bailey, but both came into their own in the thirties. Tea's relaxed drawl was the perfect compliment to his facile blues-tinged trombone.

Fats Waller wasn't your conventional singer, but the same forceful rhythm and joiedevivre of his piano playing shines through his vocals. While we're on singing pianists, let's mention Nat "King" Cole again.

And while we're on unconventional singers, let's move up to the Dixieland revival period and pick up the hoarse shouting approach of Turk Murphy, whose powerful vocals were, like Teagarden's, cast in the same mold as his fruity sliphorning. Turk's sometime colleague in the Yerba Buena Jazz Band was the marvelous Clancy Hayes, whose Crosbyish singing gave new life to many previously neglected tunes that are now staples of the West Coast revival Dixieland style.

I could go on, but these names will do for now and I have a couple of other stories to tell you. Before I do so, however, and even though I haven't dealt with the contemporary scene, I want to mention one present-day singer who hasn't appeared much, if at all, on the West Coast festival circuit and whose name might therefore be unfamiliar to many of you.

George Buck's various labels include a number of releases featuring Barbara Lea. They display a poised singer with a lovely voice who has superb taste in selecting worthwhile but underrecorded material.

I told you that the persons mentioned herein do not comprise an exhaustive list of singers I admire. However, one omission is so glaring that I feel compelled to explain it.

When all-time great jazz figures are being cited, there are certain names that always turn up on everyone's list. Some of them are not artists to whom I personally prefer to listen, but I have no trouble understanding why they are cited.

For example, though I don't care for bop, I can understand it enough to appreciate the nature of the changes wrought by Dizzy Gillespie and Charlie Parker. Parker might just have been the second most influential jazzman of all time (behind Armstrong), while Gillespie is one of the most technically gifted trumpeters of his era. Both deserve the adulation they have received.

Similarly, I don't listen much to Art Tatum because I think that he too often let his blinding keyboard dexterity take precedence over creative thinking. However, Tatum was probably the most technically accomplished pianist jazz has ever known. I consider his 3/21/33 "Tiger Rag" for Brunswick to be the single best recorded piano solo I've ever heard. Tatum clearly ranks with jazz' immortals.

However, I have been unable to reach the same conclusion with respect to Billie Holiday. I am obviously missing something that everyone else can easily hear, but I find her voice not particularly pleasant and her articulation and pitch frequently erratic.

I have dutifully bought the recordings that most jazz commentators rank among her best, the small combo sides with Teddy Wilson, and listened carefully to them. The jazz is wonderful, but I don't hear Lady Day adding much to the proceedings most of the time. I have rarely gotten these sessions back off the shelf.

Thus, though Ms. Holiday is considered by some respected critics to be the greatest female jazz singer who ever lived, she has been missing on purpose from my "favorites" list. Perhaps some day I will get her message, as I eventually did in the story I am about to relate.

There is just one singer who affects me with the same emotional impact as Bessie Smith. I was first exposed to her some 35-40 years ago, when I was just beginning to dig deeply into jazz.

As many of you know, I came to Dixieland via the West Coast revivalists. Initially, I was not finely attuned to the nuances of jazz singing, but I knew how highly Bessie Smith was regarded. I had bought some of her records and was beginning to assimilate them when I read of another singer who was favorably compared to her.

Back then, you could take LPs into a booth in the store and audition parts of a few tracks. So, following the lead, I listened to this second singer. However, she wasn't singing with a jazz background. Not hearing my beloved banjo and tuba, nor much other jazz, and not fully knowing what to listen for, I bypassed the album. Shortly thereafter I saw this artist in a feature film and had the same experience.

As the decades went by, I became immersed in all aspects of Dixieland and eventually developed a taste for a music closely related thereto - pre-war (or "country" or "acoustic") blues, which includes certain types of religious music. I'll elaborate on blues & gospel in another column, but for now, I'll say that this interest brought me full-circle back to the artist I had bypassed many years ago.

When Columbia brought out a special boxed set of her material in 1991, I decided to take a chance on the audiocassette version. After about four tracks, I went back to buy the CD version as well for my permanent collection, all the while kicking myself for the many years during which I was missing out on this artist.

Now I rarely take an automobile trip without at least one of the cassettes from C2T 47083 "Gospels, Spirituals & Hymns" by Mahalia Jackson, and I am in the process of trying to acquire as many of her recordings as possible. Ms. Jackson may not be performing jazz songs, and she may not be singing with jazzmen behind her, but she can, and often does, outswing anyone you'd care to name.

Listen, for example, to the power and drive of "Roll, Jordan, Roll" in that collection. And if you can get all the way through "I Found The Answer" without being moved by the passion, joy and resonant beauty in that voice, you're more hard-hearted than I.

I have occasionally talked to fans who tell me that they don't like vocals. Having heard some of the "vocalists" who've made it onto records and festival stages, I can see how some listeners might be discouraged in that respect.

However, as I've said, the voice is an instrument. Deciding that you don't want to hear it, no matter how well "played", makes as much sense as deciding that you don't want to hear a band with a trumpet, or a trombone, or piano, or some other instrument that, like the voice, can be handled badly or can be handled so well that you'll be transformed by it.

The singers recommended herein are among those who have made me realize how enjoyable jazz singing can be. Perhaps if you sampled a cross-section thereof, you'd find additional riches in our music.

If you want to investigate the subject in depth, Friedwald's book, mentioned above, is a good place to start. It's written in a conversational fan-oriented style, talks about all the right people, gives you leads to names that will be new to you, and even includes a useful discography (unfortunately, mostly of LPs, difficult to locate today). Its only deficiency is that Friedwald does not tell you in so many words what he thinks jazz singing is, nor does he always tell you what you should be listening for with respect to the individual singer he's discussing.

However, I've given you a definition of jazz singing in today's column that should keep you on the right road. Let me know how you come out.

TEXAS SHOUT: HOW DIXIELAND JAZZ WORKS

Bessie Smith 1920s
Photo by Elcha - N. Y.

Ma Rainey with Rabbit's Foot Minstrels 1923
Photo by George Hoefer

Jazz Singers

Ella Fizgerald   1946
Photo by Robert Asen

Maxine Sullivan   1983
Photo by Ed Lawless

Mildred Bailey   1931
Photo courtesy Metronome Magazine

Mahalia Jackson   1950s
Photographer Unknown

TEXAS SHOUT: HOW DIXIELAND JAZZ WORKS

Lee Wiley 1930s
Photo courtesy of Metronome Magazine

Barbara Lee 1990
Photo by Andrew Wittenborn

Louie Armstrong 1950s
Photo by William Gottlieb

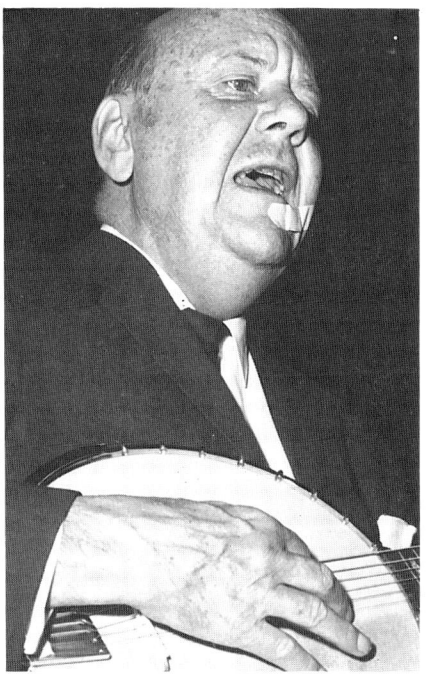

Clancy Hayes 1960s
Photo by Ed Lawless

CHAPTER 31   WESTERN SWING AND SPANISH TINGE

Two terms you'll encounter as you read your older-style jazz festival programs are "western swing" and "Spanish tinge". What types of music do these describe and how do they fit into the older-style jazz picture?

By "older-style" jazz, I mean the types of jazz played at festivals covered by *WCR*, i.e., Dixieland and swing (which I will refer to collectively in today's column as "D/S"). "Dixieland" is the generic term covering several styles of jazz utilizing the jazz vocabulary and conventions of the twenties, while "swing" is the generic term describing jazz styles utilizing the jazz vocabulary and conventions of the thirties. For reasons set forth below, I need to distinguish D/S, for today's purposes, from bop and other more advanced jazz forms.

A band is playing western swing when it plays jazz licks, which may or may not be improvised, over a country/western rhythm, i.e., a rhythm section using the types of shuffle and back-beat characteristic of country bands rather than jazz bands. A band is using the Spanish tinge when it plays jazz licks, which may or may not be improvised, over a rhumba, tango, samba or other Latin beat.

Thus, although these two musics contain non-jazz features, they both utilize devices to which jazz fans can relate. It would seem logical, then, that there should be a place for each at broadly-based jazz festivals.

In fact, as we all know, Igor's Jazz Cowboys, a highly-polished show band playing both western swing and straight western music, is one of the most visible and popular acts on the D/S festival circuit. Similarly, Guatemala's Paco Gatsby, a band that, in large part, plays D/S figures above Latin rhythms, has been a successful attraction for D/S festivals that can afford to import the combo.

The popularity of these bands has caused controversy in these pages and elsewhere. Why?

Well, if you've been a faithful reader of this column, you'll be familiar with my view that the thing that distinguishes D/S from other similar types of music is its approach to rhythm, i.e., the notes of D/S are articulated in a manner generating a particular kind of passionate forward movement described by the jazz community as "hot and swinging". Unless the music is played with that type of rhythm, it isn't D/S.

As explained above, western swing and Spanish tinge are not played to this special type of jazz rhythm. Thus, for our purposes, though they may have jazzy characteristics, neither is jazz.

(Since the bossa nova craze of the sixties, modern jazzmen have made many records with Latin rhythm which are promoted as jazz and apparently are accepted as such by modern jazz fans. Of course, modern jazz deliberately set out to break some of the commonly accepted rules of older-style jazz.

TEXAS SHOUT: HOW DIXIELAND JAZZ WORKS

Although I have trouble with the concept of jazz being played in anything other than jazz time, I do not claim to understand the rules of the various styles of modern jazz, a type of music that doesn't do much for me. For that reason, I'm limiting my discussion of "jazz" in today's column to D/S.)

Look at the subject this way: If you start playing a jazz solo in the middle of a country band, you're producing jazzy country music, not countryish jazz. If you want countryish jazz, then you should play fiddle or bluegrass licks to a jazz beat as, for example, the Dixieland Jug Blowers did in the twenties.

Similarly, if a trumpet, clarinet and trombone improvise "Ja-Da" to a rhumba beat, they're producing jazzy Latin music, not Latinish jazz. If you want Latinish jazz, then play bullfight-type trumpet figures, or melodies with a Latin sensibility, to a jazz beat as, for example, in "Cielito Lindo" from the LP "Orange Kellin In New Orleans" , Center CLP-7.

The most familiar example of Latinish jazz is undoubtedly the Dixieland flagwaver "Panama", composed by Wn. H. Tyers (who was from the West Indies), originally published in 1911, as a slow four-strain piece, with introduction and tag, entirely in Latin rhythm. However, generations of jazz bands closing sets with this one have probably made it difficult for most of us to visualize "Panama" as consisting of Latin themes played to jazz time.

My conclusion that western swing isn't jazz is generally supported by record producers and sellers, who usually group western swing bands with the country/western elements of their catalogs rather than with the jazz elements. Moreover, western swing is typically not included in jazz discographies.

Similar statements can't be made for Spanish tinge because, except for Paco Gatsby, I am not aware of any D/S-oriented combos that have made Spanish tinge the major portion of their repertoires. The questions of how to promote records by such combos, or where to put them in discographies, really haven't come up as yet. However, I feel confident that, if they ever do come up, they will be dealt with in the same way as western swing.

I doubt that many readers will be upset by my conclusion that western swing isn't jazz. Quite a few Dixielanders don't care all that much for western swing, anyway.

However, more may be disturbed by that conclusion regarding Spanish tinge. After all, since the earliest days, Dixieland musicians have occasionally played tunes to a Latin beat. Jelly Roll's lovely ""New Orleans Joys" and "The Crave" are regularly heard at Dixieland festivals. And what jazzman hasn't played Handy's immortal "St. Louis Blues", with its haunting Latin-rhythmed second strain?

In that respect, let me state emphatically my belief that such music does belong in the repertoire, and that there is nothing wrong with using it to spice up, and add variety to, the program. Any music which draws heavily from D/S can successfully be presented to D/S fans, thereby enhancing everyone's good time and broadening the audience's appreciation of the artists who contributed to D/S. Doing so is analogous to playing Scott Joplin's waltzes, marches and other non-rag compositions at ragtime festivals, where such selections are welcomed by ragtime aficionados.

However, I also believe that, if we consider D/S to be an art form, then we ought to understand what kinds of music belong to it and what kinds don't. Moreover, if one has that understanding, then one is better able to appreciate the nature of the current controversy over the "legitimacy" of certain bands on festival programs.

◊ ◊ ◊ ◊ ◊ ◊ ◊ ◊ ◊ ◊ ◊ ◊ ◊

To recap, we have concluded that neither western swing nor Spanish tinge can properly be called Dixieland or swing, even though both forms of music incorporate jazzy elements. Having reached that conclusion, we can see all the shouting in proper perspective regarding the presentation at jazz festivals of western swing and Spanish-tinged combos, specifically Igor's Jazz Cowboys (representing western swing) and Paco Gatsby (Spanish tinge).

On the one hand, we have fans who are unhappy about attending festivals that claim to emphasize older-style jazz only to discover that there are bands on the bill that don't play it. On the other hand, we have fans who (1) respond to the jazzy parts of the two musics, (2) recognize that each shares common characteristics with Dixieland and swing, (3) observe that other non-jazz musics which also share common characteristics with Dixieland and swing (such as ragtime or ordinary popular music of the twenties and thirties) have for years been regularly presented at older-style jazz festivals without complaint, and (4) wonder what all the fuss is about.

Personally, I have no problem with Dixieland festivals hiring non-Dixieland bands that play music having common characteristics with Dixieland. Further, I'm not about to criticize festival producers for booking acts that a significant proportion of their patrons wants to see. All I ask is that the music be properly described in the program and publicity, so that a newcomer sitting in front of a country/western, blues, swing, ragtime or other non-Dixieland band will know what he's hearing and won't think it's Dixieland.

Actually, the debate between the "purists" and the broader-based jazz fans is, in today's scene dwarfed by the fact that many festivals calling themselves "jazz" or "Dixieland" festivals are supported in large part by folks who have no commitment whatsoever to Dixieland, swing or any kind of jazz - people who, when they get there, often make sure to avoid the jazziest artists. This situation portends grave implications for the future of our music; I have previously covered it in a separate column (see "Texas Shout" for November 1990, dealing with non-gentre music on festival programs).

I am discussing this subject today because, when Igor and Barbara Glenn last visited our home in Mendenhall, he dropped off a review copy of the Jazz Cowboys' fourth audiocassette, a 41-minute session titled "West of Dixie". While I doubt that it will convert the Igor-bashers in the crowd, I think that this release makes more imaginative use of the septet's blend of jazz and country elements than the three previous volumes.

Side One is the western swing side, offering an interesting contrast between jazz clarinet and country-picked mandolin as the two chase their way through

TEXAS SHOUT: HOW DIXIELAND JAZZ WORKS

"Washington & Lee Swing". A Dixieland front line grabs the fourth chorus, and we then get four choruses of jammy solos, in the middle of an otherwise western rendition of "Black Jack County Chain". A Dixielander will easily be able to relate to the Cowboys' version of "Midnight In Moscow" while discovering something I didn't know, namely that it has a lyric.

Side Two opens with a brace of straight Western vocals. Then it tosses in a provocative duet between mainstreamish edgy saxophone and shuffly country guitar on "Georgia On My Mind", moves into two amiable "stunt" tracks performed by Igor without accompaniment, and ends up with a couple of slick stir-'em-up cuts that are more show-biz than anything else.

In short, there's a little bit of everything here, all delivered with the Cowboys' usual panache. I have no doubt that Igor's many fans will go wild over "West Of Dixie". It's $12 postpaid from Glenn Enterprises, Inc., 2101 East Balboa Drive, Tempe, Arizona 85282.

When I'm at a festival where Igor shares the bill, Nancy and I usually drop in, say "Hello" and hear a few tunes. His music is not our first choice, but we recognize a well-organized, high-energy performance when we see one. When we leave, we can readily understand why the room is packed.

Are you unhappy about the direction the festival scene has taken in recent years? If so, there are some things you can do to reduce your blood pressure when the topic comes up.

First and foremost, you can make a point of letting festival producers know exactly which bands you want to see. Doing so is particularly important today, when transportation costs for some bands may exceed all their other costs put together.

Many festival producers, if not given any other help, are going to confine themselves to bands that are proven attractions or are located reasonably close by. Before producers commit to making the transportation investment required to bring in Band A, they need to have reassurance that there are fans who will attend the festival when Band A is on the bill.

If Band A is one of your favorites, you simply must, in current circumstances, take the trouble to go to bat for it at every opportunity. Further, you should be sure to attend the festival if Band A is booked, and urge your friends to go along.

Next, if a festival doesn't have enough bands on the lineup to keep you occupied for the full weekend, don't get upset. Just cross it off your itinerary for that year and drop the producers a line to tell them why you're doing so.

Let's face it. The landscape is dotted with music festivals, covering everything from classical to heavy metal, that you aren't going to attend. What real difference does it make if times change in a way that adds a few more to that list?

If you find yourself at a festival where the biggest crowds flock to bands you don't like, look at the bright side. Yes, I know that seeing all those people cheering a band you can't stand appears to be an implied insult to your personal taste. However, you might be thankful that the producers are broad-based enough to book bands you like even though your choices may not always draw as well as some of the headliners.

Also, you might be thankful that the venues with the loud, cheering crowds and the long lines at the door aren't the ones you're planning to visit. After all, most large festivals are going to have some bands you won't have time to see. As long as you're not going to see them anyway, what do you care about the kind of music that they play?

Moreover, why shouldn't the bands you're missing be very popular bands? If they are, their popularity attracts paying customers who help subsidize the hiring of your favorite artists.

Finally, if you are sufficiently concerned and have the time, you could become involved in some aspect of festival production in your area. Make yourself available for one of the volunteer positions, try to gain an understanding of the business/economic elements of running a festival, and strive to reach a point at which you can have some hand in the decision-making process.

In any event, don't blame the bands for being popular. They are doing exactly what they've been hired to do, and what the audience attending their shows expects them to do.

When Frankie Laine takes the stage at Sacramento, the crowd wants him to sing "Mule Train" and his other hits, not haul out a trombone and try to play tailgate (which he won't be able to do as well, probably, as many other musicians at the festival). Producers hire western swing bands like Igor's Jazz Cowboys, and Spanish-tinged combos like Paco Gatsby, to do the acts for which they have become well-known; it is absurd for "jazz police" or anyone else to urge such performers to behave otherwise.

My show consists of ragtime and Dixieland jazz. If I ever get hired to play the Strauss waltz festival, or the bagpipe festival, or the Gregorian chant festival, what the audience is going to get during my portion, like it or not, is ragtime and Dixieland jazz. If my act proves to be really popular, and I become a big name on the Strauss waltz/bagpipe/Gregorian circuit, I suppose many purist fans of those musics are going to be unhappy and complain about me in their official periodicals.

However, what am I then supposed to do when the next Strauss festival producer wants to hire me? Refuse the gig? Try to become a Strauss expert and deliver something I wasn't hired to do?

Now ask yourself how those questions apply to Igor's Jazz Cowboys and Paco Gatsby. Maybe then you'll feel more comfortable about putting the subject out of your mind and tossing another of your favorite Dixieland albums on the record player.

TEXAS SHOUT: HOW DIXIELAND JAZZ WORKS

Igor's Jazz Cowboys *Photo from Igor Glenn*

Paco Gatsby Band 1985 *Photo by Ed Lawless*

CHAPTER 32 BLUES

Dixieland jazz drew many elements from various types of music that preceded it. Even if you choose to limit your listening to Dixieland alone, you will inevitably find yourself rubbing elbows with several of these non-jazz musics, such as brass band marches or Latin-rhythmed compositions.

The non-jazz music most frequently encountered by Dixielanders is, of course, ragtime. Ragtime is a regular part of the presentation of many Dixieland bands. Also, ragtime piano sets are commonly included on the bill at Dixieland festivals.

Next on the list, for those who continue to dig deeply into dixieland, is Blues. Because this term has at least three meanings in the musical community, let's begin by defining what's meant by "blues" for purposes of today's column.

The first meaning of "blues" refers to a musical selection or performance that conveys a feeling of melancholy, regret, longing or similar emotion to the listener. Hearing it, you might say that the performer "has the blues" and, indeed, you might be moved some way toward that position yourself if the rendition is sufficiently convincing.

The second meaning of "blues" describes a tune which has a certain type of musical structure. Typically, that structure is a variation on a three-phrase, twelve-bar chorus (if played in double time, twenty-four bars).

However, eight-bar blues are quite common (the refrain to "Trouble in Mind" being a familiar example), as are sixteen-bar blues (often built like the chorus to "How Come You Do Me Like You Do" or to "(I Wish I could Shimmy Like My) Sister Kate". A sixteen-bar blues may have a few extra bars added to its final phrase (called a "turnaround" or "sweet mama" ending), "Sister Kate" again providing a common example thereof.

Among Blues aficionados, longer works, even when bluesy in feeling and performed by acknowledged Blues performers, are not conventionally thought of as blues. Thirty-two-bar numbers, though often found in the repertoire, tend to be regarded instead as pop songs.

When this second meaning is used, the performance need not create a blue mood. The boisterous set-closer "Weary Blues", for example, or the bouncy "Canal Street Blues", qualify as blues because they are constructed according to the conventions of blues composing.

Today's column focuses on the third meaning of "blues", i.e., as a term that refers to a specific musical genre just as "Dixieland" refers to jazz using a pre-swing jazz musical vocabulary. We're talking about the music you will find if you enter your local record store and browse through the section labelled "Blues". For ease in understanding, when I use the word herein with this third meaning, I will write it "Blues", with its first letter capitalized.

| TEXAS SHOUT: HOW DIXIELAND JAZZ WORKS |

The Blues section will include two rather different-sounding types of music. One is referred to as "acoustic", "pre-war", or "country" Blues, while the other is, naturally, "electric", "post-war", or "urban" Blues.

Country Blues is typically heard on unelectrified instruments, played by a solo guitar/vocalist or at most two or three people (the additional instruments being, perhaps, piano, violin, or harmonica - called a "mouth harp" or "harp" by Blues fans). Urban Blues is often performed on electric instruments by a Blues band, consisting of some combination of vocal, lead guitar, rhythm guitar, keyboard, harp, bass and drums. Urban Blues did not really come into its own until just after World War II, which explains the aforementioned "pre-war" and "post-war" labels.

Blues is primarily a vocal idiom. There are instrumental Blues rides, of course, but the overwhelming bulk of Blues recordings are vocal.

Thus, to appreciate Blues fully, one must be willing to pay attention to the lyrics along with the musical setting therefor as well as the vocalist's timbre and skill at conveying his/her message. As with any musical performance, the success thereof is judged by whether these elements do or do not come together to create a unified, valid visualization of the material that strikes a strong emotional response in the listener.

As I said, the dedicated Dixielander, as he/she becomes more of a completist, will inevitably be exposed to Blues. Johnny Dodds' fans will collect his appearances with Blind Blake and the Dixieland Jug Blowers. Ma Rainey buffs will acquire her sides with Tampa Red and Georgia Tom, the Tub Jug Washboard Band and Papa Charlie Jackson (who also recorded with Freddie Keppard). King Oliver completists will own his accompaniments to Texas Alexander. Louis Armstrong admirers - everyone reading these words - will hear Lonnie Johnson playing with the Hot Five (indeed, Johnson is on 78s with Duke Ellington and Eddie Lang as well). I could go on, but the list is very long, and you take my point.

As I collected Dixieland recordings, I eventually developed a liking for Blues. In fact, in recent years, I've probably purchased more Blues LPs and CDs than jazz.

However, it is only very recently that I have made a conscious effort to comprehend Blues and to read works devoted entirely to it. I came to like Blues accidentally, through brute force, because the music kept insistently knocking on my door while I was trying to shut it out and listen to the Dixieland elements of the performances.

Some of you are, I'm sure, traveling that same road and are going to reach the same destination. Thus, I'd like to offer a few tips that may make the journey easier, perhaps hastening the day when you will gain the ability to appreciate Blues in more depth.

First of all, don't start with urban Blues. If you're coming to it cold, based entirely in Dixieland, an urban Blues band is going to sound too much like rock n' roll. You will be turned off immediately by its heavy, insistent, riff-based beat. (In fact, the evolution - or deterioration, depending on your taste - of urban Blues into rhythm-and-blues and then into rock n' roll is quite clear, even to an unsophisticated listener.)

If you absolutely must hear some urban Blues, try starting with Arhoolie CD 305, "Ball N' Chain" by Big Mama Thornton, an excellent big-voiced belter evocative in some ways of the immortal Bessie Smith. On six of its sixteen cuts, Ms. Thornton is backed by the most important and influential urban Blues band ever, that of guitarist Muddy Waters, so you will get a fair shot at deciding whether you like the idiom while appreciating a stirring singer.

Personally, I am just beginning to get my arms around urban Blues. I still find much of it rather noisy and monotonous, and am picking my way very carefully through the record racks, guided by a couple of highly regarded periodicals which I'll mention below.

Country Blues will be much more accessible to a Dixielander. I have enjoyed it for at least ten years.

However, it took me longer than it should have to reach this point. That delay occurred because, paradoxically, I was initially exposed to two of the acknowledged greats in the field, Blind Lemon Jefferson and Charlie Patton.

Jefferson's recordings were included on a couple of LPs in Riverside's wonderful Jazz Archives reissues from the 1950s and 1960s, a series which I acquired and listened to avidly. While I am now able to comprehend his compelling blend of high-pitched whining vocals and pleading guitar, back then Jefferson was much too different from the Dixieland I was hearing on the other Riverside albums. Moreover, the sides being reissued were somewhat scratchy, making Jefferson's already slurry diction nearly incomprehensible.

The same thing occurred when I sampled Charlie Patton, considered by some to be the all-time greatest Mississippi Delta Blues singer. His thick dialect, difficult enough on its own, was noticeably immersed in surface noise, causing him to come across as someone mumbling lyrics I couldn't understand to an accompaniment that seemed relatively unchanging from track to track.

The trick is not to plunge right into Blues, but to begin with artists who work more closely to the jazz-Blues border. That way you will hear much music to which you can easily relate while you learn to appreciate the newer elements more gradually - without being hit over the head by them.

One way to get there is through the piano. Start, for example, with Art Hodes (my favorite living jazzman) who, though he is first and foremost a jazz player, is one of the bluesiest jazz ticklers you'll find. Once you've picked up on what Hodes is doing, get some of the relatively recent solo or small band sides with the late Sammy Price, much of whose playing is predominantly blues with a strong jazz element. Or try Eurreal "Little Brother" Montgomery, who could perform equally effectively with Dixieland bands or Blues artists.

Then you'll be ready for the record that turned the corner for me, "Texas Barrelhouse Piano" by Robert Shaw. (I have it on LP, but Arhoolie must have released this much-praised album on CD by now.) Shaw worked rowdy Texas roadhouses in his youth, retired from music to run a grocery store, becoming sufficiently successful that he was able to maintain a pure barrelhouse Blues style over the years by playing in his living room for his own amusement.

| TEXAS SHOUT: HOW DIXIELAND JAZZ WORKS |

This March 1963 solo session drips with juice, roots and authenticity that's only hinted at by the titles of some of his pieces - "Put Me In The Ally", "The Ma Grinder", "Whores Is Funky" and "Here I Come With My Dirty, Dirty Duckings On". If you can't appreciate Shaw, you'll never like Blues piano.

Another avenue to the Blues is through jug bands. Although usually comprised of country Blues performers, they have an easy-rolling loose rhythm which jazz fans will readily grasp, not to mention their infectious don't give-a-damn high spirits.

There were three great jug bands in the twenties. Start with the Dixieland Jug Blowers, which used enough "legitimate" instruments that it is listed in jazz discographies. Moreover, you will hear the unbelievable Earl Mcdonald, to my mind the Louis Armstrong of the jug, who sounds at times like he's playing a slide tuba! Then you'll be ready for the next two, the bracing Memphis Jug Band and the most countryish of the trio, Cannon's Jug Stompers.

The heart and soul of country Blues lies with its singer/guitarists. To sample these, I think it is critical that you start with ones whose lyrics can easily be understood. Try picking up something by Lonnie Johnson, Blind Blake and Papa Charlie Jackson.

Johnson, one of the most prolific Blues artists of all time, had a lovely, clear voice and impeccable diction. He was also a superior guitar player by any standard, his historic duets with the great Eddie Lang being much prized by jazz fans. He retained his skills throughout a long career during which he recorded a wide variety of material, both blues and pops.

Blind Blake's rich baritone is also a pleasure to hear and easy to grasp, while his guitar playing ranks with that of the best country bluesmen. Jackson's instrument was the banjo, which made it easier for me as a Dixielander to relate to him, while his material displays a solid streak of the hokum songster tradition, nicely balancing the more traditional blues for someone new to the field.

As I write, a record producer in Austria, Johnny Parth, is in the process of releasing multi-volumed CDs containing, in chronological order, the entire recorded output of many early country Blues artists. Like George Buck, Parth controls several labels, the most common being RST and Document. These labels would be available from Blues specialty dealers, such as Down Home Music, Inc. 10341 San Pablo Avenue, El Cerrito, California 95430; Jazz Record Mart, Eleven West Grand Avenue, Chicago, Illinois 60610, phone (312) 222-1474; and a mail-order firm, Roots & Rhythm, 6921 Stockton Avenue, El Cerrito, California 94530, phone (510) 525-1494.

Today's collectors can eliminate digging and duplication, such as I went through during the LP era, by picking up Parth's complete chronological sets on the Memphis Jug Band, Gus Cannon and the Jug Stompers, Blind Blake, and Papa Charlie Jackson, plus seven volumes of Lonnie Johnson's earliest sides.

A more widely-available domestic label, Yazoo, also has sampler CDs containing the best 78s by most of these artists. Yazoo is distributed by Shanachie Records, P.O. Box 208, Newton, New Jersey 07860, phone (800) 497-1043.

To help in compiling record want lists and locating sources, try an excellent new magazine that concentrates on country Blues, *Blues Review Quarterly,* Rt. 2,

Blues

Box 118, West Union, WV 26456, $12/yr. The leading U. S. Blues periodical, published every other month, is *Living Blues,* The Center For The Study of Southern Culture, The University of Mississippi, University, MS 38677-9836, $18/yr. *Living Blues* concentrates almost entirely on contemporary artists, principally urban Blues figures.

Dedicated country Blues collectors will eventually need a copy of the principal discography thereof, Blues & Gospel Records 1902-1943, by R.M.W. Dixon and J. Godrich. The latest (1982) edition is published by Storyville Publications and Co., Ltd., 66 Fairview Drive, Chigwell, Essex, England 1G7 6HS. Storyville's current postpaid price therefor in U.S. dollars (a check drawn on a U.S. bank is O.K.) is $49.30 plus, if you wish, $3.50 for registration to insure safe arrival.

Another useful reference to the field is *Blues Who's Who,* by Sheldon Harris. Published in 1979, it contains capsule biographies of a comprehensive list of blues singers, both historical and present-day. A trade paperback edition is available for $25 postpaid ($30 foreign) from Sheldon Harris, 2111 Ave. W., Brooklyn, NY 11339.

I have been meaning to talk to you about blues for some time. I was moved to pick up my pen upon the arrival of a review copy of a superb new CD that, while it remains pretty much in the jazz category and would therefore be easy for all of you to enjoy, conveys the unbuttoned flavor of jug band music. It is Flying Fish FF 70589 "Beat It, Blow It, Strum It, Hum It!" by the Sunshine Skiffle Band.

This is a ten-or-eleven piece aggregation including several veterans of the Washington, D.C. Dixieland scene, such as cornetist Dave Robinson (who here also plays comb, kazoo, alto valve trombone, tambourine and slide whistle), clarinetist Don Rouse, and leader Gil Carter (normally a drummer, but as a Skiffler slaps a steamer-trunk-like contraption called a rhumba box). Just about everyone doubles on some kind of instrument, the full arsenal covering fiddle, banjo, harmonica, saw, two washboards, gutbucket (a washtub bass), jug and even whistling. Various sidemen handle vocal chores, going from Henry Stinson's clear-toned crooning to Carter's husky hollering.

As you can see, the Sunshiners have plenty of resources at their disposal, deployed here with imagination and a dead-center understanding of the jug-band idiom. Each track has some different kind of musical combination presented along the way: "Breeze" opens with a poignant clarinet duet; "Orange Blossom Special" is a country-fiddle showcase; "Boodle-Am-Shake" has a raucous group-scat improvised ensemble; and "Crazy Words, Crazy Tune" incorporates - is the world ready for this? - both a kazoo duet and a slide whistle duet.

This wide variety of effects maintains interest throughout the disc's 52 minutes. Furthermore, they are intelligently placed, each effectively underscoring the general message of the song.

Best of all, every note communicates the impudent zestful joy of this type of music. If I were reviewing this uplifting album in my "This Month's Records" column, I would give it my highest rating of five stars. Flying Fish FF 70589 is available in compact disc format @ $16 postpaid, audiocassette @ $11, from Gil Carter, 3450 Ordway Street NW, Washington, D.C. 20016.

Because I perform in the D.C. area with some frequency, I have crossed paths several times with the Sunshine Skiffle Band. Thus, I can report, for the benefit of festival producers who want to try something new, that, once this good-natured off-the-wall crew starts to roll, there is no way you can sit in front of them without coming away refreshed and entertained.

Bessie Smith " Chirpin' The Blues" 1920s Sheet music

Muddy Waters 1950s *Photo from Red Ferns*

August 1993 West Coast Rag.

CHAPTER 33   REFERENCE BOOKS

This is the fourth, and probably last, in a number of "Texas Shouts" dealing with Dixieland and ragtime publications. The February 1991 column covered books analyzing the music. February 1992, popular histories. February 1993, periodicals. Today, references.

Nearly any book about our music can be used as a reference on some point or other. Thus, let's start out by defining terms.

For today's purposes, a "reference" is a book like a telephone directory or dictionary. That is, a significant portion, maybe all, of its text is not meant to be read front to back, but to be dipped into when the need arises to settle some point or other.

As with the previous columns, the fact that I do not mention a particular publication is not intended to be a slight. I have only encountered a fraction of the many books about Dixieland, ragtime and related music. However, readers who are interested in getting deeper into the subject may get a helpful starting point from knowing about some volumes which I have found particularly useful over the years.

Out of the small shelf of ragtime references, I find myself referring most often to *Rags and Ragtime: A Musical History*, by David A. Jasen and Trebor Jay Tichenor. It is a checklist of rags, including copyright date and original publisher, together with capsule biographies of the best-known ragtime composers.

Capsule biographies are all you'll find in *Who's Who In Jazz*, by John Chilton, and *The New Edition Of The Encyclopedia Of Jazz*, by Leonard Feather. My copy of the latter is dated 1960, but I believe that there has been an update since.

If you are particularly interested in biographies of New Orleans musicians, seek out *New Orleans Jazz: A Family Album*, by Al Rose and Edmund Souchon and *Jazz New Orleans, 1895-1963*, by Samuel B. Charters. I understand that an updated edition of the latter is being prepared as I write these words.

Books two and three of *The Complete Encyclopedia Of Popular Music And Jazz 1900-1950*, by Roger D. Kinkle, consist of biographies of jazz artists, along with those of popular composers and performers. This four-volume work is also valuable for locating the year and composers of hit songs during the period covered.

For the serious collector of jazz recordings, the most essential reference work is some kind of discography. A discography will not only provide vital information about the records in your collection, but will also furnish you with data indispensable in locating missing items.

A discography is simply a list of recordings on a given topic. In its most common format, it will catalog in chronological order all of the known recordings on its subject, giving, for each title, the date and city of recording, the artist credit as it appears on the label, the complete personnel and which instrument (or vocal) was played by which person, the master number (including alternate and rejected takes) and the label and catalog number of at least the original issue of the side (and sometimes of reissues).

A common variant on the discography is the bio-discography. This type of reference concentrates on one artist, one band or one geographic area, including a narrative text that furnishes pertinent background on the subject as background for the discographical piece of the work. In many cases, such accompanying text concentrates on the recordings and slides over portions of the subject that did not involve recordings.

A convenient break point for older-style discographies is the early 1940s. First, there was a recording ban in the U.S. imposed by the union during that period, so that, for a while, there is a gap in the number of commercially issued recordings. Second, prior to that time, home ownership of recording equipment was uncommon, so that a reasonably comprehensive picture can be obtained from examining commercial recordings and the files of commercial recording companies. Third, substantially all commercial recordings (except electrical transcriptions designed for radio broadcast) were two-sided 78 rpm platters, so that the complexities of LPs, audiocassettes and CDs, with many performances on one release, are not encountered.

Today, the jazz discographer faces a nearly hopeless, never-ending task. Everyone owns small, hand-held recording equipment. Almost every note played by a jazzman in public these days has been recorded by someone and exists somewhere, albeit in possibly execrable fidelity.

Further, it has become normal for jazz artists to release their own recordings, often made at home on such equipment, in limited editions of 500 or 1000 copies on private labels. Such albums may sell out completely without ever coming to the attention of the larger jazz community of which discographers are a part.

The standard discography for vintage jazz is *Jazz Records 1897-1942,* by Brian Rust. This essential work is published in two volumes by Storyville Publications and Co., Ltd., 66 Fairview Drive, Chigwell, Essex, England IG7 6HS. (Storyville Publications is a prominent publisher of discographies of music from the Dixieland and ragtime years. In the remainder of this column, I will indicate by "(Storyville)" any book mentioned which is one of its publications.)

The current postpaid price of the 5th and latest (1982) edition of Rust, which may change before this column appears in print, is $97, and it is worth every penny. As a record reviewer of such material, I have felt it necessary to pony up for each successive revision upon publication, and I've never been sorry.

Brian Rust is, without question, the dean of discographers of the early jazz years. In the course of his studies, he has accumulated considerable knowledge of records of related music, much of which he has published in separate volumes. These include discographies of British dance bands (co-authored with Sandy Forbes), American dance bands and entertainment figures, plus volumes on American record labels, Victor's electrical 78s and the science of discography.

A number of efforts have been made to bring Rust's research up to more recent times. In a series of eight flimsily-bound paperbacks, now out of print, Jorgen Grunnet Jepsen made the first pass at the period from 1942 to the mid-1960s, producing a generally useful work which also foretold only too clearly that discographies covering the years of privately-produced small-label recordings and widespread home recording equipment were going to be much less complete and accurate than had previously been the case.

W. Bruyninckx has collated Rust with research on later recordings and has reorganized jazz stylistically to produce a series of discographies that cover jazz from its origins through the late 1980s. His series labeled *Traditional Jazz* includes five paperback volumes and an index, and is subject to the usual classification difficulties encountered in trying to pigeonhole jazzmen (does an artist belong in the "Swing" or the "Traditional" category?).

For better or worse, among the available options, I've elected to go with the discographies currently being authored by Erik Raben, covering jazz records from 1942 to 1980. Four volumes of this somewhat pricey hard-cover series have appeared at this writing.

Virtually every jazz figure of the twenties and thirties who is fondly enough remembered to have his/her records reissued with any frequency has been the subject of a bio-discography. In the second of these four columns, I recommended the one which best transcends the limits of the genre and is an engrossing read on its own, *Bix: Man And Legend,* by Richard M. Sudhalter and Philip R. Evans with William Dean-Myatt.

However, as far as I know, the most staggering bio-discography of them all, the Mount Everest for later entrants in the field, is the incredible *Hendersonia: The Music of Fletcher Henderson And His Musicians,* by Walter C. Allen. This unbelievable monument to years of meticulous research, now out of print (I think), includes every conceivable fact that anyone would want to know about Henderson, his recordings, his sidemen, his compositions, etc., etc.

Other bio-discographies on my shelves that have proved highly useful deal with Fats Waller (*"Fats" In Fact*), by Laurie Wright (Storyville); *James P. Johnson: A Case Of Mistaken Identity,* by Scott E. Brown with a discography by Robert Hilbert; *Turk Murphy, Just For the Record,* by Jim Goggin; *Clarence Williams,* by Tom Lord (Storyville); *Jelly Roll Morton (Mr. Jelly Lord),* by Laurie Wright (Storyville); the Original Dixieland Jazz Band and the quintets who modeled themselves after the ODJB *(The Fabulous Fives),* by Horst H. Lange, revised by Ron Jewson, Derek Hamilton-Smith & Ray Webb (Storyville); McKinney's Cotton Pickers *(McKinney's Music),* by John Chilton; *The Jazz Legacy of Don Ewell,* by John Collinson and Eugene Kramer, with seventeen piano transcriptions by Ray Smith (Storyville); and Bob Crosby's Bob Cats and big band *(Stomp Off, Let's Go),* by John Chilton.

Title and composer credits from the original 78s can be most useful to a collector, particularly if the tunes were never published or are rare in published form. *The Paramount 12000/13000 Series,* by Max E. Vreede (Storyville) and *Columbia 13/14000-D Series,* by Dan Mahony include many vintage 78s of interest to fans of our music.

If you're into uptown New Orleans, you might try to find a copy of *New Orleans, The Revival,* by Tom Stagg & Charlie Crump. West Coast revival buffs would prefer *Jazz West: 1945 to 1985,* by K.O. Eckland or maybe even *Jazz On The Barbary Coast,* by Tom Stoddard (Storyville).

| TEXAS SHOUT: HOW DIXIELAND JAZZ WORKS |

The list goes on. Some of the references on our field are highly specialized, if not esoteric. How about *German Ragtime & Prehistory Of Jazz,* by Rainier E. Lotz (Storyville)? QRS piano rolls (*The Billings Rollography,* by Ginny and Bob Billings)? *Jazz In The Movies,* by David Meeker? Where the names of some of the early jazz tunes came from (*Tell Your Story,* by Eric Townley (Storyville))? Spike Jones (*Thank You Music Lovers,* compiled by Jack Mirtle)?

Whatever your particular interest in jazz may be, there almost certainly has been a reference written about it. These are available, in most cases, only from specialty dealers and will not be found on the shelves of your local book store. While some of the books listed above are out of print, specialty dealers may well have either used copies or new ones that have been sitting unpurchased on their shelves for years. Thus, it can't hurt to ask about something you really want.

I have had good success in dealing by phone and mail with two such specialty booksellers, one in the East and one in the West. They are: OLB Jazz, a division of Oaklawn Books, Box 2663, Providence, RI 02907, phone (401) 941-6840; and Arthur L. Newman, 10325 Elk River Ct., Fountain Valley, CA 92708-5924, phone (714) 968-3706 or (714) 968-3921.

As you find your area of special interest within our music, and begin delving more deeply into it, you will discover that you need a reference work about it - both to help you keep track of what you've already located and to put you on the right track for the rest of it. If you're truly serious about this pursuit, you might as well spring for a reference now and make life easier for yourself as you go forward.

You'll also find, I think, that you're having more fun along the way and, as you accumulate more knowledge about the music and its players, enjoying it more - which is what Dixieland and ragtime, in the last analysis, is all about. Good luck.

Sept. 1993 West Coast Rag

CHAPTER 34   DOWNTOWN NEW ORLEANS

There were three styles of Dixieland played in New Orleans in the early days of jazz. In "Texas Shout" for September and October 1992, I discussed the style played by the white Crescent Citians, which embodies more or less legitimate technique, is ensemble-oriented, and has no significant blues content. The other two styles were played by Black musicians and are known as the "downtown" and "uptown" styles of New Orleans Dixieland.

The downtown style, the subject of today's column, was a relatively schooled and sophisticated music. The downtown Blacks included the Creoles, individuals of mixed African and European descent, who occupied a somewhat higher place on New Orleans' social ladder than more pure-blooded Blacks. As a result, the downtown Blacks got more exposure to "legitimate" music (such as grand opera), both in terms of musical training and in cultural background.

The jazz that they developed, not surprisingly, is a blend that draws strongly from both these "legitimate" influences and the rougher, strongly blues-based, visceral music of the uptown Blacks with whom the downtowners regularly interacted. Downtown New Orleans style is ensemble-oriented, usually calls for a reasonably demanding degree of technical skill, often involves multi-strain compositions executed with noticeable precision, and incorporates a significant blues content.

Just about all of the jazz sides waxed during the 1920s by Black musicians from New Orleans are in the downtown style. These include the 78s of King Oliver's Creole Jazz Band, Ory's Sunshine Orchestra, Louis Armstrong and his Hot Five/Seven, Clarence Williams' Blue Five and Jelly Roll Morton's Red Hot Peppers.

There are very few vintage-period recordings of uptown style. The uptown musicians were not as frequently called by their downtown colleagues to come to cities like Chicago and New York, which were the major recording centers. Not placing as high a value as the downtowners on a "legitimate" approach to technique, the uptowners were sometimes misunderstood and mistakenly believed to be inferior performers vs. the downtowners.

Recording equipment in the twenties was nowhere near as compact and portable as it is today. Undertaking a field trip to New Orleans to make records was a logistical effort for a major label housed in Gotham or the Windy City.

Moreover, times being what they were, on the occasions when such field trips did take place, the recording executives arrived in the deep South to discover little interest there in getting Black musicians on record. Celestin's Original Tuxedo Jazz Orchestra (15 sides), Sam Morgan's Jazz Band (8), Louis DuMaine's Jazzola Eight (4), the Jones and Collins Astoria Hot Eight (4) and Fate Marable's Society Syncopators (2), plus some alternatives and vocal backups, pretty much sum up the Black jazz recorded in N.O. in the 1920s, vs. the dozens of platters in the north by

TEXAS SHOUT: HOW DIXIELAND JAZZ WORKS

Oliver, Armstrong, the Dodds brothers, Morton, Noone, Bechet, Williams, Ory, et al.

Among the seven styles of Dixieland, one could make a persuasive argument that downtown New Orleans is the most perfectly balanced. For example, it has more blues than white New Orleans and West Coast revival, but not as much as uptown New Orleans. It presents soloists with technique sufficient to execute very intricate conceptions, but does not emphasize soloing as much as Chicago style. It pays attention to cleanly executed routines on tricky material, but not to the degree that hot dance does.

In making the statement about the balancing of elements in downtown New Orleans, I am most emphatically not saying that downtown New Orleans is a superior art form to any of the other six styles. In my view, each of the seven Dixieland styles has its own objectives and standards; each of those seven, when rendered by creative artists who understand those objectives and standards, has an equal claim to the attention of the discerning Dixielander.

I make the statement about the balancing of elements in downtown New Orleans because, for me, it explains why that style is the only one that nearly always receives favorable comment from the critical community. Even critics who normally do not listen to Dixieland and who are quick to condemn, for example, the relatively heavy rhythm of West Coast revival or the "illegitimate" intonation of uptown New Orleans seldom have a bad word for the downtowners.

Downtown New Orleans, you see, offers a significant proportion of something for everyone. If you like virtuoso soloing, you have Armstrong, Noone, Bechet, and Morton; crisp, cohesive ensembles - Oliver's Creole Jazz Band, the Blue Five and the Red Hot Peppers; advanced compositional structure - Morton again and Lillian Hardin (who was not from New Orleans, but played downtown style); etc.

Thus, when the downtown recordings are reissued, the critic probably focuses on those portions which appeal to his/her special interest and responds positively to them. Whether or not I'm right in this hypothesis, whenever the sides appear by the Apex Club Orchestra, the New Orleans Wanderers/Bootblacks, and the other downtown units mentioned above, they are greeted warmly, are not accused of being dated, and usually wind up at the top of annual critics' polls.

Given the nearly universal acclaim for downtown New Orleans, I can't help remarking on the fact that, of the seven Dixieland styles, downtown New Orleans is the one that has most completely vanished from the current domestic Dixieland scene and very nearly from the face of the earth. You can find plenty of individual players who are consciously influenced by certain downtown jazzmen. Nearly every sizeable Dixieland festival will include a pianist whose debt to Jelly is clear, a sopranoist reworking Bechet, many post-Armstrong lead horns, etc. However, you will look in vain for a band that, as a team, deliberately tries to work within the boundaries of downtown New Orleans.

To be sure, you will hear Morton, Oliver and the others acknowledged from the bandstand in every set. Lots of bands pick repertoire and routines from the famous downtown 78s. However, today's bands will almost always perform those tunes and routines in the West Coast revival, uptown New Orleans or British trad styles of Dixieland.

The last combo I remember seeing in person that chose to be a downtown style Dixieland band was pianist Bob Greene's Red Hot Peppers re-creation about twenty years ago. In fact, my copy of the septet's RCA Victor album, "The World Of Jelly Roll Morton", one of the last U.S. Dixieland records to be released on a major label, bears a 1974 copyright.

Europe recognized jazz as a new and valuable art form before the United States establishment did. Possibly for that reason, the situation is not quite as bleak overseas as it is stateside.

The LPs of Copenhagen's Peruna Jazzmen do a most creditable job of evoking King Oliver's Creole Jazz Band. The Swedish Jazz Kings recorded two albums for Stomp Off using the approach of Clarence Williams' combos. (Further, the SJK's cornetist, Bent Persson, is probably the closest thing you'll hear these days to the way Louis sounded in the twenties). British trumpeter Rod Mason has led (and may still) a quintet modeled after the Hot Five.

In 1992, acting as Festival Jazz Education Coordinator for the Sacramento Dixieland Jubilee, I wrote and M.C.'d a special show entitled "A Cavalcade Of Dixieland Styles". The idea was to present, choosing from the various bands at Sacto that year, as many of the seven Dixieland styles as possible, linking them with an explanatory narrative that outlined each style's origin and its musical objectives. I hoped that, by hearing the different styles side by side, the audience might enhance its ability to appreciate the diversity that the Dixieland idiom has to offer an open-minded listener.

Unfortunately, one of the styles that had to be omitted from that show was downtown New Orleans. Looking over the festival's lineup of some 100 bands from all over the world, I was unable to identify a single one that I felt would play a sufficiently pure downtown style to be used for demonstration purposes in the "Cavalcade".

Thus, I cannot end this column by recommending to festivalgoers a way to experience this very highly regarded brand of Dixieland in person. If you are a newcomer to the festival scene, you probably have heard many bandleaders praising the combos mentioned in this column when tunes are announced. Nevertheless, you probably haven't had a chance to grasp the tremendous appeal of the brand of jazz being discussed, even though you've heard lots of live versions of titles that were written or recorded by Oliver, Morton, Armstrong and the others.

Do yourself a favor. Seek out a specialty store (or check the record bar at the festival) and look for some of the recent chronological reissues by the vintage-period downtown artists. These days the record companies can often get the entire recorded output of one of these immortal combos on just one or two CDs with, I am told, remarkable clarity of the twenties' sound quality (I've long since acquired all of this material on LP, so I'm not personally familiar with the CD versions).

Once you've heard the Creole Jazz Band soar into the out chorus of "New Orleans Stomp", or the Red Hot Peppers romp through the finale of "Georgia Swing", you won't forget the experience. And if enough of us do that, perhaps we'll even create sufficient demand to bring live downtown New Orleans back to the domestic festival and club scene. What a great day that would be!

TEXAS SHOUT: HOW DIXIELAND JAZZ WORKS

King Oliver's Creole Jazz Band   1923   *Photo from Victoria Johnson*

Louis Armstrong's Hot Five   1925   *Photo from Muggsy Spanier*

Downtown New Orleans

Clarence Williams at piano 1920s *photo from The Record Changer*

Jelly Roll Morton's Red Hot Peppers 1926 *Photo from W. R. Hogan Collection*

Kid Ory's Sunshine Orchestra 1944 *Photographer Unknown*

TEXAS SHOUT: HOW DIXIELAND JAZZ WORKS

CHAPTER 35   UPTOWN NEW ORLEANS

In last month's "Texas Shout", I discussed the Dixieland style known as "downtown New Orleans". Today I'd like to talk about the other vintage-period Dixieland style played by Crescent City Black musicians, which is called, not surprisingly, "uptown New Orleans".

To give you all a quick idea of the type of jazz I'm referring to, The Preservation Hall Jazz Band, probably the most famous Dixieland band in the world, plays uptown New Orleans. I'd guess that most readers of this publication have heard that combo or its records and are reasonably familiar with its sound.

Uptown New Orleans is the closest of the seven Dixieland styles to a folk music. Its players express themselves on their instruments in highly personal ways which often pay little or no attention to the accepted "legitimate" performance modes.

Thus, to a listener conditioned to hearing schooled musicians, some uptown players may sound thin-toned or sour-toned. Tuning up within the band may not be as precise as in more schooled styles. Uptown routines may appear to have ragged edges (trumpeter Kid Thomas Valentine would sometimes start a tune by beginning to play it, letting each other sideman enter as soon as he recognized the selection).

No premium is placed in uptown New Orleans on instrumental virtuosity or dazzling solos. There are almost no screech-range trumpeters, lip-trilling trombonists, etc., in this branch of Dixieland. In many cases, soloists stick closely to the melody, adding a few phrase-end fills or decorations to personalize the chorus.

Some jazz critics are unable to make their peace with these characteristics of the music. They tend to denounce uptowners as unskilled performers who can't play their instruments.

In my view, such critics are listening to the wrong thing and are missing some highly satisfying jazz in the process. Although one often gives up technical agility, fleet runs, high notes, resonant tones, crisp section work, etc., in uptown New Orleans, one receives in exchange a very high level of communication on an emotional level with the artists. Uptown style at its best delivers a sense of righteousness, of conviction, that is most exhilarating to experience.

Uptown New Orleans has the highest blues content of the seven Dixieland styles. Said another way, it makes extensive use of bent tones, "blue" notes or other off-pitch sounds which, when properly deployed, create a unique vision of the material, transforming even a frequently-played standard into something fresh and provocative.

This branch of Dixieland emphasizes ensemble playing. On many of the classic recordings in the idiom, the band is heard in ensemble throughout. In other instances, while a "soloist" may temporarily come to the fore of the sound, quite often the other musicians will continue to play throughout the solo, though at a subdued volume.

TEXAS SHOUT: HOW DIXIELAND JAZZ WORKS

The style comes out of a dance hall tradition and is strongly audience-oriented. Uptown musicians often engage as a matter of course in activities that some musicians in other styles consider demeaning, such as marching through the crowd, dancing around the stage or presenting good-natured hokum/comedy numbers.

Putting a premium on entertaining the paying customers without compromising the integrity of their music, many veteran uptowners see no reason to avoid such crowd-pleasing antics that will heighten the hilarity of the show. Again Kid Thomas comes to mind, with his "Milk Cow Blues" routine in which, he does both the male and female vocal, as well as clarinetist Willie Humphrey's bumps and grinds while soloing on "Li'l Liza Jane".

The uptown repertoire also largely comes out of the dance-hall tradition. It focuses primarily on vintage pop tunes rather than compositions specifically written to be performed by Dixieland bands, although the Dixieland standards are played as well.

Further, in keeping with their audience orientation, of playing what the crowd wants to hear, the uptown bands are willing to play requests, even ones for familiar evergreens that revivalist Dixielanders claim are overplayed. Indeed, The Preservation Hall Jazz Band regularly closes its shows with "When The Saints Go Marching In".

For me, many of these characteristics though regarded in some circles as deficiencies, operate to make uptown New Orleans a very accessible, easy-to-enjoy music. Uptown New Orleans makes a point of inviting the listener into the action.

When it's hitting on all cylinders, its emotional power and zestful drive are irresistible. Personally, I'll never forget the last time I saw the Billie and De De Pierce unit of The Preservation Hall Jazz Band, digging in and whipping the audience in a University Of Delaware concert hall into an absolute frenzy.

For reasons related in last month's column, very little uptown New Orleans was recorded during the twenties. The style first attracted widespread notice during the Dixieland revival of the early forties, specifically with the initial recordings by one of its most important figures, trumpeter William Geary "Bunk" Johnson.

That session took place on June 11, 1942 in a third-floor piano storeroom of Grunewald's Music Store in New Orleans. Included in the septet along with Johnson were three other musicians who were to become the archetypes of uptown New Orleans on their instruments: clarinetist George Lewis, trombonist Jim Robinson and banjoist Lawrence Marrero.

Johnson was not an active musician at the time of that recording and essentially used Lewis's band for that purpose. It went on to achieve national fame.

Following Johnson's death in 1949, the septet, under Lewis' leadership, became the flagship band for uptown New Orleans during the 1950s and one of the most influential Dixieland bands in jazz history. All over the world today, there are combos playing the Lewis repertoire, with each sideman trying his best to replicate the licks of his counterpart in Lewis' most celebrated lineup: trumpeter Avery "Kid" Howard; Lewis; Robinson; pianist Alton Purnell; Marrero; bassist Alcide "Slow Drag" Pavageau; and drummer/vocalist Joe Watkins.

Uptown New Orleans

The Johnson and Lewis combos pretty much had the field to themselves well into the fifties. However, with the inauguration and subsequent success of Preservation Hall, other fine uptown musicians and bands started appearing more frequently on records, such as trumpeter De De Pierce and his wife, pianist/vocalist Billie Pierce; clarinetist Albert Burbank; banjoists "Creole George" Guesnon and Emanuel Sayles; alto saxophonist "Cap'n" John Handy; drummer Josiah "Cie" Frazier; and trumpeter Percy Humphrey and his brother, clarinetist Willie Humphrey.

Primus inter pares among these was probably Kid Thomas' Algiers Stompers, a raw-edged, fiery team that was the most important uptown combo during the sixties. Its personnel, including trumpeter Kid Thomas Valentine, tenor saxophonist Emanuel Paul, trombonist Louis Nelson, bassist Joseph Butler and drummer Sammy Penn, became icons of the idiom, while the band itself spawned a number of imitators.

In many cases, devotees of this style who followed in their idols' footsteps tended to copy the routines on the records. Such imitation sometimes went so far as replication not only of obvious clams made by the individual players on the original 78s but also of devices which (as discussed below) may not always have been the best ones.

By contrast, the uptowners strongly influenced a number of British jazzmen, specifically trumpeter Ken Colyer and trombonist Chris Barber, who began performing in the 1950s an uptown-derived style, but modified somewhat to suit their artistic leanings. Their approach in turn developed its own followers and became a Dixieland style known as "British trad". British trad is the most recent Dixieland style to emerge, and deserves a separate column all its own.

The uptown scene was dominated for so long by the Johnson and Lewis combos that, in some circles, their way of performing seems to have been viewed as the only "correct" or "legitimate" mode in this genre. For the consideration of combos whose tastes lean toward uptown New Orleans, I'd like to mention a couple of devices which, in my view, did not always work to the benefit of the ride.

Lewis' vocalists tended to sing two-chorus vocals in which the same lyrics were sung successively twice without interruption. To me, singing the same chorus twice in a row amounts to playing the same solo twice in a row, something you never hear because it prevents the performance from building and developing.

If you are going to have a two-consecutive-chorus vocal, then the vocalist should sing a second chorus that has different lyrics. If the vocalist is going to sing the same chorus twice, I think it better for the two vocal choruses to be separated by some kind of instrumental passage.

In order to keep fast tunes from ending too abruptly, so that the ride doesn't seem to run into a brick wall at top speed, most bands adopt some kind of closing device that puts an exclamation point at the finale. These include "double endings" (playing two extra bars of ensemble on the tonic chord), "turnarounds" moving to a "six (VI7)" chord on the last measure and playing the last four bars again), scored tags and a host of other effects. One of the most common has the drummer playing a four-bar break at the end of the last chorus, after which the ensemble returns for a final four or eight bars.

| TEXAS SHOUT: HOW DIXIELAND JAZZ WORKS |

The Lewis band, from time to time, would end a tune with a four-bar drum break and then play an entire full ensemble chorus as a windup. Most of the time, I find the playing of a full chorus after the break to be anticlimactic.

A properly functioning combo should have developed the ride to its maximum intensity on the last chorus. It is extremely difficult to maintain or increase that kind of emotional pitch for yet one more chorus, especially after the relaxation afforded by a short break.

Both of these devices, the two-chorus repeated vocal and the full-chorus ensemble after the drum break, were picked up by uptown revivalists in the sixties. However, they were not adopted by the British trad bands and they have pretty much faded from the current scene.

Nevertheless, it is worth raising the points here. The uptowners created some immortal jazz and rightly inspired many followers. However, if the music is to remain vital, it can't be perpetuated by mere imitation.

Those who perform it today need to maintain creativity and independent judgment regarding the music. They should continually ask themselves whether this or that element of the performance should be kept in the act. These two devices, in my view at least, are ones that revivalist uptowners should think through very carefully before deciding to emulate.

Today's uptown jazzmen/women naturally turn toward recordings of their favorite artists for source material. The tunes recorded by Bunk Johnson, George Lewis, Kid Thomas Valentine, Billie and De De Pierce, etc. have become staples of the contemporary uptown repertoire.

In some cases, the pioneering musicians did not fully remember the tune as the composer originally wrote it. In those cases, they simply made up the missing parts. This procedure will work well enough as long as everyone in the band has the same understanding of what melody and chords are to be played at any given time.

Sometimes memories were sufficiently faulty that what emerged was an entirely original composition. Bunk Johnson's 1942 recording of "Bluebells Goodbye" for example, is almost surely an attempt to recall "Bright Eyes. (Good Bye.)" (1905), words by Harry H. Williams, music by Egbert Van Alstyne. However, Johnson undoubtedly got the song mixed up in his mind with "Blue Bell" (1904), words by Edward Madden, music by Theodore F. Morse, also a march-like tune with a lyric about a man bidding farewell to his love. The result, "Bluebells Goodbye", is in fact a brand new tune that doesn't resemble either of its sources in more than a superficial way.

In such cases, jazz bands wanting to play those numbers will, of course, use the early uptown records as a model. They are the definitive versions of these "new" titles.

There are other cases where pioneering uptown bands have played standard tunes, ones familiar to most Dixieland players, and not followed the accepted versions of the chords or melody. In such instances, revivalist uptowners have typically tacitly "corrected" the music and used the standard practices.

Some tunes occupy a middle ground. These are selections that are not particularly obscure but which are primarily played only by uptown New Orleans Dixielanders, and where the common practice is to follow the recordings rather than the sheet music. One example that readily comes to mind is "Ice Cream".

"(I Scream - You Scream - We All Scream For) Ice Cream" (1927), by Howard Johnson, Billy Moll and Robert King, is a clever novelty ditty about a college for eskimos. As originally written, the lyric to the first chorus is (spelling and punctuation per the original song sheet):

> I scream, you scream,
> We all scream for Ice Cream
> Rah! Rah! Rah!
> Tuesdays Mondays
> We all scream for Sundaes
> Siss! Boom! Bah!
> Boola Boola Sasparoola
> If you've got Chocolet
> We'll take Vanoola
> I scream, you scream,
> We all scream for Ice Cream
> Rah! Rah! Rah!

George Lewis' drummer/vocalist Joe Watkins obviously did not remember this lyric and instead sang what seems to me to be meaningless gibberish. Here is Watkins' version, from the first chorus of his vocal of June 18, 1953 as recorded on Delmark DL-201:

> You scream, I scream
> Everybody wants ice cream
> Rock, rock my baby rock.
> You scream, I scream
> Everybody wants ice cream
> Rock, rock my baby rock.
> Osceloa, R.C. Cola,
> Everybody wants a Pepsi-Cola.
> You scream, I scream
> Everybody wants ice cream
> Rock, rock my baby rock.

To me, it is perfectly obvious which of the two lyrics has the superior claim to be rendered. Nevertheless, despite the fact that the sheet music to this tune is reprinted from time to time in folios of twenties songs, the Watkins version is essentially the only one heard from Dixieland stages.

Similar discrepancies occur in tune titles. "Panama" (1911) by William H. Tyers and "Hiawatha (A Summer Idyl)" (1901) by Neil Moret (pseudonym for Charles N. Daniels) are commonly played by uptowners under the respective titles "Panama Rag" and "Hiawatha Rag". However, as indicated, the word "rag" does not appear in the title of either. Moreover, from a musical viewpoint, neither one is in fact a rag - "Panama" is written in entirely Latin time, while "Hiawatha" is completely unsyncopated.

Along the same lines, the familiar Dixieland flagwaver "Weary Blues" (1915), by Artie Matthews, is frequently played by uptowners under the title "Shake It And Break It". Apparently this title comes from a line of a lyric sometimes sung to the chorus which begins "You shake it, you break it, you hang it on the wall, ..."

I point out these "errors" not to criticize the pioneering uptown musicians, who created immortal jazz and some of my favorite performances. Those musicians were not schooled and were certainly not musicologists.

I mention them because I believe that, as we follow their footsteps in light of information easily available today, we need not necessarily adopt the same practices. I see no reason, for example, why today's musicians shouldn't play a tune under the title the composer gave it.

Why create audience confusion by playing "Weary Blues" as "Shake It And Break It?" Especially when "Shake It And Break It" (1920), words by H. Qualli Clark, music by Signor Friscoe Lou Chiha, an entirely different number, was recorded by a number of famous jazzmen during the vintage years and is still played today?

For that matter, some possibility of audience confusion is created by playing "Panama" as "Panama Rag". There is, after all, a piece titled "Panama Rag", a ragtime piano solo written in 1904 and published as by Cy Seymour (believed to be a pseudonym for W.C. Polla). The rag is currently in print in a folio from Dover Books and probably is heard occasionally at ragtime gatherings.

With respect to actual changes in the music itself, as with the lyrics to "Ice Cream", I believe that a jazzman ought to try, if reasonably possible, to present the number as its composer wrote it. That is, I think the proper starting place is the published sheet music, which is not as hard to locate for many selections as one might think. During the sixties, when I really started digging into this music in earnest, I was amazed at the number of times I would try calling a New York publisher about some tune from the twenties to discover that it was still in print and could be sent to me for seventy-five cents plus postage.

Sometimes, after examining the music or comparing it to recorded versions, an artist will decide that certain modifications need to be made if the piece is to swing comfortably as a jazz vehicle. I have no problem with such decisions, as long as the artist has given the subject some independent thought. I have trouble with mindlessly copying what someone - even one of the all-time great jazzmen - happened to do one day years ago in a recording studio for reasons we can never know (which might include, for example, being tired or preoccupied and thereby not bringing his best skills to bear on what he was doing).

I have gone through this sermon because the uptown style is the branch of Dixieland that has, in its original source recordings, the largest number of pitfalls of this type for those who are coming along behind. Let's keep the best parts of that heritage by all means, but remain alert to areas where we can add elements that will enhance it.

Before leaving this subject, I want to touch on two elements of the mythology of uptown New Orleans. One deals with the alleged primacy of the style and the other deals with its view of elderly musicians.

Uptown buffs are known to claim that this style was the first known jazz style and that all later Dixieland styles, and indeed all other subsequent jazz forms, are somehow less pure and authentic. I doubt that anyone can be certain which of the three New Orleans Dixieland styles came first or how quickly the other two followed in its wake.

Still, the claim for primacy of uptown New Orleans seems plausible enough to me because, as I have previously mentioned, it is the least technically sophisticated of the three. However, that fact surely is of no more than historical interest and does not support any kind of implication that the style itself has some sort of superior claim to the attention of jazz buffs.

The artistic merit of jazz styles does not in any way depend on their chronological age. All styles, when performed by skilled artists who understand the genre, are equally "authentic" examples thereof.

A mediocre rendition of uptown New Orleans Dixieland, or any other style, is mediocre no matter how you slice it. Such a performance is not more worthy of our time than a superior performance in Chicago, West Coast revival, etc., just because uptown New Orleans appeared on the scene earlier. Similarly, mediocre swing or bop performances have no claim to superiority over outstanding Dixieland performances just because swing and bop are later styles and are, in the eyes of their supporters, more "advanced" or "up to date" than Dixieland.

It is commonly believed by the jazz community that Bunk Johnson and the other musicians who sparked interest in uptown New Orleans were elderly musicians. This notion has been romanticized in some circles into a hagiology that seems to consider Dixieland musicians of advanced age, particularly Black musicians from New Orleans, as having some kind of special understanding of the "authentic", "original", "correct", or whatever, way to play jazz. I have no doubt that much of The Preservation Hall Jazz Band's appeal to the non-jazz audience comes from its implicit (and sometimes explicit) fostering of ideas along these lines.

While the uptowners of the 1940s revival were no longer youths, they were not old men. On December 1, 1945, the time when Johnson's most fondly recalled lineup was in the process of making a series of recordings for Decca and Victor that are usually ranked with his best, the average age of the seven musicians was 48 years and 1 month.

While playing a musical instrument is an activity that calls for a certain amount of physical strength and stamina, it is not so demanding that middle-aged people should be considered to be in danger of losing their talents. Indeed, the average age of many Dixieland bands on the festival circuit today is well above 48, including quite a few of the most popular and creatively potent units. As has been demonstrated time and again, jazz musicians in their fifties are still at a time of life when they can be expected to perform at peak.

This is not true, on the average, when musicians reach their seventies and eighties. Of course, we can all cite many great ragtimers and jazzmen who continued to create great music in those years - Doc Cheatham, Bob Haggart, Alton

TEXAS SHOUT: HOW DIXIELAND JAZZ WORKS

Purnell, Yank Lawson, Milt Hinton, Art Hodes, Louis Nelson, Wild Bill Davison, Eubie Blake; the list is a long one.

However, advancing age affects different people in different way. There have been many other truly elderly artists who, for one reason or another, did not retain the manual dexterity, breath control, imagination and other talents that are required to play worthwhile jazz.

I would be the last to deny such performers the adulation and acclaim that they have earned through a lifetime of distinguished contributions to our music. I have many times gone out of my way to attend appearances by artists whose jazz has given me much pleasure even though I knew before leaving the house that the show would be a dim echo of days gone by - and I thoroughly enjoyed myself in the bargain.

However, I think it is important to keep such matters in perspective. Given that we would all like to attract more fans to our music, we should recognize that we are not helping our cause in that respect by representing below-average outings by superannuated musicians well past their primes as examples of something our friends should admire for itself alone.

I am taking the trouble to make this point because I can't forget what happened the last time Nancy and I attended a concert by The Preservation Hall Jazz Band. On that evening several years ago, the lineup included a musician who had made historically important recordings in the vintage years.

While I was grateful for the opportunity to see him live for the only time in my life that I did so, my enjoyment was quickly dissipated upon discovering that he was so feeble that he was not only barely able to play his instrument but also could hardly struggle to his feet when the front line stood up for the out chorus. He died shortly thereafter.

We spent much of the concert feeling rather sorry for this gentleman. We also were considerably disturbed to observe that a band which presents itself to the general non-jazz public - the bulk of the audience at this particular show - as preserving the true jazz heritage would include in its presentation someone who was so clearly incapable of delivering on that promise.

That was the sixth time I had attended a concert by the PHJB. The first five were memorable. Thus, we may be placing too much emphasis on one night's experience. However, we were so put off by what we saw that we have yet to be able to bring ourselves to attend another, even though the band appears annually at a theatre about a half-hour from my home.

Perhaps, as is sometimes asserted, the veteran uptown musicians of the 1950s and 1960s were maintaining a form of jazz that they had played since the turn of the century and which was free of intervening influences. However, that is not the case now.

Musicians in their seventies today were born in the late teens and twenties. Many of them absorbed their initial jazz influences during a period of nationwide radio broadcasts and record distribution, at a time when the cutting edge of jazz was beginning to change from Dixieland to swing.

There cannot any longer be a significant reason to regard elderly musicians as special keepers of the flame of any Dixieland style. Indeed, many of the third-and-fourth generation revivalists on the scene today, most of whom learned the music in the same way as many of today's "elderly" musicians, are doing a perfectly splendid job in that respect.

Records in the uptown style are fairly easy to find in any record store that emphasizes jazz. However, for comprehensive one-stop shopping by someone new to the idiom, I'd suggest contacting George H. Buck, Jr. and requesting a copy of his free catalog. The address is 1206 Decatur Street, New Orleans, LA 70116, phone (504) 525-1776.

Among his stable of labels, particularly on American Music, G.H.B. and Jazzology, George has many records of uptown New Orleans. These include all of the great names in the field, each of whom can be heard performing at his/her best on one or another of George's releases.

Preservation Hall Jazz Band 1950s *Photo by Dan Leyrer*

TEXAS SHOUT: HOW DIXIELAND JAZZ WORKS

Kid Thomas Valentine 1960s *Photo by Ed Lawless*

Billie & De De Pierce 1950s
Photographer Unknown

Bunk Johnson 1938
Photo by George Hoefer

CHAPTER 36 BRITISH TRAD

The Dixieland revival that began in the U.S. in the early forties spread to England fairly rapidly despite the obstacles of wartime. By 1943-44, British pianist George Webb was recording with a combo that certainly sounds as if someone therein had been listening to Lu Watters' 78s.

Bunk Johnson's recordings of that period also didn't take long to get across the pond. By 1949-50, the Crane River Jazz Band was performing an uptown New Orleans-derived Dixieland style. Two of its members were cornetist Ken Colyer and clarinetist Monty Sunshine.

In order to get closer to the source of his musical interests, Colyer took a job as a seaman and jumped ship when he reached New Orleans in 1952. Before the authorities caught up with and deported him, he had spent as much time as he could learning jazz at the knees of George Lewis and other seminal uptowners.

Colyer returned in 1953 to something of a hero's welcome from the British Dixieland community. He found a band waiting for him, a piano-less sextet with himself, Sunshine and trombonist Chris Barber in the front line.

That version of Ken Colyer's Jazzmen was one of the all-time great British Dixieland units. While it did not stay together long (breaking up in 1954), it was highly influential on up-and-coming British Dixielanders.

Two first-rate bands emerged from the breakup, one led by Colyer and one by Barber (with Sunshine in the personnel). While both leaders perpetuated the basic sound they had created together, Colyer favored a somewhat looser, more uptown-leaning approach, while Barber tightened the routines and the instrumental voicings.

Of course, there have been lots of good bands over the years. However, the Colyer/Barber matchup and its two immediate successors inspired imitators among their countrymen.

It is the widespread attempt, over a sustained period, of disciples to play more or less like a specific model that creates a jazz style. A band may be the most original combo that ever took the field, but if no one follows its lead, the stylistic ripples it makes will never mature into tidal waves.

As units led by clarinetist Acker Bilk or trumpeter Kenny Ball became popular, even to the point of making the pop charts once in a while in the U.S., common characteristics thereof began to be noticed. Dixieland bands exhibiting those characteristics have come to be known as "British trad" bands.

British trad is the seventh, and so far the last, distinctive Dixieland style to have appeared on the scene. One can hear it today in the playing of, among others, the popular Climax Jazz Band from Toronto (perhaps the purest post-Barber team extant), the Phoenix Jazzers from the Pacific Northwest, Monty Sunshine's Jazz Band and the Albion Jazz Band, a reunion septet formed to carry forward the Colyer approach to jazz.

TEXAS SHOUT: HOW DIXIELAND JAZZ WORKS

(Oddly enough, you are less likely to hear it from Barber himself, though he is still going strong. His crew is now called a Jazz & Blues Band, and is as likely to play New Orleans rhythm 'n blues a la Professor Longhair as vintage 1950s British trad.)

Because Colyer and colleagues were trying to emulate the uptown New Orleans style (which I discussed in the two previous "Texas Shout" columns), British trad has a lot in common with uptown. British trad players play very compatibly onstage with uptown artists and typically perform much of the usual uptown repertoire.

However, if the differences between those two styles are subtle, they are nevertheless real. While uptown New Orleans is almost a kind of "folk Dixieland", as I discussed in my previous columns, British trad is more consciously an art music.

British trad pays more attention to "legitimate" intonation, to cleanly executed routines and to playing tunes designed primarily as jazz vehicles (rather than as popular songs). For example, Barber's band recorded in its early days a number of tunes by Duke Ellington, a composer not played much by uptowners. Further, a British trad band may voice the front line instruments in harmony for certain passages, something the uptowners almost never do.

Another distinguishing, and controversial, feature of most British trad bands is the role given to the banjo in their rhythm sections. Colyer's and Barber's combos often did not have a piano, so their only chord instrument was the banjo.

Their rhythm was mounted on a metronomic four-four from the banjo, usually somewhat prominent in the mix, supported by the bass and drums. Even when a piano is present, the listener frequently hears the banjo as the principal rhythm instrument.

For some reason, perhaps the humidity coming across the English Channel, the banjos on the early British trad recordings produced a somewhat tinny and unresonant sound. As the pioneering bands were imitated by their disciples, this particular banjo sound became de rigueur for the style.

Those who respond to British trad don't give a second thought to the banjo timbre - it's an integral and accepted part of the action, just as football has goal posts instead of a pitcher's mound. However, there are quite a few critics who can't get past it and who dismiss British trad units (and miss a lot of good jazz in the process) amid complaints of "clanging", "scraping" and other epithets directed at the banjoist.

In the July 1990 "The Letter Drop" column of *WCR*, reader Francis Eaton requested that I explain the differences between the various Dixieland styles. Well, Francis, it has taken a while, but today's column on British trad finishes the job.

For your reference, hot dance was covered in the February 1990 "Texas Shout", Chicago in July-August and September 1991, white New Orleans in September-October 1992, West Coast revival in November-Holiday 1992, downtown New Orleans three issues ago and, as mentioned, uptown New Orleans in the two previous columns. I hope all of you are now prepared for the examination.

British Trad

Seriously, though, before leaving the discussion of Dixieland styles, there are a few general thoughts that I think are worth leaving with you. These deal with the question of categorizing the music in the first place. Is this just an academic exercise, or is there some useful purpose in doing so?

I think that more widespread recognition of the seven Dixieland styles, and their various objectives and characteristics, is important. I see it as the best way not only to expand one's own enjoyment of the music but also to dampen the infighting and factionalism that has, for as long as I've been interested in the music, crippled the Dixieland community from effectively marshalling whatever economic power it has.

Most Dixieland fans I've encountered tend to like only one or two styles. They are quick to lump together all of the other styles (the ones they don't like), without recognizing any differences between them, as consisting of players who are doing the wrong thing.

I believe that the more you know about something, the more likely you are to enjoy it. If you prefer the powerful West Coast style, for example, you're missing a lot if you - as so many Watters/Murphy devotees are prone to do - criticize Chicago musicians as a bunch of soloists who play the same tunes all the time and who value technique above musicality.

Why not try digging a good Chicago band, recognizing up front that, because Chicago is solo-oriented, you may well see some virtuoso players who have the ability (if you give them a chance and listen with an open mind) to show you new facets of tunes you think you've heard to the point of exhaustion? If you go in with that attitude, without a predisposition to immediately find fault with a band that doesn't have a banjo or tuba and isn't going to play "Elephant Wobble" or "Sud Buster's Dream", you might come away very pleasantly surprised at what you did hear from the musicians.

If you're a fan of hot dance, with its intricately-voiced section passages and quick, precise changes in tonal colors, you may have been turned off by the uptown New Orleans musicians, with their sometimes home-grown techniques and distinctive tones. You may already have written them off as people who can't play their instruments.

How's about forgetting about those complaints for a few sets, and letting these artists do what they do best, communicate with you on an emotional level, giving yourself up to be swept away in the momentum of a full-throated uptown rideout or the fragility of a George Lewis-ish clarinet singing the blues? You might see musicians exposing their inner selves in a way that shows you depths of the music that few hot dance arrangements ever captured.

In short, if you say you like Dixieland, you should realize that all seven styles I've covered belong to that music you say you like. They all use the same musical vocabulary and conventions, i.e., those developed by jazzmen prior to the onset of swing in the thirties. Each style has chosen to do something a little different with that vocabulary and those conventions, something that is worth doing, something that is easily accessible to you if you already like any Dixieland at all and if you'll just take the time to understand what's going on.

TEXAS SHOUT: HOW DIXIELAND JAZZ WORKS

If you do so, you will gain a new appreciation of the wonderful diversity within the Dixieland community and you will have broken down your own barriers supporting the factionalism that hurts our music. There are too few Dixielanders as it is without further fragmenting our numbers.

Yet, how many of you don't go to your local Dixieland club when it presents a style that isn't your favorite? And how many of you then complain when not enough members turn out (for the same reason) to see the band you really enjoy?

Within a few hours of my home, there are several clubs that present Dixieland on a more-or-less regular basis. One of them, an organization with well over a thousand members, heavily emphasizes one style in its presentations. As the overall Dixieland audience has decreased during the 1980s, this sizeable group has had difficulty getting much more than 100 people to attend its regular concerts (i.e., events that aren't multi-band weekend spectaculars).

By contrast, another of these societies, less than half the size of the one just mentioned, regularly draws close to two hundred to its recurring concerts, and attendance is increasing. Why? This second society takes the trouble to present good bands that play all styles of Dixieland (and, on occasion, swing).

When Nancy and I go to its concerts, we always see essentially the same central core of happy faces. The members know that whatever the society presents will be worth hearing; that if the style presented today isn't their favorite, a style they like will soon get its fair share on the bill; and that all the club members are ultimately on the same side of the fence. Specifically, if each member boycotts a style he doesn't like, none of the concerts will be economical and in the long run the society will be in trouble.

In today's precarious climate for Dixieland, I see this attitude as the only sane one to take. We have simply got to stop fighting with each other. If you agree and if you're willing to go out and help support the styles your fellow club members and festivalgoers like, so that they will reciprocate, you might as well learn something about those styles so you'll have a better time.

I'm not saying you have to go to everything that's around, or that you will like every band you hear. I'm certainly not saying that you should spend hours on end forcing yourself to listen to music you don't understand.

I'd say you should take it a little at a time. Try one new band for one set at each festival you attend, or a new style a few times a year at your local jazz club, making sure that whatever style you're sampling is represented by a combo that is regarded as a good one musically (not always the same as being popular with crowds).

When you go, don't plan to force yourself to like the music right away. Instead, enter with the goal of understanding why other people think that this type of jazz is worthwhile.

If you do, I'll bet that you'll wind up appreciating aspects of Dixieland that you never thought much about previously. You'll find some bands you'd never heard before that you'll want to hear again. And you'll get even more fun out of your interest in Dixieland.

As a closing caution, I should point out that we are talking about Dixieland jazz, an element of popular culture, something which does not easily lend itself to drawing bright lines. Many bands operate around the common borders of the various Dixieland styles and can't readily be pigeonholed into one style or another.

That's as it should be. Each band should be trying to find its own distinctive voice, taking whichever bits and pieces of the music seem most appealing, and forging them into something fresh and new. Thus, many Dixieland bands won't fit precisely into any one of the seven styles, and there's no reason why they should.

For example, The Grand Dominion Jazz Band works within its own marvelous blend of British trad and uptown New Orleans. I hear all three New Orleans styles from time to time in the music of the Golden Eagle Jazz Band, with the emphasis sometimes flowing from one to another in mid-rendition. The Hot Frogs combine the force of West Coast revival with the outgoing mood of white New Orleans.

If these, or similarly cross-styled bands, should ever inspire hordes of conscious imitators, we might even wind up some day with a new eighth style of Dixieland. However, I don't think that will happen. The Dixieland community is dwindling in size and no longer has the common channels of communication that it had in the sixties.

In that respect, the experience of the New Black Eagle Jazz Band is instructive. When it came on the scene in the 1970s, it quickly became the most influential Dixieland band of the last twenty years. Its sound, a core of uptown New Orleans balanced around the edges with British trad and downtown New Orleans, was new and valid in the field.

If it had appeared in the forties or fifties, we might have a "Boston trad" or "New England revival" style at festivals today. However, other bands did not decide to imitate the Eagles as a team. What happened was that other combos took elements of the NBEJB's presentation and incorporated them selectively into already developed ensembles.

Thus, we hear many bands today (I'm a member of a few myself) playing tunes that were brought back to the repertoire by the Black Eagles. Quite a few combos have modified their approaches to rhythm to bring them closer to the Eagles' gliding four-beat that shifts into two-beat virtually on a free-form basis. The Eagles' understated approach to front-line polyphony is less evident elsewhere, but I still hear its influence from individual horns here and there.

The Eagles were our best shot for a new style, and none developed. In fact, the Eagles themselves don't sound today quite like they did in the 70s.

Moreover, I think it is significant that all seven Dixieland styles emerged in the forty years between the first jazz recording and the takeover of the pop charts by rock in the mid-fifties. No new style has emerged in the nearly forty years since.

However, seven styles is more than enough for each of us to enjoy lots of Dixieland in its delightfully unpredictable diversity. I find much to like in all of them and I hope you will come to feel the same way.

TEXAS SHOUT: HOW DIXIELAND JAZZ WORKS

Ken Colyer *Photo courtesy of Bob Erdos, Stomp Off Records*

British Trad

Monty Sunshine
Photo by Dan Polin

Chris Barber, (Margaret Thatcher), Dave Morgan and Kenny Ball   1980s
Photo courtesy of Bill Reid

Climax Jazz Band   1980s   *Photo by Dan Polin*

Grand Dominion Jazz Band, *Photo courtesy of Bob Pelland*

New Black Eagle Jazz Band 1980s *Photo by Dan Polin*

CHAPTER 37   WILL DIXIELAND COME BACK?

Frequently after a gig, a fan will come up to me and ask "Don't you think Dixieland is going to make a comeback?" Sometimes the question is bolstered by a comment like "After all, all things come around".

I truly wish I could agree with such good folks. Besides, I don't want to say anything that throws a damper on the good time they're having. So, I respond with something positive but noncommittal, such as "That would really be great, wouldn't it?" or "I sure hope so." However, you and I are alone here where we can let our hair down. Thus, I'm going to tell you what I really think about this issue.

Let me warn you that my thoughts are not optimistic. I don't want to appear to have a negative attitude, but I want to be honest.

Besides, I think that, in order for the Dixieland community to address its problems properly, it needs to get those problems clearly understood. After all, just because I can't think of the solution doesn't mean that someone out there can't do so if we can just get the situation in proper focus.

To begin with, what would be meant by a "comeback" for Dixieland? How would we recognize it if it happened?

After all, Dixieland jazz, like other areas of show business, has always been an uncertain profession at best, subject to the vagaries of popular taste and the ups and downs of the economy. We all have heard the stories of famous Dixielanders having to exist on transparent sandwiches and sleeping on the floors of colleagues' apartments.

However, when I first became interested in Dixieland as a teenager in the early 1950s, most of our largest cities, and many others not so large, had at least one tavern that, like Condon's or Ryan's in NYC, provided a daily living for a house band of Dixieland musicians. Major record labels were interested in maintaining a complete line of music, issuing LPs on a regular basis by name Dixielanders like Phil Napoleon, Eddie Condon, Yank Lawson and Bob Haggart. Dixieland artists who had achieved recognition among the broader general public, like Louis Armstrong, Red Nichols and Jack Teagarden, led bands that toured theaters and clubs, giving steady employment to their sidemen.

In short, in those days, while Dixieland had its insecurities, there was a regular market for it on some level. A musician who liked Dixieland had reason to think that, if he was just good enough to crack a club house band or name combo, he'd be able to get along.

To me, that would be the standard by which to judge a comeback for our music. That is, Dixieland hasn't "come back" until it offers a viable alternative to someone contemplating a career in music.

TEXAS SHOUT: HOW DIXIELAND JAZZ WORKS

Doesn't that put us on too commercial a basis, you ask? I don't think so. Anything short of the standard I propose leaves us where we are now, at a point where the only people who choose to become professional Dixielanders are those whose internal makeup drives them to play the music regardless of the consequences. If the only new Dixielanders we're going to get are those who would sign up anyway, how can the music have "come back" in any meaningful sense?

If that is the standard, we can now see in retrospect that Dixieland died sometime in the late 1960s or early 1970s. Moreover, though it's hard to imagine anything deader than dead, the scene has steadily deteriorated since.

It was during the sixties that the major labels, and even the larger minor labels, began to abandon Dixieland jazz. That was the decade in which many of the famous pioneering Dixielanders died or became inactive. Their touring bands and recording dates were not taken over, to any noticeable extent, by the next generation of Dixielanders.

Instead, the recording scene shifted to independent labels run on a quasi-hobby basis by Dixieland fans. Tours started to ebb into occasional weekends of concerts for the geographically adjacent Dixieland clubs that were springing up, mostly in the East. Instead of Dixieland night clubs, annual festivals of varying size began to dot the landscape.

Today, except for New Orleans and Orlando, where Dixieland and nostalgic music are part of the attraction for the large tourist trade, our big cities no longer have clubs that offer a house band - the same personnel every night - playing Dixieland five or six nights a week. Again, except for New Orleans and Orlando - and casinos, where Dixieland is sometimes used to facilitate the action but where few of the patrons are attending specifically to hear it -, Jim Cullum's San Antonio-based septet is the only full-time every-night Dixieland aggregation I can think of offhand. (Readers will undoubtedly write to mention others I've temporarily forgotten, but there aren't many such combos, and you take my point.)

As for records, the majority of the Dixieland records being made today, even by some of the most popular names on the circuit, are produced by the musicians themselves. Most of the independent labels concentrating on Dixieland have, at this writing, issued only a handful of albums, the principal exceptions being George Buck's and Bob Erdos' operations. (Further, I understand that Bob, having established one of the highest-quality Dixieland catalogs ever and having paid his dues to our music far beyond just about all of his contemporaries, is beginning to look toward the day when Stomp Off's release schedule will be cut back to allow him to get on with some well-earned activities in other areas.)

Outside of The Preservation Hall Jazz Band, which has a mystique that sustains it apart from the band's makeup at any given time, there is no Dixieland band recording for a major label or regularly touring large theaters. Even Preservation Hall's touring group may not be on the road that often, or appearing with a set personnel, although (not having followed PHJB recently) I can't be sure of those points.

While the festival scene has blossomed since the sixties, one only has to do the arithmetic to see that it isn't providing, and can't provide, a living for musicians. Even the most active bands rarely play as many as 30 three-day festivals a year. The normal musician's fee for such a schedule is not a living wage, and the sale of

Will Dixieland Come Back?

records (at least for a sideman) doesn't add much to the total. Further, regular sidemen with busy festival bands have trouble keeping steady musical jobs back home because their employers don't want them running off every other weekend.

Finally, if you read the standard Dixieland periodicals and stay in touch with the industry gossip, you have to come away with a bleak picture of the Dixieland employment picture. I don't want to name names, but I recall a few years back hearing a well-known player with a top-name professional band saying he was thinking about getting a real estate license to help make ends meet. The other day I heard of a musician who had "joined" a "full-time" band, though his first gig therewith would not occur until a tour scheduled some two months after his joining.

A coterie of free-lance Dixielanders, mostly in New York City, New Orleans and Orlando, seems to be getting by. However, the grapevine throbs with tales of world-famous Dixieland musicians looking for casual festival gigs, playing club dates for peanuts, and moving hither and yon in hopes of landing something that will last for a while.

Like it or not, this is the situation in which we find ourselves today. Is Dixieland likely to deteriorate further, or is a "comeback" in the cards?

To get a handle on that subject, I find it instructive to examine demographic data available to me from several surveys taken in recent years. The sources are diverse not only geographically, but also in universe covered, including a West Coast jazz festival, a British jazz periodical and two East Coast Dixieland clubs. Yet, after making a few rough adjustments to the results to concentrate on the Dixielanders, they seem to have come out about the same way.

The New Jersey Jazz Society, a long-standing club devoted to pre-bop jazz, principally Chicago-style Dixieland and small-band swing, reported its survey results in the December 1990 issue of *Jersey Jazz*. Age Of Members Responding: Over 70 - 20%; 60-69 - 45%; 50-59 - 23%; 40-49 - 7%; 31-39 - 4%; Under 30 - 1%.

The Potomac River Jazz Club in Washington, D.C., also a long-standing society, focuses almost exclusively on Dixieland in all of its styles. Club Director Maury Cagle, in a 6/25/93 conversation, reported to me the breakdown of those who answered a 1988 club survey question on members' ages. 70 or over - 10%; 60-69 - 39%; 50-59 - 32%; 40-49 - 13%; 30-39 - 4%; 20-29 - 2%. A followup in 1991 was even more skewed toward the elderly, with no one responding in the 20-29 bracket, and nearly 70% being 60 or over.

Jazz Journal International, an almost-50-year-old British periodical that is one of the world's best jazz magazines, covering all types of jazz except the most anarchic free-form modern stuff, broke down its readership in April 1992. Over 70 - 3%; 61-70 - 25%; 51-60 - 44%; 41-50 - 21% 31-40 - 5%; 30 or Under - 2%.

In 1991, the Sacramento Jazz Jubilee which draws heavily from the nearby community, presenting a cross-section of excellent Dixieland bands along with non-Dixieland headline acts whose names will be familiar to the locals (e.g., Frankie Laine), took a survey of attendees. During a phone call on 5/11/93, the festival's Executive Director, Roger Krum, told me that the age category results were: Over 65 - 25%; 45-64 - 53%; 25-44 - 19%; Under 25 - 3%.

I'd make a few "guesstimate" adjustments to the above data to try to focus on Dixieland fans. For example, because *Jazz Journal* covers bop, it should have a higher proportion of readers in their forties (who would have been forming their musical tastes as kids when bop first made it big on records after World War II) than *Jersey Jazz,* which doesn't pay much attention to bop. Similarly, because Sacto's Jubilee is the biggest thing that happens all year in the city, it naturally gets somewhat more of a cross-section of the general public than would a meeting of the local Dixieland club.

Even without such allowances, it seems clear enough to me that a good three-quarters of the audience for Dixieland is over 50. I'd "guesstimate" from these figures that probably two-thirds of it is over 60 and that virtually none of it is under 40 (that is, the younger half of the U.S. population includes no significant amount of Dixieland supporters).

These results are hardly surprising. The literature has been filled in recent years with concern about the aging of Dixieland musicians and their followers.

It's seeing the precise numbers that put the dimensions of the problem in focus for me. They also tell me something about the likelihood of a "comeback" for Dixieland.

Let's suppose that I'm right in my guesstimate, and that two-thirds of the Dixieland audience is over 60. The four surveys cited all show a dramatic fall-off going from ages 60-69 to 70 and over, probably because infirmity, or the grimmer ravages of time, begin taking a toll in earnest as people go from their sixties to their seventies.

Thus, to put it bluntly, we are going to lose a significant proportion of our audience over the next ten years. Even an optimistic reading of the four surveys indicates that the loss is likely to be on the order of 15%, if not more.

Most Dixieland festivals and societies work close to a break-even basis. They can't afford to lose 15% of their attendees. Major changes in the scene are on the horizon.

My prediction is that, ten years from now, Dixieland festivals and societies will have done one of three things: (1) substantially changed emphasis with respect to the type of music they present, (2) substantially reduced the scope of their operations, or (3) folded. You can already see early-warning indications of these developments today.

Back in February 1993, *West Coast Rag's* front-page headline asked "Is It Time To Change Direction?" The article observed that attendance was dwindling at some societies and noted festivals that were going into the red.

Some festivals have already changed direction. Sacramento no longer calls itself a "Dixieland Jubilee" and books headliners who have little or nothing to do with Dixieland. On Sacto's biggest days, its largest venue, the Convention Center, is programmed almost exclusively with non-Dixieland acts or with show bands which may include some Dixielandish licks among their production numbers.

Will Dixieland Comeback?

Without naming names, several other festivals, even some that call themselves "Dixieland" festivals, clearly prefer to hire primarily with an eye toward building crowds rather than the style of music being performed. Personally, I have no trouble with their doing so. I think it is inevitable, given the statistics cited above, that if you want to continue to maintain a profitable large-scale festival in the near future and book any Dixieland bands at all, you are going to have to bring in popular non-Dixieland or quasi-Dixieland acts to pay the freight.

If you don't want to do so, you're going to have to cut back drastically. A number of festivals, mostly in the eastern part of the country, are one-stage festivals held in a hotel ballroom that seats, say, 500 people. These festivals stick to Dixieland, staying afloat by hiring three or four organized out-of-town bands at maximum, possibly filling in around the edges with a set or two by a local combo.

Is there anything that can be done to reverse this trend? When discussing this subject, some well-meaning fans have tried to be reassuring by telling me things like "What comes around goes around".

I appreciate their sincerity and cheerfulness, but such a slogan represents a do-nothing, head-in-the-sand philosophy. It is not true that what comes around goes around. Plenty of obsolete forms of popular music that once were on solid ground are deader than doornails - Victorian parlor ballads, reveries, Indian intermezzos, cakewalks, schottisches, etc. No one thinks they will "come around" again, and they in fact are not going to do so.

If we let nature take its course, Dixieland might well go the way of, say, wooden flute ensembles, being sustained via periodic get-togethers in the homes of a few aficionados, played for the music's sake alone. Don't laugh - it could happen.

For example, while I recognize that some performers and composers are still able to get a significant part of their incomes from ragtime, in some respects ragtime (a music many *WCR* readers love, myself included) is not far from that status today. Today's ragtime societies rarely present concerts at which the artists are paid.

They typically meet periodically at a central location, sometimes a member's home, where ragtimers from beginners to professionals play without pay for each other. Even major ragtime festivals usually have several performers on the bill whose fees do not begin to cover their expenses for the event or who may be appearing without a fee essentially for a place on the program and a chance to stay in touch with the ragtime community.

Further, we are kidding ourselves if we think that, once people reach age 40 or 50, their tastes will mature and they will come to appreciate the merits (which seem so obvious to us) of Dixieland jazz. The crowds cheering Frankie Laine and the Ink Spots at Sacramento did not, by and large, leave the room to catch the Dixieland bands, becoming hooked on our music and seeking out the local Dixieland society. They went back home and listened to their Frankie Laine and Ink Spots records.

Along those lines, following *WCR's* "Change Direction" article cited above, "The Letter Drop" contained some follow-up letters expressing sentiments to the effect that Dixieland jazz will remain popular as long as folks like to dance and have a good time, or that as long as Dixieland jazz is fun and exciting, people will pay to see it. I wish it were so, but I can't agree.

TEXAS SHOUT: HOW DIXIELAND JAZZ WORKS

That's because your conditioning plays such a large part in shaping your definition of a good time. I suppose that folks in Tasmania or Tibet like to dance and have a good time, and enjoy fun and excitement, but that doesn't mean there is a pent-up demand for Dixieland in those locales. My daughter spent many evenings during her early twenties at discos dancing and having a good time until all hours, but no Dixieland was played there (nor, despite her lifelong association with Dixieland through me, did she bring her friends to Dixieland gigs).

I got out of high school in 1954, just when early rock 'n roll, which was in those pre-Beatles days a commercialized form of rhythm & blues, was about to take over the hit parade. At my high school dances, we danced mostly box steps to fox trot rhythm and today have no difficulty dancing to Dixieland (which is played at the tempos of fast, slow and medium fox trots).

However, while at college in 1955-58, as I sat in my fraternity lodge watching Dick Clark's "American Bandstand", I saw the participants dancing to such things as the Twist, the Madison, the Philly Dog, and other rhythm steps that go with an early rock 'n roll shuffle, not a fox trot beat. If you are between, say, 45 and 55, and your early dancing years were conditioned by "American Bandstand"-type music, you are not going to feel comfortable dancing to Dixieland no matter how well played.

In that connection, look at what happened when Uncle Yoke's Black Dogs burst on the scene. It was the first band to appear at Dixieland festivals that devoted a major part of each show to tunes with a New Orleans rhythm & blues beat.

Even after allowing for the fact that the Black Dogs were all superb musicians, with impeccable credentials as Dixielanders and an infectious sense of showmanship, they took the audience by storm compared to other bands with comparably skilled sidemen and presentations. Why?

I saw the answer the first time I heard the Black Dogs do Huey "Piano" Smith's old hit "Don't You Just Know It". As Tom Hook shouted the call, I realized that nearly everyone in the audience knew the tune and was singing the response. These were folks relating to the beat that fueled the hits of Fats Domino and Little Richard, the tunes to which they grew up and danced, with which they felt much more at home than the Dixieland numbers on the Black Dogs' program

Now I'm starting to see other bands turning up at festivals with some 1950s New Orleans rhythm & blues tunes in their books. The audiences are responding strongly to such material, even when it is rendered by combos that, to put it kindly, are less talented than the Black Dogs. I can even think of one group that, in my view, has become popular out of all proportion to its musical merits primarily because of its adoption of an approach that takes closer aim at post-1954 pop styles than at Dixieland or any other kind of jazz.

I believe that, as folks in their forties mature into their fifties and sixties, they are likely to bring their music along with them, not adopt ours. Unless we do something to get them refocused, these good people will naturally gravitate toward bands that incorporate more modern elements into their shows, as did the Black Dogs.

If we need a younger audience, what can we do to attract it? Several Dixieland societies in recent years have been sponsoring jazz assemblies in the schools. Some, like the Sacramento Dixieland Society, have gone further, maintaining instructional

Will Dixieland Comeback?

sessions to teach youngsters to play our music. These are laudable efforts to reach people while their musical tastes are still being formulated.

I support such activities 100%, if for no other reason than my belief that the schools should be exposing children to all aspects of our nation's cultural heritage, in which Dixieland jazz looms large. However, in terms of attracting the audience needed to replace those disappearing at the older end of the scale, they do not appear to me to be successful.

Although these programs haven't been going on for a real long time, they have been running long enough to have exposed several years of students to the music. As far as I can see, these youngsters have not graduated from school and elected to join local Dixieland societies or to attend Dixieland festivals in any numbers that are likely to make a difference on the scene.

The exceptions are those who have been taught to play the music, and thereby are getting more immediate and direct rewards therefrom. I am seeing graduates of the Dixieland instructional programs showing up at societies and at festivals, as well as on stages as performers. However, we are not attracting others of their age who simply want to listen.

I dealt at length in this column in April 1991 with the musical reasons why young people (i.e., anyone whose musical tastes were primarily conditioned by the post-1950s pop charts) have difficulty relating to Dixieland jazz. Space prohibits me from going through that reasoning here, but let me give you an example that may illustrate why the in-school programs are not bringing more of a young audience to the Dixieland scene.

Suppose you were a youngster who, once a year during your school days, was treated to an assembly in which a band demonstrated Japanese Kabuki music. Do you think you would, through that exposure, have sought out Kabuki records or performances when you graduated and were on your own? Not likely.

We face a similar problem with our youth. The type of "music" prevalent on pop charts today, if it operates according to any rules at all, utilizes conventions so different from Dixieland and other pre-rock styles that they might as well be Japanese Kabuki music as far as youngsters are concerned.

Not long ago, I played a gig in which a member of the band was in his thirties, a solid Dixieland player with a number of recordings and festival appearances to his credit. During a break, he was chatting with Nancy at our table about the scene.

She told me that, after looking around at the white-haired folks comprising essentially all of the audience, he expressed concern that people his age were not on hand. He not only missed having his friends and contemporaries in the crowd (particularly women his age, to pinpoint his exact concern), but also was clearly wondering whether, in ten or twenty years, there'd be anyone left to listen to him. Good question.

I've given this subject much thought over many years, and I don't have any answer to the problem. However, in talking over this article with Nancy, she came up with a thought that, on first blush, makes sense to me. For what it's worth, I'll pass it along.

Noting the statistics quoted above, she suggests that the Dixieland community should regard young people not as being schoolagers, but instead as anyone under

40. Let a person under 40 join the local Dixieland club for half-price for the first two years, or attend society concerts for one or two dollars, or attend free if brought by a member over 40.

Not bad. Folks in their thirties and late twenties are more independent than schoolagers and have some money to spend. We sure aren't getting any of them now, and we could have worse problems than having too many of them flooding our club meetings. They might even balance the economic scales a bit by spending more on food and drink than our over-40 set.

If you have another suggestion, I'd love to hear it. In the meantime, though, there are some things we can do to make the best of the situation.

I used to get annoyed when I saw "Dixieland" festivals hiring non-Dixieland acts, especially if they wound up getting bigger crowds than the Dixieland bands. I don't get annoyed any more.

If the non-Dixieland acts are good ones, with good musicians and interesting presentations, and they aren't trying to palm themselves off as Dixielanders, that's fine with me. If they weren't at the festival drawing people, there'd probably be fewer Dixieland bands on the bill, or maybe no festival at all. I'll use the weekend to enjoy the Dixieland, skip the acts that don't appeal to me and not lose any sleep over the programming mix.

Second, to return to a topic I've discussed frequently in this column, the Dixieland community needs to stop fighting within itself. If the various Dixieland styles keep looking down their noses at each other, every one claiming that the others are missing the boat, we will simply continue to divide ourselves up into even smaller fragments, each slowly wasting away. Such bickering hastens the day when we'll have to enjoy the music by ourselves in our living rooms.

Within a few hours' drive from my home are no less than four organizations that present concerts of older-style jazz. In the twenty-plus years I've been supporting them, I don't recall a single instance in which, for example, two of them held a joint concert to present a band neither could hire individually. I doubt that there ever has been a single conference call between the four societies at the start of the season to try to coordinate dates or arrange block bookings for certain artists on specific weekends.

As I write, three of the four have been bemoaning regularly in their periodicals about poor attendance at club events. Yet, each one more or less goes its own way, occasionally feinting in the direction of trying to avoid scheduling conflicts or maybe picking up a band another is hiring on a given weekend (if the bandleader calls around to set it up).

I wrote a letter to one of them, published in its newsletter, complaining because, on one Sunday afternoon, several of these societies scheduled concerts at nearly the same time. Believe it or not, the response was, in most cases, that a representative called me (not the other clubs), to assure me that his club was happy to cooperate with the others, but they wouldn't cooperate with his. Figure that one out.

We can pick at each other and help drive our favorite music into oblivion or we can get together to keep it going while we, at least, are still here to play it and enjoy it. After that time, I guess we won't care what happens to it.

Will Dixieland Come Back?

Uncle Yoke's Black Dog Jazz Band   1980s
Courtesy of Steve Yocum

TEXAS SHOUT: HOW DIXIELAND JAZZ WORKS

Preservation Hall Jazz Band, St. Michelle Winery, Wa.   1980s
Photo by Dan Polin

Colleen & Harry Galland 1980s
at Sacramento Jazz Jubilee
Photo by Dan Polin

April 1994 West Coast Rag

CHAPTER 38   MOVIES

Not long ago I learned of the recent discovery of a clip of sound film that shows a few seconds of Bix Beiderbecke soloing on cornet. I haven't seen it yet, but the news reminds me of some experiences with vintage films that might be of interest to *WCR* readers.

As many of you know, Nancy and I are deeply into movies. We watch over 300 features a year, almost all of them via cable or VCR.

(We gave up going to the theater. Not only is it expensive, but the audiences are often loud and otherwise rude. Further, the films are sometimes projected at the wrong aspect ratio. If we want to see films at the wrong aspect ratio, we can do it more cheaply and comfortably at home.)

Years ago I was historian and host for the last vintage film society to function here in Wilmington. A fair amount of the courtship between Nancy and myself occurred at drive-in double features (no off-color remarks, please). The first summer of our marriage, we drove an hour to Germantown several times a week to a movie house that was showing a summer of classic-period features.

Shortly after we were married in 1971, we began attending special film fans' weekends. These are much like Dixieland festivals, except that instead of digging various combos from dawn until the wee hours, attendees watch rare old (usually pre-1940) movies and sometimes meet stars or other persons active in the production thereof.

In recent years, we've been attending a fabulous function in Syracuse every March, the Syracuse Cinefest. (For information thereon, contact Phil Serling, 215 Dawley Road, Fayetteville, NY 13066, phone (315)637-8985.) Most of the time, we watch the films projected in 16 millimeter in a hotel ballroom, but once during the weekend Phil takes us out for special 35 mm screenings.

In 1993, the special showings were at a restored downtown movie palace. A highlight was to be "Her Sister From Paris", a 1925 silent from the Library Of Congress collection that turned out to be a delightful Constance Talmage-Ronald Colman romantic comedy. We were promised some early Vitaphone sound shorts, but were not told what they would be.

Imagine my amazement when one of them turned out to feature Red Nichols! I couldn't readily identify the entire sextet, but banjo/guitarist Eddie Condon (who also sings two vocals) and reedman Pee Wee Russell are unmistakable. Five numbers are played, the second a ballad in which Nichols is joined by two trumpeters. The show ends with "China Boy", a romping ride that's hotter'n a pistol.

I couldn't believe it. Here, captured on sound film at the very beginning of their careers, when no one had any reason to think they would become legendary figures

~ 225 ~

TEXAS SHOUT: HOW DIXIELAND JAZZ WORKS

of jazz, were Condon and Russell, not to mention Nichols, a personal favorite of mine, still young but already well known.

The twenties, the decade of most interest to hard-core Dixieland buffs, was almost over before sound film came along. The principal groundbreaking developments in Dixieland had already gone by. The main body of jazz was starting to incorporate changes that would evolve into swing. There are a few films of great jazz figures from that period - the famous Ellington and Bessie Smith shorts come to mind -, but nothing at all of such magical and important groups as, say, the Red Hot Peppers, the Wolverines, the Hot Five, etc.

A similar experience took place a few months later, at the 1993 convention of the Society for Cinephiles, held over the Labor Day weekend each year. (To get wired in, contact Society For Cinephiles, P.O. Box 1632, Hollywood, CA 90028.) One of the features was a 1915 silent, "The Whirl Of Life", a tongue-in-check biography of Vernon and Irene Castle, with the Castles themselves in the leading roles.

It was engrossing enough to see these two artists, whose influence on the popular musical styles of the 1920s was considerable. However, as the topper, the feature closes with an extended dance routine by the Castles in a nightclub.

If you watch the corner of the frame, you'll see bits and pieces of the Castles' regular accompanists, the orchestra of James Reese Europe, perhaps the most important Black musician in New York City during the early years of this century. Parts of the band are also shown in full-frame closeup for a few seconds.

The movie, as I've said, is silent. Nevertheless, it is of considerable interest to anyone concerned with jazz history, as it presents live footage of Europe, whose Society Orchestra made in 1913 the first recordings by an all-Black dance band. Probably also in this sequence somewhere is Ford Dabney, composer of "Shine" and a number of fine piano rags, who was Europe's pianist and assistant director.

The film includes a brief closeup of the drummer, maybe Buddy Gilmore, a featured Europe sideman. In an earlier tavern sequence, a Black instrumental trio is shown on stage, probably also members of Europe's aggregation.

I've been a movie buff all my life, my parents taking my sister Dallas (also a nickname) and me to every film that appeared at the Edge Moor (the closest movie house to our neighborhood), except for the really scary movies (which we saw anyway at the Saturday matinee). I've also been crazy about Dixieland and ragtime since I was a kid decades ago.

However, I had never heard of "The Whirl Of Life", nor did I know that there were any extant movie scenes of James Reese Europe. I asked Miles Kreuger, who introduced the film and who knew Irene Castle personally, if the jazz world was aware of the existence of this movie. He didn't know the answer specifically, but told me that the feature was no secret, having been a part of the Museum Of Modern Art's collection for (I think he said) at least some thirty years.

This incident reminds me all over again how little intersection there is between the vintage film community and the vintage jazz community. To be sure, there is a small handful of people who specialize in collecting film footage of jazzmen. There is even a book attempting to list appearances by jazzmen in the movies, *Jazz In The Movies*, by Donald Meeker. (It doesn't list "The Whirl Of Life", either because

Meeker didn't know about it or because Europe was really a pre-jazz personality and might have been thought to be outside of the scope of the book.)

However, despite the recent proliferation of music videos, including ones concentrating on jazz and ragtime, there is relatively little discussion of jazz on film in the present-day jazz periodicals. (The excellent British magazine *Jazz Journal*, is an exception, having carried a regular column on the topic for years.) Similarly, jazz films are not commonly presented as part of Dixieland festival weekends, possibly because (from what I know of the few attempts to do so) such presentations are poorly attended.

This latter situation is unfortunate. With most of the great pioneering players no longer around, seeing them on film is an easy, inexpensive and accessible way to appreciate their talents.

We have many people today not only attending jazz performances, but even posing as authorities on the subject, who really are not very well grounded in what they're seeing or talking about. Some exposure to the great musicians on film might go some way toward relieving that situation.

I got my first indoctrination into the byways of jazz film collecting over twenty years ago, during a discographical conference that Nancy and I attended at Rutgers University. It included a fascinating seminar thereon, together with film clips, by Ernie Smith, an expert on jazz films. Two of the points Ernie made that day stuck in my mind.

First, he said that, if you are interested in jazz, and if you are watching a movie in which instrumentalists appear in the shot, you must condition yourself to stop watching the main action immediately and begin looking around the edges of the frame. He reminded us that in many cases, unless the musicians are featured performers in the film, the players are just there for atmosphere, will be on screen for a few seconds at most, and then only in an incidental way. You will have virtually no time to try to identify them.

Second, and I think I'm recalling this point correctly, he said that, in the earliest films, if Black musicians appear on screen, there is a good chance that they are real musicians and not actors. I believe his theory was that it was easier and cheaper for the film companies to hire organized Black bands, which already had instruments and uniforms, than to bother with recruiting Black actors and outfitting them.

It was shortly after that conference that Nancy and I attended our first Cinephiles convention, in Washington, D. C. We were overwhelmed at the large number of rare movies spread out for our delectation (calling for agonizing choices between different films being shown simultaneously in the two screening rooms), the inclusion of rediscovered features we had been led to believe were lost (we were astonished to see "White Gold", a 1927 silent with Jetta Goudal), and the chance to meet live big-name stars of the old days (Leatrice Joy, star of C.B. DeMille's "Saturday Night" in 1922, still looked like a million dollars and exuded high class from every pore).

Thus, we were still starry-eyed as we settled in to watch an early 1920s version of "Camille" starring Alla Nazimova and Rudolph Valentino. Perhaps, then, and with Ernie Smith's admonitions still fresh in my mind, I thought I saw what I hoped I would see in this film and not what I actually saw. However, I'm getting ahead of my story.

TEXAS SHOUT: HOW DIXIELAND JAZZ WORKS

"Camille" contains a sequence in which the leading character goes to a casino and is taken ill. The set for the casino is a highly stylized two-story affair, with a small triangular opening in a second-story wall overlooking the gambling floor.

As the scene opens, we are given a flash of this opening in closeup, which was just big enough to hold the three Black musicians crowded into it. As the image flashed by, I whispered to Nancy "That looked like Johnny Dodds!".

We both went on the alert, but the musicians only appeared once more on the screen, in a distance shot. They were briefly seen as they leaned out of the alcove to watch the crowd gathered around the collapsed Camille.

Immediately after the showing, we went out in the lobby and looked up the film in an American Film Institute catalogue at the convention's main desk. As we expected, there was no cast credit for such a fleeting glimpse of the musicians.

Upon returning home, I compared the date of the movie as shown in our convention program with the date of the famous 1921 photograph of King Oliver's band taken during its California tour. I was excited to find that the timing seemed to allow for the possibility that at least some members of Oliver's combo could have appeared in the casino sequence of "Camille".

I have repeated this story to Ernie Smith and to every other collector of jazz films with whom I've come in contact. I've also asked a few of the film people at our film weekends about it, but they are, understandably, not as interested in using their limited time to track down this detail of jazz history as they are to track down more central points of film history. If anyone has ever followed up this matter and either confirmed the identity of the musicians, or obtained a still print of the frames involved, I'm unaware of it.

I seem to recall that, in addition to the clarinetists, one of the "Camille" musicians was playing a banjo. I think the third musician was a pianist, sitting so as to face the right of the frame with the piano obscured behind the wall of the alcove.

However, the shot went by so fast that I can't be sure of anything. Lil Hardin was Oliver's pianist on that trip, but if there was a pianist in the frame, it went by so fast that the sex of the player did not register on my memory.

Most likely, I was the victim of a fevered imagination combined with a star-struck sensibility. However, until the musicians in Valentino's "Camille" are identified, the story is a good one for cold winter nights.

Moreover, silent or sound, wouldn't it be something if there was motion picture footage - albeit silent and extremely short - of even a segment of Oliver's immortal Creole Jazz Band? If, sixty years after his death, we can come up with a sound sequence on Bix, maybe such a dream isn't beyond the pale after all.

May-June 1994 West Coast Rag

CHAPTER 39   RECORD REVIEWING REDUX

In the mid-1960s, though I had loved ragtime for about a dozen years, I had practically nothing to show for it. I had yet to meet another ragtimer. There was virtually no published ragtime music on the market. I bought all the ragtime LPs I could find, but they comprised a mighty slim shelf.

One day, while thumbing a magazine at a newsstand (I think it was *High Fidelity*), I saw a review of an LP of ragtime piano solos by Tom Shea, a name I didn't then know. Anything that smacked of ragtime was good enough for me, so I bought the periodical and ordered the album. The seller was listed as The Ragtime Society, with an address in Toronto.

When the disc arrived, it was accompanied by material describing the Society. The group had not only produced this record, but also published a periodical about ragtime and even reprinted some of the old sheet music. I joined right away, while ordering back issues of the newsletter plus all available Society products.

I was delighted to discover an organization doing something to support this nearly forgotten music that I enjoyed so much. I would have been happy to help out, but there didn't seem to be much I could do at a distance.

Shortly thereafter, the great ragtime and barrelhouse pianist Knocky Parker recorded four LPs of vintage rags, most of which were otherwise unavailable on vinyl. When I got my copies, I was surprised to find that, in two respects, they differed from what I had expected.

First, probably to get more titles on each platter, Parker usually omitted repeats, Well, I could live with that aspect of the set.

Second, probably to get variety into the show, the performances were spliced between strains. For example, the first strain might be on piano accompanied by string bass, the second on harpsichord accompanied by tuba, the third on celeste accompanied by banjo, etc. I found this practice distracting and thought others might also.

I painstakingly listened through the four recordings, noting which rags were played by which combinations. The results were edited into a record review which I sent to The Ragtime Society, knowing that many Society members would unhesitatingly buy the set on the strength of Parker's reputation and wanting them to know what to expect. The review was published in the November 1966 edition of the Society's newsletter.

At that point, I realized that I had about as comprehensive a collection of U.S.-produced ragtime LPs as was available. I figured I could help out the Society by keeping it apprised of new releases.

So, each time I acquired a new ragtime record, I wrote up a review and sent it north of the border, becoming the Society's regular reviewer. My wife and I then

TEXAS SHOUT: HOW DIXIELAND JAZZ WORKS

began attending the Society's annual Bash, at which John Norris, publisher of *Coda* (Canada's leading jazz magazine) maintained the record bar.

We got to know John and his second in command, Bill Smith, on these trips, both at the Bash and via visiting the record shop they then operated. John soon asked me if I would write reviews for *Coda*.

I had subscribed to *Coda* some years previously and had let it lapse because its focus was too much on modern jazz for my taste. I explained my position to John, who told me that they really wanted to cover all jazz styles, would give me the records along with a free subscription, and had been planning to add a knowledgeable writer on older-style jazz to the staff. On that basis, I agreed (and have been a *Coda* writer ever since).

Soon artists and producers began giving me records to review. Needing an outlet for the reviews, I wound up writing for a small older-style jazz magazine called *Jazz Digest*.

That periodical eventually ceased publication. In the meantime, I had done a few concert and festival reviews for *The Mississippi Rag*. Thus, I became a *MR* reviewer in 1978.

For the next dozen years, I estimate that I wrote about 40% of *MR*'s record reviews, plus some commentaries on festivals, books and music folios. Shortly after "Texas Shout" was inaugurated for *West Coast Rag* in 1989, my record reviews moved to *WCR* as well, in a column titled "This Month's Records" (TMR).

Except for *Coda*, which still sends me the records it wants me to review, I rarely review records sent to a publication. I have all I can do to stay even with the ones sent directly to my home. I haven't made an official count, but I'd guess that, since the first one in November 1966, I've had more published reviews (many hundreds) of recordings of ragtime, Dixieland and closely related music than any other U.S.-based writer.

Wanting to give the musicians the fairest possible shake, I confine my reviews to music in which I have a special interest. If I receive an album which, on a cursory listen, falls outside that area (typically, it'll be a modern jazz recording), I'll note its availability in TMR, but will not comment on it qualitatively or assign it a ranking in my one-to-five star system.

Some recordings pose difficult questions as to whether or not they should be reviewed in a column essentially for fans of Dixieland and ragtime. For example, an item may have some tracks within the scope of TMR, but others outside it. Or, an artist whose main activity and reputation has been in Dixieland and ragtime may come up with an album consisting partially or primarily of other types of music.

Nevertheless, if I review an album in TMR, I assume that the readership wants to know where it stands judged as a Dixieland or ragtime record. If it isn't all that jazzy (or raggy), whatever its other merits may be, it won't get a five-star rating from me.

For example, suppose the South Frisco Jazz Band issues a CD of grand opera, with Vince singing arias from "Don Giovanni" and Bob's tuba reproducing the basso solos. South Frisco fans may well flock to it as a change-up from SFJB's usual raunchy post-Watters two-beat, and it may get a standing ovation at the Met, but it is unlikely to get many stars in TMR.

Record Reviewing Redux

I would have thought these principles were well enough understood by my readers to go without saying. However, some time back I received a review copy of an album from a friend of mine, a fine musician who leads a well-known, highly regarded band on the festival circuit. The recording consisted of tunes with a generally religious/spiritual orientation, played in Dixieland style but with more restraint than on the combo's previous releases.

After describing the album's several worthwhile points, I felt obligated to say that it was tamer than usual. This assessment, as indicated above, resulted in a below-average overall rating on my five-star scale.

A few issues later, the letters column included a note from my friend in which he agreed with my opinion that the recording was not as hot as usual. However, he seemed somewhat put out with me for saying so, stating that I had missed the point of the album.

Perhaps I did, and if so, I regret the error. I do try hard not to criticize artists for failing to do something that they aren't trying to do in the first place.

On the other hand, I believe that TMR readers are essentially looking for information that will lead them to superior recordings of ragtime and hot Dixieland jazz. I don't want to mislead anyone into spending money for something that doesn't rank high by that standard, regardless of how good it is in other ways.

These remarks stem from two sources. First, in discussing possible topics for "Texas Shout" with *WCR*'s editor, Woody thought you might be interested in hearing how I found my way into record reviewing. Second, I have received another religiously oriented album by a famous Dixieland band and I don't want to make the same mistake - if mistake it was - or leave you with any misunderstanding about this one.

HHZ-120, "Feelin' The Spirit: The Queen City Jazz Band Plays Gospel" is a September 1992 studio session rendered with the QCJB's customary first-rate musicianship and showmanship. Big-voiced Wende Harston shows all over again, in her four outings, that she knows how to sell a song.

Those who have Queen City's previous releases will certainly want to hear their heroes doing something a little off the beaten track. However, hard-core QCJB fans do not need a review from me or anyone else to get them to buy the album, which is available in CD format @ $17 postpaid, or audiocassette @ $12, from H.H. Zeno Productions, P.O. Box 1273, Littleton, CO 80160.

However, if you are not a Queen City completest, but are a Dixieland fan looking for the biggest bang for your record dollar, I would think you'd want to know that (1) the running time is about 42 minutes, a little light for a compact disc and (2) only about half the cuts are played in jazz time. The other half include two pretty waltz-hymns, a terminally cute sing-a-long featuring a children's chorus, and a couple of heartfelt arresting vocals by Ms. Harson in, respectively, rhythm & blues and march rhythm.

In those circumstances, I would have trouble telling Dixieland buffs that HHZ-120 was an above-average purchase, no matter how appealing it might be otherwise. I'd feel constrained to award it no more than two stars if I reviewed it in TMR. Fair enough? Do we understand each other better now?

| TEXAS SHOUT: HOW DIXIELAND JAZZ WORKS |

As an aside, I can't help noting that I have now encountered two religious albums by respected Dixieland units that, on the whole, contain less hot jazz than those bands' established norms. Perhaps that fact explains something I've wondered about recently.

When The Rent Party Revellers were asked to work up a Sunday morning show for the 1989 Shasta festival, I had not yet seen one by another jazz band. I assumed that, because the show would be a regularly scheduled Revellers set at the festival, the audience was entitled to a full measure of hot jazz.

Thus, I picked a program of tunes that would fit in with the uplifting nature of the occasion, but ones with a wide-open construction to allow us ample room for hard-driving rent party Dixieland. Believe me, we did not pull any punches in performing them.

Our show proved popular and was repeated at other festivals, at which we started to get requests for recordings thereof. Dan Jazz Productions waxed it as performed at the 1992 Santa Rosa festival. The album has sold very well whenever we present our "Hymn Sing".

Conversely, if we are not doing the show, Nancy tells me that fans who approach our record table looking for Revellers albums sometimes pass "Hymn Sing Live!" with hardly a glance, telling her that they don't like such recordings. I wondered why they felt that way, but now I think that these folks have been conditioned by other combos to expect that religiously oriented Dixieland records aren't going to be as jazzy as usual. Well, you live and learn.

In last month's "Texas Shout", I told you how I got into record reviewing and how my "This Month's Records" review column operates. These comments lead into a broader question of how readers should use record reviews. The answer is that, if you are using the reviews as a guide to shopping (which is what they're for), you should remember that, though they are supposed to represent informed opinions, they are hardly absolute.

I recently reviewed a CD by one of the biggest contemporary names in uptown-style New Orleans Dixieland. I loved the album and gave it top grades.

The editor of a well-known jazz club newsletter, a fine jazz writer and musician (whose preferences favor Chicago style), later reviewed the same album, disliking it so much that, in his review, he wondered if the music was properly classifiable as jazz. A third reviewer, for one of the largest independent Dixieland periodicals (who gives so many mixed and unfavorable reviews that I personally wonder if he really likes Dixieland very much), gave the album a generally negative rating but noted some positive elements about it.

All three of these reviews were of the same disc, by seasoned writers, yet they came out in three quite different places. How is the reader supposed to harmonize that situation?

Record Reviewing Redux

You don't. You recognize instead that there never has been a recording, and never will be one, that every reviewer likes. If I praise a record to the skies, one thing I can be sure of is that there are other reviewers out there who, if they are required to review the same record, will hate every note on it.

Thus, you look for a reviewer whose tastes mesh with yours in such a way that his/her reviews can be relied on as a guide for buying records. Usually such a reviewer will be someone whose tastes coincide with yours, but you may find that the opposite works as well.

To illustrate: Nancy and I, pursuing our hobby of watching movies, have learned that Julie Salamon of *The Wall Street Journal* and Janet Maslin of *The New York Times* are almost always in line with our views. If either of them really likes a film, we'll put it on our list of movies to see, and we're rarely disappointed.

However, a few years back, we subscribed to a periodical which had, among its movie reviewers, one who just loved obscure, slow-moving art films. We learned that, if this reviewer went into orbit over a feature, we should avoid it at all costs because we'd be bored out of our minds.

Similarly, one of our area's newspapers, a while ago, had two movie reviewers whose tastes were reverse barometers to ours. If they recommended a film, we wouldn't care for it, and if they disliked it, we'd often enjoy it.

For that reason, there's no point in getting all bent out of shape if you read a record review that pans an album you enjoy. First of all, if you aren't going to use the review as a basis for your own shopping, the review isn't written for you anyway. Second, there are probably other reviews out there of the album, some pro and some con, that you aren't going to run across, so what difference does it make if you happened to read this one and not one of the others? Just turn the page and concentrate on the next article.

There are those who have great difficulty accepting the fact that one of their favorite artists or recordings has received a negative evaluation in print. Such folks are quick to assume that the reviewer is biased, or has some hidden agenda or axe to grind.

I've received letters, some being remarkably abusive in tone, accusing me of all sorts of malevolencies regarding my record reviews. One reader will tell me that I'm biased in favor of something, while another will come along to say that I'm biased against it. Someone else imagines that I'm using reviews to surreptitiously promote my own gigs by tearing down performances by other, supposedly competitive, artists.

This latter accusation reflects a significant misunderstanding regarding the impact of Dixieland record reviews these days. Such reviews appear in small-circulation periodicals and have virtually no economic impact on the artist or the record.

Most people who buy a Dixielander's or ragtimer's records do so at in-person performances, wanting a souvenir of the occasion and not knowing or caring what some reviewer may have said about the albums. Similarly, festival producers usually hire musicians as the result of seeing live shows, or hearing audition records and making up their own minds apart from published reviews.

TEXAS SHOUT: HOW DIXIELAND JAZZ WORKS

Unless there are extraordinary circumstances in the picture, a rave review in *WCR*, *The Mississippi Rag* or a large Dixieland club periodical, one written by a well-known and respected reviewer, might produce a one-time blip of ten to twenty orders for the recording. So much for the "economic power" of record reviewers.

With respect to bias, such claims are, of course, always justified, but not usually in the sense that the irate fans think. Naturally I'm biased, in the sense that I have certain musical likes and dislikes. So do all other record reviewers, and so do all of you.

The better reviewers, however, understand what their preferences are and try to discount for them in some way so as not to be unfair to the artist. For example, some reviewers won't write unfavorable reviews.

While I respect the reasoning behind such a policy, and while I personally dislike writing unfavorable reviews, I think that failure to deal candidly with weaker elements of the recordings does not properly service the needs of the record buying-public. If all the records are good ones, how do readers learn how to discriminate between Dixieland that is routine, average, superior and outstanding?

In my own case, I try to figure out what the artist is trying to do on his/her own terms, and judge as best I can whether the effort was successful regardless of whether I personally prefer the approach being taken. I'll sometimes also comment on whether I think the objectives are worthwhile, but try to do so in a way that the reader will have enough information to disagree with me and buy the record anyway if his/her inclinations don't square with mine.

Thus, I can think of a few instances in which I've given top grades to recordings which I knew I would never get off the shelf again. Typically, these are in jazz styles that seldom make it to the top of my listening-for-pleasure list, such as swing tinged with early bop.

In any event, most record reviewers I've read, whatever their deficiencies, are sincerely trying to give each recording their best, most honest appraisal. In fact, if any reviewer truly displays a hidden agenda that causes reviews to be slanted a certain way without regard to the music, the Dixieland/ragtime community usually sniffs out such problems in short order and the reviewer over time receives fewer review copies.

Readers who have trouble accepting the points just made sometimes wind up taking time and energy to write letters like this one, which came in not too long ago:

> "Dear Mr. Wyndham:
>
> I read with considerable disgust your snide review of [albums by Artist X]. I've followed Dixieland and ragtime music (especially the festival circuit) for many years, and purchased several of [X's recordings]. I found them to be not only highly entertaining, but [X] is one of the best technicians I have heard in years, and is consistently inventive and musical in his arranging. Your assertion that [the letter quotes the unfavorable portion of my review] is insulting and in fact smacks of some professional jealousy. ...

> Mr. Wyndham, lest you think I'm totally biased in MY opinions, I also have purchased your tapes in the past, and although I've found them interesting in their historical content, the technical peaks you reach in your vocals and piano playing do not even approach the lows on [X's recordings]. In other words, haul the log out of your own eye, or off your own piano keyboard before attempting to pick the splinter off of other's.
>
> Very truly yours,"

Speaking of letters, another reader (whom I'll call Y), who also disagreed with my assessment of X's recordings, made the following provocative comments in his epistle:

> "To validate my expenditure for [X's recordings], I played them at a recent party, and they passed the shoulder-bobbing, ear-pleasing and foot-patting test with flying colors. This may not be as sophisticated or cerebral as Tex's system, but it sure did make everyone feel good.
>
> One doesn't have to be a great chef to know when food tastes good.
>
> Maybe reviewers shouldn't be musicians or have any talent at all ..."

Y makes some points here that are worth discussing. Let's start with Y's query as to whether or not there is any advantage in having reviews written by musicians.

On the surface, it would seem that a review written by a musician ought to be more worthy of the reader's attention than otherwise. However, in the last analysis, I side with Y.

Perhaps a musician can add certain bits of color to the text that will make the review more interesting. I play along with every record I review before putting on the earphones for the second and more important review listen. I learn things about the recording by doing so that might not be apparent to a non-musician; sometimes that information finds its way into the review.

Similarly, a musician/reviewer, at least if he/she has been around for a while and an active part of the scene, may well have gotten to know some or all of the musicians on the record. While this situation can create awkward situations for those who are reluctant to criticize their friends, it does allow for the possibility that some backstage anecdotes might fit into the review, enhancing its general appeal.

However, the bottom line in any review is the quality of the judgment and how clearly that judgment is conveyed in writing. Musicians have no corner on either. Being a musician doesn't mean that you can write well. Further, as we all know from some of the execrable bands we've seen from time to time, it also doesn't mean that you have good taste.

TEXAS SHOUT: HOW DIXIELAND JAZZ WORKS

My all-time favorite jazz record reviewer, now retired I believe, is John S. Wilson, who wrote for, among other publications, *The New York Times*. If Wilson was able to play music, he never mentioned that fact in any of his writing that I can recall.

Nevertheless, Wilson had a broad and deep knowledge of our music, impeccable taste, and the ability to set down his thoughts in unmistakably clear prose. As Y puts it, "One doesn't have to be a great chef to know when food tastes good."

With respect to Y's shoulder-bobbing test at his party, Y is certainly on the right track. The ultimate test of any recording, or other artistic performance, is whether it strikes an emotional response in its audience.

If you like a record, painting, movie, etc., it makes no difference what anyone else says about it - you'll get your money's worth out of it. However, I would respectfully suggest that Y's criterion is really not sufficient for a prospective buyer of jazz records, unless one has unlimited funds.

Y does not tell us who came to his party. Perhaps all the guests were experienced jazz fans who sat down and quietly listened to the recordings. In that case, we would certainly have to give some weight to their reaction.

I think it more likely, though, that the recordings were played as background for a general gathering of Y's friends, some of whom knew something about jazz and ragtime (but many didn't). Most of them were probably chatting to each other, munching, drinking or engaging principally in other activities while the recordings were being played.

In that case, I think you'll find that virtually any recording of pre-rock American non-classical, non-ethnic music - such as marches, twenties pops, banjo solos, blues, Dixieland, swing, polkas, thirties dance ballads, country music, etc. - will, even if not performed with much depth, get guests at a general party to tap their feet and bob their heads. Most such music, at least on the surface, when played with rhythmic cohesion, has a sufficiently outgoing quality that it will brighten a party, even though it might not stand up on a close listen by aficionados thereof.

Put another way, being able to get a general and inattentive audience in a better mood is virtually a rock-bottom minimum for a ragtime or Dixieland record. Except for the few I own where the rhythm section is obviously out of synch, just about any one of the thousands of recordings on my shelves, including some really bad records that I wish I'd never bought, will accomplish that purpose.

Indeed, that is one of the functions of the elevator music typically piped through office buildings. It puts everyone in a better mood although no one claims that it will survive critical listening.

Thus, I don't believe that you can truly "validate" your expenditure for a recording by playing it as background at your next cocktail party for your non-jazz-loving friends and observing whether any of them tap their feet. You'll be buying everything that comes on the market if that, and that alone, is your standard.

Why go through this argument? Certainly not to disparage Y, who makes some good points, and who commendably took pen in hand to defend a favorite musician.

~ 236 ~

Record Reviewing Redux

However, I often hear variations of Y's basic claim - that, if I can tap my feet or snap my fingers to the music, if it conveys an upbeat spirit, then it is worthwhile. This is a seductive position, but I think it puts its values on the wrong things.

Except in very special circumstances, if a ragtime pianist or Dixieland band has such poor rhythmic coordination that listeners don't tap their feet, bob heads and be of a sunnier disposition, then it isn't even out of the starting gate. It doesn't deserve to be on record at all. If we value our music as an art form, we need to seek out artists who not only give us the basic minimum, but who have something new and worthwhile to say in the bargain.

Anyone can produce yet another recording that's just like dozens of others in our collection. Given that none of us can afford to buy everything that's out there, and that we wouldn't have time to listen to all of it anyway, we should be trying to invest our recording budget in those sounds that go the farthest beyond the basics.

It is in this area that a record reviewer whose tastes coincide with yours can help. Reviews can sort through the plethora of available recordings, leading you to ones that will not only facilitate the action at your party but also provide more lasting rewards when you're listening by yourself for the umpteenth time.

Further, if the reviewer is a good enough writer, he/she should be able to heighten your own awareness of fine points of the music that have hitherto escaped your attention. In that case, you will get even more satisfaction from both your purchases and your attendance at live concerts.

One could ask why have record reviews at all anymore, given that they have the minuscule economic impact discussed above. It's a good question, one I mentioned in my previous "Texas Shout" columns on record reviewing (September and October 1990).

Let's not revisit that one today, though. Enough's enough.

TEXAS SHOUT: HOW DIXIELAND JAZZ WORKS

CHAPTER 40 COMMON THEMES

I can't remember where I saw it, but I recall reading that there were certain musical themes in common circulation among early ragtime and jazz musicians, ones which no one person seems to have composed, that were considered fair game for anyone in the community to sell to a song publisher and claim on a going-forward basis. That is, nobody got too upset if Musician A sold a composition containing one of these musical notions which, from that time on, was regarded as his.

If I am right in my recollection, I can understand how this situation might have come about. At the turn of the century, Tin Pan Alley was in its infancy. There may not have appeared to be much return to be made out of selling songs for publication, particularly in the Black areas of towns like Sedalia, Missouri, or New Orleans, both of which were not near big sheet music publishing centers. What money there was in ragtime and Dixieland mostly came from gigs.

Anyway, for whatever reason, if you listen to or play Dixieland and ragtime for very long, you will become aware of some of these anthems which turn up from time to time in various pieces, some of them quite well known. There are far too many of them to mention in one column.

However, talking about a few of them might be interesting in itself. Also, it might get your ears a little more attuned to do some detective work on your own as you listen in the future.

Let's get the framework in place before we start. You can find piles of different tunes that have the same chord pattern (*Jersey Jazz* has just finished running a serialized article listing dozens of similar songs, many of which are new melodies based on standard patterns). For example, there are thousands of variations of the twelve-bar blues.

Other recurring Dixieland chord patterns include those for the choruses to "(I With I Could Shimmy Like My) Sister Kate", "How Come You Do Me Like You Do", "When The Saints Go Marching In" and "Bill Bailey, Won't You Please Come Home?" Each of these four different chord structures occurs in more jazz tunes than we could begin to discuss here. I'm generally excluding that type of similarity from today's column.

We're not talking about cases where, for one reason or another, a tune's composer recorded it under two different titles, or recorded it under one title and published it under another. Jelly Roll Morton, for example, did those things on several occasions.

Finally, let's also exclude instances where, consciously or unconsciously, something has been stolen wholesale. The tune titled "Egyptian Fantasy", credited to Sidney Bechet, is an illustration thereof. It was actually written by Abe Olman in

> TEXAS SHOUT: HOW DIXIELAND JAZZ WORKS

1911 and comprises the first two strains of his pseudo-Eastern instrumental entitled "Egyptia".

Incidentally, while I don't condone plagiarism, I can understand what Bechet might have been thinking at the "Egyptian Fantasy" session in 1941. He may well have felt that, as long as nobody remembered "Egyptia" anymore (I don't think it was a big hit in the first place), why not get a few extra bucks or prestige or whatever by claiming authorship?

In 1941, as now, jazz records usually didn't sell in huge quantities, so it was unlikely that the royalties on "Egyptian Fantasy" would be worth a lawsuit to claim even if anyone noticed. And if someone told Bechet that over fifty years later, jazz fans all over the world would still be listening to that side, Bechet probably would have wondered what he was smoking.

Now let's cite a few instances. You won't be surprised to find that three pioneering names in our music, W.C. Handy, Jelly Roll Morton and the Original Dixieland Jazz Band (hereinafter "ODJB") are going to pop up with some regularity.

In fact, Handy and Morton intersect on our first example, a tune that must have been floating up and down the Mississippi after the turn of the century. Morton recorded it as "Winin' Boy Blues" and also used it as a strain of his "Tom Cat Blues".

Handy, who openly admitted that he got many musical ideas from itinerant musicians passing through Memphis, used the same motive in 1909 as a campaign song for E.H. Crump, who was running for mayor of the city. It was then titled "Mister Crump", but we now know it as the second strain of Handy's famous "Memphis Blues". (Because the first strain is often omitted by today's Dixieland bands, let's make clear that we're talking about the theme that accompanies the lyric "Folks, I've just been down, down to Memphis town, ...")

For another use of the "Winin' Boy/Mister Crump" theme, see "The Camel Walk Blues" by Ebon Gay, published in 1919 by Stark Music. Also relevant, though the "Winin' Boy" melody is not expressly stated, is the chorus to "Keyhole Blues", recorded on May 13, 1927, by Louis Armstrong and his Hot Seven.

In 1938 and 1939, Jelly waxed a tune titled "Don't You Leave Me Here", the 78 listing "Morton" as the composer. This melody must also have traveled the inland waterways. It appears in two ragtime piano solos published in 1909: "Rag Medley No. II: Strains From Flat Branch", by Blind Boone, published in Columbia, Missouri, and "I'm Alabama Bound", by Robert Hoffman, published in New Orleans.

I'm not sure just when Jelly appropriated it. However, if the sleeve of my French LP reissue of the side is to be trusted, "J.R. Morton" was listed as the composer of "Don't You Leave Me Here" as early as 1927, when it was waxed by Charlie Johnson's Original Paradise Ten.

Ragtime also supplied another of Jelly's popular evergreens. "Buddy Bolden's Blues" is a strain in one of my favorite solos, "St. Louis Tickle", by Theron C. Bennett, published in 1904 (under the pen name of "Barney & Seymour").

When Jelly Roll recorded "Georgia Swing" in 1928, the label listed as co-composers "J.R. Morton - S. Pecora". The latter is trombonist Santo Pecora, who was in the New Orleans Rhythm Kings a few years earlier when the NORK recorded

Common Themes

the two strains of "Georgia Swing" as part of a multi-strain piece called "She's Cryin' For Me". However, one of those two strains clearly has its origins in the ODJB's "Soudan", recorded in 1920, as well as in the chorus to the well-known Crescent City creole anthem "Eh La Bas".

While we have Morton and the ODJB on stage together, let's move on to "Tiger Rag". Everyone knows that Morton said he created this number by jazzing up strains of an old New Orleans quadrille. It was first recorded in 1918, by the ODJB, with its trumpet player, D.J. LaRocca, getting composer credit.

Morton and the ODJB each put their distinctive spin on "Tiger Rag", to be sure. However, it has been reported that the tune was commonly played in New Orleans from the earliest days of jazz under titles like "No. 2" and "Jack Carey".

In fact, one doesn't have to be a great musicologist to hear, in the opening portion of "Tiger Rag", a re-working of the first strain to "Get Out Of Here (And Go On Home)", the closing theme of the first jazzman anyone knows about, cornetist Buddy Bolden. It shows up again, in slightly altered form, as the B theme to King Oliver's "Chattanooga Stomp".

For that matter, the first strain of "Chattanooga Stomp" clearly derives from the first strain to the ODJB's "Fidgety Feet". And while we're on Oliver, let's mention that the first strain to "Mabel's Dream" (a tune recorded by Oliver but credited to Ike Smith) is the same as the first strain to the ODJB's earlier "Lazy Daddy".

Before we leave Handy, Morton and the ODJB, let's pause for Handy's 1915 work "The Hesitating Blues". The itinerant musician who passed through Memphis with this tune must have circled through Louisville as well, because its main motive makes up the refrain to "Hesitation Blues" published that same year in Louisville, with Scott Middleton and Billy Smythe listed as co-composers.

In 1921, Handy published "Loveless Love", which uses the familiar "Careless Love" as its chorus, preceded by a verse structured in 12-bar blues form. I'd guess that it is this publication which causes many uptown New Orleans-style bands to open their renditions of "Careless Love" with a couple of run-throughs of the twelve-bar blues, though usually not following Handy's or any other commonly accepted melody.

Similarly, in 1914, a number titled "The Long Lost Blues" appeared with lyrics credited to H. Alf Kelley and music to J. Paul Wyer. Its chorus is the old standby "Bucket's Got A Hole In It". Years later, on George Lewis' version of "Bucket's ...", the band plays a verse that turns out to be the verse from the sheet music of "The Long Lost Blues"! Now, just as with "Careless Love", when uptown-style New Orleans Dixielanders play that verse on "Bucket's ...", whether they know it or not, they're really (in one sense, at least) playing "The Long Lost Blues" instead.

In 1926, pianist Lillian Armstrong was credited as composer of the eight tunes recorded by a wonderful band known by two names, the New Orleans Wanderers and the New Orleans Bootblacks. One of those was a straight-ahead two-themed swinger called "Gate Mouth".

For the chorus of "Gate Mouth", Lil drew on a notion that seems to be everywhere among Dixielanders. It was published in 1917 as the chorus to

TEXAS SHOUT: HOW DIXIELAND JAZZ WORKS

"Mama's Baby Boy", listing John A. St. Cyr and Armand J. Piron as co-composers. The Wanderers/Bootblacks' trombonist, the great Kid Ory, carried it into the revival period as "Do What Ory Say". Lu Watters' Yerba Buena Jazz Band waxed it as "Get It Right". The mid-1970s version by Don Kinch's Conductors' Ragtime Band comes on under the whimsical title "Taiwan Ahn".

Let me emphasize that these various examples need not be plagiarism, but probably represent musicians drawing on more or less common property and giving it their own individualistic interpretations, something that is a specialty of the best Dixielanders. "Winin' Boy Blues" and the second strain to "Memphis Blues" really have a quite different feeling, even though they come from the same source and differ significantly only in one spot (where Jelly uses a minor chord while Handy uses a major). Similarly, "Buddy Bolden's Blues", at its typical slow pace, paints a much different musical picture than Theron C. Bennett's ragtime version.

Besides, as I said, nobody got too bent out of shape about these ideas being borrowed. Well, almost nobody. It has been reported that Louis Armstrong claimed to have written "(I Wish I Could Shimmy Like My) Sister Kate", and was so annoyed at A.J. Piron's name appearing on the song sheet as sole composer that Satchmo would never perform the selection!

You may think that this kind of analysis is musical navel-gazing. However, I find it interesting to try to dig out the origins of some of these tunes we like so much, and to notice how several of them pop up here and there in different costumes.

There are lots more examples, but the foregoing will do for now. I've showed you how to play the game, and you can have some fun finding your own recurring themes. Besides, I want to end this column with the most bizarre example I've yet encountered of unconscious tune-borrowing.

Most of you have heard, at festivals or on record, a number entitled "Red Flannel Rag". It's a three-strain piece, with an introduction and a strangely-harmonized interlude, that is credited to Turk Murphy. Once past the four-bar introduction, "Red Flannel Rag" is identical in all significant respects to "Lazy Luke", a ragtime piano solo composed by George J. Philpot, published in Boston in 1904, a decade before Turk was born.

At a St. Louis festival in the late 1970s, I had a chance to ask Turk about it. He told me that he'd never heard of "Lazy Luke' or George J. Philpot, and asked me to send him a copy of the music, which I promptly did. When we next met, Turk agreed that the tunes were identical.

He was at a loss to explain it. Turk felt sure that he had written "Red Flannel Rag".

Personally, I have no reason to doubt Turk's sincerity. First, his reputation in all quarters was that of a square-shooter. Second, his stature as a composer of quality Dixieland tunes was so secure that there was no reason for him to steal an old ragtime composition.

My guess is that, when Turk was a kid, someone in his neighborhood liked to play "Lazy Luke", or had a record or piano roll of it, so that Turk became exposed to the tune subliminally. Decades later, it emerged as an "original" composition.

Common Themes

    Stranger things have happened. I've heard it said that everything you've been exposed to is still rattling around in your brain somewhere, waiting for you to discover how to get access to it.

    Maybe we're lucky we can't do so. Can you imagine having to relive your memories of the ten worst bands you ever heard? On that note, let's call it a day.

TEXAS SHOUT: HOW DIXIELAND JAZZ WORKS

Rent Party Revellers   1990s   *Photo by Dan Polin*

Golden Eagles Jazz Band   1990s   *Photo by Charles V. Passela*

CHAPTER 41   ROUTINES

Any musical group requires a system to tell its members two things at each step of every performance: (1) which strain, theme or portion of the composition is to be played and (2) which instrumentalists are supposed to be playing it. In Dixieland bands, the members refer to that system as the "routine" or, less frequently, the "road map".

(It is also sometimes referred to as the "chart" or "arrangement". However, for purposes of today's column, I will use those terms only when referring to a score that has at least all of its ensembles, and maybe the solos as well, completely written out or otherwise preplanned note for note.)

Combos develop routines in a number of ways. Some, of course, use written arrangements, so that the instrumentalist just has to be able, as Jelly Roll put it, to read "those little black dots".

Many Chicago-styled bands, which are primarily solo-oriented, are less concerned about the intricacies of routines than they are about quickly getting to the solo parts of the rides. Many of them do quite well with only a single basic routine, one that specifies the solo order. An example might be: opening ensemble; solos by clarinet, trumpet, trombone and piano; closing ensemble.

Other combos may not want to write out charts, but still wish to present their audiences with more variety in routines. They might have separate road maps for each tune.

To illustrate, whenever such a unit plays Tune X, its routine will be: ensemble chorus, piano solo, ensemble verse, trumpet half-chorus solo, trombone half-chorus solo, clarinet-banjo full-chorus duet (other rhythm instruments out), ensemble chorus. Tune Y will also have a set routine but a different one, Tune Z different yet, etc.

If you don't want to plan your routines in advance then you need a code to designate on the spot who's supposed to do what. The most common of these has the on-stage leader pointing to the next soloist when it's his turn. This is the method used by almost all pickup or jam bands.

These spontaneous systems are often fine-tuned by adoption of a mutually understood set of hand and/or verbal signals that the leader can use to introduce various devices into the rides. These effects might include a key change, a move to a different strain, or musicians coming in and out of the action.

All of these ways of operating are "right" ways. Many first-rate combos can be found using each of them.

Despite what some devotees of various Dixieland styles will tell you, there is no one best way to set routines for your band. Whichever one you adopt will be fine, as long as your group always tries to produce jazz that strives to be hot, swinging and inventive.

I've said many times in this column that improvisation is not necessary to good jazz. There have been, and will continue to be, many worthwhile jazz performances in which every note has been specified in advance.

However, I doubt that you will ever find me interested in participating in any of them: I get my biggest jazz band kicks from being part of a group that has, to the maximum extent possible, the freedom to take the ride where, at that unique point in time, it wants to go.

Lots of musicians respond to a well-wrought arrangement, are able to play it over and over with the proper feelings of spontaneity and swing, and gain satisfaction each time they do so. I respect such views, but I'm not turned on by them. If we all know in advance what we're supposed to play, I'd just as soon skip that tune and go on to something else.

I feel much the same way with set-piece routines. Even if the notes aren't specified, I would eventually become bored playing in a band where, for example, in every rendition of "Papa Dip", the clarinet played the first half of the third chorus and I played the second half. The clarinetist may be the greatest stickman in the world, but I'd soon start to wonder what I might come up with if the preceding soloist, once in a while, played a different instrument, or if I played the first half of the chorus occasionally, or if everybody dropped out on my solo except the bass or ... You get the picture.

These feelings crystallized when I came to recognize that Dixieland is the branch of jazz in which the largest number of musicians can function effectively on stage without any type of arrangement. A seasoned Dixielander learns to assimilate the output of as many as seven other improvising musicians and to instantaneously improvise a line that will enhance and complement their efforts. By contrast, more advanced forms of jazz use such complex lines and dense chords that, without a chart, things start to get noisy above five or six sidemen.

After extended experience in combos from duets to octets that have varying kinds of instrumental makeup, a skilled Dixielander will enlarge that special talent. He/she will develop an instinct for performing in a way that turns the group in which he/she is functioning at the moment into a fully realized unit, one that sounds complete with whatever instrumentation is being heard.

I like to be in bands that get the participants to use that enlarged ability as much as possible. In such combos, any musician might suddenly find himself playing either entirely alone or with any combination of the others, being forced into a new "ensemble", a new context in which he/she must, together with whoever else is playing at the time, create something that will be meaningful and still keep the ride developing in larger terms.

Decades ago, I began operating along those lines with my Wilmington, Delaware-based Red Lion Jazz Band. It turned out that verbal signals worked fine with the Red Lions because we jammed together every week at my home. Thus, we got to know each other's styles intimately. The sidemen became used to listening for my verbal cues and executing them cleanly on the spot.

Routines

I tried the same verbal signals with The Rent Party Revellers, but ran into trouble doing so. The Revellers are a bigger band than the Red Lions (octet vs. septet), and have a more aggressive approach to Dixieland. It was hard for me to be heard on stage.

To compound the problem, the Revellers are a "reunion" band that only comes together a few times a year. The sidemen were not as used to my methods as the Red Lions, so I had to work harder to be sure everyone was picking up the signals.

Things came to a head the first time we played a week-long festival, at St. Louis in 1985. Halfway through the week I was starting to lose my voice from shouting vocal cues during the sets.

Our pianist, Dick Shooshan, came to my rescue by presenting the Revellers with a set of hand signals. Maybe he invented them on the spot, maybe he'd been using them for years with the Golden Eagles, but in any event they were what we needed.

I've used them ever since, adding a few new ones of my own, and even stealing a few others (e.g., a hand signal, to cue rhythmic afterbeats, I picked up while subbing with The Buck Creek Jazz Band). I still use voice signals for some things, but not so much, and I don't get hoarse anymore.

Several of you have asked me to explain the onstage signals that I use to call routines during performances by combos I lead. Actually, variations of most of these devices are in rather common usage among bandleaders and, I would think, shouldn't be hard to figure out by someone in the audience who pays close attention. Thus, I doubt that many of you would be much interested in a detailed description thereof.

However, a brief discussion of the basic philosophy behind these techniques might give general readers a little better understanding of what's happening on the bandstand and thereby enhance their enjoyment of our music. Maybe it will get a few bandleaders thinking about ways to keep their own presentations fresh. Anyway, here goes.

The Rent Party Revellers have one ground rule regarding onstage routines. It is my job to get the signal to each sideman. No Reveller is supposed to drop out, or re-enter, just because he hears someone else do so. He/she has to get the word from me.

With that lead-in, the Revellers' hand signals operate to cue the band regarding the number of choruses to play, which musicians are to be playing at any given time, and (in two instances) when a pre-set sub-unit of the band is to perform. In addition to those, I have a set of signals, some verbal, some by hand, to tell the drummer what kind of ending to use.

If the cornetist and drummer in a Dixieland band know what kind of ending is coming up, they can structure what they play to cue the other musicians to end the tune accordingly. I won't outline each of those signals, but they provide methods to end tunes in about six or seven ways. Using a variety of endings makes it appear that the band is employing arranged passages but leaves the freedom to get right up to the closing bars before settling on the ending that's the "right" one for that particular tune on that particular day.

As for verbal signals, at the start of the tune, when it's quiet, I can easily cue the number of opening pickups, at which point the trombone, piano and tuba will know just what to do. Also, that's a good time to cue the first solo, or maybe the first two.

We have a few other basic understandings that we've developed over the years. However, the ones described above will do for purposes of today's discussion.

There really aren't a lot of them, and most are fairly obvious. Indeed, the average combo is likely to use most of them to some extent at one time or another.

(There is one exception to that statement. Some combos use various numbers of fingers pointing up or down as a way of indicating keys.

The Revellers don't do that because, with few exceptions, we don't change keys for a given strain during a performance. We believe we can get enough different things going by regrouping our eight players without spontaneous key changes. Thus, we feel free to use these standard "key change" signals for other purposes.)

If you've occupied a stageside seat during a Revellers' set, you'll hear me tell the band at the start how we'll get into the tune, and who will be playing during the first solo chorus. After that, most of the time, nobody, not even me, knows for sure what will be happening. At each step, though, we try to build on what's gone before while steadily striving to show the audience a fresh framework for the tune.

It's a risky way to operate. However, in my opinion, taking chances is a sine qua non of creating the best jazz. Not all chances work, but when each sideman is on his toes, ready for the next challenge, you'll find that more of them work than otherwise. Further, because surprises can occur at any time, everyone - musicians and audience - gets caught up in the process.

Dick Shooshan told me once that he'd heard it said that the best jazz is played right on the brink of disaster. I couldn't agree more. If you only listen to bands that never take chances, you'll never hear any wrong notes or the type of mix-up that jazzmen call a "train wreck", but you probably won't hear any truly great jazz either.

In the dozen or so years that the Revellers have been exposing these devices on the circuit, I think I've seen some bands increasing their spontaneous use of subunits and other changes in tone combinations. However, I haven't yet seen a band that regroups the musicians as often or as radically as we do.

I sometimes wonder why not. Have today's Dixielanders become so conditioned to the sounds on their favorite records that they are afraid to try any others?

Don't other bandleaders become curious, for example, about what might happen if the next chorus were a tuba solo accompanied only by the clarinet and cornet? Or a trio of clarinet, alto and banjo? Or the trombone and clarinet (with full rhythm) taking turns backing each other's solos on the first and second half of the chorus? Or front line only with the rhythm entering on the first beat of the second half of the chorus?

Routines

The possibilities are literally endless. Some of them turn out so gloriously that the thrill sticks in your mind for years.

There is one catch, however. To make such wide use of spontaneous effects, the leader needs to learn how to think several choruses in advance. It took me quite some time of working with the Red Lions to get used to doing so.

You need to think far ahead because, for example, if you believe it might be interesting along the way to try an unaccompanied tuba solo, followed by an unaccompanied saxophone-tuba duet, then an unaccompanied clarinet-saxophone-tuba trio before breaking the tension with a trombone solo with full rhythm, you can't wait until the performance is half over before getting into the sequence. You'll have already used up too many of your soloists and lost the chance to build the ride properly.

Also, you can't organize a routine like that one with just two or three bars to go. You need to start doing so while there's time to get everyone properly cued. Otherwise, the execution will be sloppy.

Even after all these years, when I'm leading a band on stage, I'm concentrating exclusively on the routine once the rendition begins. That's one of the reasons why I don't play cornet solos. I'm too wrapped up in keeping things on track.

(If you hear me playing cornet without one of the other front line horns playing, it's always part of a special effect, either a chase or a subunit. I've never particularly sought this somewhat left-handed distinction, but I'll bet I'm the only cornetist who's been with a major festival/cruise band for over ten years and who's never played a full-chorus improvised solo backed by the entire rhythm section.)

The Red Lions could probably tell you piles of stories about how oblivious I get to anything that isn't a part of the music happening onstage. For example, in our early days, a patron had a heart attack and died while we were playing a restaurant gig. Once the commotion died down and we prepared to resume, I was about to announce the next tune on our preplanned list when our pianist leaned over, tapped me on the shoulder, and suggested that maybe it wouldn't be quite comme il faut to kick off "After You've Gone".

Most of you haven't seen the Red Lions. However, let me wrap up this somewhat technical column on, I hope, a light note by relating a couple of instances that some of you witnessed.

I was leading a jam session at a festival, the band comprised of wonderful players, all friends of mine and good-hearted people. It turned out that they had arranged to play a practical joke on me on our set-closer by ignoring my signals; instead they followed routines cued behind my back by one of the other sidemen. Quite a bit of the audience, in fact, was in on the joke before we took the stage.

I'm afraid I rather flattened the event without meaning to. I was, as usual, thinking so far ahead on the ride that I was unable to bring myself to do anything other than try frantically to straighten out what I perceived as missed cues caused by my own failure to communicate properly.

I remained in that confused state until the performance struggled to its conclusion. Once offstage, with the pressure off, I realized right away that I was being given a friendly leg-pull.

| TEXAS SHOUT: HOW DIXIELAND JAZZ WORKS |

The second occasion is an instance that just got funnier the longer I remained in my cloud. It occurred during the last Revellers' set at the 1992 San Diego festival.

The next group at the venue was Dick Shooshan's Golden Eagle Jazz Band. Though Dick was, naturally, playing with the Eagles that weekend, he is also, as mentioned above, one of the Revellers' pianists. I thought I saw Dick enter the hall and wanted to call him up to sit in, but all of a sudden he seemed to have disappeared.

It turned out that Dick had worked his way around the room's perimeter, getting up to the bandstand without my seeing him and taking over the keyboard from Ed Metz halfway through our next-to-last tune. Now Dick and Ed are both great players, but their styles are very different. Most leaders would have heard the difference right away.

Nevertheless, because nothing was going wrong, and because the piano solo had already been played by Ed, I did my usual thing and concentrated on working the other sidemen through various combinations until we finished. Then, still wondering what had happened to Dick, I announced the closing number and counted it off.

Ed, meanwhile was standing right by the stage in full view of me and of the audience, which was chuckling away at my single-mindedness. We started the last tune, at which point Ed, still without his presence registering on me, started walking back and forth in front of the bandstand, about two feet in front of my horn.

Finally, it came time to cue the piano solo. I turned to discover Dick, rolling it out with a big smile on his face, and the audience in gales of laughter. I can still hear Dick saying, as I was packing up after the set, "Man, are you FOCUSED!"

Ed Metz   1990s
Photographer Unknown

Oct. 1994 West Coast Rag

CHAPTER 42 "TRADITIONAL"

If you read these pages regularly, or much else that discusses our music, you'll run across a number of terms of art. They will be used freely on the assumption that readers know what these terms mean. Examples include "Dixieland", "uptown New Orleans", "Chicago style", etc.

Unfortunately, while these terms enjoy common usage, you will rarely find anyone setting down precise musical definitions thereof. As a result, there is a great deal of miscommunication and misunderstanding regarding our music. Someone will use such a word with the idea of making a certain point but various listeners/readers, because of the lack of common definitions, will receive different messages.

I first noticed this phenomenon as a youth when, having discovered Dixieland jazz and ragtime, and having no one in my home town to explain them to me, I paid close attention to LP liner notes and to the volumes on the jazz shelf of the public library. I soon discovered that much of what was said therein not only didn't square with other sources, but also didn't square with what I was hearing on the records.

Take the word "Dixieland". Many people who like older-style jazz have a knee-jerk reaction against that word. Initially, I tended to side with them.

However, over the years, I came to recognize that, for better or for worse, the most widely recognized, most accessible term for describing pre-swing jazz is "Dixieland". When I used it with the general public, everyone knew what I was talking about. It helped my Red Lion Jazz Band get gigs to say we played "Dixieland".

Popular culture does not always bestow names on its elements that are the ones their devotees would have selected. No one who thinks jazz is an art form can be very happy with the fact, considering the origins of the word, that it is called "jazz". But, like it or not, nothing can be done about "jazz" at this late date.

"Dixieland" is the same way. Jazz that uses the conventions and vocabulary employed by jazzmen prior to the innovations that came in with swing are playing "Dixieland". It is a broad umbrella term that includes seven distinct Dixieland styles, such as hot dance, Chicago, etc.

By the way, most people I've talked to who claim to hate the term "Dixieland" are unable to give me any well-thought-out reasons for disliking the word. If I ask them to tell me what "Dixieland" means, they usually start off discussing musicians who wear striped vests or funny hats.

I'll say right now that anyone who needs to know what a band is wearing in order to identify the music that it's playing is someone who doesn't know what he's

TEXAS SHOUT: HOW DIXIELAND JAZZ WORKS

talking about. Further, if "Dixieland" bands wear funny hats, then there must not be any "Dixieland" bands any more; I've been around the scene for some time, and I can't think of a single band these days that regularly wears hats at all, much less funny ones.

(The wonderful St. Louis Ragtimers, being a ragtime band and not a Dixieland band, don't count, although I think their hats fit their rollicking onstage personality perfectly. What about the pith helmets sometimes worn by Don Neely's Royal Society Jazz Orchestra? Would anyone be foolish enough to say that, when RSJO wears the costume using the pith helmets they're playing "Dixieland", but when they play the same chart in another uniform they're playing some other kind of music?)

I don't want to rehash the term "Dixieland", because I covered it in my very first "Texas Shout" (see the November/December 1989 *WCR)*. However, to give you an idea of the type of miscommunication I'm talking about, I'll share a brief portion of a letter I received not long ago.

The writer claimed to be a regular reader of this column, although he attributed some opinions to me that are the exact opposite of those I've frequently taken herein from time to time. Either I don't express myself clearly, or he isn't paying attention. Anyway, his rather contentious epistle said, in part:

"... Jimmie Noone's group didn't play 'dixieland' as we know it. They used an alto sax lead by Doc Poston; no trumpet, no trombone. But they sure enough played hot jazz.

"Similarly, my favorite recording - the one I play when I'm in the dumps and ready to quit the music - features Sidney Bechet and Muggsy Spanier with Wellman Braud on bass and Carmen Mastren on guitar. That's all. Dixieland? Hardly. ..."

Those comments prompt me to make the following point very clear all over again: The style of jazz played by a musician is determined by one thing and one thing only - the musical conventions and musical vocabulary employed during the performance. If those conventions and vocabulary do not use any elements introduced by swing and later jazz styles, then the performance is, in the lexicon used in this column since its inception, a Dixieland performance.

Anyone who thinks he can tell what style of jazz a band plays simply by knowing its instrumentation, without listening to it, needs to go back to Square One and start re-learning our music. Of course you can play Dixieland without a trumpet, or without a trumpet and trombone, or without a clarinet, or with two trombones, or ...

As it turned out, my correspondent and I weren't all that far apart in the essentials. His letter goes on to say, "Hot jazz is what we ought to be talking about here". I couldn't agree more, but that term is not precise enough. Swing when properly played is hot jazz - hot as blazes - and so is bop.

We need a title for our music that is less inclusive than "hot jazz". Like it or not, I haven't found a better one than "Dixieland".

Among the most common terms that older-style jazzmen use to describe their music is "traditional jazz". After much thought, I have decided that this term no longer has a useful meaning in the older-style jazz community. In fact, I think that it is starting to become a divisive term that causes more heat than light.

~ 252 ~

"Traditional"

I haven't found any good use for "traditional" that isn't served better by some other term that is more descriptive, less ambiguous, and less emotional. As a result, I try not to use it any more.

I'd like to see the Dixieland community also start to downplay the word "traditional". I'm going to use the rest of today's column to explain how I came to that position.

It was a long journey for me because, as I understand it, "traditional jazz" was coined by Turk Murphy, my all-time favorite musician and one of my earliest musical idols. When I was getting started in Dixieland, Turk could do no wrong.

Turk's style of Dixieland was one that he helped create as the trombonist for Lu Watters' Yerba Buena Jazz Band. I suppose that Turk intended "traditional jazz" to be the descriptive name for that style.

However, as I said before, the public doesn't always bestow on us the nicknames we prefer. Ever since I've followed our music, the branch of Dixieland played by Watters and Murphy has always been referred to as "San Francisco style" or "West Coast revival style". The jazz community never accepted "traditional" as being limited to the jazz of Watters, Murphy and their disciples.

However, the term didn't go away. That's because "traditional" is a word that has a highly charged emotional connotation. Like "classic", the word "traditional" suggests something that is time-honored, that has the approval of the ages, that has long and respectable roots.

Thus, everyone wants to be able to claim that the jazz he likes is "traditional". For example, the earliest type of "modern" jazz, the style of bop played by Dizzy Gillespie and Charlie Parker in the early forties, is now a half-century old and sounds rather conservative when compared to some of the anarchic music (I almost said "noise") appearing in the jazz bins in record stores. I've met early bop-style musicians who told me with a straight face that they play "traditional jazz".

Moreover, the term "traditional", in my view, has too often tended to exacerbate the kind of divisiveness in the Dixieland community that keeps us from acting together in our own best interests. There are those who believe that, if the kind of jazz they like is "traditional" - that is, has the legitimacy and authenticity of being based on long-established principles -, then the jazz they don't like must somehow be suspect. So they waste time fussing about whether this band or that band is or is not "traditional", as if that conclusion reveals anything about a combo's musical merits.

Take for example, the excellent festival staged each August at Santa Rosa, one which has a reputation among festivalgoers of being a "traditional" festival. After the 1993 event, a really first-rate affair (it was one of those rare occasions when Nancy and I had a chance to hear at least a few tunes by every band on the bill), one of the directors had to endure a lengthy harangue from a fan about whether one of the featured groups was "traditional". If it played good Dixieland, who the devil cares? (Believe it or not, the combo in question included former Murphy musicians, so one would think that such a band would be "traditional" if anything was).

Another Santa Rosa official had to deal with a fan who vociferously asserted that a different band, one that plays top-drawer Chicago style, was not "traditional". That particular complaint - that Chicago style is not "traditional" - is one I hear from time to time. It finally made me decide that the term "traditional" is doing the Dixieland community more harm than good.

If "traditional" is supposed to describe jazz that has the legitimacy of having been grounded in the jazz age, let's face it, Chicago style is not only traditional, but it also has a better claim to being traditional than two of the so-called "traditional" styles. Chicago style was actually played in the twenties, for Heaven's sake, while West Coast revival didn't come along until the forties and British trad was not heard before the fifties.

I can understand that, because Chicago is the only Dixieland style that is primarily solo-oriented, it might be useful to have a generally accepted shorthand term to distinguish Chicago style from the other six styles. I try to use "non-Chicago", an expression that leaves no doubt as to what is meant.

Still, "non-Chicago" may sound a bit technical, or maybe a bit negative. A suitable alternative word to refer collectively to the six non-Chicago styles would call them "revivalist" styles. After all, when the Dixieland revival started in the forties, Chicago was the only Dixieland style that didn't need reviving. It was still being played commercially at a fairly visible level. Thus, the other six styles are "revivalist" styles, a term which, in today's scene, I believe is less emotionally charged than "traditional".

While we're on more neutral-sounding terminology, let's return to the people who hate the word "Dixieland". As I said, I think you're shooting yourself in the foot by abandoning this widely understood word, but if you can't say "Dixieland" without gritting your teeth, why not say "early jazz" instead? Because Dixieland is the earliest form of jazz, you're not likely to be misunderstood by anyone with a smattering of knowledge about our music.

Are the points made above mere ivory-tower academia of no useful purpose? If you think Dixieland jazz is little more than a suitable background for dancing or for consuming a couple of beers, maybe so.

However, if we think our music is a legitimate art form, one that's worthy of attention for its own sake, one that can touch deep emotions in its listeners, one that can send echoes through the decades to stir our passions, one that is capable of generating new and meaningful expressions, then it's high time we began behaving accordingly. One way we can do so is to develop, as have other art forms (painting, literature, classical music, etc.), a commonly accepted, clearly defined vocabulary that will provide the basis for intelligent analysis and discussion of Dixieland. At least for the present, I favor leaving "traditional" out of it.

CHAPTER 43   FATS WALLER, ETC.

I grew up, and went to college, only about 120 miles from Times Square. However, in those years I had neither much money nor convenient access to transportation, so a trip to New York City was a big deal for me. As a result, I only once attended Eddie Condon's nightclub during his lifetime.

I had a ball. It was one of the few occasions, up until then, that I saw big-name Dixielanders live. The band was great.

To make the evening extra special, I decided to see if the combo would play a request for me. The Condon mob had just released its "Eddie Condon's Treasury of Jazz" LP, which included the first commercial version of "Duff Campbell's Revenge" a composition by my favorite musician, Turk Murphy. I longed to hear it played live.

I knew that "Duff" was a difficult and unusual tune, and I suspected that the band had learned it just for the recording. So, I thought I should have a second choice ready that would be, I believed , a sure thing.

Thus armed, I approached the stage just as the sextet was setting up after a break. I asked trombonist Cutty Cutshall, who was sitting at the side of the bandstand, if he would play a request for me.

Cutty readily assented and asked what I wanted to hear. When I mentioned "Duff Campbell's Revenge", his face fell. "Gee, he said, " we read that one off in the studio. I don't think we'd remember it."

"O.K.", I replied, "how's about playing something by Jelly Roll Morton?" To my amazement, Cutty's face fell again as he mumbled "Gee, I don't know. What did he write?"

As I started down the list of standard Jelly tunes, Cutty immediately brightened with recognition. He chose "Wolverine Blues", spoke briefly to the band and they kicked off the set with a red-hot version that put just the right icing on the cake for me that evening.

That incident was my first exposure to a phenomenon which still catches me off-guard at times. Many Dixieland musicians, even famous full-timers who make a living from the music and have devoted their lives to it, don't know and don't particularly want to know who wrote the tunes they play every night.

I now understand why this happens. Almost everybody who comes to Dixieland does so by hearing someone else play it, either live or on records. Something in them responds to the music, and they are moved to create it themselves, initially desiring to replicate the sounds that caught their ears.

Thus, their initial focus is upon assimilating the style and repertoire of their favorite jazzmen. To do so, you just need to listen and practice. You don't need to

TEXAS SHOUT: HOW DIXIELAND JAZZ WORKS

know anything about the tunes themselves except how to reproduce the notes thereof.

As time passes, anyone getting deeply into Dixieland inevitably settles on numbers that he/she particularly enjoys. Moreover, if a player is doing the right thing, he/she eventually stops replicating others and starts to develop his/her own personal vision of the music. In doing so, he/she will choose certain compositions that seem especially compatible with that vision.

At that point, I would think that the player would naturally take the trouble to find out who wrote the tunes. He/she might do so out of respect for the music itself; after all, without the composers, we wouldn't have anything to play.

But beyond that objective, if you particularly like a certain tune, wouldn't you want to know who wrote it, on the assumption that this composer may well have written other things you'd particularly like for which you could be on the lookout? It doesn't happen that way very much, a fact which continually surprises me.

Possibly because I am a pianist and am seeing things from a pianist's perspective, or possibly because most popular tunes are published in vocal/piano editions, I think that pianists are somewhat more finely attuned to focusing on composers than the average Dixielander. Still, I can't help but notice how securely many musicians are locked into the records. That is to say, they associate a title primarily with the artist who recorded it and are inclined to believe, if that artist has any reputation at all as a composer, that he probably wrote it as well.

For example, Fats Waller made a particularly well-remembered 78 of "I'm Gonna Sit Right Down And Write Myself A Letter" (1935), lyric by Joe Young, music by Fred E. Ahlert. If I had a nickel for every time I've heard some bandleader announce Fats as the composer of that piece, I would have retired years earlier than I did. Moreover, Ahlert was not exactly an unknown composer, having had a long and productive career on Tin Pan Alley that included the creation of several other standards such as "I'll Get By", "Walkin' My Baby Back Home", "Where The Blue Of The Night" and "The Moon Was Yellow".

(As an aside, I often see misattribution of composer credit to Louis Armstrong, but for a different reason. There are those who see "Armstrong" listed as a composer and assume that Louis is meant. Actually, Satchmo did not compose all that many selections - though his wonderful "Someday You'll Be Sorry" and "Swing That Music" are standards, and it has been said that he was the actual composer of "(I Wish I could Shimmy Like My) Sister Kate".

However, his second wife, Lillian Hardin Armstrong, was one of the all-time great composers of Dixieland tunes. If you see "Armstrong" as a composer credit, there's probably a better-than-average chance that Lil, not Louis, is intended.)

Speaking of Fats, and of misattribution of Fats as a composer, jazz folklore is filled with tales of Waller's raising the price of cab fare, a meal or a drink by selling melodies on the spur of the moment to various publishers (allegedly sometimes re-selling themes he'd already peddled elsewhere). No doubt certain of these got reworked by the publishers' house arrangers or composers into songs that may or may not have had Fats' name on them when they appeared in print.

Laurie Wright's authoritative bio-discography of Waller, *"Fats" In Fact* (1992, Storyville Publications) contains a full page of titles that, at one time or another,

Fats Waller, Etc.

someone has asserted to be composed by Fats. Wright cites every such example known to him, including some which (to use his words) seem "wholly fanciful".

One of those, the one I believe I've seen attributed to Waller more than any other, is "I Can't Give You Anything But Love". Ernie Anderson, who knew Fats well, has written that Fats sold it to composer Jimmy McHugh for quick cash. Franz Jackson has been reported to have said the same thing about "On The Sunny Side Of The Street", which came along in 1930, two years after "I Can't ...". At any rate, McHugh is the composer on the song sheet for both numbers.

In his 1992 volume, *Black And Blue: The Life And Lyrics Of Andy Razaf*, biographer Barry Singer attempted to nail down the authorship of "I Can't ...", assessing the available evidence and ultimately concluding that "It is impossible to say." Let me preface this discussion by saying that I have no new discoveries regarding that tune or "Sunny Side".

In show business, anything is possible. However, though it may be presumptuous to question someone close to Fats (like Anderson), I'm inclined to take such claims with a grain of salt, and here's why.

Let's begin by noting that, though McHugh was a professional manager for Mills Music during the 1920s, he wasn't some unknown office boy who might have put his name on something in the files. He was one of the top songwriters of his era, having as early as 1924 composed tunes that are still played today.

We all know his famous ballads "Don't Blame Me" and "I'm In The Mood For Love". Dixielanders regularly choose to jam on such McHugh evergreens as "When My Sugar Walks Down The Street", "Blue Again", "Exactly Like You" and "I Can't Believe That You're In Love With Me". Revivalist combos occasionally essay such McHugh swingers as "Baltimore", "Everything Is Hotsy Totsy Now" and "The Lonesomest Girl In Town". In sum, McHugh was an established, highly successful composer who had no need to buy or otherwise appropriate someone else's tunes.

Further, "I Can't Give You Anything But Love" was the biggest hit from the score of "Blackbirds Of 1928", for which McHugh wrote all the original tunes. As far as I know, more pieces from that show are still played by Dixieland bands than any other musical stage production of the twenties - seven of them to be exact. In addition to "I Can't ...", I know of fairly recent recordings of "Diga Diga Doo", "Doin' The New Low Down", "Here Comes My Blackbird", "Baby", "I Must Have That Man" and "Magnolia's Wedding Day".

All of those songs swing like mad and were written at the same time. They are clearly cut from the same musical cloth, seemingly the work of the same musical mind, so it seems unlikely to me that one of them is a ringer. Yet, to my knowledge, no one has ever suggested that McHugh is not the composer of the other six.

Finally, although Fats was certainly a master practitioner thereof, he was not the only composer of his day who was gifted at writing catchy pops with simple rhythmically-oriented melodies that continue to attract older-style jazzmen. Walter Donaldson, for example, is my pick for the composer who, during the ten years that comprised the twenties, probably wrote more tunes still played today by Dixieland bands than anyone else. Also, you won't get through a Dixieland festival without hearing a number of works by Irving Berlin.

TEXAS SHOUT: HOW DIXIELAND JAZZ WORKS

McHugh belongs in that category. In fact, though he was white, it was surely his well-known (in the industry) knack for writing the kind of number that would fit the styles of the Black entertainers who made up the cast of "Blackbirds Of 1928" that got him the assignment to compose the show's music. In fact, Fats himself later waxed, in fondly recalled renditions, two McHughs not yet mentioned, "I've Got My Fingers Crossed" and "Spreading Rhythm Around", but no one is claiming Fats wrote those.

Similarly, I've heard it said that James P. Johnson and not George Gershwin wrote "Liza" (from Gershwin's 1929 musical "Show Girl"). Perhaps that rumor has its roots in the fact that stride pianists like to play "Liza", finding its open melody and chord structure particularly compatible for typical stride variations. Of course, there are lots of tunes that lay well for stride piano that weren't written by a strideman.

I think the "Lisa" claim is nonsense for two reasons. First, by 1929, Gershwin was one of Broadway's most celebrated figures; like McHugh he had little to gain and a lot to lose by stealing material. Second, of all the great Broadway names, no one had more affinity for older-style jazz than Gershwin, who loved our music. His "Oh! Lady Be Good!" and "Summertime" are now Dixieland jam standards, while his "I Got Rhythm" (along with tunes based on the chord pattern thereof) is virtually the national anthem of swing jam sessions. He had plenty of ability to write our kind of music.

In short, I am highly skeptical of such assertions, particularly when they are made after all of the principals have died. I can't prove anything either way, but until someone can, I'll go with the published song sheet as far as the McHughs and Gershwins of the world are concerned.

How do such stories get started? I have a couple of ideas thereon which I'll share with you after I vent one other peeve of mine regarding Fats Waller legends.

It is an article of faith among some Waller commentators that Fats was forced by record producers to play worthless pop ditties of the day and that his humorous vocalizing and spoken asides on his records were a way of protesting such treatment. The unspoken assumption seems to be that, if Fats had been left alone to do what he wanted to do, his recordings would have been somehow better, based on stronger material, and more "serious" (thereby being more worthy of attention by a "serious" jazz fan. To me, this kind of thinking flies in the face of what we know about Fats personally, and also of his overall recorded legacy.

To begin with, by all accounts, Fats was an ebullient, irrepressible and irresponsible personality, one who lived entirely for the moment, never planned ahead, loved to kid, and kept everyone around him in good spirits. His recordings are consistent with that view, as he seems unable to restrain himself from joviality no matter what he's playing, be it one of his immortal standards or one of those so-called "worthless" ditties.

Fats Waller, Etc.

We all know such people - good natured, easy-going folks who never seem to take things seriously and, with their spontaneous wit, constantly light up the room. Naturally, jazz has its share of them, and Waller was one of them. It's as simple as that.

Further, from what we know of Fats' appearances where he seems to have had a freer hand in selecting repertoire - such as air checks, or piano solo sessions without his hot little backup group, Fats tended to gravitate to the same handful of numbers, often his own works like "Honeysuckle Rose", "Ain't Misbehavin'", "I'm Crazy 'Bout My Baby" and "Blue, Turning Grey Over You". This picture is consistent with that of many older-style jazz players who have certain tunes with which they feel particularly comfortable and who play (and record) those numbers over and over again, sometimes with little variation on the solos.

Fats was not a student of pop music the way some of today's older-style jazzmen/women are, compiling lists of obscure gems that he was dying to get on record. He entered the studio with little or no advance planning (e.g., Eddie Condon's famous story about Waller's "The Minor Drag" date).

Had Fats been left to his own devices, we'd probably be left with hundreds of Waller records re-waxing about twenty tunes instead of the rich and varied discography we have. And he still would have been kidding around. I know which choice I prefer.

Further, as to those "worthless" tunes, Waller was a nationally famous recording artist for RCA-Victor, one of the biggest labels in the country, a company that could and did command access to the latest and best from the songwriting industry. Moreover, we're talking about the 1930s, the time when the craft of writing popular music probably reached its all-time peak.

Many of the selections recorded by Fats may not have gone on to become standards, and they may have had the type of sentimental lyric that causes discomfort in certain areas of jazz criticism, but they contained plenty of musical red meat. Indeed, Fats' recordings have provided a gold mine for jazzmen looking for high-quality but underplayed material.

When someone today comes up with a new rendition of something Fats did back then, he/she's usually praised for doing so, not castigated for resurrecting "worthless" titles. For that matter, when guitarist Marty Grosz, probably our foremost keeper of the overall Waller ambiance in his bands, inserts some of his own very funny, dry wit into the rides, everybody (rightly) gets a big bang out of it. They don't go around wringing their hands because poor Marty has to take out his frustrations on the dreck he's been given to play.

We've headed in several directions today, so let's take time out to recapitulate. We started this essay noting that many jazz players don't know or care who wrote the tunes they play. Having concluded that discussion, we found that it led into some idle thoughts regarding misattribution of composer credits, a topic clouded somewhat by rumors that famous white composers stole from Black stride pianists.

Then, by stream-of-consciousness thinking generally forgivable when employed by persons of my advanced age, we wandered into another area of rumors about a Black stride pianist, one who reportedly was laughing to keep from crying.

TEXAS SHOUT: HOW DIXIELAND JAZZ WORKS

Many of these rumors seem like nonsense from a common-sense viewpoint, but they keep getting repeated in the literature.

What's going on here? I've said before in these pages that there is a lot of material written about jazz that just isn't so. Part of those fairy tales result from the hidden agendas of some jazz commentators. Three such viewpoints regularly recur in the literature, and I see them at work in the matters discussed above.

First, there are those who regard jazz as a serious matter. They are most comfortable with lyrics that talk of no-good lovers, broke-and-hungry people and the like. The higher the blues content in the music, the more they like it.

Conversely, such folks are discomfited by anyone who seems to be having fun with our music. They are quick to claim that jazz played by a band that wears eye-catching uniforms must necessarily be trivial; that songs with upbeat lyrics about, say, flappers and sheiks, or sentimental romance, lack the proper depth; and that any device which seems to add humor to a performance, no matter how well it might enhance the emotional pitch of the ride, is corny or Spike Jones-type irrelevancy.

To illustrate: If you play an obscure jazz instrumental for one of these types, and preface it with the statement that the tune is titled "Gritty Hawg Jowls", they'll leap to tell you how gutty, earthy, and low-down it is. However, if you tell them instead that they're about to hear a number called "Dimpled Kiddie Smiles", and then play the same rendition, they'll ask you to take it off before it ends, claiming it's the fluffiest, most trivial thing they've ever heard.

When Fats starts clowning around on his titles, even when the jokes are truly witty and contribute to the general hilarity and heat of his wonderful little combo, our doomsayer critics can't laugh along with the rest of us. They have to find some other reason supporting the humor. Hence, we hear about poor Fats, suffering for his art, taking out his frustrations on the material.

Of course, such a viewpoint refuses to consider jazz on its artistic merits. Jazz, like any other valid art form, is capable of expressing the full range of human emotion, from the most euphoric and cheerful, through the most tender and romantic, to the most despondent. There is no reason why a performance which concentrates on the brighter end of that spectrum has any less claim on our attention than the reverse, provided the results are done with originality, heat and swing - always a hallmark of any Waller recording.

Second, there are those who really want to keep the music for themselves. They complain that jazz musicians don't as a rule get rich and famous, but when one does, they can't handle it. They rapidly assert that the artist has "sold out", "gone commercial" or the like.

To those folks, it is inconceivable that the jazz community, once in a while, could produce a Fats Waller or a Louis Armstrong, someone with immense jazz talent who also had the type of stage personality that endeared him to the public in general, one who could reach the people without compromising his artistic integrity. So when Fats tosses off one of his hilarious asides, or Louis breaks into that big-eyed grimace during a vocal, such actions can't be interpreted to be part of a natural style, but must be seen as demeaning condescension to the public's inevitably bad taste.

Fats Waller, Etc.

I don't buy that view, either. If all a jazz musician had to do to become rich and famous was to "sell out", there would be plenty of Dixieland musicians over the years, just barely scraping by, who would be rushing to do so at the first opportunity.

As I have said before in these pages (see "Texas Shout" for August 1990), entertainment for its own sake is a perfectly valid objective for a jazz band. The trick is to find a way to entertain while still playing the kind of music you prefer, an ability with which Fats and Louis, for example, seem to me to have been naturally gifted.

Thirdly, and finally, while one brings up racial topics very gingerly these days, it is common knowledge that there has always been a strong streak in jazz criticism of Crow Jim (i.e., prejudice in favor of Blacks). Entire books have been written which essentially dismiss all white jazzmen/women out of hand, usually taking the view that even the best of them are pale ripoffs of Black performers.

Part and parcel of this school is the notion that virtually every Black performer has to be seen as some type of victim, no matter how famous or successful he/she became. Those who subscribe to this view are quick to believe that, for example, well-known white composers really got to the top by stealing themes from the Wallers and James P,s of the world.

Well, being a Black jazz musician never has been a bed of roses, particularly in the twenties. Black artists were, in fact, treated inexcusably with regularity by unscrupulous whites who were in a position to do so. For example, on several occasions, I remember listening to Eubie Blake tell about working conditions for Black vaudevillians so cruel and harsh that our hearts bled to think of them.

In short, there are plenty of well-documented shameful instances of racial discrimination in our music's history without going around looking for more, or finding reasons to make up some without any sort of hard evidence. Did Fats have to face the indignities of bigotry? Without a doubt. However, that conclusion doesn't make me inclined to believe that he, and not the credited composers, actually wrote all, many, or even any of the tunes with which Fats is most closely associated.

Those three filters for viewing jazz - that it must be "serious", that it cannot be commercially popular without being suspect quality-wise, and that discrimination against Black musicians is a major part of the answer to nearly every meaningful question related to our music - have been thrown up time and again by those who would like to dissuade you from listening to certain musicians, Dixieland styles or specific performances. Be aware of those theories, give them the value they deserve, but don't be seduced by them.

There is no general proposition about jazz that will tell you anything reliable about whether a given musician, band or performance will be worth hearing. Listen for yourself to the jazz with open ears and an open mind. Then decide on the merits of the music, not on pop sociology.

And if Fats, or Marty Grosz, or The Firehouse Five Plus Two, or anyone else, cracks a joke on a recording, I have a bit of advice for you: it's perfectly O.K. to laugh and still conclude that the overall ride was a great, hot, swinging jazz rendition.

TEXAS SHOUT: HOW DIXIELAND JAZZ WORKS

James P. Johnson   1940s
Photo from The Record Changer

Fats Waller   1930s
Photo from The Record Changer

George Gershwin   1920s
Photographer Unknown

Feb.-Mar.-Apr. 1995 West Coast Rag

CHAPTER 44   LEARNING TO PLAY

The techniques used to teach musical instruments today are nothing short of amazing. School-age children are regularly taught to sight-read flypaper, spend all evening in the screech range, and generally execute with regularity things thought to be impossible in the twenties.

This phenomenon is an outgrowth of the stage band movement, which really started to grab hold in our high schools in the sixties. Although the teachers thereof typically pay no attention to Dixieland, believing that jazz really started with Charlie Parker, one has to admire what they've taught their charges and to wish that such instrumental coaching had been available in our day.

This thought got me to reminiscing about the home-grown ways in which many of today's veteran Dixielanders, obsessed with a desire to play our music but unable to find anyone who would teach it to us, learned how to operate our instruments. I'll share some of my own stories on that topic with you in a moment, but before I do so, I want to make a point about technical virtuosity and jazz playing.

No one in his right mind denigrates technique. We all practice diligently to maintain the technique we have and to try to expand it.

All jazzmen yearn for the chops to reach up one more half-tone, play one more closing chorus, toss off a dazzling run, etc. We can't help feeling a touch of envy when we hear highly skilled jazz technicians, and when we see their startling accomplishments being rewarded with thunderous applause.

From an audience viewpoint, technique is readily recognizable, easily accessible, and highly exciting. If a trumpeter steps up on his first solo and hits double-high Z-sharp with a big fat tone and ringing volume, and then manages to squeeze 473 cleanly articulated notes into every beat, even a tin ear in the crowd will be forced to take notice.

Such an accomplishment deserves recognition and gets it. Even so, a Dixieland fan should be careful to remember a number of things regarding instrumental technique.

First, there are many impressive players who are unable to resist putting their entire bag of tricks into every solo. One need not disparage their talents to find this practice getting old fast. Once you've shown the audience everything you can do on the first tune, what's left for the second?

When I encounter such a player, I usually jump to my feet after the opening number, applaud warmly on the next, begin to experience deja vu on the third, and start looking to see who's playing at the other venues on the fourth. It's not how many notes you play that counts, but playing the right notes that pays off in jazz. Technique is useless if it is not put to the service of creating a distinctive, valid and fresh vision of the material.

Second, the rules of Dixieland were set down before these super-fancy techniques were known to exist. Someone who deploys, to an excessive extent in a Dixieland framework, the busy lines and extreme ranges available to modern technicians will upset the balance of the band.

There is a place, to be sure, in Dixieland for dramatic highs, fleet runs and angular out-of-chord notions. For example, I wish I could hit a high concert Eb on my cornet. I encounter occasions when it seems right to do so; instead I need to invent an alternative way to make my musical point.

However, such occasions don't come up that often, and if I spent the whole gig up around that Eb, the other Dixielanders in the band would be unable to do their jobs, which is to find something to blend with my lines. In short, compared to more advanced jazz forms, where instrumental virtuosity is more highly valued for its own sake, there aren't so many times when it will really advance the ball for a Dixielander in a meaningful way.

In fact, many immortal Dixielanders had techniques that probably wouldn't pass muster in today's high school bands. Jim Robinson is one of Dixieland's most imitated trombonists, not because of the notes he played (which are fairly easy to replicate), but because he had a matchless gift for selecting notes that drove the combo forward relentlessly. Muggsy Spanier is reported to have joked that he never hit a high C in his life, but that doesn't keep jazz history from placing his name high on the list of all-time hot lead Dixieland horns.

Third, while all Dixieland players would like to have more technique, it should be recognized that, in the wider musical community, technical virtuosity is fairly common. Schools like Juilliard, Berklee and North Texas State turn out dozens of musicians annually who have technique coming out their ears and who possess much more of it than the typical Dixielander, including many famous ones, can begin to approach.

If you really want to applaud technique, you're reading the wrong publication and attending the wrong concerts. You should be listening to, among other things, modern jazz or classical music. If you want to listen to Dixieland, you should be looking for bands and musicians who can surprise you, who seem always to have something special to say, even if they manage to say it with a couple of half notes in the mid-range followed by a long rest.

Stage bands weren't around in 1945 when I was eight years old and in the fourth grade at a suburban public school. That fall, Mr. Pleasant School sent around a letter to parents saying that piano lessons were available for a nominal charge. My parents signed me up, even though we did not then have a piano at home, over my protests (the lessons were given on part of the lunch hour and I wanted to go out on the playground).

We took the "Visual Method". There was one piano in the room, an upright with its keys wired to a replica of a keyboard on its top. We sat at wooden blocks carved to represent about two octaves on a piano keyboard.

The teacher struck a note on the piano, it would light up on the replica, and we would place our fingers at that spot on the wooden block. Once a period, we came up to the real piano so the teacher could see if we were doing it right.

Learning To Play

Those of us who didn't have pianos were given folding cardboard keyboards to take home. We would spread it out on the dining room table and practice fingering. (I still have my keyboard, though fortunately for me, my folks acquired a piano shortly thereafter from a business associate who was getting rid of his furniture following a divorce. For that matter, I still have that piano.)

I took the Visual Method through the fourth grade and for a few weeks into the fifth. It taught me how to read music as well as how to recognize a major, minor and seventh chord (but it did not teach any theory or chord progressions).

My parents then had me take private lessons, but within a few months I was bored by the finger exercises and simplified classical pieces with which I was confronted. We did not have much music in our home, and the titles meant nothing to me. Besides, none of my friends wanted to hear me play "Santa Lucia" or "The Blue Danube".

So I stopped taking lessons. However, just about that time, I heard some piano music on the radio. (Remember, in the late forties, commercial radio played all kinds of popular music, by contrast to today's scene, where rock predominates.) I had no idea what it was, but I thought it sounded great. I wanted to play piano that way.

I went to Wilmington's largest music store where, believe it or not, the last song plugger in our city was still going strong. Able to read anything at sight, she stood behind a small counter with a piano and piles of colorful music sheets displayed in racks behind her. If a piece caught your eye, she would demonstrate it for you on the spot.

I tried describing the music I'd heard on the radio. I had no idea that it had any kind of a name, but the lady was very patient with this enthusiastic child. (I told this story once at the office, only to have a colleague speak up and say "That was my mother!" Small world.)

She eventually figured out that I was probably talking about ragtime, a type of music that was then dead as a doornail. She walked behind her music racks and started rummaging through a drawer. I could see her blowing dust off the song sheets as she examined them.

She emerged with reprint copies of "Smoky Mokes" and "Maple Leaf Rag". Once she played them for me, I knew that this was the music I'd heard and gleefully snapped up both of them.

You couldn't keep me away from the piano. My parents, bless their hearts, must have had the patience of Job, because they never once complained about hearing these same two songs over and over, hour after hour.

"Smoky Mokes" is a fairly easy cakewalk which I soon got under control, but "Maple Leaf Rag" is hard and my little hands had a lot of trouble pushing down those thick cluster chords in the trio. It would take me about forty-five minutes just to get through it once (played accurately up to tempo, it should take about three). Then as I only had the two tunes, there wasn't much else to do but try it again. Never a word from Mom or Dad, unless I was holding up dinner.

I couldn't find any more ragtime commercially in those days, but I did buy some simplified pieces that sounded like they had some similar elements. I remember particularly two easy-to-play boogie woogies. Still, I was limited to the printed scores until an unforgettable day that opened wide the doors of popular music for me.

I was in junior high school and a member of the cast of a Saturday morning kids' radio show on WILM. I would banter with Harry Hubbel (dressed as Wilmo The Clown before a live studio audience) and maybe play a little piano or do a recitation

One day at rehearsal, when just the two of us were in the studio, Harry said "Tex, do you know how to play piano by ear?" "No." "There's nothing to it. You can play any song using only four chords."

I was dumbfounded. Remember, my Visual Method had taught me nothing about chord progressions. However, I was certain that more than four chords were needed to play all of the songs in the world, and I said so. Harry then left me slack-jawed by sitting down at the piano and running off a long string of popular hits, all of which needed only four chords.

I now realize that the basic building blocks of pre-rock pops are a major chord on the tonic note (called a I chord), a major chord on the fourth note of the scale (a IV chord), a seventh chord on the fifth note of the scale (V7) and a chord on the second note of the scale which might be either a seventh or a minor chord (II7 or IIm). Thousands of twelve-bar blues use only the I, IV and V7 chords. Harry, of course, was selecting only tunes that would work with the four basic ones, but he could go on like that indefinitely.

Suddenly the whole universe of music seemed within my grasp. I quickly memorized the chords, which were in Harry's favorite key of F: F, Bb, C7 and either G7 or Gm.

Now I no longer had to live with "Smoky Mokes" and "Maple Leaf Rag". I would pick out the melody to a tune I wanted to play. If it wasn't in F, I would immediately transpose it to F, so that I could apply the "magic chords" to it.

(Although I can now play the piano easily in any of the common jazz and ragtime keys, to this day F seems especially comfortable for me at the keyboard. Moreover, it took me a while to become completely weaned from F.

When I got to college, and was initiated into jamming Dixieland tunes, I'd be thinking something like: "If this tune were in F, the next chord would be a Db - three whole tones down from F, but we're playing in Ab, so that means I need to go three whole tones down to an E chord." I still can't believe I could make that intricate thought process work while playing at high speeds, but it got me through until I reached the point where I automatically knew progressions in the different keys.)

You would be astonished at all the tunes that got played with Harry's four chords. "Stardust"? No problem. "1812 Overture"? Piece of cake.

However, my ear soon began telling me that, for some tunes, none of the four chords would work. I tried others. If I was harmonizing a D note in the melody, I would try a D chord of some kind. If that didn't work, I'd try some other chord that had a D in it. Eventually after months of this process, I taught myself, by brute force, the circle-of-fifths chord progression, the basic progression used in American popular music prior to the Beatles.

Learning To Play

By this time, as a result of reading *They All Played Ragtime*, I had discovered what ragtime was, and via 78s by The Firehouse Five Plus Two, I was into Dixieland jazz. I couldn't do much more than play melody and chords to tunes, but a friend of mine at school had taken lessons in popular piano at a downtown studio. His name was Rick Cordrey, later to spend fifteen years as pianist for my Red Lion Jazz Band and then to become the first 88er for the Buck Creek Jazz Band.

In another session I'll never forget, Rick was kind enough to come to my home after school and show me some of the tricks he'd learned at the Horace Hustler studios. I came away with one special effect for each hand - voicing the treble in octaves to get a bigger sound, and a "fake bass", rolling my left hand without moving it on the keyboard, to get a light-but-accurate rhythm at fast tempos.

I practiced these incessantly (for some years I could play treble runs faster in octaves than in single notes, just the reverse of what is comfortable for most pianists). However, now that Rick had alerted me to looking for pianistic tricks, I was able to pick up others from records and even invent a few of my own.

I was on my way. My patchwork method was a cruder school than Juilliard, and I've often wished I had more formal lessons (it sometimes took me years of fooling around at the keyboard before I understood a fact that a teacher could have taught me in five minutes), but at least I had enough grounding to play some gigs, form a band, and even investigate methods of getting sounds out of other instruments than the piano.

The Visual Method was not my first exposure to music lessons. For unimaginable reasons, when I was in the third grade, my father bought a mandolin from a colleague at his office with the notion that I might like to play it. Perhaps he thought I might become a gondolier some day.

I took a few lessons, but I had about as much interest in the mandolin back then as I do now. Thus, that experiment was rather short-lived.

It did have an unforeseeable payoff, however, because it gave me some familiarity with the mechanics of stringed instruments. When I became interested in Dixieland, I taught myself to strum a ukelele that I found around the house. Eventually, in the mid-sixties, I wound up playing rhythm banjo for a Drexel Hill, PA-based Dixieland band, The Good Time Six.

I found my way to the cornet by a similarly circuitous route. When I was in the seventh grade, my parents decided that I should learn the trombone, so I was taken to the junior high school band director with that thought in mind. However, my arm was not yet long enough to reach the seventh position, so I was handed instead a baritone horn, a valve instrument that plays in the same range as the trombone.

The literature for baritone exerted the same compelling attraction for me as had the literature for the mandolin four years previously. Exit one baritone horn.

Segue to midway in the eleventh grade, when I had become very much interested in music. I decided that I wanted to play in a group with other musicians, so I went to the office of our high school band director and had a conversation along the following lines:

> "I would like to play in the band."
> "What instrument do you play?"
> "Piano"
> "We don't have a piano in our marching band"
> "I know. However, if there is an instrument you need played, and you'll show me how to play it, I'll give it a try."
> "Have you ever had lessons on any other instrument?"
> "A few years ago, I had some on baritone horn."

Enter the baritone horn again. I commenced weekly lessons and held down the second baritone horn chair in the Pierre S. du Pont High School band until the end of the year, at which time a wonderful thing happened. The entire trombone section graduated.

Mr. Beymer handed me a trombone before summer recess along with an instruction book, informing me that, upon the commencement of school in the fall, I would occupy the exalted first trombone chair.

I was ecstatic, especially as I was now able to play a Dixieland instrument along with my FireHouse Five Plus Two 78s, of which I had a complete set. I quickly matched the slide positions to the baritone's valve fingering and, each day, played along with every single FH5 side.

My turntable was mounted on a combination 78 rpm player and reel-to-reel tape recorder, so it was hardly a precision instrument. Moreover, I have no mechanical ability at all, being the sort of person who is defeated by a thumb tack.

(My wife won't even let me hang a picture at home. Were I to attempt the task, it would soon became a Laurel & Hardy plot - within a half-hour, the basement would be flooded, the ceiling would be on fire, and the garage would be reduced to splinters.)

As I toiled along with the FH5, I couldn't help but notice that they functioned in what seemed to me to be rather unusual keys. Nearly all the tunes were in B natural, F sharp or E natural.

Oh well, I thought, mine is not to reason why, especially if this is the way I'm going to master this exciting music. As you have guessed by now, my miniscule mechanical skill fell far short of clueing me in to the fact that the turntable on my record player was revolving somewhat faster than 78 rpm.

However, for a while after that time, I could play tunes more comfortably in those impossible keys than in the most common Dixieland keys of B flat, F natural and E flat. I can still play brass instruments without much trouble in B, F# and E as a result of that experience, so I suppose I gained something from it.

During my last year at college, I picked up an old rotary-valve tuba for $20 (and made $25 playing it that same night). It was an Eb tuba, but I never bothered to re-learn the fingering. Instead, I pretended it was a baritone horn and transposed the chords, just as I had done with the piano - that is, if we were playing a tune in Bb,

Learning To Play

I'd assume it was in F and improvise a tuba part accordingly. I still play Eb tuba that way, though I haven't been on any tuba gigs in years.

Swarthmore College had a small music department, all 100% classical. My thirst for knowledge about music was so great that, as electives, I took a year of classical musical theory and a year of classical music composition. Neither taught me much that was of value in Dixieland or ragtime, but I do have one special memory from each course.

One day the theory teacher was late, and I was whiling away the time by noodling some blues on the classroom baby grand. When he entered, the professor passed behind the piano bench and whispered in a friendly but firm way, that in the future, the department's piano was not to be subjected to that kind of music.

As an assignment in my composition class, I wrote a short piece for a classical string quartet. I didn't retain a copy, as it was just ordinary homework to me.

A few weeks later, at an all-college assembly sponsored by the music department, I was quite surprised to hear Professor Swan announce that the next number would be a string quartet composed by Tex Wyndham. It was both amusing and satisfying to see the amazed expressions on the faces of students around me as they realized that the leader of the campus Dixieland band was involved in such highbrow activities.

By the time I reached graduate school, I was a fairly competent tubaist and tailgate trombonist. During the 1962-63 school year, I worked six nights a week at Your Father's Mustache in Boston, playing solo piano upstairs two nights, playing trombone with and leading a Dixieland band two nights, and playing a variety of instruments behind the three-banjo sing-a-long combo two nights.

One afternoon, my first wife came rushing back to our Ellery Street apartment to tell me that a cornet was in the window of a thrift store two blocks away. Once again, the price was $20.

My previous experience with a lead horn was on a battered trumpet a friend gave me in high school. It had been in some sort of accident that had broken the tailpipe and bell loose. They had been soldered back on the leadpipe side of the horn, so it had a rather strange look to it, and it leaked badly, but it did play, and I fooled around with it some. (It now hangs over the door to my music room.)

However, cornet was what all the vintage-period Dixieland bands used, and I was taken with the idea of owning one. My band's trumpet player, whom I used as a consultant, informed me that, if all the valves and slides worked I could hardly go wrong for $20. Thus, I added the cornet (which was an old department store house brand model, but in excellent shape) to my arsenal of instruments with the banjo band.

Once again, I never bothered to re-learn the fingering to conform to parts written for Bb trumpet/cornet (the standard size horn). In trumpet music, if you want a Bb trumpet to sound a "Bb", you write a "C" on his score. Not for me, though.

I associate the fingering with the notes that come out of the horn. When I see a "C", that's what you'll hear. Thus, I can sight-read melodies on the cornet from piano-vocal song sheets or concert-pitch lead sheets, but can't play a written cornet part without painstakingly going over it in advance.

TEXAS SHOUT: HOW DIXIELAND JAZZ WORKS

I only had to play a couple of cornet tunes a night at Your Father's Mustache, so I had no particular need to develop much technical facility. However, a few months later, I graduated and returned to my home town of Wilmington, Delaware to begin my career in Du Pont's finance function.

I also started gathering musicians weekly to my home to jam some Dixieland tunes. After a year, people started offering us gigs, and The Red Lion Jazz Band was born, first taking the field at a Du Pont Treasury Division office party in July of 1964.

I played trombone and piano on the initial two Red Lion gigs. It soon became obvious though, given the limited number of Dixielanders available in Wilmington, that I would have to play melody if I wanted a band that could handle the type of repertoire I had in mind. I couldn't be dependent on the scene to provide me with a reliable supply of lead men who knew the West Coast revivalist tunes.

Thus, essentially out of self-defense, I took up cornet in earnest. Despite steady practicing, I never seemed to be developing much range or endurance. I probably should have sought lessons, but having figured so much out for myself up to that time, I decided to try some home-grown therapy.

Looking in the mirror, I concluded that I didn't have very much lip covering my two front teeth. It appeared that I had more lip room over on the left side of my mouth.

Well, I thought, Wild Bill Davison plays on the side of his mouth, and he's one of my favorite musicians. If it's good enough for him, it's good enough for me. So, I moved the mouthpiece over to the left and, once I got used to it, the new position seemed to be a better one. It's been there ever since.

In fact, I remember the night a fan brought a high school trumpet teacher to see the Red Lion Jazz Band at our regular monthly gig at the Hotel Du Pont's Green Room. I was told that the first thing the guest said upon observing me in action was "That guy has the worst embouchure I've ever seen."

The snare drum snuck in there somewhere, thought it had nothing to do with jazz (but it may have helped with the washboard, with which I later dabbled on an amateur basis). I was still a trombonist when I first reported to the motley assemblage laughingly referred to as the Swarthmore College Marching Band.

Swarthmore had only 900 students at the time, so the band was, to put it kindly, a loosely organized, less than imposing ensemble. We would gather Saturday morning before the game with whoever showed up (as many as 30 on a good day), pick a few tunes for half-time and rehearse our "formations". Eventually, we would walk out on the field and rearrange ourselves into a series of amorphous globs while the stadium announcer, who had been carefully primed, triumphantly told the audience what we were supposed to be representing.

The snare drum is the crucial instrument in such high-jinks because it is setting the time to which the others are marching in step. Fortunately, Ted, our snare

Learning To Play

drummer, was all that we could have hoped for, but he graduated at the end of my freshman year. (Believe it or not, I next saw Ted 32 years later at Friday Harbor when he walked out of the audience after a Rent Party Revellers' set and reintroduced himself.)

Not to worry. The incoming freshman class included Freddie, who appeared to have impeccable credentials as a drummer, so we gathered that fall for our first drill with confidence.

Snare drummers in a marching band commonly strap the drum to their left leg to keep it from swinging around while they're simultaneously marching and drumming. Freddie, it turned out, had done lots of concert work, but had never attempted to drum with his snare bobbing up and down on his leg.

After an hour of stumbling and skipping across the gym trying in vain, along with the others, to march to the spastic rhythms Freddie was emitting, I approached the long-suffering area music teacher who had been dragooned by Swarthmore into the thankless job of trying to make the Marching Band into something that might get by on a foggy day. The following conversation ensued.

>"How's about me strapping on a drum for the game tomorrow to help Freddie out?"
>
>"Can you play a snare drum?"
>
>"No, but I can keep steady time. Freddie can do all the fancy stuff."

After a prayerful glance Heavenward for aid in appraising his obviously distasteful alternatives, he agreed. Thus, I became, for the next three years, probably the only person who ever led a college band drum section without being able to play a sustained roll. I still can't and never did learn what a paradiddle is.

While we're on miscellaneous instruments, I became enamored of the bass saxophone as a result of two fine Riverside LPs, a contemporary one by Carl Halen's Gin Bottle Seven and a reissue by the California Ramblers. In the 1960s, the bass saxophone was even rarer than it is now. In fact, I had never even seen one.

However, I figured that I'd have a better chance of finding one in Boston than in Wilmington. So, one morning shortly before graduating from business school, I put in the four hours required to call every music store in the Boston yellow pages.

Two of them had bass saxophones on hand. One horn had been ordered new from France, but had been sitting unpurchased for so long that the owner, unwilling to let a sucker off the line, offered to knock $360 off the retail price if I'd drive downtown and buy it. The other was a used Conn that the owner had, mirable dictu, acquired that very morning and had not yet priced - and his store was across the street from the first one!

I did not know how to play a saxophone, my sole experience with reed instruments being a few squawks I had elicited from a World War II metal clarinet that somehow wound up in my growing stack of instruments. So, I asked the reedman in my band if he would be my expert in making the choice.

Tom tried both, stating that the used Conn was every bit as good as the new horn, and that if he could get such a bargain on a baritone sax, he's buy it in a minute. Thus for $295, I got a bass saxophone, a hard case, a box of reeds, an instruction book, an adjustable metal saxophone stand with rollers, and a harness so you could play it standing up if you had the physique of Godzilla. The store's prices were so good that I also purchased a straight soprano saxophone that day for another $95.

I was driving an MGA, which barely has room for two people, let alone a bass saxophone, so we folded back the roof, sat the horn upright in Tom's lap (where it topped out at a level about twice as high as the car), pulled out into the bumper-to-bumper Boston rush hour traffic and crept back to Cambridge as a sudden downpour soaked us both (but not the horns).

The hard case was the size of a small coffin, and our apartment was about the size of a large broom closet. The only place big enough to store my bass sax was the middle of our living room floor, where it resided for the few months left until we moved.

If you know how to play Dixieland tuba lines, you can translate them to the bass saxophone fairly easily. I played my first gig on it less than a week after buying it. It's really a fun instrument to play but, as with the trombone and tuba, the demands of the cornet and piano have kept me from it except for one gig about twenty years ago.

Actually, piano is my first love. Next to spending time with my wife Nancy, playing piano is the thing I enjoy most.

I quickly learned to sight-read lead sheets on piano, but never had to do much in the way of reading piano scores because ragtime, the only piano music that interested me much, was almost completely unobtainable commercially during the 1950s. I remember staying up two straight nights until the wee hours, in those pre-photocopier days, handcopying Scott Joplin's "The Cascades" that a friend lent me, because it was the only way I knew to acquire the music to it.

The reading came in 1963, when Max Morath privately published *100 Ragtime Classics*, a thick folio containing a cross-section of the best Missouri Valley classic rags. I got four copies, so I could play everything in this marvelous volume without having to turn any pages.

Max had picked rags ranging from easy to demanding, and it was that variety that got me through the agonies of getting comfortable with reading. I worked on the easier numbers until I was at home with them and then discovered that a few slightly harder ones in the volume had thereby come within my grasp, and so on through the entire contents.

Now, because I am used to the conventions of ragtime scoring (and because I never bother with much of anything else), I can pick up a fairly challenging rag at sight and usually get something out of it. However, if you put some other kind of music in front of me - say a simple church hymn scored in half notes - I may still wind up puzzling it out the way I did so many years ago with "Maple Leaf Rag".

Piano comes much more easily to me than the cornet, which I find to be a devilishly high maintenance instrument. If someone had told me, back in the mid-sixties when I first turned to cornet, that I would one day be the cornetist with a major-league Dixieland band appearing regularly at national festivals and cruises, I'd have wondered what he was smoking.

Learning To Play

Much as I enjoy playing with the Red Lions, I begrudge the practice time I have to put in on the cornet. I told myself, back in 1964, that I would hang up the horn after 25 years (if the Red Lions lasted that long), and concentrate on the piano.

Then, in 1982, The Rent Party Revellers came along. The RPR has proved to be a dream come true for me. I'm having too much fun with the Revellers to think about stopping. As long as they stay on the boards, I'll probably keep squaring off against the cornet for an hour or so each day.

I suppose that most aspiring Dixielanders hope for a day when they can get up on a stage with a band full of ace jazzmen/jazzwomen, play the living daylights out of a bunch of tunes, and leave the crowd cheering. I've been very fortunate in that respect. As a member of the Revellers, that experience now happens to me several times a year. Let me tell you, it's just as much fun each time as it was when the Revellers first took the stage in December 1982.

Anyway, that's the saga of how one Dixieland-struck kid fought his way into playing music, via a series of coincidences, determination, and jerry-built ad hoc musical systems, in those days before the advent of high school stage band programs and jazz colleges. I think many Dixielanders my age could tell you similar stories.

Now in our late fifties, we're too old to start over. Many of us missed out on the teaching devices widely used today in public schools that could have given us better technique more quickly. The ones we devised on our own were constructed of dreams, spit and baling wire. What we did was analogous, in a way, to experiences of some early Dixielanders who, entranced by jazz, made guitars out of cigar boxes and drummed on kitchen chairs.

On the other hand, we were forced to pay close attention to what we wanted to say with our music, because we were on our own to figure out how we were going to get the chops to say it. Maybe that's not too bad a trade-off, after all.

[Author's Note: You might find it interesting to know that, based on the amount and type of feedback I received, I believe that the chapter you have just read was the most popular of all the "Texas Shout" columns. This result surprised me because, though I tried to include some material of broader application (such as the discussion of the four "magic chords"), I considered it basically a fluffy good-natured piece of nostalgic chit-chat.

After writing the essay published in November and December 1994, I told *WCR*'s editor that (1) I felt I had covered all of the topics I really wanted to discuss in "Texas Shout" and (2) I was accordingly planning to close down the column. Woody was unhappy at hearing such news and asked me to keep "Texas Shout" going a while longer. "Learning To Play" was my first effort in that direction.]

TEXAS SHOUT: HOW DIXIELAND JAZZ WORKS

CHAPTER 45   JOHNNY ONE NOTE

Remember the 1937 Rodgers & Hart song "Johnny One Note"? From the show "Babes In Arms", it told of a singer who, as his name implies, could only sing one note. However, he sang it so magnificently that all who heard him were mesmerized - even traffic stopped and Niagara Falls stood still.

If Johnny One Note really existed, I think a lot of us would be curious to hear a recording of what he sounded like. I suspect, though, that we would be perfectly satisfied to have a 78 rpm recording of Johnny. It would contain only two renditions, each subject to a time limit of about three minutes.

If Johnny had come along during the LP years, his album would run some 45 minutes. By that time, his act, good as it was, would probably start getting a little old for most people.

How about a full 70-minute CD of Johnny? I rather think that the average listener would be unable to make it through to the end without his/her mind wandering for the last half-hour of the journey.

There always have been a lot of Johnny One Note (henceforth J1N) artists on the scene. These are individuals, combos, etc., who have learned how to do one thing superbly well.

Before records came along, you didn't need to be more than a J1N. You were doing a fifteen-minute turn at a vaudeville house, moving on after a few days to a new location, and not returning for some time. When you did come back, the audience, recalling your previous triumph, was usually perfectly satisfied to see you do the same thing with which you entertained them for fifteen minutes last year.

78 rpm records worked much the same way. Even a very popular artist would have new platters released no more frequently than every few months. The buyers thereof wanted the performer to touch base by doing his/her specialty with only slight variations.

Making a 78 was much like making sequels in the movies today. Now we go to see "Rocky Part XXXVI" because we want to see the stars doing much the same thing we liked so much the first time. We only want a tiny difference, just enough to keep deja vu from overtaking us.

By contrast, the era of long-playing recordings and CDs is a difficult one for JINs. Instead of having to plan just an individual performance or two, the musician needs to produce something that unfolds in a way that will keep his//her audience engrossed for a duration of over an hour.

The overall product, as well as each individual ride, needs to be assembled so that it will hold the listener's attention. How should the program proceed in terms of faster vs. slower numbers, instrumentals vs. vocals, full-band sides vs. subunits or

TEXAS SHOUT: HOW DIXIELAND JAZZ WORKS

features, and whatever other options are available? Do it the wrong way and, even if each cut works on its own, you run the risk of having your purchaser reach the end of your album in a disinterested, negative frame of mind.

I see this effect fairly often when I encounter chronological compilations of recordings by an artist from the vintage years - not the great ones, like Louis, Bessie, Bix, Fats, Jelly, et al. They transcended the restrictions of 78 marketing so that we can hear them on CD without becoming distracted for an instant.

This result does not occur, though, for the majority of performers, those highly competent jazzmen who nevertheless did not possess the genius of the above-named immortals. Take for example, the legions of very fine boogie-blues pianists or blues singers who tended to record 12-bar three-chord pieces, often with little or no variation in tempo or key. While I enjoy hearing their reissues, in many cases the track-to-track differences are so minor that, by the time the album ends, I have trouble remembering just which title was which (maybe my difficulty merely reflects the initial stages of senility, but I doubt it).

I can live with this situation as far as reissues are concerned. I make a sort of automatic allowance for the fact that the artist was doing the right thing for the technology of the time. It isn't fair to criticize these JINs for failing to (1) anticipate a 70-minute CD and (2) produce a body of material that would flow in exactly the right way when compiled into one.

I have more trouble making such an allowance for today's performers. Yet, what is a JIN of the 1990s to do?

Most artists of interest to *WCR* readers sell the bulk of recordings at their in-person performances. This situation forecloses the option of sharing a CD with another musician whose talents might provide the balance that would make the disc more enjoyable overall and would set our JIN's unique abilities into sharper focus.

That's because much of the audience for a live performer really doesn't want to pony up a CD price for a recording that devotes only half (or less) of its running time to the player they've just seen. The excitement of attending an in-person concert tends to mask the JIN aspects of the show, aspects that don't really emerge clearly until the disc is playing in the living room without the cheering crowd, the you-are-there thrill.

How should a reviewer deal with a new JIN album? If each separate rendition clicks standing alone, should he/she give it an above-average rating and tell all of you to spend your money on it? Or should he/she acknowledge being bored beyond description at hearing the same thing over and over for some 15-20 selections and admit that the recording is probably going to spend the rest of its life on the shelf?

I thought of writing about this topic when a couple of CDs arrived at my home that more or less fit the JIN category. I had planned to close these remarks by giving you a couple of real-life examples.

I've changed my mind. The records really are pretty good if you approach them the right way, usually by not trying to listen intently all the way through at one sitting. Besides, I don't see any purpose in saddling someone with the doubtful honor of being a JIN.

Johnny One Note

Jazz literature is filled with comments about the "limitations" of 78 rpm records, meaning the necessity to complete the performance within about three minutes. Yet, many immortal jazz renditions were created within those "limitations". It's hard to visualize how they could have been improved, no matter how much additional time was available.

By contrast, for practical purposes, we can now play as long as we want to when making records. Still, most Dixieland and ragtime rides on CDs nevertheless wind up being not much more than three minutes anyway, usually coming in somewhere around four.

Perhaps there is something about the idiom that dictates economy most of the time, vs. more modern forms of jazz which take much longer to complete a ride. Or, maybe because the vintage recordings that attracted them to Dixieland are on the shortish side, today's musicians might be conditioned to complete their statements somewhere close to the old durations. At any rate, you never see 10-chorus Dixieland solos, but they're all over the place in modern jazz.

At any rate, now that we are free of the limitations of 78s, we have a new set of problems, those dealing with planning a 70-minute program that stays afloat every step of the way. Seems a bit ironic, doesn't it?

I suppose, though, that we live in a time when, it has been said, "The medium is the message." Perhaps that thought is the only one we need to sum up today's musings.

Sooner or later you'll find yourself with an album that, for reasons you can't quite identify, doesn't satisfy you the way it should. All the performances are up to standard, maybe even better. Yet, you reach the end of the playing time lost in daydreams, possibly feeling a little exhausted.

In that case, perhaps the artist really isn't to blame. The fault may lie entirely with the format in which today's market requires the artist to appear. Anyone for bringing back vaudeville?

TEXAS SHOUT: HOW DIXIELAND JAZZ WORKS

Joe "Fingers" Carr 1950s
Photographer Unknown

Trebnor Tichenoir 1990s
Photo by Andrew Wittenborn

Marvin Hamlisch
Photographer Unknown

June 1995 West Coast Rag

CHAPTER 46   CONTEMPORARY RAGTIMERS

Ragtimers aren't what they used to be. I'm not saying they're better or worse, mind you, just different.

I discovered ragtime in the 1950s through two sources. One was the wonderful book *They All Played Ragtime*. It happened to be on the library shelf of music books through which, as a youngster trying to learn about this music, I was systematically reading my way. I was captivated by the brilliantly told and researched story of what was then America's completely forgotten popular art form.

The second was the music of Joe "Fingers" Carr (a pseudonym used by pianist Lou Busch for recording ragtime). Carr's performances were usually of vintage pop tunes played in a two-fisted virtuoso novelty ragtime style with a breezy rhythm accompaniment. They were popular enough to support a string of albums for Capitol during the early LP years and to get occasional radio play - about the only ragtime consistently heard on popular music stations back then.

(Incidentally, the recordings of Carr and other ragtimers of that period, such as Johnny Maddox, are unfairly dismissed by many of today's ragtimers. This injustice occurs because a major portion of the current ragtime community, for reasons stemming from developments of the early 1970s (discussed below), has been conditioned to accept an incorrect belief - namely, that shallow commerciality taints any ragtime performance which deviates much from Missouri Valley/Joplin-style ragtime played per score with a fair amount of academic restraint.)

A lot of ragtimers my age will tell you that these two influences were the ones that started them down the ragtime highway. Unfortunately, it didn't do us much good. There was no organized ragtime community in those days. Also, the music simply wasn't available, either in published sheet music form or on record.

If you were a pianist looking for classic rags, you were limited to a couple of commercial folios. *The Ragtime Folio*, from Melrose Music, contained nine rags from John Stark's legendary catalog, including works by Joplin, Scott and Lamb. *Play Them Rags!*, from Mills, contained thirteen pieces - a few Joplins plus a number of Tin Pan Alley rags, some, unfortunately, of no special distinction.

Beyond that pair of collections, you were on your own, sifting through the antique store/auction/flea market circuit, if you had the time and dedication. I didn't have the time, or indeed much money for sheet music, while in high school and college. Thus, I could have counted on the fingers of one hand the number of additional legitimate ragtime piano solos I'd managed to collect after years of nursing a consuming interest in ragtime.

The same was true of recordings. There were, as mentioned, ragtime LPs of popular standard songs, but no one was recording the rags celebrated in *They All Played Ragtime*. You could read the book and be tantalized by its descriptions of

| TEXAS SHOUT: HOW DIXIELAND JAZZ WORKS |

the delights of "The Easy Winners", "Efficiency Rag", "St. Louis Rag", "Ragtime Nightingale", etc., but just try to hear them. In fact, I had graduated from college, law school and business school before I even met another person who could play a classic-period ragtime piano solo.

By the 1960s ragtimers had begun trying to find each other. St. Louis' Trebor Tichenor, a formidable force in ragtime today, was involved with a publication called *The Ragtime Review*. A bit later, some folks in Toronto established The Ragtime Society, which became the principal focal point for ragtime from the late sixties through most of the seventies.

Not surprisingly, the ragtimers who gathered in Toronto for the Society's annual Bash were primarily historically oriented. Because we had little first-hand exposure to the idiom, we were spending much of our time simply trying to find the old pieces, to understand what they were all about and what kind of people wrote them. We were sheet music and record collectors.

Few of us were composers. Except for Trebor and the late Tom Shea - and, of course, Eubie Blake, a pioneer who never stopped composing - virtually no one was writing much new ragtime.

Then, through an incredible series of coincidences, a marvelous thing happened, something beyond our wildest expectations. In the early 1970s, three completely independent projects focusing on Scott Joplin came to fruition: (1) The New York Public Library financed the first publication of Joplin's collected works. (2) A college in Georgia sponsored the first full-scale public production of Joplin's opera "Treemonisha". (3) Joshua Rifkin, a young pianist, recorded an LP of Joplin's rags, played with proper academic attention to the scores, for the classical Nonesuch label; as a result of rave notice by *The New York Times*' classical reviewer, the album shot to the top of the classical charts.

These developments had two beneficial effects. The legitimate musical establishment began focusing upon ragtime, principally Joplin's oeuvre. The general music market became alert to the possibility that, at least for the time being, there appeared to be the chance to make money out of ragtime.

One of the New York Public Library volumes - the one with all the rags - was published in a soft cover version for sale in music stores throughout the country. Classical pianists began trying to duplicate Rifkin's success by recording Joplin.

(By the way, playing ragtime accurately per score is no great trick for a classically trained pianist. While there are many technically demanding rags, quite a bit of quality ragtime, including several Joplin works, isn't particularly difficult. Ragtime, which came along before commercial radio and at a time when few people had many records, couldn't have become as popular as it did unless the published music was within the grasp of the average parlor pianist of the day.)

These two flurries of interest in Joplin led to an even more unbelievable break for ragtime. Arranger Marvin Hamlisch was commissioned to adapt Joplin's music for the sound track for a major Hollywood film.

If the film had been a flop, believe me, today's ragtime scene would probably be very different from the way it is. How, I don't know, but there can be no dispute that the shock waves from this film still reverberate through ragtime today.

Contemporary Ragtimers

As everybody knows, the movie turned out to be a winner in every way. "The Sting" (1973) won seven Oscars, including Best Picture. Hamlisch's single of Joplin's rag "The Entertainer" (which became popularly known as "The Sting") rose to the top of the hit parade, the last piece of ragtime to occupy that exalted position.

(As a side note, the ragtime/jazz community has the perverse propensity to bemoan the fact that its music isn't commercially popular and then berate any jazz or ragtime artist who becomes popular as having "sold out" and "gone commercial". Thus, it became de rigueur in some ragtime circles to disparage Marvin Hamlisch as having perpetrated some kind of evil pollution upon Joplin's pristine art.

The fact is that Hamlisch was commissioned to rework Joplin's music for the film using the format of Gunther Schuller's 1973 Red Back Book LP for the Angel label by The New England Conservatory Ragtime Ensemble. Had he not taken the assignment, it would have gone to someone else, someone who is unlikely to have equalled the splendid job Hamlisch did (as the film's sound track LP demonstrates).

Hamlisch's music is faithful to the period scoring and to the spirit of Joplin's inspiration while adding immeasurably to the flow of the movie. Who can forget, for example, the evocative way the solo piano playing the closing strains of "Solace" brings out the longing in the film's "love" scene (remember, nothing in this story turns out to be what it seems at first).

Further, on Oscar night in 1974, when Marvin Hamlisch first stepped up to the podium to accept an Academy Award for his work, he made sure to use a few seconds of his very limited time to pay specific tribute to Scott Joplin. Watching the show live, I thought that was a very high-class un-Hollywood-like thing for him to do. I have never seen Hamlisch given any credit for this generous statement, heard worldwide, by anyone in the ragtime community.

At any rate, Marvin Hamlisch's work wound up providing ragtime with a public visibility for which it could never otherwise realistically have hoped. The ragtime community owes him a debt of gratitude. It's high time somebody stood up and said so.)

For a short time, the country was ragtime crazy. The boom didn't last, but it did leave behind some lasting benefits for ragtime.

First, it brought a lot of vintage ragtime back into print. Major publishers combed their files for material to gather into folios that appeared on music counters everywhere. Except for ones dealing with Joplin, they sold very poorly and were not maintained in the catalog. However, for a short time, literally hundreds of rags, in nearly all of the vintage ragtime styles, could be picked up for a song at your nearest music store.

Dover Publications, a New York book publisher specializing in reprinting material no longer under copyright, is the only one that has kept its ragtime on the market. Through Dover, as of this writing, one can own over 200 turn-of-the-century rags, including all of Joplin's and most of Scott's and Lamb's. The collections concentrate on Missouri Valley and early folk rags, but taken together, Dover's folios contain more rags than most professional ragtimers have at their fingertips.

Second, as mentioned, the "legitimate" musical establishment's attention was caught by ragtime during the 1970s boom. Some portion of it still spends time on ragtime. Professional concert pianists occasionally include rags in their recitals, almost always Scott Joplin's and often as encores or throwaways, but the rags are there. Conservatory-trained pianists are showing up on the ragtime circuit, something that almost never happened prior to "The Sting".

Third, the publicity showered on ragtime coaxed some composers out of the woodwork, a trend that has lasted to the present day. As in the past, today's compositions range from brilliant to execrable. Many are hopelessly derivative of Joplin and other Missouri valley composers. Some, proclaimed by their composers to be rags, aren't at all, consisting of a few ragtime syncopations stuck into the middle of arch-modern licks.

Even so, this is a marvelous thing for ragtime. The music will become a museum piece unless there are people willing to write new works in the idiom.

Ragtimers can only rejoice in these developments. We hoped for years to have ragtime taken seriously by "serious" musicians, and now it is, though perhaps not to the extent we'd have desired. Similarly, we longed for the day when neighborhood music stores would again carry ragtime on their shelves, and now they do. However, like most of life, these uppers are not entirely without their down sides.

There isn't much point in discussing the negatives at length because ragtime has now become so pervasively a hobby music. There is virtually no one left making a fulltime living exclusively from ragtime. Even major ragtime weekends depend to a significant extent on the willingness of featured artists to perform without pay or at less than out-of-pocket cost.

In these circumstances, where economic viability is frequently a secondary or irrelevant factor, the community is inevitably going to drift in whatever directions the whims of the relatively few movers and shakers in the field dictate, regardless of what commentators may write. Sad to relate, nothing anyone says about the scene makes much difference anymore.

Let me just briefly note, then, that I believe a disproportionate emphasis has been given to Scott Joplin since "The Sting", even though he is unquestionably ragtime's all-time greatest composer. For example, most record stores, if they have any ragtime at all, have ragtime browsers devoted almost exclusively to Joplin. Someone who only casually comes into contact with the music could easily be misled into believing that worthwhile ragtime pretty much begins and ends with Scott Joplin's compositions.

Nevertheless, as true ragtimers recognize, Joplinesque/Missouri Valley classic ragtime is not the only ragtime style. Even within that style, (1) both Scott and Lamb produced quite a few rags that are in every way the equal of Joplin's finest and (2) other ragtime-era composers, though perhaps not as prolific or consistent, left us a wealth of ragtime that is also comparable in quality to top-rank Joplin.

Further, the emphasis on Joplin encourages the already-existing tendency of the ragtime community to focus on ragtime piano solos while regarding ragtime songs and other ragtime compositions as of secondary interest. However, as Ed

Berlin points out in his excellent book *Ragtime: A Musical And Cultural History*, "... songs were the most conspicuous species of ragtime ...". In addition, ragtime was commonly composed for all musical formats, from solo xylophone to full concert band.

It also disturbs me that so many ragtimers who've come to the music since 1973 have little knowledge of or interest in the artists who were keeping it alive during the 1950s and 1960s. Quite a few of these pre-"Sting" revivalists are still around and capable of providing quality entertainment at ragtime weekends.

Lastly, I regret that ragtime functions, like Dixieland festivals, are now being invaded to a significant extent by non-genre music, that is, music which isn't ragtime. I understand why this change is occurring (see, e.g., "Texas Shout" for April 1990). However, I don't happen to live near any ragtimers, and when I go to a ragtime festival, I'm dying to hear live ragtime, not light classics, Latin numbers, etc.

Anyway, ragtimers aren't what they used to be. I guess that's to be expected.

However, ragtime itself never changes. We can haul Charles Hunter's "Just Ask Me" from 1902, Charlie Straight's "Hot Hands" from 1916, Billy Mayerl's "Virginia Creeper" from 1925, Joe "Fingers" Carr's "Rapscallion Rag" from 1952, Max Morath's "One for Amelia" from 1964, David Thomas Roberts' "Roberto Clemente" from 1979 and all of the others off our shelves, depress the notes exactly as these fine composers set them down for us years ago, and experience the same uplifting experience that captivated audiences when these works appeared. I suppose that's what really counts after all.

Ubie Blake 1970s
Photo by Ed Lawless

TEXAS SHOUT: HOW DIXIELAND JAZZ WORKS

Rosy McHargue 1950s
Photo - Self Portrait
Courtesy of Floyd Levin

Rosy McHargue 1996
Photo courtesy of Don Jones

CHAPTER 47   AGING MUSICIANS

A lot has been written in recent years, some of it in this column, about the effects on the scene of the aging audience for Dixieland jazz. Relatively little note has been taken of the fact that the same thing is happening to the musicians.

I want to talk today about the way the graying of the Dixieland musicians' pool is affecting festivals, repertoire and recordings. To orient you properly for this discussion, I'd like you to start by taking a minute to ponder a couple of questions.

First, make a written or mental list of your personal choices as the top rank of the organized Dixieland bands. Specifically, I mean those bands which you like so much that, to see them in person, you will leave your home town for a weekend and spend some $500-$1,000 per couple (assuming you drive and stay at a hotel; it'll be more if you have to board a plane to get there).

We are talking about Dixieland here, so only list Dixieland combos. Do not include the country, blues, swing, etc., bands that are on the festival circuit, no matter how popular they are and no matter how much you like them.

My guess is that you will write about thirty names on your list, give or take a few. Nancy and I wound up with twenty-five. Everyone's picks will be different, but I'll bet that a core group of something like twenty bands will appear on most people's lists.

Now count the names from the East Coast. The total will probably be close to a third of your basic throwdown. We had eight, plus another five from cities located on the Mississippi River. You'll likely be left with somewhere between one to two dozen bands in the two U.S. western time zones.

Now go back to your original list and break it down another way. This time, note the bands that have been in existence ten years or less. You'll see just a handful. We had only five.

What conclusion can you draw from this exercise? For one thing, you'll observe that, during the last decade, the number of top-rank bands has not increased at a rate anywhere near matching the proliferation of festivals that desire to book top-rank names. We have more festivals chasing pretty much the same small bunch of combos.

(This situation does not affect a regional festival - one that annually hires those bands which operate in its geographic area for a weekend get-together. Regional festivals are primarily interested in putting on the same show each year for their neighbors and are not looking to draw very many fans from long distances. Nothing at all wrong with doing so, of course - everyone has a good time without too much expense and the Dixieland torch is kept burning in the vicinity.)

TEXAS SHOUT: HOW DIXIELAND JAZZ WORKS

The large multi-stage national festivals are still pretty much concentrated within shouting distance of the West Coast. (Can anyone tell me why? I've never been able to figure that out to my satisfaction.) Thus, the situation of many festivals chasing the same small number of bands is even worse than it appears at first. That's because importing a band from a distant time zone involves the expense of not only air fare, but also, depending on the starting and ending times of the festival, an additional night or two in the hotel for the sidemen.

Only a few festivals have been able to bring several bands across the country at one time and still stay afloat. More commonly, the lineup sports just one or two distant bands as headliners, with the bill fleshed out by groups from the same or an adjacent time zone.

We are seeing fewer even of this second, less broad-based, type of festival. I know of three West Coast weekends that used to hire one East Coast band each year but (probably due to air fare increases) seem, as of now, to have stopped doing so. There may be others.

Thus, for many West Coast festivals, instead of chasing the thirty or so bands on your initial list, they're really chasing the twenty or so top outfits in the two western time zones. Is it any wonder that, from time to time in "The Letter Drop" column, we see complaints from fans about festivals hiring the same bands all the time?

Unfortunately, those letter-writers are absolutely right. Even worse, there really isn't anything, given the current limited availability of sure-fire top-draw bands, that can be done about it.

I'm sure all festival producers would love to hire a whole bunch of those fine but more remote units that haven't yet been seen on their stages. However, if they can't do so without putting their festivals in financial peril, they won't - and they shouldn't.

But, you ask, couldn't the lineups be shored up by a more varied mix of second-rank bands? My guess is that this procedure is being followed already, but you don't really notice it because the second-rank bands aren't ones that particularly attract you to attend the festival in the first place - although you're perfectly happy to be entertained by them for a set or two once you get there.

As an aside, I'll mention another factor relevant to that point. To be sure, there are a few second-rank bands that are clearly on their way up. My observation, though, based on decades of reviewing records and attending festivals, is that the gap in ability between the top-rank and the second-rank bands has become very wide and is getting wider.

With many of today's second-tier groups, including some well-known and popular ones, I find that I've heard everything they're going to say after just a few tunes. However, this is a subject for a different column, one that I probably will never write because the topic is too depressing for me to contemplate at much length.

At any rate, if you took a trip last month to see a festival featuring bands A, B and C, and you're feeling less than enthused about the prospect of making another this month to see bands B, C and D, and you think you probably will save the money next month because that one's starring bands A C and D, there's really no point in getting all hot under the collar about the situation. It comes with the territory on the festival scene these days because, as with the audience, new blood is not entering the Dixieland musicians' pool at the rate it used to 40-50 years ago.

Now let's talk about the repertoire and recordings. If, over the past 20 or so years, we had been getting the same number of young jazzers coming to Dixieland as in the 1940s and 1950s, what tunes would they be playing?

A fair number of those musicians would have learned the music the way Dixielanders of my generation did. They'd have heard a broad range of the basic recordings in the field and assimilated the standard repertoire.

At least some of them would have continued to feature the tried-and-true evergreens in their live shows and recordings. Further, those recordings would, given the vitality of youth, contain a full measure of the heat and swing that not only are the essence of jazz, but are the characteristics that brought most of us to jazz in the first place.

Instead, where are we today" Let me give you some examples.

Not long ago, I was talking over administrative details with an official of a festival that had hired The Rent Party Revellers. As we discussed the upcoming weekend schedule, I happened to mention that the Revellers like to balance our sets, covering both standards and seldom-heard compositions. We're just as likely to render "Nagasaki", "I Got Rhythm" or "China Boy", for example, as "Yankee Doodle Blues", "I Got A Misery" and "Brown-Skin Mama".

I was somewhat surprised to hear a sigh of relief over the phone. The official said that, after discussions with his festival's board of directors, he'd been asked to talk to a few bands. He'd been planning to include the Revellers because he suspected we'd be receptive to his request. Boiled down to its essentials, he was hoping to find at least a few bands who would promise to play, during the weekend, some tunes that the folks in the audience would know.

It turned out that the festival's chairman, a Dixieland player of wide experience over several decades, had recently been in a band that shared a concert with a nationally-known well-traveled combo. The other band's program consisted entirely of selections that the chairman not only didn't know, but had never heard of.

By contrast, the chairman's band rendered a mixture of familiar and offbeat numbers. He couldn't help noticing that the tunes receiving the loudest applause were the standards performed by his group.

His festival is fairly large, one that can't be sustained by the dwindling number of hard-core Dixieland buffs. It must draw heavily from the general public in the surrounding area to stay solvent.

He recognized something that too many Dixielanders have chosen to ignore in recent years: no matter what else we may do, our first priority must be to entertain the audience. If the crowd wants to hear some tunes it recognizes, something that will make our music more accessible to non-Dixielanders, then we are fools (especially in this declining market for Dixieland) not to accommodate its perfectly reasonable desire. Hence, the chairman sent out the word to ask the musicians to help the audience have a good time by programming at least a few bits of reasonably familiar material.

TEXAS SHOUT: HOW DIXIELAND JAZZ WORKS

Note that no special requests for any specific titles were made. No one was asked to wear costumes, parade through the audience, play the trombone with a foot, or do anything else that might make a performer uncomfortable - except for those performers who have the odd notion that the expectations of paying customers have to take second place to their own agendas.

I can't help noting that this festival is one that hires Igor's Jazz Cowboys with some frequency and that, whatever else you may think of Igor's music, if you can squeeze your way into his packed venues, you will hear a program containing a significant percentage of tunes that strike a responsive chord in a general audience. Can it be that Igor does, indeed, have something important to teach revivalist Dixielanders? While you ponder that point, let's cite a couple of other incidents.

◊ ◊ ◊ ◊ ◊ ◊ ◊ ◊ ◊ ◊ ◊ ◊

Incident One. Not long ago I was playing a gig with a lineup that included a musician in his twenties. A skillful player, he has become deeply interested in our music to the point where he is now an official of a Dixieland club and a member of a festival-quality band. However, his regular combo is one of those that worships at the cult of obscurity and will not add a tune to its book if it thinks that the number is currently being played by another band anywhere in the world.

We were working with a roughly sketched tune list, but about halfway through the second set, we hit one of those what-shall-we-play-next stage pauses. I suggested "Memphis Blues", but our young friend didn't know it. Undaunted, I tried "Ida", but with the same result. Astonished that anyone could reach his level of ability without mastering such staples, I gave up at that point and let him make the calls for the rest of the evening.

Incident Two. A while back I was on lead with a combo that finished a set with a rousing "Clarinet Marmalade" to the general approval of all present. One of the sidemen was an excellent seasoned Dixielander, a member of one of the most famous and widely traveled units on the circuit. As we left the bandstand, he mentioned to me in a bemused way that he didn't think he's played "Clarinet Marmalade" in fifteen years.

My jaw just about hit the floor. I spent the next break, and a fair amount of time since, asking myself two questions: How could such an experienced in-demand artist have gone so long without playing "Clarinet Marmalade" or any other tune in the standard repertoire? Why would anyone want to go fifteen years without once participating in a rendition of such a can't-miss hot number as "Clarinet Marmalade"?

What's going on here? If you put these two incidents together, you can see the answer.

Those top thirty combos we listed at the beginning of this column consist of a pool of some 200-300 musicians, mostly age 50 or over. The majority thereof is on the revivalist side of the fence and came to the music in the 1950s and 1960s.

At that time, it was still true that, by and large, the music of such greats as Oliver, Armstrong, Morton and Dodds was not in common currency in the Dixieland community. Bands such as Turk Murphy's, Bob Scobey's, the Red Onions, the Dixieland Rhythm Kings, and Firehouse Five (all of which also played the standards, don't forget) were introducing such material to the wider Dixieland audience by putting it into their regular books and recording it.

These outfits hooked a later generation of musicians, many of whom proceeded to develop and then religiously embrace an absurd dogma: that obscurity in itself is a virtue, that there is something wrong with playing the established Dixieland favorites, and that a band is making unacceptable concessions to commerciality if it plays requests or anything else the audience actually wants to hear. They have been assiduously following those misguided principles for the past 20-30 years.

In the process, they have succeeded in virtually stamping out the standard repertoire from large segments of the Dixieland community, so that veteran musicians can now go fifteen years without playing a given standard. Even worse, the few young people who are attracted to our music are coming in somewhere in the middle, unexposed to the selections that once formed a common jazz vocabulary, learning tunes that nobody else knows, and unable to be fully functional outside of their regular bands. Can anyone in his right mind think that this situation is a healthy long-term one for Dixieland?

(Frankly, if a jazzman tells me that he won't play the standard repertoire, I believe he's really saying that his stock of imagination and creativity has become so exhausted that he can't show you something you haven't heard before without the help of a tune that's new to you. He's running on empty.

This topic actually belongs in a separate column, another one that's really too depressing to write. However, anyone who listens to as many records as I do should have no trouble concluding that a disheartening number of well-known revivalist Dixielanders have long since said everything they have to say and have been reworking the same favorite licks through the same solos for years. This problem is less evident at in-person performances, where the immediacy lets you forgive chord-running more easily, but it hits you between the eyes on the records.)

Now that the standard repertoire has been driven underground, have the obscurantists replaced it with anything? No. The lemming-like search for more unknown titles just goes on. To show you what I mean, let me recount one more true-life adventure.

All new recordings purchased for our collection get their first spin while we're eating breakfast. We have them in the air, with one ear on them, just to get the lay of the land before we do the hard listening.

When recordings come in for review, if they are clearly appropriate for my review column, they go on the review shelf. However, if there is any doubt, they also get the breakfast treatment. We run through each one fully once, and if it turns out to be outside my scope of interest, I don't review it but just note its availability in "This Month's Records".

My wife Nancy is a knowledgeable and perceptive listener. We frequently comment to each other on various aspects of the breakfast serenades.

Sometimes the review copies turnout to be modern jazz of a type so jarring, noisy and unpleasant that it sounds like 65 minutes of someone torturing a cat while a string bass noodles in the background. Nancy and I both wonder if anyone really enjoys such musical anarchy, but she realizes that I need to check out the album all the way through, just to make sure the last few tracks don't make an unlikely turn into Dixieland territory.

Not long ago, we acquired one that seemed highly promising. The personnel consisted of top Dixielanders, artists frequently seen at festivals and mentioned in these pages. Several are long-standing friends of ours, so we anticipated delightful sounds as an aid to digestion that morning.

We were soon disillusioned. The disc was rife with pedestrian material, obscure to be sure, but deservedly so - trivial vintage pops, imitations of personality entertainers, marginalia from the old days -, rendered with no spark or buoyancy whatsoever.

As I was suffering through yet another soggy version of a tune better left in its grave, and wondering why such fine musicians were wasting their time with it, Nancy spoke up. She said, for the first, and so far only, time in our twenty-plus years of breakfast jazz listening, "Do we have to listen to this album to the end?" I then realized that it was time to write this column.

Anyone who's seen me perform knows that I am the first one to appreciate a neglected gem. However, we have long since left behind the 1950s and 1960s. The discographies of the great vintage bands are no longer a secret to Dixieland musicians and haven't been for decades.

Nevertheless, many aging revivalist musicians and revivalist-oriented record producers can't tear themselves away from the supposed virtues of continued rediscovery. Their obsession with refusing to record anything anyone's ever heard of is now becoming detrimental to the scene.

A finite number of songs were recorded and written in the twenties. Surely we have no need to "rediscover" every one of them, right down through the fourth-rate Tin Pan Alley hackwork that is now being dredged up in some circles.

Said another way, after decades of combing old records and sheet music for overlooked treasures, we have bands that are simply choosing, by default, tunes that everyone else has rejected after three or four decades of revivalist research. I doubt that there are many fans on the scene who care to listen to such leftovers.

Moreover, because the opportunities for regular work for full six-or-seven piece bands have constricted substantially in the last three decades, many of today's recordings are being made by one-time-only studio groups that confront the material for the first time at the recording session. The results often show only too clearly that they are not only struggling to get acclimated to the particular personnel of the day, but also attempting to overcome the additional substantial handicap of doing so while learning the tunes on the fly. From the uninspired readings given with increasing frequency, it is equally obvious that most of the team isn't particularly turned on by the forgotten pieces that the titular leader has elected to resurrect for the occasion.

Recordings produced this way are not only below par in quality on an absolute scale, they are going the wrong way in terms of today's vital need to attract new fans to Dixieland. Few enough people outside of our community will buy an album by a nonexistent band that contains no titles which they recognize. Those that do

Aging Musicians

purchase aren't likely to come back for more once they're been subjected to the often plodding interpretations thereof.

As I have said before in this column, the fact that a tune is obscure is very likely to mean that it wasn't so good in the first place, not that it is an undiscovered masterpiece. This is especially true today with respect to titles waxed in the twenties by jazz artists, nearly all of which have been reissued somewhere since the dawn of the LP era. If one of those ditties hasn't been picked up by now, it probably doesn't deserve to be.

Somebody needs to say out loud that, if our journey of rediscovery is not actually over, we are far enough down the road to rest awhile and consolidate our gains. If you look through the catalogue of Stomp Off or G.H.B./Jazzology, just to name our two biggest labels, you'll find literally hundreds of perfectly good tunes that have been recently revitalized, recorded once or twice, and then abandoned, relapsing back into oblivion to make room for the less meritorious stuff being waxed now.

Can't we concentrate on learning some of those for a while? I'd like to propose a moratorium on revival of unknown selections, and suggest a couple of rules of thumb that ought to lead to improved recordings.

If you have a regular organized band, please plan your albums the way the original revivalists typically did. If you're going to wax a tune, first put it in your book and play it for a while until everyone is comfortable with it and knows what he/she wants to say about it.

Then, if you record it, tell yourself that you will continue to feature it on your gigs. After all, you found this tune and inflicted it on the rest of us. If you don't care enough about it to keep it alive, why should the rest of us pay any attention to it?

If your band is going to be a one-shot recording-only team, make sure that at least 75% of the titles you record are ones that will be reasonably familiar to every sideman before he/she gets to the studio. Such a procedure will go a long way to insure that the date will have a satisfactory measure of heat and swing.

If there is a bright spot in all of this, it is that (revivalists will wince at these words) the above-described problems are not especially evident on the Chicago side of the Dixieland scene. Chicagoans, being solo-oriented, have always understood that repertoire, charts and all the other frills mean absolutely nothing when measured against creativity, heat and swing.

A searing version of "When The Saints Go Marching In" has more artistic merit on the jazz scale than a less full-blooded ride on the most complex and obscure work you can name. If you do not agree wholeheartedly with that statement, you do not fully understand what Dixieland jazz is all about and you may unwittingly be contributing to its demise by encouraging the practices criticized above.

Have I beaten these points, some of which I've discussed before in this column, to death by now? Maybe so, but we need to wake up and smell the coffee.

Dixieland is going up in flames all around us. It is our turn to put out the fire by recruiting the next generation.

However, too many of us are, unintentionally to be sure, pouring gasoline on the conflagration by perversely refusing to do for today's audiences the very things that our idols did when we were first exposed to them, the things that drew us to Dixieland decades ago. We have got to stop behaving in this suicidal way, or Dixieland itself will be reduced to ashes.

Spiegel Willcox 1990s
Photo by Dan Polin

George Probert 1990s
Photo by Dan Polin

CHAPTER 48   GOVERNMENT SUBSIDIES

In the spring of 1994, two bills had been introduced in Congress. One would have declared 1995 the centennial year of jazz. The other would have purchased land by the Federal government and funded the site as a national park for jazz.

There was no action occurring on either bill, due to lack of supporting messages to Congressmen from their constituents. In order to inspire such activity, members of the jazz community interested in those matters attempted to "get out the vote".

As one of the few Dixielanders in the Wilmington, Delaware area known outside of the Delaware Valley, I received a number of phone calls in furtherance of this purpose. I said that I'd be happy to spread the word, meaning that I'd try to remember to mention the situation at my weekly Red Lion Jazz Band rehearsal and on any other of the limited occasions around here when the subject might be appropriate.

This was not a sufficient response for one caller, whom I'll refer to as X, a prince of a fellow, a friend of mine, and someone who has devoted more time in aid of Dixieland jazz than just about anyone I know. He was happy to hear that I'd spread the word, but he also wanted to know if I personally supported these causes.

Remembering the story of George Washington and the cherry tree, I didn't lie. I said that I was opposed to both of them, briefly outlining my reasons therefor (explained more expansively below).

X was obviously nonplussed. While he acknowledged that he could agree with at least some of my reasoning, he said he was extremely disappointed to discover that I felt the way I did. He said that he supported both measures because he was "for" jazz. In fact, he said that more than once.

The implication was, I guess, that if you are "for" jazz, you must support these bills. Thus, if you do not agree with them, your true colors are exposed; you are not really a person who is "for" jazz - not even if you've been doing the various jazz-related things I've been doing for nearly all my life (which I won't summarize here, but are known to many of you and have been touched upon in past "Texas Shout" columns anyway).

Now I really don't think that X believes, upon reflection, that I am some kind of fifth columnist in the jazz ranks, a secret viper in jazz's bosom. He was just caught so off guard that he blurted the first thing that came to mind that might be used to change my opinion.

However, my reasons for opposing these ideas are ones that I've pondered for many a year, regarding the way the jazz community interacts with the normal civilian world. I think they have much broader implications than the disposition of these two proposals.

Thus, though I never thought I would ever write a "Texas Shout" dealing with politics, I'd like to share them with you. In order to save Don from reams of irate responses in "The Letter Drop", I'll start by recognizing that many of you, like X, will not agree with me. I respect your opinion, hope we're still friends, and will be happy to buy you a beer sometime while we sit down and chew over the subject.

Fair enough? Here goes.

Let's start with the declaration of 1995 as the centennial year of jazz. X's only stated reason, in our conversation, for backing this measure was his opinion that it would operate to give jazz a wider degree of visibility on the national scene.

By the time this article sees print, we will know if the measure passed, and whether it accomplished that objective. I'll bet that it didn't.

I suppose that the readership of *The American Rag* is much more alert to matters affecting jazz than the general public. Yet, do many of you remember, or did you ever know, that in 1987, Congress adopted a resolution declaring jazz a national treasure?

That declaration was reported in many Dixieland-oriented publications. Was it also reported by your local newspaper, radio or TV station? Did anyone in your locale stage any special jazz activities to mark the occasion? Was the jazz scene in your area benefitted to any noticeable degree by Congress' action?

Congress makes all kinds of pronouncements of this type. It has probably decreed a national pickle day, a national donut month, a national ice cream week, etc. Does your local media make you aware of such declarations? Do you know when such events come up on the calendar? Do you eat more pickles, donuts, ice cream, or whatever it is, on these anniversaries?

I'll estimate, and I think I'm on the low side, that 98% of you answered "no" on all counts. So much for the visibility of a Congressional declaration of the centennial of jazz.

But what harm could the declaration do, you ask? Why not take the time to support the effort? How can doing so possibly hurt our cause?

The answer to those questions lies in my deep-seated belief, formed from decades of observation of the jazz scene, that (1) the Dixieland community is very small compared to other power groups in this country, and hence does not have a great bankroll of political influence to spend and (2) it should not use up any of this capital unless something concrete and positive is going to accrue to jazz as a result of doing so. Declaration of 1995 as a centennial of jazz will, I wager, not result in a single paying gig for a jazzman anywhere, cause any new music to be commissioned, lead to the production of even one new recording, etc.

I have no desire to belittle the activities of anyone who wishes to exert himself/herself on jazz' behalf. Further, I hope that these remarks do not cause me to be perceived as mean-spirited.

However, I believe that the impetus behind such movements is based on the mistaken notion that there is much of anyone left in the real world who cares what

Government Subsidies

people think inside the Washington D.C. beltway. As I see it, Congressional declarations about jazz won't accomplish anything other than lulling elements of the jazz community into assuming that jazz has been moved forward in some important way. Actually, we will have gone to the well and consumed some of the water just to make a symbolic gesture.

If we're going to activate the Federal government to do something for jazz, let's get specific. Surely there are many things the government could do that would result in concrete benefits for jazz.

I confess that I have not compiled a list of them because of my feelings regarding government and the arts, set forth below. However, just picking an idea out of the blue, why not use our small pool of political capital to encourage our government to negotiate with Canada a way of reducing the hassle and cost attendant to gigs in that country by U.S. jazz musicians?

If a U.S. jazzman is hired to play a Canadian gig that is receiving widespread Canadian publicity (so that customs officials are likely to know about it), special papers have to be supplied in advance and filled out for display at the border when the U.S. musician enters Canada. A fee is due at that time of, I believe, 125 Canadian dollars. Also, if recordings are being brought in for sale at the gig, a special duty must be paid (which is not refundable with respect to records brought back to the U.S. that weren't sold).

Further, as combos playing the Victoria festival will attest, the 125-dollar/musician fee is reduced if the musicians in a band all cross the border at the same time. There is a sort of "group rate" discount, which makes it advisable for the band members to gather at the airport, wait around until all sidemen have arrived, and enter Canada together.

Otherwise, as when a musician wants to come in a day or week early for personal reasons, he/she's stuck with the fee. Certain festivals (such as Victoria) will not reimburse the expense in that case.

This situation obviously makes it more costly and inconvenient for Canadians to import U.S. jazzers. It also raises prices (thereby reducing sales) of the records to be sold at the gig. Which cause do you think is more worthy of calling your Congressman, this one or declaration of a centennial year?

After all, your Congressman is a busy person and he isn't going to keep giving you everything you want. The jazz community needs to pick its targets carefully before trying to mobilize the government. Doing so isn't cost-free, though it may appear that way in a vacuum, not set alongside other issues.

Well, you say, how about that national park? There's a tangible thing that would stand as a monument to jazz. Tex, you're not going to tell me that such an institution would be an empty gesture.

You're right, I'm not. I'm opposed to that one for an entirely different reason, one that reflects my basic view of the purpose of government as an institution.

TEXAS SHOUT: HOW DIXIELAND JAZZ WORKS

Let me begin by saying that if - and this is a big if - the government is going to fund the arts, then Dixieland should get its fair share thereof, which it doesn't do now. Similarly, if - another big if - the government is going to pay someone to sit around and tinker from time to time with postage stamp designs, then Louis Armstrong is long overdue to be honored thereon.

(As an aside, this is a perfect example of the Federal government's unerring instinct for grasping the wrong end of the stick. A respectable case can be made that Satchmo is the most important and influential musician ever born in our country, yet at this writing his image has never graced a U.S. postage stamp - although this disgraceful situation may have been rectified by the time this column appears. By contrast, the question of which pose of Elvis Presley (!!!) should appear on a stamp was deemed of sufficient importance that the postal service conducted a national referendum on its two choices - and then, if memory serves, printed both versions anyway.)

However, my deeply held view is that government should do the absolute minimum required to govern and, in all other respects, leave us alone to get on with our lives. I think that using tax dollars to support the arts is not required for the task of government. In particular, I am opposed to using tax dollars to fund the arts, including funding Dixieland jazz and ragtime.

Let's put aside the fact that our Federal government currently runs a substantial deficit and needs to find ways to cut spending. Let's also overlook recent well-publicized fiascoes in which Federal funds were used to subsidize activities so far removed from a rational definition of "art" that, except for being propped up by the government, they would have disappeared instantly into the oblivion they deserve.

Even if we had intelligent governmental officials (an oxymoron?) running the show, I wouldn't go for it. I think that, if an art form can't make it in the commercial marketplace, then it should be maintained on a hobby basis (as Dixieland and ragtime have pretty much been for decades now).

Further, if there aren't enough hobbyists interested in it to keep it alive, then it might as well fade from the scene. Why should our tax dollars be spent to preserve something for which no one cares much?

An aspect of the problem that is rarely discussed revolves around the situation that, in a free economy, virtually any element of popular culture, once it has had its day, can be viewed as "art", a part of our heritage that needs to be saved for posterity. These include matchbox covers, advertising materials, automobile hood ornaments, doll houses and their furniture, soft drink bottles, kitchen reamers (to crush juice from fruit), teddy bears, railroad cars and engines, comic books, mustache cups, on through an endless list of everything you could name, even entire buildings (we already pay for maintaining those now as, I believe, National Historic Sites).

You and I might think that Dixieland jazz, one of America's earliest native-born art forms, obviously ought to rank higher on the scale than many of these other items. However, I'll bet someone who has spent his life collecting old model trains wouldn't agree. I'm sure he's just as opposed to having his tax money spent on Dixieland jazz as I am to having mine spent on model trains.

Government Subsidies

Yet there isn't enough money to preserve everything that could legitimately claim to be art. I wouldn't be presumptuous enough to say that my special interest outweighs someone else's. Government officials, of course, love to make such sweeping decisions, but who trusts them anymore to come close to getting things right?

Thus, I think it best to let each "art" community take care of its own to the extent that it wants to do so. If it doesn't want to do so, then it shouldn't try to extract money from folks who don't care about it.

Let's say, though, that government is going to fund the arts. Does that mean that a national park for jazz is our most pressing need in this respect? Not in this household.

As most of you know, Nancy and I are deeply committed movie buffs. We particularly enjoy silent movies.

Most silent movies were filmed and printed before safety stock was invented. They were produced on nitrate-based film, a highly inflammable substance that, if not maintained at exactly the proper temperature and humidity, will deteriorate into dust. Even under ideal conditions, nitrate film does not have an unlimited shelf life.

I can't pinpoint the source, but I recall reading that, partly as a result of fires and inappropriate storage, over 90% of all the silent films ever made no longer exist. Of the remainder, there are quite a few in the vaults of film archives around the country that, for lack of funding, aren't being preserved on safety stock and are slowly but surely wasting away.

We are not talking here about a side issue like a national park for silent movies. In this case, the art form itself has substantially disappeared from the face of the earth. Unless funds are found, and soon, to do the job of conversion, some of the small portion of it still around is going to suffer the same fate.

Thus, much as I love Dixieland, if I were going to advocate spending money on arts in which I am personally interested, I would much rather see the funds to go toward the immediate and pressing need to preserve what silent movies remain to us. As a fan of fantasy and horror literature (we've been to the World Fantasy Convention ten times), much of which was originally published decades ago in pulp magazines printed on the cheapest possible paper, I feel much the same way about trying to save pulps that would otherwise crumble to pieces.

Let's assume that we're past that point, though, and have decided that we will use government funds to support Dixieland jazz in some way. Is the establishment of a national park for jazz our first choice? Which others were considered?

Nancy and I have had a little experience with such monuments. I'll preface the tales by conceding that this is anecdotal and may not represent the generality. Also, I don't know how much, if any, public money was involved in these instances.

On our first trip to New Orleans, we discovered that we were in the midst of the French Quarter festival, a delightful affair in which excellent Dixieland bands were playing all day for the public's free enjoyment at stages set up along French Quarter streets. One would think that, at such a time, interest in Dixieland jazz among the general public would be heightened.

TEXAS SHOUT: HOW DIXIELAND JAZZ WORKS

It was a pleasant spring afternoon, a good day for a walk. So, after enjoying some jazz, we decided to try to locate the New Orleans Jazz Museum, containing rare and valuable memorabilia associated with some of our favorite musicians. It turned out to be in a building not far from the musical action.

We were fascinated by the instruments, sheet music and other items displayed from the early days of New Orleans jazz. We had plenty of time to examine them, because while we were there, no more than three other people were looking at the exhibits.

After we left the museum, we took another short walk to a park containing a large impressive statue of Louis Armstrong. It was quite a lovely setting: we lingered a while and even took our pictures with Pops. During the entire time we were at the spot, there wasn't another human being anywhere in sight.

Perhaps we were there on an off day, but I doubt it. At any rate, whatever those two projects cost, it didn't seem to us as though the public was extracting much value therefrom.

We've had essentially the same experience when we visited other establishments commemorating important Dixieland figures. For example, we were the only ones in attendance the time we stopped at W.C. Handy's birthplace and museum in Florence, Alabama.

Would a jazz national park suffer the same fate? Would the funds to be earmarked for Dixieland be better used to, say, preserve sheet music cover art? To reprint rare jazz tunes in commercial editions so that today's Dixieland bands can get access to and play them? To fund oral history interviews with important veteran jazzmen/women? To finance a search for the fabled trunk left behind by Scott Joplin that just might contain his lost opera and other unpublished manuscripts? To produce recordings so that the public can more easily appreciate the heritage of Dixieland jazz (to my knowledge, there never has been a U.S.-produced reissue album devoted entirely to The Halfway House Orchestra of New Orleans, one of my all-time favorite bands)? To present Dixieland concerts? To establish courses at which Dixieland history and performance are taught?

As I see it, these questions are not easily answered. I very much doubt that the Federal government is in a better position to weigh alternatives than the jazz community itself.

Thus, I think that the government should stay out of the whole business and let members of the jazz community utilize their private funds as they see fit. The same goes for the model plane community, the rare books community, the cigar band community, and so on down the line.

There you have my view. If you disagree, fine. If you think I'm somewhat to the right of Attila The Hun on this topic, that's O.K., too. We'll kick it around over that beer I mentioned.

Tell me, though. After reading my thoughts on this subject, do you really see me as someone who isn't "for" jazz? Have I actually been kidding myself all these years?

CHAPTER 49 "DIXIELAND" REVISITED

In the first "Texas Shout" (published November-December 1989), I argued that "Dixieland" is the preferable generic name for jazz that confines itself to the musical conventions and musical vocabulary employed within the jazz community prior to the development of swing. I touched this subject again in October 1994 while suggesting that, for a variety of reasons, "traditional" and "trad" have not proved to be useful alternative words for that purpose. Today I want to revisit this topic one more time.

Why am I continuing to beat this horse, you groan? Well, anyone who reads this publication has to know that Dixieland has been on life-support for over twenty years. A number of festivals have already pulled the plug by dropping the word "Dixieland" from their names and/or booking popular non-Dixieland acts (country/western, blues, concert-in-the-park, vintage pop, barbershop) to maintain attendance.

In these circumstances, Dixielanders' first priority, if we're to keep any presence on the scene at all, has to be recruiting new devotees, both listeners and players, from outside our ranks. We can't sensibly begin this task if we don't even agree on the name of the music we're supposed to be urging those outsiders to seek out.

Specifically, we will not help our cause if I use one term and you use another - or if we both use the same term but mean different things. We also will make life more difficult for ourselves if the term we select is one that has a different or alternative meaning in a non-jazz context.

I don't want to repeat the October 1994 column, but these problems explain why "traditional" has not proved suitable. First, the standard non-jazz meaning of "traditional" would imply to most people that any jazz over fifty years old, such as the early bop of Charlie Parker, may justifiably claim to be "traditional" (and indeed is considered as such by fans of more recent jazz forms). Second, nobody, inside of Dixieland or out, knows what "traditional jazz" means.

In the latter respect, "traditional" (or "trad") has never had a clearly defined, well understood, widely accepted, precise meaning within the Dixieland community. As a result, each Dixielander using "trad" or "traditional" has his/her own personal idea of what is meant by the term, a situation that exacerbates the confusion, fractionalization and infighting that (1) prevents Dixielanders from acting together in our own best interests and (2) makes it nearly impossible to use the term effectively to entice outsiders.

The same difficulties arise with words like "classic". Whether or not you like bop, you can't reasonably deny that many of Charlie Parker's bop performances are

TEXAS SHOUT: HOW DIXIELAND JAZZ WORKS

"classic" jazz rides in every sense of the word. The larger jazz community simply isn't going to let Dixielanders appropriate words like "classic" so that the only "classic jazz" renditions henceforth will be Dixieland.

We need a word that refers only to our music and which will be easily recognized as excluding swing, bop and later jazz forms. Fortunately, we have one. It is "Dixieland".

Whether or not a person likes Dixieland jazz, or whether or not a person likes the term "Dixieland", I think that most people who hear the word and attach any meaning to it at all associate it with music that comes out of the 1920s. They may not recognize it as jazz, but they usually don't confuse it with the output of Benny Goodman, Dizzy Gillespie, the Beatles, Elvis, Maria Callas, Eddy Arnold, etc.

That's a great start for us. We should build on it.

Nevertheless, I have discovered that there is a strong resistance, an irrational one in my opinion, to the term "Dixieland" in some quarters and an equally strong reluctance to give up the sloshy term "traditional". Thus, I want to confront directly some of the claims I've heard, not specifically addressed in my two prior columns, when I ask the question "What's wrong with 'Dixieland'?".

One *WCR* commentator wrote that he was comfortable enough with "Dixieland" in general, but had difficulty believing that the big band jazz style of the twenties fits under that term. I can understand where he's coming from.

Viewing with the 20/20 hindsight of the 1990s, we see big band jazz as part of a continuum that peaked with the big swing bands in the thirties and continued into progressive and more advanced big band jazz forms. We now tend to think of the "big" jazz bands of the twenties (which usually had about ten pieces) as the opening end of that largely non-Dixieland spectrum. Thus, some of us may have trouble accepting the fact that those beginnings of big band jazz are really Dixieland outfits when considered in terms of the music they played.

The big band jazz style of the twenties, popularly known by the somewhat misleading term "hot dance", was the subject of my third "Texas Shout", published in the February 1990 *WCR*. That column says, among other things, that hot dance is a form of jazz in which the musicians (1) confine themselves to the musical vocabulary and musical conventions that existed in the jazz community prior to the development of swing and (2) codify those musical devices in head or written arrangements for sections and ensembles, so that only the soloists are given a spontaneous choice of which notes to play.

If one keeps that definition in mind, I think it's easier to recognize that hot dance is, indeed, a Dixieland style. If a band is playing licks that characterize it as a Dixieland band, the type of music it's playing doesn't change just because those licks may be written down or memorized so that they can be exactly replicated. Similarly, while hot dance bands tend to be (but need not necessarily be) larger than the typical Dixieland combo, it should be clear that the type of music being played doesn't change simply and solely because the size of the band changes, as long as everyone continues to use the same musical vocabulary and conventions.

Remember also that, as I have said many times in these pages, though most Dixieland bands employ a lot of improvisation, improvisation is not a sine qua non

"Dixieland" Revisited

of Dixieland or even of jazz. There have been, and will continue to be, many performances easily recognizable as jazz (including Dixieland) which are fully arranged throughout. Some "hot dance" rides fit that description, but are not thereby disqualified from being a part of Dixieland jazz.

Hoping that the foregoing explanation helps you over the hurdle of classifying hot dance as, in fact, one of the seven Dixieland styles, let's briefly consider a possible red herring in the discussion of the desirability of "Dixieland". I refer to the fact that not long ago the Sacramento Jazz Jubilee dropped the word "Dixieland" from its name. Other festivals may have followed suit, but offhand, I can't recall any.

I bring up this point just to head off any claim that Sacto is opposed to the term "Dixieland" as such. The change was made, as the festival's publicity made crystal clear, because the festival's presentations became so broad-based that Sacto could no longer accurately be called a "Dixieland" festival or be described by any of the other words that are considered synonymous with "Dixieland".

A glance at the headliners spotlighted in the front of the festival's program book in recent years reveals that the top acts at Sacto, the ones that have been drawing the largest crowds and which have been getting expanded festival time, are vintage pop artists (like Kay Starr), blues, zydeco, country/western, Latin, barbershop, big-band dance and other similar forms of music; none of these is even jazz, much less Dixieland. The general public, the audience that Sacto is trying to attract, wouldn't expect to find such acts at a "Dixieland" festival, so naturally the word was dropped from the festival's title.

Anyway, to the extent that Sacto or other festivals have removed "Dixieland" from their names, I do not see this action as being indicative of a groundswell of aversion to the word itself among producers. It is instead a realistic reaction to the fact that our music, by whatever name, doesn't do much anymore to draw very large crowds.

By the way, we're very fortunate that Sacto continues to be run by the local Dixieland club members. These good people, to their credit, have continued to proclaim their commitment to our music and support that commitment by hiring annually, along with the other artists, more Dixieland bands than any other U.S. festival.

If Sacto ever gets turned over to, say, the Sacramento Chamber of Commerce or tourist bureau, I have no doubt that it would (1) drop the word "Jazz" from the festival's title, re-christening it the "Sacramento Jubilee", (2) get rid of about 20 of the least popular Dixieland bands, replacing them with regional combos that play 1950s/early 1960s rock or R&B, (3) salt away the remaining Dixieland acts into a few Dixieland-only sites and (4) sit back and watch attendance increase. Let's hope that Roger Krum and his wonderful staff remain on the job for a good long time.

TEXAS SHOUT: HOW DIXIELAND JAZZ WORKS

Having disposed, to your satisfaction I hope, of a couple of the less prevalent arguments against the word "Dixieland", I now want to address the most poorly thought out, dumbest, most baseless objection to the word, and the one that is always tossed out first by people who don't like the term. They will claim that "Dixieland" is indelibly associated in the public's mind with musicians who wear straw hats, striped blazers, striped vests and/or similar so-called period attire and who play shallow trivial music.

This statement is made as if it is incontrovertible truth and as if it means something significant. It is supposed to end the discussion. The time has come for true supporters of our music to confront and destroy this deep-seated myth face to face.

So many questions are raised by the striped blazer assertion that it's hard to know where to start asking them. For example, in my earlier columns I wondered how a style of music could in any way be defined by what the musicians are wearing when they play it. More to the point, just exactly what is supposed to be wrong with striped blazers anyway?

I'll be willing to bet that nearly every festival or club that presents Dixieland, whether it favors the term or not, has at one time or another advertised one of its events with a drawing depicting a musician in a straw hat, striped blazer or striped vest. This practice reflects the common-sense viewpoint that, if there is an image that suggests a wholesome good time to potential attendees, why not make use of it?

For that matter, I know of no festival or society concentrating on pre-swing jazz that refuses to hire bands which wear straw hats, striped vests or striped blazers. Nor am I aware of one that prohibits musicians or members of its strutters' groups from wearing such attire to its functions.

Come to think of it, at this writing there are several highly regarded, well-traveled bands on the circuit that wear blazers with some regularity, though usually solid-color ones. Should we thus conclude that blazers are really O.K. after all as long as they aren't striped? Precisely what is this magical quality of stripes which, when they are applied to a jazzman/woman's blazer or vest, causes musical notes to curdle upon emerging from the instrument?

In any event, musicians have to wear something on the bandstand. Striped blazers, in my book, look a lot better than the costume considered de rigueur in certain circles of the British trad style, where the artists apparently are trying to create the impression that they have just rushed onstage after having spent the last eight hours underneath the car changing the crankcase oil.

I love British trad along with the other six Dixieland styles. However, I much dislike the custom adopted by those British trad bands who make a special point of looking like ragamuffins, even when playing in expensive concert halls.

I can swallow my bile regarding the disrespect that is thereby shown to the music and also to the audience (which has usually taken the trouble to dress more suitably for the occasion). However, I can't forgive the fact that these bands are doing nothing to attract outsiders to our music.

Unless they're hoping to convert grunge rockers to Dixieland, they ought to know that few members of the general public are going to go out of their way to

"Dixieland" Revisited

patronize scruffy-looking musicians. Indeed, quite a few potential Dixielanders may be so turned off by an out-at-elbows appearance that they won't take time to appreciate the music. Dixieland isn't healthy enough to tolerate such a cavalier attitude by its practitioners.

Next questions: Just exactly how did Dixieland get this striped blazer image? When did it happen? Which bands and musicians, specifically, were responsible for it? How many of the general public really remember those artists? Why can't the image be erased over time by the good bands that have come along in the interim?

Ask these questions the next time some anti "Dixieland" type incants the straw-hat/striped blazer dogma. You won't get any well-focused answers. These folks just assert that "Dixieland" equals striped blazers equals shallow music as if everyone with any knowledge of the subject ought to agree.

I've seen it written that the striped blazer connection was made in the fifties, though no specific names were accused. Well, I was collecting Dixieland in the fities and sixties. I don't recall that there were hordes of schlock bands destroying Dixieland jazz at that time.

I do remember, though, that there was something of a commercial resurgence of Dixieland in the fifties, lasting about ten years before jazz started to fade, like other pre-rock music, in the glare of Beatlemania. A key band in that revival was The Firehouse Five Plus Two, which regularly appeared in firemen's uniforms.

However, the FH5 is (rightly) idolized in the current festival scene, so I guess it couldn't have been one of the bands that ruined "Dixieland" with its costumes. Or are the anti-"Dixieland" folks saying that if everyone had only worn firemen's uniforms instead of striped blazers, they wouldn't have a problem with the word?

I also remember that several record labels, in the early days of 12" LPs, promoted their Dixieland recordings with cover drawings or photographs of the musicians in costumes. Capitol, for example, did so with regularity on albums by, among others, Pete Daily, Bob Crosby, Ray Bauduc, Jack Teagarden, Sharkey Bonano, Red Nichols, Jack Teagarden and other fondly recalled jazzmen.

Are these great players the villains who are supposed to have prostituted our music? If so, why do used copies of those LPs, the ones which haven't been reissued on CD, draw such high prices on the collectors' market? Besides, what influence do performers have over the way record producers promote albums?

In the early days of high fidelity, the Audio Fidelity label released an immensely successful series of LPs by The Dukes of Dixieland, many of which had special themes and came in jackets showing the band in costumes consistent with the themes. Are these the cause of the striped blazer curse? If so, how do the anti-"Dixieland" people deal with the fact that the band itself, the Assunto brothers edition of the Dukes, was one of the best Dixieland bands of its day, one that would mop up the floor with most of today's Dixieland bands in head-to-head competition, one that created such lasting fame for itself that a version of the Dukes has stayed on the boards pretty much ever since?

In fact, the popularity of the Dukes' Audio Fidelity LPs raised the consciousness of a sizeable slice of the general public toward Dixieland. We'd be very lucky if a Dixieland band came along today that duplicated its success, no matter what kind of costumes it wore or how it was marketed.

TEXAS SHOUT: HOW DIXIELAND JAZZ WORKS

By the early 1960s a string of sing-a-long banjo clubs had sprung up across the country in chains with names like The Red Garter or Your Father's Mustache. The mandatory uniform for the musicians included a striped vest. Were these night spots the culprits who trashed Dixieland?

The difficulty with that idea is that a fair number of today's Dixielanders about my age (late 50s) spent some time working in these clubs, myself included. Every one of them I've talked to has positive memories of the experience.

Although the music played by the resident banjo bands was vintage pop, not Dixieland (I doubt that many people thought it was Dixieland), most of the venues did book legitimate Dixieland bands on weekend afternoons or on slow nights. These establishments thereby provided lots of work for Dixielanders of their day and attracted respectable crowds to a scene where the audience was immersed in Dixieland-influenced music. Striped vests or not, all Dixielanders would be much better off if the banjo sing-a-long fad were to recur.

Does the stigma on "Dixieland" stem from pizza parlors? I doubt it. Before the 1960s-70s, when Dixieland took hold for some years in pizza and other fast-food emporia, there was already a faction abhorring the word.

I suppose we've all seen glib disparaging comments about a "pizza parlor image", but frankly, what's wrong with playing in a pizza restaurant? Has there ever been a Dixieland artist stupid enough to turn down a paying gig just because pizza was sold on the premises?

Nobody has any trouble with our music being played in bars. Why is there supposed to be something demeaning about playing it in a family situation where booze isn't the main entree?

Besides, like the sing-a-long clubs, the pizza joints provided steady employment for Dixielanders for many years. Our community owes them a debt of gratitude.

In fact, in acknowledgement of the support these eateries gave our music, the owner of the Shakey's chain was honored a few years back as the Sacramento Jazz Jubilee's official emperor. Like it or not, it's too bad for us that you don't hear much Dixieland any more in pizza parlors.

I've tried and tried to get people to give me facts about the origin of this striped blazer slander, but without success. It is simply another piece of phony jazz lore, one of those things that just isn't so about Dixieland that gets mindlessly repeated by people who ought to know better.

However, suppose it all were true? Let's pretend that the word "Dixieland" really does mean shallow music played by silly bands wearing gaudy clothes in which the trombonist always works the slide with his foot and the trumpet player fingers his horn upside down? What if the impossible happened and some other word than "Dixieland", say "traditional" or "classic", were widely recognized by today's general public to mean high-quality, uncommercial, deep, twenties-style jazz?

Sooner or later bands would come along that were 100%-schlock outfits trying to get a free ride on our pristine image by claiming to be playing "traditional" or "classic" jazz. Given that the public doesn't always bestow its acclaim on those most worthy, some of those schlocky bands would become popular and start getting more

"Dixieland" Revisited

bookings than the excellent more deserving bands. These shallow bands would thereby tarnish the hard-won image of "traditional" or "classic".

What are we supposed to do then? Go through the same process? Decide that "traditional" or "classic" now means schlocky music and start down the long road of converting the public to some other word? Of course not. So let's make the most of "Dixieland", the word we already have.

In the years since I wrote that first column about "Dixieland", I've probed all of the reasons people have given me for disliking the term. None survives close analysis.

Not finding any other explanation for resisting "Dixieland" that satisfies me, I have concluded that the anti-"Dixieland" folks really, deep down inside, want to be part of an elite in-group that can congratulate itself on appreciating some music known by a term only they understand. Such an attitude is, of course, totally self-destructive in terms of the Dixieland's community's urgent need to recruit new supporters from outside our ranks.

However, Dixielanders regularly engage in much self-destructive conduct, e.g., lack of cooperation between geographically adjacent Dixieland clubs, pointless infighting among supporters of different Dixieland styles. I suppose one more instance of it won't make much difference.

Therefore, if you have some burning compulsion to do so, you might as well keep on proclaiming that "Dixieland" is shallow trivial music, that you don't play it or listen to it, and that you really are involved with jazz described by some other term that you need to explain to the neophytes in the crowd. However, as far as I'm concerned every time you mouth that litany, you're loosening one more plug in Dixieland's already fragile life-support system. Whether you know it or not, you're part of the problem.

Dukes of Dixieland   1950s
Photo by Bob Witt

TEXAS SHOUT: HOW DIXIELAND JAZZ WORKS

Firehouse Five Plus Two
1960s
*Photo courtesy of
Contemporary Records*

Parasol Parade
Sacramento Dixieland Jubilee
Photo by Dan Polin

CHAPTER 50   SUBSTITUTES

I doubt that many of you think of an organized band in terms of its substitutes. However, substitutes are among the most critical elements needed to sustain a combo's viability.

Show business is probably subject to more uncertainties than most occupations. Even in the ranks of full-time professional outfits, sidemen come and go without much warning and occasional emergencies require a fill-in.

This situation is exacerbated with respect to Dixieland, which is almost entirely a part-time affair, even for many of its top names. The limitations imposed by one's day job (particularly getting enough vacation time to play out of town) as well as the other claims of personal life often interfere with musicians' ability to take gigs, even very attractive ones.

Jobs don't grow on trees these days for Dixieland bands. Thus, any leader needs to cultivate a stable of qualified backups, people who can step in without lowering the quality of the show which his/her band's clients have come to expect. If you can't find them, either the standard of your performance (and maybe your reputation) takes a beating or, just possibly, you'll have to turn down some work for lack of players.

Locating such subs isn't easy. There aren't as many people as there used to be who know how to play idiomatic Dixieland at all, let alone play it well.

Even for groups that operate essentially on a jam basis, everyone needs to feel comfortable - both stylistically and personality-wise - with all of the sidemen/women if the team is going to jell. Further, many of today's combos perform uncommon selections or use intricate routines that can't be grasped on the fly, no matter how talented the substitute.

Thus, an intelligent band tries to establish an environment that will make outsiders want to work with it and want to return after the experience. After all, if you're not satisfied with the sub, you can always put him/her lower on your call list. However, if he/she is a hobbyist, playing to a large extent for fun, and is so uncomfortable on your gig that he/she won't take another with you, your options are narrowed.

[Similarly, on those (hopefully few) occasions when a regular member has to be replaced, the leader should make every effort to handle the changeover without creating the kind of bridge-burning ill feeling that will make it impossible to use the musician as a sub in the future. Why cut yourself off from someone who knows your routines?]

Anyone subbing with my Red Lion Jazz Band gets the red-carpet treatment from all hands. We try to include the new face in our between-set conversation, make his/her companion feel at home, never criticize the sub's performance, always end the evening assuring him/her that he/she did a great job, etc. If the gig's budget allows and the substitute has come very far, we try to toss a few extra bucks in his/her direction to cover some of the gasoline and/or tolls.

One would think these principles would go without saying. However, things don't always work that way.

One time I was called to play cornet with a relatively new group. One of my front-line companions apparently had become so used to the way his regular lead man phrased everything that he became unsettled when he didn't hear me playing the familiar notes at the familiar volume and attack.

After virtually every phrase, I was getting sotto voce instructions to play louder, softer, this way, that way, etc. Of course, I tried my best to comply. After all, a substitute is supposed to help the band put on its best show; any advice the regulars can offer in furtherance of that purpose is most welcome as far as I'm concerned.

However, I soon realized that my colleague had impossible expectations. Moreover, he was driving me up the wall and ruining my evening.

I could have bitten my tongue, counted the hours until closing, and then elected to be otherwise engaged on subsequent calls from that crew. However, I decided that the problem was essentially due to the group's inexperience. So, to try to point it in the right direction for the future and to save my sanity for the time being, I got the leader and one of his more seasoned sidemen in a corner at the second break.

I told them what was going on and the effect it was having on me. I said that if they weren't happy with my performance, they were perfectly free to drop me from their substitute list. I repeated the request that I always make when filling in, that if I'm not doing something the way they prefer it, let me know and I'll do my best to change it.

But I also said that I was tired of having a sideman constantly whisper in my ear that there was something wrong with everything I was doing. I observed that the gig was turning into the job from Hell, and that, unless the scene brightened fairly quickly, they should not expect me to be interested in playing with them again. I closed with my view that, if they are going to treat their substitutes this way, no capable musician would be willing to put up with it a second time.

To their credit, my friends appreciated the advice. They got the situation cured on the spot. We all enjoyed a cordial relationship thereafter. In fact, I continued to sub with them until, their key players having moved away, the group disbanded.

You can't avoid the need for substitutes. Even with The Rent Party Revellers, a band that was formed to play just a few festivals/cruises a year which would be contracted far in advance, we soon learned that, if we were going to book even an abbreviated schedule, we had to bring additional sidemen into the project to deal with conflicts caused by our personal lives and local band commitments.

The Revellers are an eight-piece band. However, at this writing, there are sixteen sidemen/women on our mailing list, top players who are current on all our lead sheets and routines so that we can play with any combination of them without having to change our act or suffer a deterioration in its quality.

Substitutes

(For those who are interested, when we get a gig the Revellers fill the chairs strictly on the basis of seniority with the band. Every hand is a first-rank performer, so it would be senseless to try to choose among them on any other basis.)

My Red Lion Jazz Band works with a number of local musicians who will fill in, or sometimes just drop in, on our Tuesday night rehearsals. We thereby have the luxury of drawing our substitutes from a pool of artists who know our routines.

Some bandleaders will take a gig if they're not engaged personally and then put the band together from available sidemen. I don't work that way. Whether it's the Revellers or the Red Lions, I always tell the client that I'll call back to confirm as soon as I have the others lined up.

I won't take any chances. If I take a gig, I want to know in advance that I can deliver a band that will perform up to snuff. As a result, I have (fortunately rarely) elected to turn down a gig because I couldn't put together a team that satisfied me.

Conversely, I have occasionally had clients who want to dictate which sidemen I should hire for their gigs. I won't let them do so, responding that, when they contract for the Red Lions or the Revellers, what they're entitled to is a band that will deliver the kind of show for which those groups have become known. It's my job to fulfill that promise and how I do so is strictly up to me.

Of course, when I make up a tune list, I keep in mind the musicians who are booked for the job. Some titles have routines or aspects that play to a certain substitute's strong points, so I'll program those. I make sure that, if any tricky material is planned, I'll have time between sets, between numbers, or even during the rides, to get the proper cues to the fill-in so that everything goes smoothly.

On rare occasions, I have encountered a festival that tries to exert a sort of quality control by including a clause in its contracts that purports to give the festival some say in a band's choice of substitutes. I can understand the producer's desire to insure that the festival gets a group whose performance will be consistent with its reputation or its audition tape.

However, once it's hired a band, a festival usually has only one legitimate interest at stake and that is to be sure that it stays within its budget. If a substitute becomes necessary, the festival has a right to expect that the substitution will not significantly increase the amount it intended to pay for the band. For example, a bandleader should not be surprised if a festival refuses to pay transportation involved in replacing a local musician with one who lives across the country, or replacing a journeyman performer with an internationally known artist whose fee is much higher.

Beyond that point, I believe a festival is out of line if it tries to dictate sidemen to a bandleader on artistic grounds. If it has begun advertising the band, it has little choice but to let the leader go with the replacement with whom he/she is most comfortable.

If it hasn't placed ads, the festival might elect to cancel the band's invitation if it isn't happy with the substitute. Before doing so, though, it should weigh the effect that such an action is likely to have on its relations with bands it wants to book in the future, knowing that, as mentioned above, occasional substitutes are inevitable in today's scene. Besides, the festival should recognize that it and the leader are really

TEXAS SHOUT: HOW DIXIELAND JAZZ WORKS

on the same side when substitution becomes necessary - both want to give the audience the best show possible in the circumstances.

Does a Dixieland band sound different with a new face in it? Of course it does. Given the significant degree of improvisation in most Dixieland performances, some change in sound is unavoidable.

However, different doesn't mean better or worse. Eddie Condon's groups with Bobby Hackett on lead didn't come on the same way as those with Wild Bill Davison, Max Kaminsky, Muggsy Spanier or Johnny Windhurst, but they all rendered red-hot, top-drawer Chicago style jazz. That's the only thing that counts.

Again, one would think these points are self-evident. However, some time ago, I read a letter of complaint by someone who had attended a festival set by one of the country's top units, one which for that particular weekend had two musicians replacing its regular sidemen. Both of them were highly talented artists, well known on the circuit.

The complainant believed that he had somehow been misled. He was unable to make his peace with the changed lineup and was blaming the band and the festival. As I recall, he said something to the effect that the band shouldn't have taken the gig, or that it shouldn't have been advertised under its usual name, or that prospective attendees should somehow have received advance notice that violence had been done to the group's usual personnel.

This view is totally unrealistic. In the current scene, there is simply no way to avoid the need for a substitute from time to time.

You judge a band by whether it plays well and gives you a good show, regardless of who's in it, recognizing that the ensemble will be affected to some extent by any change in personnel. If it fails to produce those things, for whatever reason, then your remedy is to stop going to see it.

If it fails often enough, producers will stop hiring it, regardless of the lineup proposed for any particular gig. Indeed, I can think of one artist who regularly brings out bands made up of the best musicians in his branch of Dixieland, but in poorly organized pickup jam bands whose shows have been so uneven that at least some festivals have put his name rather far down the call list.

By the way, with respect to the individual cited above who complained so vociferously about substitutes, Nancy and I happened to attend that festival and to have heard a set by the band in question. The subs were so skilled, and so compatible with the regulars, that we regarded the program as the best thing we saw during the weekend.

I can't help but conclude that the complainer was listening with his eyes, not his ears, and that as soon as he saw new faces on the bandstand he made up his mind in advance that the show would be unacceptable. All I can say is, if you can't handle a band that uses a substitute or two from time to time, you're not going to be hearing much Dixieland over the long haul.

March 1996 The American Rag

CHAPTER 51   MELODIC IMPROVISATION

Author's note: The following material was written for publication in mid-1997 as an addendum to my "This Month's Records" column. For reasons that will become clear, I am reprinting it as a lead-in to this chapter.

[I'd like to use my remaining space to restate some points made in the March 1996 edition of my "Texas Shout" column. (For new readers, "Texas Shout" was a series of essays about the music that ran in this publication from 1989-96.) As some of you will recall, that article offered certain comments on soloists who construct their solos in a melodic and tuneful way and on those who do not.

I included in the text thereof a portion of a previously published letter that touched on that topic. I did so because I thought I could save myself some work by using something I already had on hand.

In retrospect, I see that I should have written the whole piece from scratch. My letter was designed to accomplish a different purpose. I didn't do a good enough job of writing the new material in a way that melded it seamlessly with the terminology used in the letter.

As a result, some of my readers came away with an imperfect grasp of what I was trying to say. So, I'm going to take another crack at setting forth in clearer terms those parts of the column that caused confusion.

It may help if you think of a Dixieland solo as a form of speech, speech expressed in music. A person's normal speech is made up of groups of words, called sentences, separated by pauses. A soloist's "speech", the solo, is made up of groups of notes, called phrases, also separated by pauses (often the spots at which horn players take breaths).

A spoken sentence may be any length. The same is true of a musical phrase.

Although it is possible for a phrase to last a full chorus or even longer, a typical soloist's phrases are usually much shorter. A Dixieland phrase is commonly two or four measures long.

For reasons explained clearly enough in my original March 1996 column, a Dixieland solo must make frequent contact with, or reference to, the notes in the underlying chord pattern. Said another way, the solo must, first and foremost, adhere as a whole to the tune's basic harmonic structure. Otherwise, all or parts of it will sound "wrong".

Within that overall mandate, each phrase played by a soloist will fall into one of three categories:

(1) It repeats, or is a fairly obvious paraphrase of, the tune's melody as written by its composer.

(2) It does not use the composer's melody, but is a phrase that by itself, is tuneful, melodic and singable - something hummable or something to which one could easily add lyrics. (As a subcategory thereof, a soloist may, often for humorous effect, play a phrase from the melody of some other well-known tune, a phrase that happens to fit the chord pattern on which he is improvising. This practice is known as "quoting".)

(3) It is not tuneful, melodic or hummable, but consists of bent notes, growls, rasps, leaps, jabs, riffs, blizzards of notes (such as busy clusters, triplets or extended eighth-note runs) and other devices that are primarily rhythmic rather than melodic in nature.

All soloists regularly use all three types of phrases to some degree. However, over time, almost every soloist develops an approach to improvisation that draws heavily from just one of the three categories. Thus, when you appraise a given soloist's body of work in its entirety, you can usually place him/her without much difficulty as a soloist who liked to build most of the solo out of one of those three types, using the other two types for occasional flavoring.

In the uptown New Orleans style of Dixieland, it is a common practice to construct the bulk of a solo by paraphrasing the composer's original melody. This procedure is also followed, but to a much more limited extent, in the British trad style, a style which is significantly derived from, and therefore sort of a first cousin to, the uptown New Orleans style. In the other five Dixieland styles, soloists usually create their own phrases and make relatively little use of the ones written by the composer.

In all seven styles, soloists who elect neither to repeat nor to paraphrase the composer's original melody overwhelmingly wind up creating solos comprised predominantly of the third type of phrase listed above - the type that is primarily rhythmic rather than melodic in nature. Examples of such artists cited in my March 1996 column included Jim Robinson and Wild Bill Davison.

Artists whose improvised solos consist mostly of the second type of phrase listed above are extremely rare. Those who are good at it are almost nonexistent. That is the reason why performers in this very exclusive company - I would rank Bix Beiderbecke and Sidney Bechet among them, as I said in my March 1996 essay - are so highly rated by the jazz community.

Perhaps the foregoing is a more successful attempt at explaining what can be an elusive concept, particularly to a non-musician. A discerning listener of Dixieland responds to and appreciates the differences in soloists described above, even if only at a subconscious level. Thus, it seemed to me to be worthwhile to take another stab at the topic in the hope that the explanation will hasten some of you along the path to discerning listenerhood.]

Melodic Improvisation

From time to time, I encounter persons who want to say that an integral, if not defining, characteristic of Dixieland jazz is melodic improvisation by soloists rather than improvisation based on the chord pattern of the piece being played. This is a seductive concept for reasons set forth below.

Unfortunately, it is also completely inaccurate. As I will explain, whether or not a Dixieland musician chooses to create a new melody when soloing, he/she must, as a first priority, produce something that fits the chord pattern being played by the rhythm section, particularly the chord instruments (piano, banjo, guitar). Thus, all Dixieland improvising is primarily chord-oriented.

It is true that there are some Dixielanders who improvise melodically. However, it is fallacious to generalize from this minority and expand the notion of melodic improvisation into something inherent in and essential to our music.

First, let's make sure we know what we mean by "melodic improvisation". We are not talking about a soloist who chooses to repeat the melody written by the composer, personalizing it via tonal shadings, fills and other decorations.

Doing so is a common convention of the uptown New Orleans Dixieland style and is also adopted by some soloists in other styles. I respect and enjoy the practice, recognizing that it takes great talent to do effectively, but it is not the type of melodic improvisation that I want to discuss today.

For our purposes here, I mean an improvisation that emerges as a logically constructed new song, a coherent chorus-length singable tune (that fits the basic chord pattern) - such as Frank Trumbauer and Bix Beiderbecke each created on their immortal recording of "Singin' The Blues (Till My Daddy Comes Home)". Incidentally, the fact that these two solos were learned note for note by hordes of jazzmen over the years ought to provide your first clue that the skill of melodic improvising is much rarer in Dixieland than many works of jazz literature - often highly romanticized - would have you believe.

Why do these romantics embrace the notion of improvising on the melody? There are two main reasons. First, "melody" is a word that carries an emotional charge in addition to its technical meaning. Second, there is some misunderstanding about what is or is not a melody in the first place.

You can see this dichotomy in the dictionary definition of "melody". From a technical viewpoint, mine accurately enough defines melody as "a rhythmic succession of single notes organized as an aesthetic whole". However (here comes the emotional charge), an alternate definition is "a sweet or agreeable succession or arrangement of sounds" [emphasis added].

Many people discussing Dixieland run these two notions together when discussing melody. To them, melody has a connotation of being pleasing.

Obviously, then, the more of it they can say is in the music they like, the better that music must be. Similarly, if the jazz they like involves melodic improvisation, then it must be more pleasing than jazz which does not and which they don't like.

It is common for these folks to use this approach as a way of putting down bop and other post-bop jazz forms which, to them, do not have melodies that please. Some of them say that such music has no melody at all.

| TEXAS SHOUT: HOW DIXIELAND JAZZ WORKS |

Actually, modern jazz solos are often much more melodic, as that term is understood musically, than Dixieland solos. Saxophonists and pianists in modern jazz typically spin out lengthy lines that are much more like song melodies than the two-bar and four-bar phrases that comprise the overwhelming bulk of Dixieland solo improvisations.

These modern jazz lines are frequently angular, busy, dissonant vs. the harmonic pattern, jagged, and in other respects responsive to conventions of modern jazz that many Dixielanders do not find pleasant. However, whether or not you like such lines, there is much more melody to those ideas than there is, for example, in the two-bar riff that forms the basis for the chorus to the Dixieland evergreen "Royal Garden Blues".

In fact, modern jazzmen/women are commonly forced to improvise on the melody. The chords used in some modern jazz tunes employ very high harmonics and odd intervals, setting up ambiguous harmony that won't clash with anything the soloist wants to play. In those cases, he/she has little other than the melody on which to base the improvisation. But I'm getting ahead of my story.

In May 1991, *WCR*'s publisher Woody Laughnan sent me a copy of the May 5, 1991 *IACJF Networker*, the newsletter of the International Association Of Classic Jazz Festivals. Woody wanted me to know that a "Texas Shout" column of mine had been reprinted therein.

Reading the rest of the publication, I observed that the group was struggling to define "classic jazz" in order to explain to prospective members the type of music it supported. Two definitions had been offered for the membership's consideration, including this one: "Classic jazz is that form of jazz wherein improvisation is based upon the melody as opposed to being based upon chordal progressions."

On May 10, 1991, I sent a letter to Phil Franklin, IACJF's Chairman, to thank him for reprinting my article and for his kind remarks about it. Not being able to keep my nose out of other people's musical business, I added some thoughts regarding the suggested definitions.

If memory serves, Phil printed my letter in a subsequent *Networker*. Anyway, the portion of my remarks therein most pertinent to today's column reads as follows:

> The other definition, one which requires "classic jazz" to have improvisation based on the melody and not on chord progressions, reflects a fundamental misunderstanding of how the music works. Persons who improvise in the older styles of jazz, presumably the "classic" ones, are virtually forced to keep the chord pattern in mind while doing so.
>
> That is because Dixieland jazz typically has rhythm sections with relatively louder instruments playing the chord pattern behind the solo. If the soloist chooses to play out-of-chord notes as part of a melody line against the rather insistent sound of a tuba or banjo, and if he keeps it up for very long, the solo will start to sound "wrong". That statement is still true, but to a lesser degree, if his backup is the softer-edged guitar and string bass.

Melodic Improvisation

As jazz evolved, less emphasis was placed on the practice of expressly stating the chords. For example, pianists during the thirties were more inclined to play single-note treble figures with occasional part-chord jabs in the bass.

In the more advanced jazz forms, bands may well have no chordal instrument at all. Ornette Coleman made his first big splash with a combo consisting of trumpet, saxophone, bass and drums.

Such an instrumentation gives, say, the saxophone soloist maximum freedom to play pure melody, because the trumpet and bass sound only two notes against him. Any combination of three notes will make some kind of chord, so it's almost impossible in that context for the soloist to hit notes with a "wrong" sound. In fact, some of the "free Jazz" that came along in the sixties was played without any sort of advance agreement among the musicians as to key, chords or tempo!

Given that the earlier styles of jazz are those in which the soloists must pay the most attention to the chord pattern, for the above reasons, the suggested definition manages to miss the point in yet another direction. All jazz soloists play with relative degrees of emphasis on melody and rhythm. Rarely does a soloist consistently emphasize those two elements equally.

To name two that quickly come to mind, Sidney Bechet and Bix Beiderbecke were highly melodically-oriented soloists. Their solos always sing to you.

Conversely, Wild Bill Davison (one of my all-time favorites), whose solos sometimes consisted of unique combinations of shrieks, jabs, bent notes and rasps, was a rhythmically-oriented soloist. Some of his solos do not sing to you at all (are practically unsingable, in fact), but instead roll right over top of you with their sheer drive and excitement. A major name on the current scene, who shows more than a little of Bill in his style, is the excellent Ernie Carson, whose solos are often built up of short flurries of unadulterated rhythm based on the chord pattern, bearing essentially no relationship to the original melody.

One could go on. The great tailgater Jim Robinson created a unique solo style out of a handful of licks which he emitted with an irresistible, almost percussive muscularity, while his colleague, pianist Alton Purnell, stuck largely to treble arpeggios and jabs over a propulsive rhythmic base.

If you define "classic jazz" as jazz where the improvisation is based more on melody than chords, you will be saying, whether you realize it or not, that Wild Bill Davison, Jim Robinson, Alton Purnell, Ernie Carson and a host of others, including the overwhelming majority of part-time Dixielanders who make up so many of the bands that play for your members, do not play it. Also, many modern jazzmen will be able to say, quite accurately, that because they improvise melodically, they play "classic jazz". That result, I think, is not the one you're looking for.

Let me close by amplifying the points in my letter with a few observations drawn from thirty years of reviewing recordings in all styles of early jazz, including taking careful notes on every solo played thereon. There is no question that the overwhelming majority of soloists on those records are primarily rhythmically oriented, as were Wild Bill Davison and Jim Robinson, described in the letter quoted above. Their lines tend to be made up of short loosely related phrases (fitted to the underlying chord pattern) that push and pull at the beat while, via tone coloration, also setting up and easing other types of tension.

This result is consistent with the way most jazz artists approach soloing. Few of them go into a solo with a clear idea of how they're going to start, much less how they're going to structure the entire outing. Their solos consist in large part of spur-of-the-moment responses to factors impacting them at the time, such as what the accompanists are playing, audience response, the acoustics of the room, etc.

Improvising jazzmen/women are occasionally asserted to be spontaneous composers. Perhaps that statement is true in a strict-construction sense. However, an improviser does not usually "compose" as most people understand the term - consciously creating and polishing a carefully worked out, poised, musical statement.

Thus, melodic improvisation, far from being a sine qua non of early jazz, is actually a rather rare commodity in it. I suspect that this rarity is the reason why especially gifted practitioners of melodic improvisation, such as Bechet and Beiderbecke, are so admired by players and fans alike.

To be sure, highly talented rhythmic soloists, like the wonderful cornetist Muggsy Spanier, are revered by the jazz community and rightly so. However, they are seldom put on as high a pedestal as the melodic improvisers because there are many more of the former than of the latter.

In sum, don't be misled by a claim that, as a rule, Dixielanders improvise on the melody or are melodic soloists. It sounds good, but it doesn't square with what you'll hear from the stages and on the records. Worse, if you're striving to deepen your appreciation of the idiom, it will head you in the wrong direction.

Frank Trumbauer 1930s
Photo from Downbeat

CHAPTER 52   MAJOR LABELS

In the second "Texas Shout", printed in the January 1990 *American Rag* (then called *West Coast Rag*), I lamented the absence of Dixieland recordings from the general marketplace. The issue is an important one, so perhaps it's worthwhile rechecking the scene as it stands today. Also, as has happened so often over the years, *WCR/TAR*'s pages have carried some attempts at dialogue on the subject that indicate once again how desperately the terminology in our field needs clarification.

Let's deal with the second subject first. In the February 1994 "Texas Shout", which discussed the somewhat gloomy future of Dixieland jazz, I remarked that, with the exception of the recordings on Columbia by The Preservation Hall Jazz Band, there seemed to be no interest in producing new Dixieland records by the major labels. A few months later, one of my esteemed colleagues indicated that the situation wasn't quite that bleak, citing individual recent releases on Discovery, Good Time Jazz, Telarc Jazz and MusicMasters as evidence of some slight interest among the "bigs".

With all due respect to my friend, I think we have here another example of Dixielanders using the same words to mean two different things. A "major label", as I use the term and as I believe it is used in the commercial recording industry, refers to a label like RCA Victor or Columbia, i.e., one that is represented by some kind of recording in every record store in the country.

These are large corporations with thousands of recordings in their current catalogs. They record everything that is likely to sell in appreciable quantity: rock, classical, country, soundtracks, original casts of musicals, religious, etc. If you go to the record shop that is most convenient to your home, be it a small mom-and-pop store, a specialty store, mall store or whatever, it will have something in stock that you can buy and take right home on Columbia, RCA Victor or any other label that qualifies as "major".

As I understand record industry parlance, it recognizes only two kinds of labels, "major" and "independent". An independent label may have released many records or only a handful.

For example, George Buck's catalog over the past forty years covers hundreds of issues and all branches of our music. You can typically find a few of George's CDs in the jazz sections of large chain record stores in our biggest cities. However, lacking the clout and breadth to get his product into just about every retail record outlet, George is classified by the industry as an independent.

For the record industry's purposes, Dixieland labels may be grouped into two categories, those which have arranged for national distribution and those which have not. I do not know how such arrangements are made, but I feel certain that virtually any label, even one with a very tiny catalog, can have its recordings distributed nationally.

TEXAS SHOUT: HOW DIXIELAND JAZZ WORKS

If such distribution has been arranged for, then a local record store is in position to obtain the record for someone who orders it. That is, even if your neighborhood outlet doesn't stock the record you want, it will be able to locate the recording in a computer file or other source; get the catalog number, price and pertinent address; and place a special order for your copy.

If national distribution has not been arranged for, then, as far as your local record store is concerned, the item you want doesn't exist. You may have seen the CD at a festival and made a note of the artist, label and catalog number, but taking that information to your local store won't get you a copy. Neither the store nor its supplier has any way of locating the label's address or the price of the record.

The overwhelming majority of the U.S.-produced Dixieland jazz records are in this latter, commercially nonexistent, category. They are produced by the artists themselves or by their fans, primarily to be sold stageside at live performances. The hassle involved in placing such records into a national distribution system, not to mention the percentage of profits that are drained off by the middlemen, keeps these records in an underground distribution system consisting of living room mail order and stageside sales, supplemented by a few copies placed with specialty mail order dealers patronized by knowledgeable Dixieland collectors.

Against that background, let's consider the assertion that Good Time Jazz, for example, is a "major" label, one of the "bigs". I am choosing Good Time Jazz for this illustration partially because it is a label that many of you know.

I want to make it clear at the outset that I am not in any way derogating the considerable achievement of one of the most revered, and rightly so, names in Dixieland jazz recording history. Some of my earliest Dixieland acquisitions were on Good Time Jazz and they still rank with my all-time favorite albums. I have a complete run of the label's LPs and have such high regard for GTJ that I will buy anything thereon which contains material new to my collection, even if I have to suffer some duplication in the process.

Good Time Jazz's releases appeared during about a twenty-year period from the 1950s to the 1970s. It issued 78s, EPs, and 10" LPs, most of which wound up being reissued in its 12" LP line, on which nearly 60 platters appeared.

Although this material has resurfaced on CD over the years, GTJ did not release another newly-recorded album for about a quarter-century, one by the Silver Leaf Jazz Band in 1994. Since then, a few additional CDs have been produced.

It hardly needs to be said that, although Good Time Jazz's catalog contains immortal core records of West Coast revival Dixieland, sides that have withstood the test of time, it cannot be considered a "major" label when it has produced less than 100 LPs' worth of recordings in a half-century and when you can count the new ones (i.e., not reissues) on your fingers and toes. Good Time Jazz is, like Delmark (its Dixieland series), Sackville, Jazz Crusade and Arbors, a small jazz specialist's label.

It is understandable that some Dixieland fans could be misled into thinking that these labels are bigger than they are. If you live in or near one of our largest cities, you probably have access to a Tower Records or other large chain store located therein, with browsers on several floors or spread across a warehouse-size room.

> **Major Labels**

Amid the plethora of modern jazz records in its racks, you will occasionally find something on Good Time Jazz, Arbors, etc. As you won't find much other Dixieland, I suppose you could conclude that these labels are the "big" ones when actually they are the ones that have done the work necessary to enable retailers to stock their records.

Most stores don't bother to do so. At the time my friend voiced his above-mentioned view that the CDs on Discovery, Good Time Jazz, Telarc Jazz and MusicMasters were marketed by "bigs", I think it unlikely that a single retail store in my native state of Delaware had any of the four in the bins available for purchase by a casual buyer.

That situation has persisted as long as I've been writing "Texas Shout". It is my main reason for revisiting the subject today.

When this column began in 1989, not much Dixieland had been released on CD. That situation is no longer true.

All of the most influential recordings of our music are now on compact disc, along with nearly everything else of jazz interest that was recorded in the twenties. However, the bulk of it has been produced in Europe on collectors' labels and virtually none of it is currently stocked in a store that is convenient for shopping by high school students or other members of the general public in your area.

If you go through the jazz section of your local mall store, you will indeed find some archetypical examples of our music, most often by Satchmo, Condon, Ellington, Bix, Fats, Bessie, Jelly, and maybe Bechet, Tea and a few others whose names are the closest things we have to commercially viable household words. Nearly all of those albums will be post-1924, i.e., electrically recorded. No recent Dixieland recordings will be on hand.

This situation is better than it was in 1989, but not by much. It is reassuring that a sample of truly great classic-period Dixieland is easily obtainable by the general public. However, this sampling is not a sufficient quantity to sustain anyone who develops a keen interest in our music. Also, the artists listed above do not represent a true cross-section of the seven Dixieland styles.

WCR/TAR's pages have been filled with articles in the intervening years regarding the crucial need to interest more fans, especially younger people, in our music. Believe me, it won't happen if the records aren't where newcomers can conveniently buy them.

It takes a while for someone to get deeply enough committed to our music to begin learning about and subscribing to Dixieland publications where specialty record dealers advertise. It takes a while for someone to get deeply enough committed to our music to begin writing away to buy records from specialty dealers.

The basic foundation of my own record collection consists of records purchased at two nearby record stores in Wilmington, Delaware while I was in high school. Although a jazz store in center city Philadelphia was about an hour's drive away, I didn't find out about it until I was just about to enter college. Moreover, taking the family car into downtown Philly just to buy records wasn't something I would have been able to do very often anyway.

TEXAS SHOUT: HOW DIXIELAND JAZZ WORKS

If those two local stores had not stocked Turk, the Firehouse Five, the YBJB, the Hot Five, the Red Hot Peppers, Bessie Smith, Condon, Pete Daily, Sharkey Bonano, the Bob Cats and the others at that point in my life when I had the time after school to pay attention to them, I probably would have become interested in something else (as did the majority of my friends) and never entered the world of Dixieland jazz. It was difficult enough back then for a youngster to swim against the tide and become a Dixielander. Think of how hard it must be now, when it is all but impossible for a youth to follow up an initial contact with Dixieland by going out the next day and purchasing records by that artist or one who plays a similar Dixieland style.

Suppose your teenage friend hears a King Oliver record at your home or on the radio in the car, or attends a high school Dixieland assembly at which an Oliver tune is played. Suppose the demonstration accomplishes its purpose, and your friend decides to stop by his/her favorite record store the next day and grab something by Oliver. How long do you think that spark of interest is likely to remain burning when no such record is on hand?

It is impossible to overstate the seriousness of this problem to the continued vitality of the scene. However, I confess that I have no solution that seems likely to work on a large scale.

Record stores are in business to make money. If Dixieland records sell, they'll restock Dixieland. However, with today's sophisticated inventory procedures, they aren't likely to restock a Dixieland record if, when it finally is sold, the computer tells them that it's been gathering dust in the browser for the past four years. As a result, except for the few Armstrongs and Ellingtons, twenties-style jazz has disappeared from all but the largest big-city stores that want to maintain something approximating a complete line.

What can you do to improve the situation? For one thing, if you accompany a youth to a Dixieland show and he/she seems interested, perhaps you could top off the occasion by buying one of the artist's albums as a present for him/her to take home. Similarly, without throwing your money away on indiscriminate record-buying, you might be alert to ways in which your experience at buying Dixieland records can help someone, young or otherwise, obtain a copy of an album he/she would like - maybe by suggesting a source of which the other person might be unaware.

For another, you might make a point of trying to order records through your local store. You will have to endure the inconvenience of the special order process, but perhaps if enough of us do so, stores will get the idea that they ought to stock a few of the newer Dixieland releases. If you have the title, artist, label and catalog number, you can find out over the phone if your nearby CD emporium can get the album for you.

I recognize that it is difficult enough these days to find retail store help that is competent, literate and genuinely interested in servicing the customer. Moreover, it seems inconvenient to copy ordering information from a review, take it to a local store and order the disc instead of sending away for it yourself. Further, commercial channels may take forever to come up with something on a small Dixieland label, when a direct mail order from you to the producer usually gets a response by return mail.

However, if we do not try to use our local stores for the recordings we want, we can't complain if those items aren't stocked. Although I don't use my local stores for special orders (fortunately, I get frequent enough gigs in large cities or at festivals with well-stocked record bars to take care of most of my Dixieland buying needs), I do check them regularly for recent blues and gospel CDs. That experience assures me that you can find reliable neighborhood dealers and establish useful personal relationships with them.

Can the efforts of a few thousand dedicated Dixieland record buyers make a dent in the practices of the retail record industry? Who knows?

Maybe all that would happen is that direct mail sales, at retail prices to the manufacturer, would be transferred into sales to record stores at distributors' prices. If so, manufacturers' receipts would go down.

However, most manufacturers of small Dixieland labels whom I know are people who are in the business principally to keep alive their favorite music. I think these producers would be more than willing to support anything that might broaden the appeal of Dixieland jazz to the general public, even if it costs them a few direct sales.

However, if you have any other ideas for putting our music easily within the grasp of folks outside our inner circle, send *AR* a note. Let's read about them in "The Letter Drop".

Let me close this essay, and recall my comment about cordial relationships with local retailers, by thanking Brad Riesau of Rolling Thunder, a record store in Wilmington, Delaware's Branmar Plaza, for sharing with me some of his experience in record distribution and retailing. It goes without saying that any misstatements or other unfortunate utterances in this column are solely my responsibility.

TEXAS SHOUT: HOW DIXIELAND JAZZ WORKS

Bob Erdos
Stomp Off Records
Photographer Unknown

George Buck
G.H.B. Jazz Foundation
Nine Labels
Photographer Unknown

CHAPTER 53   CDS: IMPORTANT VS. "GOOD"

Is it possible for a recording to be so important that it is an essential purchase for a dedicated Dixieland/ragtimer even though it contains music that is of little merit artistically? Sure. I see examples turning up on the market all the time.

I don't want to gratuitously trash something that's in the stores right now. Thus, I'll make my point with a hypothetical illustration.

The first known jazzman was cornetist Buddy Bolden, who led a band in New Orleans in 1895 that played music supposedly recognizable as jazz. Legend has it that Bolden's sound was preserved on a cylinder.

If so, the recording probably no longer exists. Anyway, it has never appeared in the Dixieland community.

If Bolden's cylinder were unearthed, it would be of inestimable importance to Dixieland research because we would be able to hear what jazz sounded like at a time close to its moment of birth. However, measured by normal standards of jazz criticism, the performance probably won't be musically worthwhile. The odds are that what we'd hear, in terms of artistic merit, would be near the bottom of the jazz scale.

I recognize that some of Bolden's contemporaries reported him to be a powerful player with a sweet tone, an artist who could touch his listeners' emotions. Still I can't help but think that someone who was in at the very beginning of jazz is unlikely to have been able to foresee how the music would unfold - its depth, breadth and technical achievements - to such a degree that his own playing could bear scrutiny by today's accepted criteria.

Since the dawn of the LP era, we have been fortunate enough to be presented with previously unheard renditions by some of the great names in our music. Alternative takes or rejected titles by artists like King Oliver, Jelly Roll Morton and Fats Waller have now been included in comprehensive collections of their 78s.

Almost all such performances waxed in the 1920s are the product of professional recording companies. Private individuals rarely possessed recording equipment in those years because it was so bulky and expensive.

As a result, the treasures that have been brought to light from the twenties provide not only useful additional perspective on the approaches of the artists involved, but also, in most cases, pleasing jazz. When the musicians appeared in a recording studio, they were likely to be as well rehearsed as was feasible, ready to perform at peak. Moreover, the studio ordinarily did its best to record everything with optimal acoustics, not knowing which takes would be accepted.

In many cases, the rejected versions are just as good artistically as the accepted one. Sometimes the luck of the draw caused a certain performance to be issued vs.

TEXAS SHOUT: HOW DIXIELAND JAZZ WORKS

another. In just as many other cases, the flaw that led to rejection is a relatively minor part of an otherwise up-to-standard ride.

Another source of previously unheard vintage jazz is airchecks from the twenties and thirties. Sometimes the radio studios themselves recorded their own broadcasts for later reuse. Sometimes private individuals preserved them on home recorders that, if too cumbersome to be transported to a gig, could at least be brought close to the radio speaker.

Live airchecks are riskier than studio recordings in terms of quality because there is no opportunity for the musician to do the number again. However, they do share some of the safeguards against substandard music as do alternative or rejected takes.

First, the artist was also aware that he/she was performing for a broad audience and should have been trying to present his/her best side. Second, though airchecks typically lack some of the resonance and overtones of a studio recording, they were produced by professional sound people who were trying to position the musicians most felicitously opposite the microphone.

After World War II, this situation changed. Recording machines were more portable, perhaps suitcase-size, and more accessible to private persons. As electronics invaded the recording industry, recorders became more compact and inexpensive.

From the sixties on, small tape units started appearing at jazz venues with increasing frequency. Today, everyone owns a hand-held recorder. Virtually every note a jazzman plays on a public gig, and even lots of private gigs, now winds up being recorded by someone.

Many of the great Dixieland pioneers did not survive into the sixties. However, two of the seven Dixieland styles, West Coast revival and British trad, did not come along until the revival period. Their founders, players like Turk Murphy and Ken Colyer, lived into the eighties. Some of Murphy's and Colyer's contemporaries, e.g., Bob Helm and Chris Barber, are still going strong at this writing.

Further, while the uptown New Orleans style was around and being recorded in the twenties, it really got its prime initial momentum from Bunk Johnson's first 78s in the early forties. Many of Johnson's best sides were produced by jazz historians such as Bill Russell using bulky but portable equipment set up in private homes or neighborhood dance halls. These platters inaugurated a reasonably steady stream of uptown buffs who descended on New Orleans over the years to document whatever was happening jazzwise at neighborhood taverns or elsewhere in the Crescent City.

As a result of all of these developments, there exist today many private amateur recordings of great Dixieland names like Ken Colyer and Kid Thomas. They were typically casually recorded at gigs by someone who set up recording equipment to preserve the goings-on for his/her own personal pleasure.

Now that a number of these immortals are no longer alive, their amateur recordings are starting to find their way onto CD. We should be grateful therefor. The sides not only supplement the finite quantity of studio sessions which these players left behind, but also provide a basis for studying an artist's approach to a tune that, perhaps, he/she never recorded commercially, or how his/her in-person show might have differed from what was selected for recording purposes.

> CDs: Important vs. "Good"

These blessings are not without their down side. Such recordings do not have the quality safeguards listed above regarding fidelity or performance.

With regard to fidelity, casual microphone placement can and often does favor certain instruments at the expense of others, giving us a wrong idea of the way the band sounded in the room. Similarly, crowd noise can be obtrusive; if you're hearing something preserved by a hand-held recorder at a table or seat out in the audience, casual conversation and other clatter will, in most cases, mask the subtleties in the music so that the featured artist's special abilities do not come through.

With regard to performance quality, at a casual gig (as compared to a studio recording or aircheck) the artist is more likely to be at less than top form. He/she may be fatigued, be dealing with difficult acoustics or an inattentive audience, getting used to substitutes or unfamiliar sidemen, trying out new ideas at the end of an evening, etc. There are a million reasons why a casually made recording would capture something that is not representative of the artist and which would not be approved by him/her for public release.

A person who owns such material, and who is moved to put it on the market, may very well be blinded to such deficiencies. Such a producer could easily be one who idolizes the musician involved and who is incapable of recognizing that there is anything less than essential about his/her every note.

As a heavy collector of Dixieland, I have recently acquired quite a few CDs by some of my favorite players, all top names in the field, that are in this category. I've listened to genius defeated by out-of-tune pianos or coping with rowdy crowds or filtered through recording processes so lacking in presence that the jazz is harsh and utterly devoid of buoyancy.

On an absolute scale, the music on some of these albums can only be described as artistically terrible. Yet, I don't regret buying them, even though I probably won't re-listen often. I much admire the musicians thereon and appreciate the opportunity to get additional perspective on their work. I'm glad the discs are on the market.

When I read the liner notes thereon, I will occasionally find apologies for the fidelity. However, the producers (perhaps understandably) never even hint that the musicians might be operating at anything less than their usual standard. Similarly, I've encountered critical reviews of such recordings in which demerits of the specific album are brushed aside in waves of generalized eulogies for the artists involved.

These aspects of the situation bother me. Fewer and fewer Dixieland records are being issued at all these days. If this kind of casual session, aimed at collector/completests, is going to take a larger part of the market, then it is more likely to come into the hands of an unsophisticated listener, perhaps someone who is sampling our music - a prospective recruit to our cause.

What is such a person going to think when he/she struggles to dig fairly ordinary jazz out of an acoustical din while reading critical commentary praising it to the skies and liner notes asserting that it is a rare treasure that should be savored for its own sake? I doubt that we'll find many such individuals electing to pursue Dixieland in depth or risking their dollars on more Dixieland CDs.

As a simple solution, I'd like to see two things happen. I recommend that both producers and reviewers (1) remain aware of the fact that the artist whose casual session is being issued gained his/her reputation not via this previously unheard date

| TEXAS SHOUT: HOW DIXIELAND JAZZ WORKS |

but through other, usually better, recordings and (2) do something to point a listener toward them.

CD producers: How's about listing in your CD insert a few of the featured player's in-print albums that reflect what the Dixieland community regards as his/her best output? A purchaser thereby (a) will have some feeling of where your album falls on the spectrum and (b) can be pointed in the right direction in the future.

Record reviewers: If you can't bring yourself to give a negative rating to this type of CD, how's about including in the text of your review something to orient your reader as to where the album fits into the overall body of the artist's work?

Doing so will not result in discouraging sales to the principal intended market, the performer's pre-sold disciples. They'll want the record no matter what it sounds like.

However, it may well keep someone who has unwittingly become exposed to a very poor recording from deciding not to delve further into our music. As you know, in this era of rap and heavy metal, we need all the fresh blood we can get.

CHAPTER 54   ART FORM VS. FUNCTIONAL

The American Rag, its readers, writers and publishers, are part of a Dixieland community strongly interested in the promotion and preservation of our music as an art form. For the balance of this column, I will refer to that community as Art Formers. It consists of, among others, musicians, fans, record producers, publishers, record collectors, writers, jazz society officials and festival promoters.

There is another Dixieland community existing alongside, but almost invisible to, the Art Formers. It was touched upon in Dan Zeilinger's excellent column in the October 1995 issue. I thought you might be interested in knowing a bit more about the structure of this second body of Dixielanders and how it works.

These folks depend on the fact that Dixieland jazz still satisfies the need that called it into being in the first place - providing infectious upbeat background for good times at picnics, advertising affairs, dances and other social and commercial functions. I will refer to them as Functionalists.

Today you will find Functionalists making a living by supplying music for shopping mall galas, conventions, theme parks, store openings, used car lots, political rallies, retirement homes, etc. They stroll around jazz brunches or jam in a corner at tavern happy hours. In fact, it turns out that, due to their efforts, Dixieland jazz is all over the place these days, being exposed to every segment of our population.

There are a number of major differences between the two communities. Let me briefly outline some of them.

Audience. The largest number of Art Formers are fans. For example, the majority of the Dixieland record community are the record buyers and collectors, not the relatively small number of musicians, engineers and producers. Many more people read *TAR* and other Dixieland periodicals than are involved in their publication. Usually (though unfortunately not always) more people attend jazz concerts and festivals than are behind the scenes or on stage.

By contrast, the Functionalists have no organized audience whatsoever. Nobody goes to a used car lot or a department store to hear the Dixielanders who have been hired to play there. Indeed, their presence is hardly ever advertised in advance. When an ad does mention music, it may not say what kind and rarely will state who's playing.

The Functionalist audience consists entirely of casual passers-by, some of whom may stay and listen for a number or two before moving along. For many Functionalist gigs, the band could probably do quite well with a total repertoire of five tunes because virtually no one hangs around for more than three.

TEXAS SHOUT: HOW DIXIELAND JAZZ WORKS

Once in a while, a listener may make a request or ask Functional musicians if they have recordings. The requests are honored (Functionalists are there exclusively to please the people), but the Functional combos usually don't have recordings because the investment required to produce them is too high vs. the virtually negligible opportunity for sales at Functional gigs.

By contrast, Art Form musicians often try to avoid playing requests, preferring to work from a pre-set program that conforms to their own objectives. Some Art Form musicians make more money from sales of recordings at gigs than the fees they receive.

Instrumentation and rehearsal. Functional combos are typically duos, trios or quartets because (1) the employer is trying to keep costs down and (2) the musician is trying to get the gig, so he prices for the smallest number of people that will provide the sound the client wants. Art Form Dixieland bands are usually six or seven pieces because the musicians are playing mostly to please themselves, typically following the paths blazed on their favorite Dixieland recordings.

Functional combos do not rehearse, although as specific musicians work together from time to time they may develop a few head arrangements to use when they're all on the same job. Functionalists are too busy trying to make a living to indulge the luxury of rehearsals. Many would just as soon relax in a non-musical environment in their off-hours anyway.

Some Art Form bands rehearse on a regular schedule. The rest rehearse at least occasionally to add tunes to the book, work on special material or sharpen up for an important gig.

Presentation. Typically, Functionalists do not put on a show in the sense that Art Formers do at jazz societies, concerts and festivals. Functionalists do not announce tunes and frequently do not sing vocals.

Functional bands will most commonly be found wearing striped vests, straw hats or other attire that helps stamp them immediately in the public's mind as Dixielanders. Playing to people who happen upon them unawares, Functionalists need all the visual help they can get to establish their genre right away. On the other hand, many Art Form musicians, for reasons that make no sense to me (see "Texas Shout" for December 1995), would slit their wrists before donning a striped vest or straw hat.

Employers. Art Formers are employed by nightspots (though this scene has all but disappeared at this writing), private functions, jazz societies and festivals. They often get the work via demand pull, i.e., the belief that there is an audience that particularly wants to see a given Art Form combo or artist. Certain bands even have fan clubs which may provide a virtually guaranteed minimum attendance.

Sometimes Art Form employers cooperate to try to facilitate the hiring of Dixielanders. For example, there is a federation of Dixieland jazz clubs in which information is exchanged and there is another of Dixieland festival producers.

Almost all work for Functionalists comes via musicians who hustle their own jobs - make phone calls, visit potential clients to drop off promotional materials, etc. Because they have no organized audience, there is no demand pull.

Art Form vs. Functional

Moreover, there is no organized network of Functionalist employers. I doubt that Sears calls Strawbridge's to see which Dixieland bands Strawbridge's hired last week. Instead, Sears' booking agent relies on his/her own personal file of contacts (which may include other stores or sources within the Sears chain).

Economics. Functional jobs pay much better than Art Form jobs as a rule. A Functionalist may play a couple of hours in a department store aisle for about double what an Art Former will get for a 9-to-1 date at a local nightclub.

Further, because most Art Form musicians are hobbyists, or at least do not rely on Dixieland jazz for their principal income, some Art Form combos will take nightclub gigs for the gate, for drinks or for next to nothing in pay. Functionalists cannot afford to sell themselves so cheaply.

One rarely sees Functional musicians at festivals for this reason. A Functional Dixielander may be able to get two gigs a day on weekends, each of which pays more than he/she would get as a typical festival sideman for the same day.

(As an aside, West Coast-based Functionalists are more likely to appear at festivals due to the comparatively high proportion of festivals there. The musician may be able to play a Functional gig early in the day and still make a nearby festival.)

Economics are important in the Art Form world because the music is the principal attraction and is thus supposed to pay its way on some level. Yes, some festivals get corporate sponsors to pick up part of the tab. Similarly, some jazz societies offer patron memberships for much the same reason or throw annual multi-band picnics to subsidize periodic concerts that lose money. Nevertheless, if the overall Art Form operation doesn't finish in the black over the long haul, whether it is a festival, concert series, Dixieland society or record label, it is probably going to close once the novelty wears off among the backers who are propping it up.

Functionalists don't have that problem. Their pay comes out of an advertising or promotional budget. Nobody expects them per se to bring anyone in the door.

Economics is also behind the Functionalists' practice of hiring each other. If Clarinetist A books a gig, the first sideman he hires is Banjoist B, and vice versa. Thus, each has to hustle only half as much to find full-time work for both. This is an eminently sensible procedure, although it does operate as an additional factor that keeps the Functional community from interacting with the Art Form world.

These are some of the principal distinguishing elements between Functionalists and Art Formers. While you're pondering them, let me offer a few general observations.

First, Art Formers commonly look down their noses artistically at Functionalists. They believe that Functionalists are playing commercial shallow music that has no lasting merit.

I suppose some of them are, just as are many Art Form musicians (as any seasoned Dixieland listener knows). However, most of the people I know who've chosen to play Dixieland, whether Functional or Art Form, do so because they love the music and want to play it as well as they can.

TEXAS SHOUT: HOW DIXIELAND JAZZ WORKS

For that reason, performing Functionalist gigs can be quite liberating. Because there is no organized audience, and no show apart from the music is required, Functionalists can play whatever they choose.

I've been on a few Functionalist engagements recently and had a ball. The other players were all veteran Dixielanders who love the music. We did whatever tunes we pleased, performing for ourselves as much as for the passers-by, and thoroughly enjoyed the gigs.

Indeed, on one of these, in a department store's menswear section, we had a quartet (cornet/piano, trombone, banjo, tuba) which, if I do say so myself, performed at a level comparable to that of many second-tier festival bands I've seen. It would, I'm sure, have been warmly received by a typical festival or jazz club audience. The gig may be commercial, but that doesn't mean the music is also.

Second, Functionalists, because they are often trying to capture an impromptu audience with familiar material, are probably doing more than the Art Formers to keep alive the standard repertoire - those well-known good old good ones that put Dixieland in the public's eye in the first place. Conversely, we all can name Art Form musicians who would rather have their fingernails torn out then render, for example, a straight-ahead hot evergreen like "(Back Home In) Indiana".

Third, Art Formers are constantly saying that our music needs exposure to younger people. Believe me, it gets plenty. There are more teenagers, young adults, thirty- and forty-somethings wandering past Dixieland combos in malls, theme parks and the like in nearly any week than hear Art Formers play in a year.

However, our music means nothing to them. The people who usually stop to listen to a few songs by Functionalists are the elderly (the same age group that forms the bulk of the present-day Art Form audience) and parents with toddlers or infants (who will also stop at the magician or the clown because they want their children to experience everything). The teenagers, young adults and other folks under 50 just keep right on moving along.

This fact reinforces my belief, mentioned several times previously in this column, that the dedicated efforts currently under way by the Art Form community to enlist younger devotees - school concerts, jazz instruction camps, youth bands, etc. - are not going to succeed to the degree necessary to sustain the commercial viability of Art Form Dixieland. The Art Form audience, currently already too small to keep our music alive in some societies and cities, will keep on aging and dying out.

By contrast, though the body of Functional Dixielanders is weighted heavily by mature musicians, there are younger players, struggling to make a living out of music and seeking any paying gig, who book Functional Dixieland jobs. Some of these neophytes, not being familiar with the repertoire or style, are having a tough time getting a foothold, but as long as the gigs are there, Functional musicians of all ages will be doing whatever is necessary to get hired for them.

Fourth, the Functional Dixieland community is much healthier than the Art Form community. I recognize that playing Dixieland for a living has always been something of a struggle, but a surprising number of Functionalist musicians are doing it.

Art Form vs. Functional

On the other hand, you can almost count on your fingers and toes the number of Art Form Dixielanders who are able to make Dixieland support them without supplementing it by teaching music, by non-musical work or by playing swing or other non-Dixieland musics. Anyone who doesn't realize that the Art Form community is disappearing at an accelerating rate is simply in major denial. One jazz society after another now hangs on by its fingernails, former all-Dixieland festivals book ever more non-Dixieland acts to stay solvent, etc.

Functional Dixieland is healthier because, as Dan Zeilinger said in his above-mentioned article, the Dixieland idiom will never die on the Functionalist side. When people want music at their events that is outgoing, uplifting, breezy and cheerful, a combo in striped vests with a banjo and/or tuba is pretty much at the top of the call list. Dixieland still has the ability, even to a crowd that never hears it otherwise and doesn't care about it in the least, to bring the same good spirits to its listeners that it did when it was being developed in the Crescent City 100 years ago.

Thus, even if every Dixieland jazz club and festival, every Art Form combo and its fans, every Dixieland periodical and every Dixieland recording vanished from the face of the earth tomorrow, the Functional Dixielanders would probably be essentially unaffected. So, if your local Dixieland band loses its gig, or your local society or festival folds, and you need a Dixieland fix, keep an eye on what's happening at hardware stores around town. You might be pleasantly surprised at what you'll find.

I want to thank the following three fine musicians, each of whom is much more experienced than I with the Functional world, for reading this column in draft form with an eye toward minimizing its errors and omissions: tubaist Norm Burbank of Beachwood, NJ, phone (908) 240-4896; banjoist Eliot Kenin of Philadelphia, PA, phone (215) 324-8263; and trombonist Matt Zimnoch of Philadelphia, PA, phone (610)874-3622. Of course, any such errors and omissions, as well as all other deficiencies in the foregoing text, are my sole responsibility.

TEXAS SHOUT: HOW DIXIELAND JAZZ WORKS

Tex Wyndham   1988   Sacramento Jazz Jubilee
Photos by Dan Polin

CHAPTER 55   LAST MONTHLY COLUMN

As I became more deeply immersed in Dixieland and ragtime, I gradually came to realize that jazz literature is filled with "facts", repeated over and over by people who ought to know better, that simply aren't so. For example, I'm sure many of you have often been confronted with the false statement that, at the time of their historic initial recordings in 1942, Bunk Johnson and his sidemen were elderly musicians.

I also observed that such literature is filled with terms of art that the jazz community freely uses on the assumption that everyone understands what is meant - terms like "Chicago style", "hot dance" and the like. You won't have much trouble finding essays that will tell you who played such music, but you'll look long and hard before you unearth anyone who's tried to gather such phrases and write down, in musical terms, exactly what they mean.

As I put together my record collection, and as I lived through what has turned out to be nearly thirty years of reviewing records, I also noticed that various "authorities" on the subject regularly were given to pronouncements that just didn't square with the music on the records. You will often hear, for example, the incorrect claim that improvisation is essential to a jazz performance. However, if that were so, we would have to exclude from the jazz category many fully scored big-band swing and hot dance rides commonly accepted as jazz by just about everybody (not to mention, perhaps, some of Jelly Roll Morton's most highly regarded sides - after all, isn't he supposed to have just wanted his sidemen to read "those little black dots?").

Finally, as I started getting away from Wilmington to attend jazz functions and play festivals, I realized that the scene was changing in a fundamental way from the one that existed when I first became a Dixieland/ragtime nut in the 1950s. Again, there seemed to be little direct discussion of this point in the several jazz periodicals I was regularly devouring.

I'm digressing too early in my tale, but let me tell you briefly why, in my opinion, so much misinformation about Dixieland gets up and running. I have met many people who say they love Dixieland. Upon closer examination, however, almost all of them turn out to love only a few of its seven styles, having no interest in, or an active dislike of, the others.

It is only human for such individuals to view Dixieland history, and to develop critical standards, in a way that conforms to their own preferences, even while telling themselves they're being objective. Thus, they come to develop a philosophy of the music that elevates the styles they like over those they don't.

For example, depending on whether the speaker prefers ensemble-oriented or solo-oriented Dixieland, I've heard assertions that solo improvisations are the essence of jazz and, conversely, that ensemble playing is the true heart of Dixieland.

TEXAS SHOUT: HOW DIXIELAND JAZZ WORKS

Both positions are nonsense. Solo-oriented Dixieland and ensemble-oriented Dixieland are simply two different, equally valid ways of utilizing the musical conventions and musical vocabulary typically employed by Dixielanders.

Similarly, depending on whether one prefers revivalist or Chicago style, you'll hear opinions stating, on the one hand, that it is better to perform tunes which haven't been commonly or frequently rendered in the past or, on the other, that you can't beat the tried-and-true standbys. Again, both are nonsense as generalities.

You should always perform the best material you know because, in the last analysis, it is what you do with it that counts. A mediocre musician or band will still deliver second-rate jazz on a neglected gem, while a superior jazzman/woman will create something worthwhile on a vehicle that has been beaten into the ground many times by lesser talents.

Finally, you will hear it said in some circles that attempts to standardize the terminology used in our field constitutes stereotyping musicians or compartmentalizing our music. In fact, we will continue to waste our time in empty disputes unless we stop using different terms to mean the same thing and using the same terms to mean different things. The music we like, and the variations of it, have to be called something and our community is long overdue in reaching consensus as to what that something should be.

For that matter, we all categorize music, and for perfectly sensible reasons. Most of *TAR*'s readership prefers music normally categorized as Dixieland, ragtime and other pre-rock forms of American popular music. If *TAR* starts devoting its coverage to music normally categorized as grand opera or heavy metal rock, it will lose those readers, even if that coverage is devoted to the best opera and rock musicians and is insightfully written.

Similarly, many of us like Dixieland and swing, but dislike more modern jazz forms. We will not go to a "jazz" concert unless we know who's playing, to insure that the musicians are ones who typically perform the categories of jazz we enjoy.

Among Dixieland fans, some love four-beat solo-oriented Chicago style and can't stand two-beat ensemble-oriented West Coast revival - and vice versa. Such folks, when attending Dixieland festivals, mentally categorize the bands and artists so that, in selecting which stage to visit, they'll wind up with the style of Dixieland they desire.

In short, classifying music - at least to some degree - is an essential part of both understanding and appreciating it. If the jazz community is not going to standardize its terminology in that respect, if different speakers continue to use the same words to mean different things or different words to mean the same thing, then meaningful dialogue about jazz cannot take place.

To return to my narrative, as the years went by, I felt that some readers might find it thought-provoking to have my take on these notions set down on paper. By the time I decided to do something along those lines, it was the mid-1980s.

In that time frame, my principal writings were record reviews, and my principal outlet for them was *The Mississippi Rag*. During the dozen years I wrote for *MR*, I was, at least by quantity if not quality, its leading record reviewer. I wrote about

Last Monthly Column

40% of the reviews published in *MR* during that period, more than three times the amount of any other *MR* reviewer.

Reviewing activity then (and still does so) took up more of my time than I really wanted to devote to it. I was reluctant to assume another monthly assignment. However, an occasional extra bit of writing didn't seem so onerous.

So, in the course of my normal correspondence with *MR* editor Leslie Johnson (one of those rare and valuable individuals who has given much more to the service of our music than she can ever expect to get back from an economic standpoint), I asked if *MR* might be interested in a once-in-a-while column under my byline that would comment on the music, the scene and the interrelationship of the two. I sent a few samples to show her what I had in mind.

It turned out that Leslie was planning a new feature, but not a regular piece by one of *MR*'s usual writers. She wanted to institute a catch-all corner where someone who wanted to write about a topic at greater length than would be appropriate for the letters page could present his/her thoughts to the readership. She thought that my essays might be used to kick it off.

Her idea seemed to fit well with my idea of writing intermittently. If I recall correctly, I suggested that the feature might be titled "Solo", and in January 1987, it was inaugurated with one of the samples I'd sent in. ("Solo" continues to this day in *MR*, but not as often. There was an initial flurry of submissions, but the flow tailed off noticeably after about the first year.)

I got more personal direct positive feedback from my readers on the four "Solo" columns I wrote for *MR* than anything I'd written up to that time. They also elicited comments on *MR*'s letters page, and even one or two "Solo" columns by other writers amplifying on points I'd made.

Nevertheless, in the summer of 1989, Leslie concluded that the type of column I wanted to write was not well aligned with the direction she had in mind for *MR* at the time. She returned two unpublished essays from her files.

I understood and respected Leslie's viewpoint and was happy enough with the outcome. However, having done the work on the two columns, I decided I might as well see if anyone else wanted them. I sent one to *Jersey Jazz*, which had published my letters to the editor over the years, and the other to *West Coast Rag* (now *The American Rag*), for which I had written nothing up to that point.

I assumed that my "occasional" column had thereby ended. However, when *WCR*'s founder, Woody Laughnan, received the submission, he phoned me to ask if I would write for *West Coast Rag* on more than a one-shot basis.

Thinking of myself primarily as a record reviewer, I felt my first loyalty in that respect was to *MR*. I replied that I was not interested in writing reviews for another periodical. Woody clarified his request by saying that he didn't care whether what I wrote were reviews or not, would I write anything regularly for *WCR*?

I thought, well, suppose I see if he wants the kind of stuff that Leslie had already tried and rejected? No conflict of interest there, I figured.

So, I said "What would you think of a column that talks about the music, the scene, and the interrelationship of the two?" "Fine."

| TEXAS SHOUT: HOW DIXIELAND JAZZ WORKS |

Thus was born "Texas Shout", which has run in every issue of *WCR/TAR* since the first column first appeared in November/December 1989. The initial one was the rejected *MR* essay I'd sent to Woody, and the second was a reprint of the other one, which had already been published in *Jersey Jazz*. After that, each "Texas Shout" has been written specifically for *WCR/TAR*'s readers.

(Incidentally, I used the name "Texas Shout" because it is both a classic-period barrelhouse tune and a nice play on words with my nickname. "Texas Shout" is a piano solo recorded in 1929 by Cow Cow Davenport.)

My goal, as mentioned, was to talk about the music, the scene and their interaction. However, along the way I have tried to give those of you who are not musicians or writers a glimpse - I hope an interesting and colorful one - of how things operate on the other side of the footlights or at the business end of the typewriter.

You will recall that I had initially planned to write a "Texas Shout" column only when the urge struck, not monthly. I told Woody that I'd keep it going as long as I could, but that I doubted it could stay in action for much more than two years. To help sustain it, I immediately sat down and made up a list of possible topics.

As it turned out, "Texas Shout" has continued for nearly seven years. Certain of the ideas wound up needing two (or even three) issues to discuss. Some of you out there supplied me with new subjects. I even thought of a few myself and added them to the list.

However, a description of the music, the scene and their interrelationship is inevitably finite. It doesn't go on forever, even though the scene gradually changes over time.

As I sit here looking at that initial list, I've crossed off everything that seems to me to be a viable basis for a full-length "Texas Shout". In fact, you may have noticed that some recent columns have been a little more anecdotal than was true of the general six-year average, although I hope still containing food for thought.

In fact, a recent experience makes me wonder whether I have been reaching too hard for topics in these latter columns, am on burnout, or losing my touch. A few readers told me they had trouble following my arguments in the March 1996 "Texas Shout", which dealt with melodic improvisation.

I don't want to rewrite the whole essay from scratch, but if you're in that category, try re-reading it with a word like "tuneful" or "songlike" in place of "melodic" and see if that procedure helps. In a broader sense, though, when my audience can't figure out what I'm talking about in this space, you can bet I'm going to do some rethinking regarding it.

I am not interested in writing about humorous gigs/incidents in my checkered musical past. Others, some of whom already grace *TAR*'s pages, do that sort of thing much better than I.

(By the way, I miss Dave Gannett's now-long-gone monthly column, don't you? He managed the difficult trick of writing knowledgeably about his topics while incorporating side-splitting humor.)

I am not interested in cannibalizing earlier columns. Those of you who've been with me through the full run are probably already weary of some of the sermons I've

Last Monthly Column

preached quite a few times: seek originality of expression within the idiom, not replication of triumphs of the vintage greats; the "standard" repertoire is a gold mine of superior material for a musician who is willing to treat every performance as a challenge to be creative; broaden your understanding of the various Dixieland styles and try not to dismiss casually fans/bands of styles that aren't your favorites; we must develop commonly accepted and defined terms with which to discuss our music; and the others. I think these are important points, but they're said clearly enough in my past columns for anyone who wants to look them up.

In short, if you've been a regular "Texas Shout" reader, you've heard everything I think you need to hear to find your way to becoming a broad-based listener/musician who can appreciate our music in all its wonderful diversity. Moreover, I've come to the end of my topic list.

Actually, I reached the end of the list in December 1993, at which time I wrote the first draft of today's column and discussed its content with Woody. He was not happy to hear the direction I was taking.

At that point, I had already written and submitted "Texas Shout" through the end of 1994. At Woody's urging, I returned to the salt mines and was able to scratch out enough more to get the column through last month's issue.

However, I have not written a fresh "Texas Shout" for some time. The possible topics that have since occurred to me just don't seem weighty enough to support an entire essay.

When one has finished talking, one should have the sense to step down from the podium. Thus, I want to tell you that I no longer intend to write a new "Texas Shout" every month. After today's column, I'm going back to my original plan of visiting you if and when the urge strikes.

"Texas Shout" has been very good to me. Woody told me, soon after it began, that it was *WCR*'s most popular feature.

In light of the several fine writers who have come on board since, that is probably no longer the case. In any event, I have much appreciated the kind words I've received from many of you about "Texas Shout" in person at performances, in "The Letter Drop" and in private correspondence/conversations.

The column has given me a visibility on the circuit that I had not anticipated. Because playing Dixieland and ragtime is my first priority where music is concerned, I'm especially grateful for that aspect of the situation.

Some fans have told me that they've saved all of the "Texas Shout" columns for future reference. One musician keeps certain of them, together with other related material, in a binder he calls his "Bandleader's Bible". A book producer once offered to finance the project if I'd expand certain themes from "Texas Shout" into a book.

These are especially gratifying developments. With regard to the book, a subject about which I regularly receive inquiries, I must tell you that I feel very complimented by the request, but I really need to cut down on my writing, which takes much more time than you might imagine.

(Actually, I've already written the book, if you want to read it piecemeal. There is at least a volume's worth of text in the full complement of "Texas Shout" columns. In fact, at this writing, the above-mentioned producer is planning to collect between two covers the entire run of "Texas Shout" from inception through today's. We'll see what happens.)

Dealing with the demands of practicing two instruments, of booking two bands and a single act, and of daily life, I have, over the years since my first published piece of jazz writing in November 1966: built a collection of thousands of LPs, including several hundred, some bought new that have been out of print for a quarter-century, which I have not yet heard for the first time; amassed stacks of ragtime and jazz sheet music that, also, remain unplayed over the decades since they first entered our house; and surrounded myself with thousands of unread books, mostly my favorite recreational reading of fantasy, horror and mystery.

I told myself that I would listen to the records, play the music and read the books when I retired. Though I've been retired for over four years, none of those things are happening.

If I'm going to get time to do them, much of it will have to come out of my jazz writing. The rest will result from cutting back on my dozens of periodicals, including some jazz magazines, thereby leaving me less well situated to write from an informed, up-to-date viewpoint. (This process is well under way. Several periodicals are already history in our household, including four dealing with music.)

As I place these words in the mail, I am heading into the preliminary stages of operations to remove cataracts from my eyes. Cataract surgery is more routine and less risky than it used to be, but this situation reminds me that I've already started benefiting from senior citizen discounts and that I ought to get racking on matters I've postponed for too long.

There are two other factors at work here. I'll mention them briefly because it depresses me to dwell on them at length.

For some time now, it has been clear that Dixieland is dying out. The scene is dwindling, as well as becoming diluted with non-genre music. The same thing is happening to ragtime.

The readership of *WCR/TAR* has, I think, shifted in accordance with this trend. This change in emphasis tells me that a smaller proportion of *TAR*'s readership is interested in "Texas Shout" - a column which, as a basic premise, assumes that Dixieland jazz and ragtime are viable worthy art forms and which attempts to set up a framework for appreciating them as such.

If memory serves, when I began "Texas Shout", "The Letter Drop" was filled with comments from readers discussing the merits of their favorite Dixieland bands. Readers' principal concerns have changed since then. For a while, "The Letter Drop" seemed exclusively devoted to a truly boring back-and-forth, carried on with quasi-religious fervor, on (1) dance floor locations, (2) listeners vs. dancers and (3), to a lesser extent, smokers vs. non-smokers.

Last Monthly Column

(By the way, the dance floor controversy is surely irrelevant by now. Most festivals dealt with it in the most practical way years ago by placing, where space permits, dance floors alongside the stage so that both groups of people can be near the band without having to be in each others' way .)

"Texas Shout" has been, in significant respect, a chronicle of the general scene. I don't see much around anymore that gives me cause for optimism.

I love Dixieland and ragtime too much to want to write continued complaints, jeremiads and obituaries about them. If that is the direction "Texas Shout" seems destined to take, I prefer to spend less time on it.

Second, there is no longer a cohesive Dixieland community. Because the music has lost its commercial viability, things have deteriorated so much that Dixieland now consists in large part of individual clubs, festival producers, record labels and bands doing whatever turns them on without much regard to each other or of economic consequences.

Twenty years ago, if a band made a superior recording, or played an outstanding show at a festival, word spread quickly through common channels of communication. Now there are no common channels, though *The American Rag* and *The Mississippi Rag* do good enough jobs in their respective markets. Nevertheless, most festivals, concerts and records are not reviewed anywhere, except possibly in a few local jazz club newsletters.

This fragmentation has reached the point where, with all due respect to you good folks who read *TAR* devotedly, nothing that anybody writes about Dixieland makes much difference anymore. In those circumstances, I'm having increasing difficulty finding a good answer to a question I periodically ask myself, especially when the pressures mount up: why am I doing this?

I'd like to believe that "Texas Shout" has caused you to think more deeply about this music that we all love so much. You may not agree with what I've said over the years, but I will guarantee you one thing: though the terminology used in this column, and the categories of jazz described herein, may not coincide with what you will hear or read elsewhere, it does square with the music that's in the grooves of the hordes of ragtime and Dixieland records that have been made throughout the decades.

The good news, for those of you who have found my columns hopelessly academic or worse, is that there will be few, if any, new ones appearing in the future. The bad news is that, according to my understanding, once the backlog runs dry, *TAR* is planning to reprint selected older "Texas Shout" essays for the benefit of subscribers who've signed up since 1989.

I'm not sure how I feel about such reprints. Like most of Dixieland, I think "Texas Shout" has probably had its day and should be allowed to rest peacefully. At minimum, as with the U.S. government shutdowns during 1995's so-called "budget crisis", we're probably better off to do without "Texas Shout" for a while and see if anybody notices its absence.

As long as I'm winding things up, I'll answer a few questions I'm regularly asked at my gigs:

| TEXAS SHOUT: HOW DIXIELAND JAZZ WORKS |

Where did the nickname "Tex" come from?

My father picked it out for me before I was born. Dad told me that, as a little boy, he went bonkers over a popular song of the day, "Good-Bye Dolly Gray" (1900), words by Will D. Cobb, music by Paul Barnes (the sheet music states that it was "Sung with Immense Success by WILLIAM H. REDMOND"). He whistled "Dolly Gray" so incessantly that folks started calling him "Dolly", a nickname Dad despised (can't say I blame him). He decided to make sure his son, if he ever had one, would bear a two-fisted nickname.

My nickname has worked well. "Tex" is a good stage name and seems to start me off on the right foot with people.

I liked it so much that I did the same thing with my son, nicknaming him "Buck", after Buck Jones, the old-time Western movie star who died while rescuing people from the Coconut Grove fire. Buck also enjoys his nickname, telling me it's turned out to be ideal for someone in his profession (aviator).

Why do you wear a red glove when you play the cornet?

The oil from one's flesh will eventually eat its way through the lacquer on a brass instrument. That's why many trumpet/cornetists hold their horns with handkerchiefs or wind tape around the valve area where the non-fingering hand grips the instrument.

In the early 1960s, I decided that a glove would be more comfortable for me. I started with a white leather glove, but it was too hot. Then I moved to a ladies' one-size-fits-all stretch glove, which works fine.

My only problem is that ladies stopped wearing that type of glove years ago. The oft-mended one I'm wearing now is the last one I have.

The red color started as a subliminal way of advertising my Red Lion Jazz Band. Now it has become a superstition with a life of its own. I never appear onstage without some piece of red apparel. I even have some red underwear to use when nothing else will get by.

You were a teacher in your day job, right?

Never was. In 1963, immediately upon graduating with high distinction from Harvard Business School, I returned to my native Wilmington, Delaware and toiled nearly 29 years in DuPont's finance function. About 2/3 of that time I held middle management jobs or middle-management-level consulting positions. From time to time, I was responsible for such things as DuPont's insurance program, its SEC filings and the financial aspects of mergers and other business combinations.

How did The Rent Party Revellers get together?

During the seventies, I played piano with a reunion band, The Bix Beiderbecke Memorial Jazz Band. Most of the sidemen lived in the New York City area, but two of us lived near Wilmington.

Last Monthly Column

I loved playing with the BBMJB. It was a hot band with a great bunch of guys in the lineup. When it played its last gig in early 1981, the sidemen having become so separated geograpahically that it was uneconomical to reassemble, I missed it terribly.

The Bix Band had played a number of festivals, during which I started formulating some thoughts on the administration of a reunion band and also met musicians who seemed to be ideal for the kind of combo I had in mind. In spring 1982, after it became clear that the BBMJB was defunct, I picked up the phone and started calling potential sidemen and concert producers. The Rent Party Revellers made our debut about six months later, in December 1982, at Johnson McRee's Manassas (Virginia) Jazz Festival.

Incidentally, as I write these words, the BBMJB is booked for a one-time-only reunion at the 1996 Bix Fest in Davenport, Iowa. I can hardly wait to get back on stage with the band.

How do the Revellers, none of whom live near each other, rehearse?

If time permits at the start of a festival weekend, we may assemble for a short time around a piano to (1) try some new things and (2) get our local bands out of our heads and the Revellers back in. In our earlier years, we sort of rehearsed by mail, sending around lead sheets and tapes of tunes in our book. We still send lead sheets once in a while, but after 13-plus years together, we don't need the tapes any more.

Why don't you write a book about the history of Dixieland jazz?

Doing so would involve research, something I hate with a passion. Avoiding legal research was one of the principal reasons why I never practiced law, despite holding a law degree and having passed the Delaware bar.

(Tony Kennedy and I studied for finals in my room three nights a week throughout Harvard Law School. We graduated in 1961 at the same level in our class, magna cum laude, at which point we made a deal: Tony wouldn't play Dixieland and I wouldn't go on the U.S. Supreme Court. Seeing the way Tony - Mr. Justice Anthony M. Kennedy to the world at large - and his fellow justices get dissected by the press every once in a while, I'm sure I got the better of the bargain.)

I've only once tried to write a piece of original research about music. Thinking that I had all the materials readily at hand and could knock it out in a couple of hours, I set out to recount the facts regarding the tune commonly played under the title "Storyville Blues". I quickly learned that nearly every sentence I drafted was filled with hidden pitfalls that needed double-checking.

Several weeks and many long distance phone calls later, I mailed the finished product to *WCR* (it's the August 1992 "Texas Shout"), telling myself that I would never do anything like that again. So far, I've kept my promise.

Those of you who've seen my shows, in which I typically introduce a tune by telling you who wrote it or recorded it, may be surprised to hear me say that I don't like research and don't consider myself a historian of the music. What I'm doing is

TEXAS SHOUT: HOW DIXIELAND JAZZ WORKS

Last Monthly Column

what many announcers do, sharing with the audience the thing about the next number that particularly interests me.

As a performer, I'm interested in finding good tunes. Thus, when I run across one, I want to know who wrote it and/or who recorded it. It seems likely that if I look for other material by those composers/recording artists I'll find other worthy stuff to play for you.

These facts, which are right there on the records or sheet music (no research required), naturally stick in my mind, just as the facts that most interest you about your hobby naturally stick in your mind. The bulk of what I know about our music's general historical background I learned from reading liner notes on my LPs and CDs.

Although I do try to stay informed about Dixieland and ragtime, most publications on my music shelves are discographies or periodicals, either in aid of my record reviewing or my understanding of the Dixieland/ragtime scene. While I will occasionally read a music book for pleasure, if it's about something or someone in whom I have a special interest, usually I'd rather read a good hard-boiled thriller or eerie vampire tale.

If you're not interested in writing a book, what about teaching jazz, say at an adult extension course, elderhostel or jazz camp?

I think doing so would be a lot of fun. The problem is that I have no idea what I would teach.

I wouldn't want to teach jazz history. Many others already do so, much better than I'd do, I'm sure. Besides, preparation of a jazz history course would require doing research.

I'd be more interested in trying to teach people how to play ragtime and Dixieland. However, I'm a self-taught Dixieland/ragtimer. To me, our music is something you master via long hours of listening, keeping your ears open, and practicing, not something a person teaches you. I can't imagine how I'd go about teaching it.

In any event, I've covered in previous "Texas Shout" essays the basic principles I followed in learning to play this music, to gain the skill of idiomatic soloing, to plan and present shows, to lead a band, etc. I don't think I have anything left to say that would be much help to a student.

I presently intend to close "Texas Shout" permanently after today. Still, like James Bond, I've learned never to say "never". Thus, I'm leaving the door open a crack in case the compulsion to write another one overwhelms me at some future date.

Either way, this is probably as close to a valedictory as I'm going to get. So, I want to thank those of you who have been so supportive of "Texas Shout" during these six-plus years. I am more grateful to you than words can express.

I also want to thank those of you who disagreed with me, or who didn't like the column, and took the trouble to let me know or to write "The Letter Drop". While I regret that some of you found it necessary to be so abusive in the process, while I felt

Last Monthly Column

that many of you hadn't really paid attention to what I'd said and while very few of you presented arguments that I found persuasive, your comments had the beneficial effect of spurring me toward exerting my best efforts to write clearly, accurately and logically. I needed that.

It's been fun. If you're in the audience somewhere that I'm playing, or we cross paths in a festival walkway, come up and say "Hello"! Keep swinging.

TEXAS SHOUT: HOW DIXIELAND JAZZ WORKS

Kid Bolden's Band before 1895 (Oldest known jazz photograph)
Standing, Jimmie Johnson, Buddy Bolden, Willy Cornish (valve trombone),
Willy Warner   *Seated.* Brock Mumford, Frank Lewis
Photographer Unknown

Publisher's Note: Despite our best efforts to prevent them, the final galley of this book contained some typesetting/proofreading errors. To our knowledge, none affects the meaning in the text. All involve format, punctuation or spelling, e. g., "Lee" for "Lea" on page 174 and "Ubie" for "Eubie" on page 283. Also, the following two pages of sheet music were intended to follow page 130 and are referred to in that chapter on "Storyville Blues". While regretting any inconvenience caused the reader by this decision, we elected not to make costly last-minute non-substantive corrections that would have significantly increased this volume's retail price.

Addendum to "Storyville Blues"

"THOSE DRAFTIN' BLUES"

Words and Music by
MACEO PINKARD
Writer of "Real Kind Mama"
"The Blue Melody" etc.

Moderato (very slow)   Until ready

VOICE (very slow)

1. Now if you've got a lov - in' man, — You'd bet-ter love him while you can — Per-haps he'll have to go to
2. You know it's gon-na break your heart, — To let your hon-ey go a - way — The nights will grow so long to

war, — To fight for dear old Un-cle Sam. They're draft-ing ev'ry man right now, — To
you, — You'll soon be look-ing old and gray. — No mat-ter how you love your man, — He's

fight the Kai-ser and his band — Be-fore they call your man, I say; — These words you ought to un-der stand; —
got to an-swer to his call — I've told you in my lit - tle way; — I'm sure you'll un-der-stand it all; —

GET THIS ON YOUR PLAYER PIANO OR TALKING MACHINE AT YOUR DEALER — GREAT!

Copyright, MCMXVIII by Griffin Music House Chicago, Ill.
International copyright secured

Sole Selling Agts. JOS W STERN & CO., New York.

Published for Band & Orchestra:
Orchestra . . . . 25¢
Band . . . . 50¢

TEXAS SHOUT: HOW DIXIELAND JAZZ WORKS